The 1940s

A Decade of Modern British Fiction

Titles in *The Decades Series*

The 1930s: A Decade of Modern British Fiction, edited by Nick Hubble, Luke Seaber and Elinor Taylor

The 1950s: A Decade of Modern British Fiction, edited by Nick Bentley, Alice Ferrebe and Nick Hubble

The 1960s: A Decade of Modern British Fiction, edited by Philip Tew, James Riley and Melanie Seddon

The 1970s: A Decade of Contemporary British Fiction, edited by Nick Hubble, John McLeod and Philip Tew

The 1980s: A Decade of Contemporary British Fiction, edited by Emily Horton, Philip Tew and Leigh Wilson

The 1990s: A Decade of Contemporary British Fiction, edited by Nick Hubble, Philip Tew and Leigh Wilson

The 2000s: A Decade of Contemporary British Fiction, edited by Nick Bentley, Nick Hubble and Leigh Wilson

Forthcoming in the series:
The 2010s: A Decade of Contemporary British Fiction, edited by Nick Bentley, Emily Horton, Nick Hubble and Philip Tew

The 1940s

A Decade of Modern British Fiction

Edited by

Philip Tew and Glyn White

BLOOMSBURY ACADEMIC
LONDON • NEW YORK • OXFORD • NEW DELHI • SYDNEY

BLOOMSBURY ACADEMIC
Bloomsbury Publishing Plc
50 Bedford Square, London, WC1B 3DP, UK
1385 Broadway, New York, NY 10018, USA
29 Earlsfort Terrace, Dublin 2, Ireland

BLOOMSBURY, BLOOMSBURY ACADEMIC and the Diana logo
are trademarks of Bloomsbury Publishing Plc

First published in Great Britain 2022
This paperback edition published 2023

Copyright © Philip Tew and Glyn White, 2022

Philip Tew, Glyn White and Contributors have asserted their right under the Copyright, Designs and Patents Act, 1988, to be identified as Authors of this work.

For legal purposes the Acknowledgements on p. xiv constitute
an extension of this copyright page.

Cover design: Eleanor Rose

All rights reserved. No part of this publication may be reproduced or transmitted in any form or by any means, electronic or mechanical, including photocopying, recording, or any information storage or retrieval system, without prior permission in writing from the publishers.

Bloomsbury Publishing Plc does not have any control over, or responsibility for, any third-party websites referred to or in this book. All internet addresses given in this book were correct at the time of going to press. The author and publisher regret any inconvenience caused if addresses have changed or sites have ceased to exist, but can accept no responsibility for any such changes.

A catalogue record for this book is available from the British Library.

A catalog record for this book is available from the Library of Congress.

ISBN: HB: 978-1-3501-4301-2
       PB: 978-1-3502-8061-8
       ePDF: 978-1-3501-4303-6
       eBook: 978-1-3501-4302-9

Series: The Decades Series

Typeset by Integra Software Services Pvt. Ltd.

To find out more about our authors and books visit www.bloomsbury.com
and sign up for our newsletters.

Contents

Series Editors' Preface   vii
List of Contributors   xi
Acknowledgements   xiv

Critical Introduction: Reappraising the 1940s   *Philip Tew and Glyn White*   1

1. Their Finest Hour? A Literary History of the 1940s   *Ashley Maher*   37

2. British Blitz Fiction of the 1940s: Another Finest Hour, Myth or Propaganda?   *Philip Tew*   59

3. Genteel Bohemia: Capable Women in Women's Fiction of the 1940s   *Deborah Philips*   91

4. The Ship and the Nation: Royal Navy Novels and the People's War 1939–45   *Chris Hopkins*   111

5. Feeling Political: Elizabeth Bowen in the 1940s   *Karen Schaller*   139

6. The Life of Animals: George Orwell's Fiction in the 1940s   *Tamás Bényei*   163

7. Masters and Servants, Class, and the Colonies in Graham Greene's 1940s Fiction   *Rebecca Dyer*   191

8. Purposes of Love: Rethinking Intimacy in the 1940s   *Charlotte Charteris*   223

9. No Concession to 'English' Taste? Refugees from National Socialism Writing in Britain   *Andrea Hammel*   249

10. Un-British: The Transatlantic Crime Film Connection   *Glyn White*   275

Timeline of Works	301
Timeline of National Events	305
Timeline of International Events	309
Biographies of Writers	315
Index	329

Series Editors' Preface

Nick Hubble, Philip Tew and Leigh Wilson

The series began with a focus on Contemporary British fiction published from 1970 to the present, an expanding area of academic interest, becoming a major area of academic study in the last twenty-five years and attracting globally a seemingly ever-increasing range of scholarship. However, that very speed of the growth of research in this field has perhaps precluded any really nuanced analysis of its key defining terms and has restricted consideration of its chronological development. This series addresses such issues in an informative and structured manner through a set of extended contributions combining wide-reaching survey work with in-depth research-led analysis. Naturally, many older British academics assume at least some personal knowledge in charting this field, drawing on their own life experience, but increasingly many such coordinates represent the distant past of pre-birth or childhood not only for students, both undergraduate and postgraduate, but also for younger academics. Given that most people's memories of their first five to ten years are vague and localized, an academic born in the early to mid-1980s will only have real first-hand knowledge of less than half these forty-plus years, while a member of the current generation of new undergraduates, born in the very early 2000s, will have no adult experience of the period at all. The apparently self-evident nature of this chronological, experiential reality disguises the rather complex challenges it poses to any assessment of the contemporary (or of the past in terms of precursory periods). Therefore, the aim of these volumes, which include timelines and biographical information on the writers covered, is to provide the contextual framework that is now necessary for the study of the British fiction of these four decades and beyond.

Each of the volumes in this Decades Series emerged from a series of workshops hosted by the Brunel Centre for Contemporary Writing (BCCW) located originally in the now-vanished School of Arts at Brunel University London, UK. These events assembled specially invited teams of leading internationally recognized scholars in the field, together with emergent younger figures, in order that they might together examine critically the periodization of initially contemporary British fiction (which overall chronology was later expanded by adding previous decades) by dividing it into its four constituent decades: the 1970s symposium was held on 12 March 2010; the 1980s on 7 July 2010; the 1990s on 3 December 2010 and the 2000s on 1 April 2011. Subsequent seminars expanding the series included the 1960s on 18 March 2015; the 1950s on 22 April 2015; the 1930s on 21 June 2017 and the 1940s on 6 June 2018. During workshops, draft papers were offered and discussions ensued, exchanging ideas and ensuring both continuity and also fruitful interaction (including productive dissonances) between what would become chapters of volumes that would hopefully exceed the sum of their parts.

The division of the series by decade could be charged with being too obvious and therefore rather too contentious. In the latter camp, no doubt, would be Ferdinand Mount, who in a 2006 article for the *London Review of Books* concerned primarily with the 1950s, 'The Doctrine of Unripe Time', complained, 'When did decaditis first strike? When did people begin to think that slicing the past up into periods of ten years was a useful thing to do?' However, he does admit still that such characterization has long been associated with aesthetic production and its relationship to a larger sense of the times. In *The Sense of an Ending: Studies in the Theory of Fiction*, published in 1967, Frank Kermode argued that divisions of time, like novels, are ways of making meaning. Clearly both can also shape our comprehension of an ideological and aesthetic period that seem to co-exist but are perhaps not necessarily coterminous in their dominant inflections. The scholars involved in our BCCW symposia discussed the potential arbitrariness of all periodizations (which at times is reflected by contributors by extending the parameters of the decade under scrutiny), but nevertheless they acknowledged the importance of such divisions, their experiential resonances and symbolic possibilities. They analysed the decades in question in terms of not only leading figures, the cultural zeitgeist and socio-historical perspectives, but also in the context of the changing configuration of Britishness within larger, shifting sets of global processes, literary, socio-cultural or political. The participants in each volume also reconsidered the effects and meaning of headline events and cultural shifts such as the Great Depression, Proletarian Literature, the Popular Front, the Second World War, the emergence of the Welfare State and the Cold War, to name only a very few. Perhaps ironically to prove the point about the possibilities inherent in such an approach, in his *LRB* article Mount concedes that 'For the historian … if the 1950s are famous for anything, it is for being dull', adding a comment on the 'shiny barbarism of the new affluence.' Hence, even for Mount, a decade may still possess certain unifying qualities, those shaping and shaped by its overriding cultural mood.

After the various symposia had taken place at Brunel, guided by the editors of the particular volumes, the individuals dispersed and wrote up their papers into full-length chapters (generally 10,000–12,000 words but in some cases longer), revised in the light of other papers, the workshop discussions and subsequent further research. These chapters form the core of the book series, which, therefore, may be seen as the result of a collaborative research project bringing together initially twenty-four academics from Britain, Europe and North America. Four further seminars and volumes have now added research-active scholars to this ongoing BCCW project, which is continuing to expand.

Each volume shares a common, although not necessarily identical, structure or format. Following a critical introduction outlining key contexts, the first chapter of each volume broadly addresses the 'Literary History of the Decade' by offering an overview of the key writers, themes, issues and debates, including various factors such as historical contexts, emergent literary practices, an introduction to relevant cultural dynamics controversies, key developments and movements. The next two chapters are generally themed around topics that have been specially chosen for each decade, and which may also where appropriate relate to themes of the preceding and succeeding decades, enabling detailed readings of key texts to emerge in full historical and theoretical context. The tone and context having been set in this way, the remaining chapters fill out a complex but comprehensible picture of each decade. In certain volumes a 'Colonial/Postcolonial/Ethnic Voices' chapter addresses the ongoing experience and legacy of Britain's Empire and the rise of a new globalization, which is arguably the most significant long-term influence on contemporary British writing. At least one chapter will focus entirely on women's writing and that particular gendered form of voice, perception and written response to both literary impulses and historical eventfulness (featuring either a cluster of female writers or one specific figure who seems to represent the dynamics of that decade). Various other chapters with a range of focuses are added according to the dynamics and literary compulsions of each specific decade, which may feature international contexts or a specific subgenre of the novel form, for instance. Each decade is different, but common threads are seen to emerge.

In the future it is planned that the Decades Series will go back to 1920 and forward to 2020, in effect reconnecting Contemporary British Fictions with their modern precursors from the aftermath of the First World War, charting a full century of transformational change through a detailed and forensic examination of its literary fiction.

Works Cited

Kermode, Frank. *The Sense of an Ending: Studies in the Theory of Fiction*. Oxford: Oxford University Press, 1967.

Mount, Ferdinand. 'The Doctrine of Unripe Time.' *London Review of Books* 28 (22), 16 November 2006: 28–30, http://www.lrb.co.uk/v28/n22/ferdinand-mount/the-doctrine-of-unripe-time: n.pag.

Contributors

Tamás Bényei is Professor of English Literature at the Department of British Studies, University of Debrecen. His main research fields are twentieth-century British fiction, crime fiction and (post)colonial fiction. He is the author of eight books in Hungarian and one in English: *Acts of Attention: Figure and Narrative in Postwar British Novels*, 1999. He has published journal articles and chapters in Hungary, Britain, the United States and other countries on Ovid, Poe, Rudyard Kipling, E. M. Forster, Agatha Christie, Anthony Powell, Iris Murdoch, Angela Carter, J. G. Ballard, Jeanette Winterson, Peter Ackroyd, Graham Swift, Martin Amis and Kurt Vonnegut. He is editor-in-chief of a forthcoming seven-volume history of English literature in Hungarian.

Charlotte Charteris is Academic Associate in English at Pembroke College, Cambridge, specializing in fin-de-siècle, modernist and mid-century prose, with a particular interest in queer studies and the aesthetics of transgression. A former Leverhulme Early Career Fellow and By-Fellow of Churchill College, Cambridge, she is the author of *The Queer Cultures of 1930s Prose: Language, Identity and Performance in Interwar Britain* (2019), as well as numerous shorter publications concerned not only with the literature and history of sexuality, but – more fundamentally – with what Christopher Isherwood once termed 'the market value of the Odd'. These include articles on Patrick Hamilton, Graham Greene, Julian Maclaren-Ross, Agatha Christie and E. M. Forster. She was the founder of Cambridge University's interdisciplinary Queer Cultures Research Seminar.

Rebecca Dyer is Professor of English at Rose-Hulman Institute in Terre Haute, Indiana, where she teaches literature, film and writing courses. As a Fulbright recipient and a visiting professor, she taught at the American University of Beirut in Lebanon (2007), conducted research at the British Library and British Film Institute (2011–12), and taught at the Université d'Orléans in France (2015–16). She has published scholarly articles in *Cultural Politics*, *College Literature*, *PMLA*, *Obsidian III*, *Cultural Critique* and *JML*, and is working on a book examining servant representations in British literature and film since the Second World War.

Andrea Hammel is Reader in German and the Director of the Centre for the Movement of People (CMOP) at Aberystwyth University in Wales. She has published widely on the social history and culture of German-speaking refugees from National Socialism who resettled in the UK, especially on women's exile writing and the Kindertransport. She leads a project on Refugees from National Socialism in Wales which is part of the Second World War and Holocaust Partnership Programme led by the Imperial War Museum London, and she is writing a book on the subject for Honno Press.

Chris Hopkins taught from 1991 to 2020, and is now an Emeritus Professor, at Sheffield Hallam University. He works on British writing between 1900 and 1950, with particular interests in women's writing, working-class writing, Welsh writing in English, popular fiction, literature and film, and book illustration. He has published *Thinking about Texts – An Introduction to English Studies* (2001, revised edition 2008), and *English Fiction of the 1930s: Language, Genre and History* (2006). His most recent book is *Walter Greenwood's Love on the Dole: Novel, Play, Film* (April 2018). He is editor of the *Reading 1900–1950* blog: https://reading19001950.wordpress.com/ and of the *Walter Greenwood: Not Just Love on the Dole* blog: https://waltergreenwoodnotjustloveonthedole.com/. He is academic consultant to the Reading Sheffield community research group: https://www.readingsheffield.co.uk. He is currently working on popular fiction and the 'people's war' and the illustrator and artist Arthur Wragg.

Ashley Maher is the author of *Reconstructing Modernism: British Literature, Modern Architecture, and the State* (2020). Her work has also appeared in *ELH*, *Textual Practice*, and the *Journal of Modern Literature*. She is Assistant Professor at the University of Groningen in the Netherlands. Before being appointed to that position, she was the Stevenson Junior Research Fellow in English at University College, Oxford, and a Lecturer at the University of Sydney.

Deborah Philips is Professor of Literature and Cultural History at the University of Brighton. She has published widely on women's writing, popular culture, cultural policy and theatre, and her published books include: *And This Is My Friend Sandy: Sandy Wilson's The Boy Friend, London Theatre and Gay Culture* (2021), *Fairground Attractions* (Bloomsbury, 2012), *Women's Fiction: From 1945 to Today* (Bloomsbury, 2006, 2nd edition 2014), with Garry Whannel *The Trojan Horse: The Growth of Sponsorship* (Bloomsbury, 2013) and, with Ian Haywood, *Brave New Causes* (Bloomsbury, 1998).

Karen Schaller is Researcher at the University of East Anglia specializing in theories of emotion, feeling and affect in twentieth- and twenty-first-century literature and culture. She has published work on Elizabeth Bowen and Sylvia Townsend Warner as well as contemporary women writers. She is finishing a monograph on Elizabeth Bowen's short stories, a study of other neglected writers and feeling mid-century, and another book on feminist feeling in the twenty-first-century university.

Philip Tew is Professor in English (Post-1900 Literature) at Brunel University London and a fellow of the Royal Society of Arts. His main publications include: *B. S. Johnson: A Critical Reading* (2001); *The Contemporary British Novel* (2004; rev. 2nd ed. 2007); *Zadie Smith* (2010); with Nick Hubble *Ageing, Narrative and Identity: New Qualitative Social Research* (2013); *Reading Zadie Smith: The First Decade and Beyond* (Bloomsbury Academic, 2013); and with Jonathan Coe and Julia Jordan *Well Done God! Selected Prose and Drama of B. S. Johnson* (2013). Tew is a series editor for the Bloomsbury Literary Decades series and Director of the Hillingdon Literary Festival. He completed a second doctorate in Creative Writing at Brunel in 2016 and has since published the following fiction: *Afterlives: A Novel* (2019); *Fragmentary Lives: Three Novellas* (2019); and a second novel, *Clark Gable and His Plastic Duck* (2020). A third novel, *Heroes and Villains*, will appear in 2022.

Glyn White is Senior Lecturer in Twentieth Century Literature and Culture at the University of Salford. He is author of *Reading the Graphic Surface: The Presence of the Book in Prose Fiction* (2005), co-author (with the late John Mundy) of *Laughing Matters: Understanding Film, Television and Radio Comedy* (2012), and co-editor (with Philip Tew) of *Re-Reading B. S. Johnson* (2007). Glyn has also published various chapters in collections and journals, and most recently contributed a chapter on detective fiction and thrillers to *The 1930s: A Literary Decade* in the Bloomsbury Decades series.

Acknowledgements

We would like to thank all our contributors for their expertise, patience and generosity when responding to our queries and guidance as this book has gradually taken shape. We have enjoyed excellent support throughout from the editorial team at Bloomsbury, especially David Avital, Mark Richardson, Clara Herberg, Lucy Brown, Ben Doyle, Laura Cope and Rachel Walker, who have been instrumental in bringing this series and its books to fruition.

We gratefully acknowledge the support of the Brunel University Research and Knowledge Transfer Committee for providing the funding which enabled the Brunel Centre for Contemporary Writing to host various events in the 'British Fiction Decades Seminar Series' during 2010, 2011, 2015, 2017 and 2018, which have led to the publication of the volumes in this book series. Without the support of administrative and catering staff at Brunel these events could not have taken place. We would also like to thank all the academics and postgraduate students who attended and contributed to the discussions at these events. We would also like to acknowledge gratefully the various staff at Enfield Library Services, Brunel University Library, the British Library, the National Library of Scotland, the National Library of Wales and other research libraries who have provided support to the contributors to this volume.

The latter stages of this project have taken place during the Covid-19 pandemic. As a consequence, unfortunately not all those scholars originally on board were able to see this project through, and we would like to thank Karen Schaller for contributing a chapter at relatively short notice. We would also like to thank all our chapter authors who have contributed to the 'Biographies of Writers' section.

Philip Tew would like to thank his son, George, an ex-colleague, Steve Barfield, and fellow volume editor, Dr Glyn White, with whom he discussed various points while developing and drafting his chapter. Glyn White would like to acknowledge Paul Duncan's ongoing work on Gerald Kersh, going right back to 'The Nights and Cities of Gerald Kersh' posted at: http://harlanellison.com/kersh/.

Critical Introduction: Reappraising the 1940s

Philip Tew and Glyn White

Socio-historical contexts

The 1940s ended with Great Britain under a Labour Government that was looking increasingly weak in a rapidly changing economic climate, and the British Empire already drastically shrunk in size and population with the loss of India in 1947 (when up to two million died and twenty million were displaced in the intercommunal strife and violence initiated by partition). In *Nineteen Eighty-Four* (started in 1944, written mostly in Jura in 1947, typed up in 1948, and published in June 1949) George Orwell presents the British Isles reimagined as Airstrip One, defined by its airbases during the war, scarred by bomb damage and inhabited by traumatized people surrounded by propaganda posters in, as Peter Lowe writes, 'a society ruined by war where the past has been either destroyed or deliberately rewritten' (311). The geopolitical landscape of Orwell's book registers emergent Cold War conditions, a new conflict with Russia as the principal enemy shielded by an 'iron curtain' – Winston Churchill's phrase from a speech delivered in Fulton, Missouri, in 1946 – across Europe and by 1949 the Soviets had tested a version of the West's most powerful weapon: the atomic bomb. All the above would have baffled most ordinary Britons in 1940, whose country was engaged in a long-feared 'hot' war against Germany (with Russia neutral until attacked in 1941), and was ruled by a coalition emerging from the foundations of the previous Conservative administration that had been unable to prevent the conflict (including the debacle of Prime Minister Chamberlain being duped by Hitler at Munich).

Given the above, one might have confidence in suggesting that no decade, including the 1910s, was so world-changing and (therefore) so unpredictable for those living through it. Discussion of the 1940s itself is often swallowed up by 'the' war – even though it was not the only war of the decade. But in order to comprehend the perspective of those living through this crisis, the Second World War needs to be remembered in the context of the 1940s as a live event in which the outcome was uncertain, before Dunkirk, the Blitz and Churchill took on the mythological meanings they seem to have acquired today (see below). As explored subsequently in this volume, fiction can help us do so. The key events remembered have almost become the equivalent of the stations of the cross, adding to the above Pearl Harbour, El Alamein, Stalingrad, the invasion of Italy, the Normandy landings, the liberation of Paris, the mass bombings of German cities, the liberation of the concentration camps and the dropping of the first atom bomb on Hiroshima. Much else is obscured and forgotten such as the sinking of the *Lancastria* off St Nazaire two weeks after the evacuation of Dunkirk in 1940 accounting for over 4,000 lives and contributing to a significant proportion of British Expeditionary forces losses, or the British attack on the French fleet at Oran that killed 1,297 sailors two weeks later, or the surrender of Singapore after only a week's fighting in February 1942 placing 85,000 British and colonial troops in Japanese captivity. Incidents on the home front such as the Bethnal Green tube station disaster of 1943 where 173 civilians were crushed to death also seldom feature in historical accounts. Moreover, the gravity of any version of the war dominates attention so easily, it leaves the latter years of the decade as if in shadow, while obscuring the fact that Britain was effectively bankrupt, owing to the United States most of a £21 billion debt incurred during wartime (which was not repaid in full until 2006). This created a crisis of convertibility for sterling reserves held abroad, and that process's suspension in 1947 resulted in drastic cuts to domestic and overseas expenditure, a contraction of trade and the economy, a loss of dollar reserves and a devaluation of sterling in 1949.

For those experiencing this decade day by day (rather than seeing it with the selective benefits of hindsight), things were very grim in the beginning, rose to a peak with victory in the war and then tailed off as its aftermath, which had started with hope and a sense of unity, gradually lost the war's sense of shared communal purpose. Throughout the war the majority of Britain's population supported continuing the struggle even, as Robert Mackay points out in *Half the Battle* (2002), when a large number on the 'home front' appeared to be unhappy with government leadership of the military campaigns – with only 35 per cent support after the fall of Tobruk (94). Nevertheless, 'People did not need to be told that the enemy was ruthless and barbaric. Once the Blitz had happened, Hitler was believed capable of any brutality' (94). This sense of unity may already have benefitted from hindsight and was certainly exaggerated for propaganda purposes during the conflict.

Dunkirk and other propaganda

Much like the Blitz spirit (see Chapter 2), the military withdrawal at Dunkirk was mythologized almost immediately, as we see in one of J. B. Priestley's popular 'Postscript' broadcasts originally aired on 5 June 1940 (a day after evacuation ended on the fourth) in full propagandist fashion:

> But here at Dunkirk is another English epic, and to my mind what was most characteristically English about it – so typical of us, so absurd and yet so grand and gallant, that you hardly know whether to laugh or to cry when you read about them – was the part played in the difficult and dangerous embarkation – not by the warships, magnificent though they were – but by the little pleasure steamers. We've known them and laughed at them, these fussy little steamers all our lives. (n.pag)

Priestley adds later another defining theme of the various myths of the conflict, 'And our grandchildren, when they learn how we began this War by snatching glory out of defeat, and then swept on to victory, may also learn how the little holiday steamers made an excursion to hell and came back glorious' (n.pag).

A heightened retrospective awareness for ideological accommodation, one that created the illusion of fellow feeling, was a matter of both nostalgia and later confusion. The apparently unifying posters for various propaganda campaigns such as 'Dig for Plenty' and 'Dig for Victory', 'Let Us Go Forward Together', 'Lend a Hand on the Land', 'Back the Great Attack' and the now classic, but rarely displayed, 'Keep Calm and Carry On'[1] foreground a shared experience but, as Ian Whittington details, the propaganda of the wartime period, in which many literary figures took part, created in reality only a grudging and partial common ground:

> British writers cast their lot with a politics of consensus whose public manifestations included the cross-party National Government, the appropriation of private property in the name of total war under the Emergency Powers (Defence) Act of 1940 and the atmosphere of collective solidarity represented by the People's War. The enemy made it easy to define what Britain was struggling against; the more difficult issue was what they were struggling for. (16)

As Whittington indicates, the popularity of Priestley's 'Postscript' broadcasts led to a democratization of radio output, and 'he went on to plant the seeds of a minor social revolution whose final form would be realized in the recommendations of the Beveridge Commission on Social Security as adopted by the Labour government after the elections in July 1945' (98). These policy initiatives would result in a radically different cultural emphasis, framing the nation's social dynamics for the whole decade and well beyond through the benefits system and the NHS, for instance. So influential was the broadcaster that Mackay argues 'the voices of Churchill and Priestley' (162) came to symbolize the wartime struggle in their appeals to patriotism, but the vision of Britain held by Priestley and other progressive broadcasters would be the one that prevailed, not that of the Prime Minister. In exploring the actuality of wartime commonality, equality and consensual effort Jose Harris writes:

> [I]n spite of high wartime taxation, the war made little permanent impact (and indeed surprisingly little short-term impact) upon the distribution of wealth; that the dramatic scientific breakthroughs induced by the war (in electronics, nuclear physics and bio-chemistry) were grafted onto an industrial base that remained ramshackle, underfunded, managerially inept and culturally hostile to advanced methods of production; that, in spite of the mass mobilisation of both men and women, the war reinforced rather than subverted traditional class and gender roles; and that the very fact of ultimate victory in the war helped to arrest rather than accelerate change, by buttressing and legitimising many obsolete and reactionary social, economic and governmental institutions. (19)

However, Harris concedes, 'If the British people in the 1940s felt themselves to be more equal and more united than ever before, then this is an overwhelmingly significant fact that no amount of analysis of income or wealth distribution can gainsay' (18–19).

The 1940s reconsidered

Over seventy years later, current views of the 1940s are shaped by what has been subsequently written and recorded in various media, as well as (of course) by our contemporaneous concerns. Because the basic objectives of the 1940s seem so immediate and specific (defeat an enemy, produce some tangible societal benefit as justification for sacrifice) it appears notably easy and 'natural' to bracket this decade off as somehow separate from the continuities of concern that normally occur between decades. The 1940s are thus often forced to form a dividing point between the two halves of the twentieth century pulling attention in different directions, while being bifurcated as a decade by doing so; everything in it is bundled into either 'before the war' or post-war, rather than looking at the decade in its own right. As Gill Plain perceptively observes:

> There are many '1940s'. For some it is and always will be the decade of the Second World War, and that conflict overshadows all other aspects of the period, not least because while hostilities ceased in 1945, the impact of the war continued to be felt – psychologically, emotionally and economically – in the state of the nation, the grief of its inhabitants and the pain of readjustment. For others, the 1940s is a beginning, not an end: the Cold War, immigration, the inception of the welfare state and the transformation of Britain as an imperial power. (2013: 1)

Any chronological periodization is further complicated in terms of positioning the conflict itself by another point that Gill Plain makes: 'The temporal span of any war cannot be confined to its literal historical duration and the exact shape of the "prelude" to the Second World War is similarly difficult to define' (1996: 35). As a consequence of the points above one might usefully extend the start and end of the decade, thereby constituting a 'long' 1940s, much as Andrew Sinclair suggests in *War like a Wasp* (1989):

> the forties properly begins in September 1939, with the declaration of the Second World War, and ends twelve years later in 1951 with the Festival of Britain and the loss of power of the Labour Party, it passes as a war and post-war decade with a brief prologue and a longer postscript of summary judgement. (286)

As a result of being the epilogue to the 1930s or the prologue to the post-war period with its own intense history, the 1940s becomes a self-contained decade in which literature of the time focused on immediate events not linked to the decades on either side. Significantly, Sinclair also describes the 1940s as a 'lost decade' in a literary context.

In literary terms, for many commentators the 1940s has emerged as a key dividing point between modernism and postmodernism, though how exactly is not so easy to evidence (see Chapter 1). The deaths of Woolf and James Joyce and the disgrace of Ezra Pound were enough to make it seem like a literary era had ended, but what would come next? Full-blown examples of postmodernism tend not to emerge in literature until the 1960s, taking their cue in Britain from the Irish writing at the end of the 1930s from those such as Joyce, Samuel Beckett and Flann O'Brien, while in the United States it was war veteran writers like Kurt

Vonnegut and Joseph Heller who took at least a decade to digest their 1940s combat experiences. If the war took so long to process, this leaves an intriguing question: to what extent can the literature of the 1940s legitimately represent it?

In this sense, perhaps this decade challenges the Literary Decades format of this book series more than most others. Bracketing off the literary output of the decade from other periods is, of course, a literary-historical convenience, but it is intriguing to find just how keen writers and commentators of the time were to do so themselves. A negative judgement on the literary 1940s seems to have set in early around 1950. This has its roots in the literary critical practices of the time and the difficulty of applying them within the exceptionality of the decade which we have already sketched. There was a sense that literature could not keep up, which might be put another way: the critical establishment was too traumatized to deal with the immediate past. All their expectations and the 'normality' of the 1930s had been totally upset.

One key aspect of the exceptionality of the 1940s literary landscape is the significant material effects of the war on the publishing industry itself (of which fiction publishing is but a small part). Book publishers' share of available paper stocks was less than 2 per cent of overall paper usage, but the remainder had to accommodate newspapers, HMSO (i.e. government publications) and periodicals including many foreign periodicals such as *La France Libre*, sponsored by the Ministry of Information, as Robert Hewison details (1977: 77). Christopher Hillard records:

> The beginning of the war was not an auspicious time to start a periodical. More than 900 magazines and newspapers suspended publication. Paper was rationed from 1940 until 1949. Under the Control of Paper order of February 1940, publishers were allowed paper in quantities up to 60 percent of their paper consumption between August 1938 and August 1939. Because Norway was Britain's principal supplier of wood and pulp, after the German invasion of Norway this allowance was cut, initially to 30 percent. By 1943 publishers were entitled to only 6.5 percent of the quantity of paper they had used in 1938–39. It also became illegal to start a new periodical, though the enterprising devised means of circumventing the ban. One way was to take over an existing publication and transform it, while maintaining nominal continuity. Another strategy was to launch what Denys Val Baker called the 'book-magazine' – treating each issue of the magazine as a free-standing book or booklet. An official at the Ministry of Information told Miron Grandea that it would be illegal for him to continue publishing *Adam* as a magazine, but that he could bring out successive volumes entitled *Eve, Cain*, and so on. (166)

As a result of their difficulties sourcing paper, book publishers had to decide what wartime readers wanted to read, never an exact science, and the number of books published dropped from nearly 15,000 in 1939 (of which 4,222 were fiction) to around 6,700 in the years 1943, 1944 and 1945 with fiction titles dropping to 1,250 (Holland 12). As Hewison indicates, worse still, on 29 December 1940 Paternoster Row in London was hit with an incendiary bomb and 'five million volumes destroyed' – the stocks of 'Hutchinsons, Blackwoods, Longmans, Collins, Eyre and Spottiswoode, Ward Lock and Sampson Low' (1977: 32)

These losses and restrictions created a shortage which according to Steve Holland meant that 'reading matter was desperately sought after by a book starved public' (14) since while the number of books published diminished between 1939 and 1945 national expenditure on books rose from £9 million to £23 million, more than doubling, according to Hewison (1977: 76). The publishing industry had become a seller's market. 'The demand for books meant that publishers were selling much of their pre-war stocks, but were completely unable to replace them. [...] By 1942 as Hewison indicates 580 out of the 970 titles in the "Everyman" series were unobtainable' (79) and by 1945, according to John St. John's history of the publisher William Heinemann, 'some 1600 Heinemann titles in demand were out of print' (308).

In order to manage these extraordinary circumstances and manage the share of paper stocks, as Hewison states, the Publishers Association put in place 'the Book Production War Economy Agreement' in 1942 (1977: 78). These dictated width of margins, amount of words on a page, the quality and weight of paper used, and 'shorter prints led to an increase in published price for books of inferior quality' (St John 300–1).

What does it mean in practice when a 'book is produced in complete conformity with the authorised economy standards'? Consider a comparison of two editions both consulted as physical artefacts in the British Library. The 1939 copy of Gerald Kersh's *I Got References* published by Michael Joseph before the restrictions applied can be compared to its 1947 Heinemann reprint. The opening 'Apology', which declares the book 'neither fish nor fowl nor red herring' (vi), is three pages in 1939, and only two in 1947, because of the type size and layout changes, thus covering a third less pages, and those pages are literally much thinner too, using lower-grade paper; hence, the 1947 version is a third of the thickness of the 1939 edition.

The content of 1940s publishing changed, too. As Rod Mengham explains, novels that were published tended to be shorter and

> The short story enabled rapid response to the constantly changing conditions of Phoney War, conscription, Blitz, blackout, evacuation, the housing crisis, and the reorganization of the workforce. Its brevity and capacity for sharp focus made it more suitable as a means of reflecting disruptions in the rhythm of everyday life and a profound sense of historical discontinuity. Both in form and content, the short story was the medium of choice for conveying a shared experience of fragmentation, unpredictability, and the psychological stress of having to live from moment to moment. (26)

What Mengham identifies here was a significant change from the previous norms of literary production. In 1941 in *The Modern Short Story: A Critical Survey*, H. E. Bates wrote that the short story 'occupies something of the place that the water colour occupies in painting' (8). Bates's urge to survey the field at the start of this decade is indicative of writers taking stock and trying to understand what Britain has to fight for in terms of literary output (others did so in a variety of fields). While the content essentially focuses on the 1930s short story from the point of view of a practitioner, Bates closes with a telling observation: 'if no other good comes out of wars, stories will' (223). Novels were not necessarily the best format to respond to the circumstances as Mengham suggests and Plain observes, 'The strongest trend in the novel of the 1940s [...] was its abbreviation, and it is the short story that demands to be recognised as the characteristic "form" of the decade' (2013: 24).

This change made the periodicals that did survive during wartime, publishing mainly short fiction, all the more influential but this changed rapidly after the war. Hewison notes that by 1947, Cyril Connolly, editor of patronage-funded *Horizon*, is complaining that the arts are moribund under the Labour government (1995: 48). Money for these areas was certainly in short supply, though this was a long-term, rather than a short-term, problem; as Hewison outlines The National Theatre, approved in 1949 and with foundations laid in 1951, was not completed until 1976 (1995: 46–8). Specifically with regard to literature, The Arts Council, formed in 1946 on the basis of the wartime Council for the Encouragement of Music and the Arts (CEMA), did not step in to save ailing literary magazines and, according to Hewison: 'Both *Horizon* and *Penguin New Writing* folded in 1950' (1977: 185).

By this date many of those active in literary circles had convinced themselves they were rightly not valued. At the beginning of the decade there was already an apparent crisis among the younger literary generation, as its chief representatives left for America. After Christopher Isherwood and W. H. Auden set sail in 1939 – to the scorn of many – the February 1940 'Comment' in *Horizon* called their departure 'the most important literary event since the outbreak of the Spanish Civil War' and interpreted it as an omen for British literature and European politics: 'Auden is our best poet, Isherwood our most promising novelist. [....] They are far-sighted and ambitious young men with a strong instinct of self-preservation [...] who have abandoned what they consider to be the sinking ship of European democracy.' New literary heroes were urgently needed.

As Mark Rawlinson states in *British Writing of the Second World War* (2000), 'much writing produced between 1939 and 1945 disappoints the desire for a reprise of the [Great War] literature of "the pity of War"' (3). Critics of the time could not point to any genuine equivalent of the First World War Poets, though there were a number of poets whose work, its promise and their short lives might seem to qualify. These were Keith Douglas, who fought in North Africa and died in action in Normandy aged twenty-four; Sidney Keyes, who had published two volumes of poetry before he joined up in 1942, to be subsequently killed in action in Tunisia at only twenty-one; and Welsh-born Alun Lewis, who apparently committed suicide in Burma in 1944 aged twenty-eight. Australian Spitfire flyer Richard Hillary's memoir of his RAF experiences *The Last Enemy* (1942) was also highly praised and his death in a crash on his return to flying – despite extremely severe injuries and reconstructive surgery – drew comparisons to the serving poets of the so-called Great War. But tragedy and talent aside, these writers did not share a common experience akin to 'the trenches' and moreover they contributed to active campaigns that brought victory even before their posthumous volumes were printed. Edith Pargeter's trilogy *The Eighth Champion of Christendom* (1945), *Reluctant Odyssey* (1946) and *Warfare Accomplished* (1947) seems to have been the swiftest attempt to catalogue the full experience of the war close to when it was occurring.

No doubt many putative writers imagined turning their experiences into novels but, as Mengham points out, first 'Censorship affected particularly the literary production of servicemen' (39), with some novels delayed until they were no longer commercially viable, and second, much literature in the 1940s foregrounded an 'emphasis on the Home Front [...]' (40). Critical effacement was the fate of any wartime literary output that was propagandist in intention, and there was little appetite or energy for undermining or diminishing the collective triumph. Writers who remained in Britain during the hostilities probably experienced a reaction such as Lara Feigel observes of Elizabeth Bowen soon after VE Day, 'Quickly, she began to look back on the war as an exhilarating period and to find what followed anticlimactic. With the threat of death removed, everyday life became less precious' (271).

When the world was rapidly changing, the war seemed to require epic factual treatment as in Churchill's (immensely successful) six-volume *The Second World War* (1948–53).

Alan Ross, in the pictorial book *The Forties*, published in 1950, was among the first to encapsulate the idea that literature of the decade had been found wanting. According to Ross:

> the first years of the war put paid to a way of writing and feeling that had characterised the whole previous decade. For the rest of the Forties English Writing was to be remarkable for untypical, sporadically brilliant individual works; for a high level of general accomplishment and a dearth of real talents. (n.pag [11])

Such an implicit (if unsuccessful) search for the canonical is symptomatic of the approach of Leavisite literary studies at that time which sought to identify authors who (for all their flaws) might represent the entirety of their age. Ross names names, though the book's picture choices may not have been his. In answer to his rhetorical question 'But who, indeed, have been the literary figures of the period?' Ross answers: 'Graham Greene, certainly, and Evelyn Waugh, converted but positive survivors in a world grasping at Catholicism on the rebound from communism. Stylists like Henry Green, Ivy Compton-Burnett, and Elizabeth Bowen.' Other literary figures mentioned are Osbert Sitwell, Anthony Powell, George Orwell, Denton Welch, Nigel Balchin, Jocelyn Brooke, Nancy Mitford and Joyce Cary.

The benefit of hindsight gives us an advantage over Ross and allows us to challenge those commentators who have dismissed much of the literature of the decade. Plain, citing Malcolm Bradbury in particular to conclude her point, says: 'in short, there was a great deal of activity in the decade, but no lasting legacy. The writers of the late 1940s ground to a halt in a haze of despair and a perverse nostalgia for a war now valorised as "a time of common purpose when writing had mattered" ' (2013: 2). In practice, in contrast, we may well decide that the harvest of the 1940s is actually rather rich and even fecund.

In this volume we will subsequently focus on many of the names Ross mentions, as well as looking to expand his list. Ashley Maher's survey (Chapter 1) which follows this Introduction considers how the decade has been revisited by criticism in the contemporary period. In the second half of this Introduction we will focus intensively on a number of writers not always associated with the decade whose experiences encapsulate a range of literary responses before introducing the chapters that follow.

Not the usual suspects

To see the literary decade of the 1940s anew it might best be approached not through the anticipated and familiar literary figures of a fading modernism such as Virginia Woolf and T. S. Eliot, or even via the Auden generation scarred by the ideological divisions of the previous twenty years, but at least initially via a writer born in 1922 who was beginning his tentative literary career during the 1940s, Philip Larkin.

Raphaël Ingelbein points to 'the considerable body of work that Larkin produced in the 1940s' (80), including his first two novels in 1946 and 1947 where bellicose realities are the backdrop to the struggles of the young. Larkin was to become far more celebrated for his later poetry, so much so he is seldom associated with this earlier period, but the 1940s left a profound impact on him and his work. He was seventeen at the outbreak of war and before university had been living in one of the areas of Coventry that was bombed from 14 to 15 November 1940, the most devastating raid to that point, killing 1,200. He hitchhiked from St John's College, Oxford, to search for his parents desperate for news and found the city still full of unburied corpses. According to Adam Piette, 'It was only when he got back to Oxford that he learned his parents were safe and sound' (232). Piette argues Larkin used the episode to sever links with the childhood he shared with an ardently pro-Nazi father (235), and thereafter only referenced it obliquely. Though the Blitz haunted Larkin's consciousness, it featured only marginally in his creative responses. In 'New Year Poem' written on 31 December 1940, the effects of war on his hometown are self-evident in the scene in which he evokes that ruined city and the effects of the Blitz:

> These houses are deserted, felt over smashed windows,
> No milk on the step, a note pinned to the door
> Telling of departure: only shadows
> Move when in the day the sun is seen for an hour [...]. (2004: 255)

The human cost, its visceral catastrophe, is displaced in typically Larkinesque fashion, but still he captures the urban suffering. On one level war meant destruction and death, its seemingly unavoidable effects, and Larkin is trapped by the moment and his disgust at the fear and loss suffered, and his own lack of direction in the aftermath.

A much more subdued, but equally bleak, wartime (and what would become post-war) austerity is captured in the opening snow storms of his second novel, *A Girl in Winter* (1947), set in a small provincial town, based on Wellington in

Shropshire where Larkin worked in his first post as a librarian. As far away from hostilities as one might imagine (as Larkin was himself variously in Oxford and later in Wellington) the narrative enumerates first the flurries of snow rapidly soiled in town, and details the drab lives of several young women librarians working without adequate heat, while living in rundown and depressing digs, yet far larger themes impinge. From the start Katherine Lind is harassed and dressed down by her superior, a permanent librarian, Miss Feather, somehow reduced and lightweight because of her name, about a supposedly missing book on Uganda, easily found and restored. Symbolically the vulnerability of all such imperial possessions seems implicit, an overarching potential loss haunting the zeitgeist, Imperial Britain easily misplaced and forgotten. Larkin's novel emphasizes the bleakness of these times, but also the capacity and requirement to sidestep all such traumatic possibilities by living in the present as Katherine attempts to do. The everyday persists, and only the unexpected disrupts the patterns of life, which it does in the commonplace occurrences. Leading home a sick colleague, Miss Green, they pass a display that evokes the ultimate cause of Katherine's malaise, the war:

> The only piece of furniture was a large double-sided stand, painted duck-egg green, for Official War Photographs. This was now covered with pictures of destroyers, aeroplanes, and tanks in the desert: sometimes urchins crept in and stared at them, or prised out the drawing-pins to steal. (21)

The symbolic reference is clear, the capitalization ironic. As Larkin indicates, the specific memories might well be fading, such an act of memorial reduced to images threatened by instability, and clearly their future status is rendered uncertain given their vulnerability after such pilfering. Larkin implies that war is subject to forgetfulness too, setting aside so much to create dominant images for such narrow and static accounts, running parallel to Katherine's effacement of her own past. The suggestion is that if the war years are to permeate the post-war period, they will do so through a diminishment, a narrowing of experience. Amid the mundanity of a provincial library the only other reminder of war is 'soldiers asking to consult the medical dictionary' (22), a pragmatic undermining of heroism. For Piette

> Larkin had come to realize that the Second World War was an event that annulled its pre-war traces, like a Lethe stretched across the space-time of European cultural memory. It worked in this way because of the sheer scale of the war and the annihilating effects of the bombing campaigns, quite literally effacing the houses, homes, and townscapes of childhood. (236)

Clearly, the trauma of war effaced memories and mental landscapes of the past too, with its insistence on the ubiquity of the present terror, displacing nostalgic return. In Larkin's poem 'On Being Twenty-six' written in May 1949, as Piette observes, 'written a year after his father's death' (237), 'slag', 'ash' and implicitly fire within the self are dominant images of his partial recollection, 'But it dies hard, that world [...]' while still haunted by 'states/Long since dispersed [...]' (2004: 57). Speaking of another reflective poem, 'I Remember, I Remember', Piette says there:

> are intimations of perplexity about sides, about direction, and about the recognizable features of his father's city: 'I wasn't even clear/Which side was which'. These lines retain the faintest trace of censored questions of allegiance as well as containing a concentrated reference to the war's annulment of his childhood. (238–9)

Displaced by the war Katherine is, in Alexander Josef Howard's words, 'the subject of misogynistic bullying' (27) by her obnoxious boss, Mr Anstey, and is acutely conscious of her status as an outsider, the text implying she is German and very possibly Jewish, aware of the English being 'characterized in time of war by antagonism to every foreign country, friendly or unfriendly, as a simple matter of instinct' (22). For Piette the novel at an unconscious level at least is 'overtly concerned with self-censorship, with shame about past and family [...]' (240). According to Ingelbein Larkin's reading of Katherine Mansfield's letters influenced the narrative and its characterization, especially her 'submission to life, her resigned stoicism' (83), but also 'Both in her foreignness and in her wintry mood of detachment [...]' (85). Katherine's life is thwarted and disrupted by the implied upheavals that she cannot overcome or even face (181), and she has conceded her fundamental loneliness (185–6), and yet now without friends she finds herself unwilling and unable to any longer contemplate 'happiness through the interplay of herself and other people' (183). Even retrieving her pre-war friends, the Fennels, and having a casual affair with the son, Robin, fail to revive her enthusiasm for life, haunted implicitly by death, echoed in the 'near eternity' (140) of the Oxford she visits, rendered timeless and deathly. At the end snowfall recurs, and the reader is aware of one day having passed in which through flashbacks, as Joan Sheila Mayne says, 'the whole pattern of her life is explored' (77). According to Larkin's narrator meaning is diminished so that 'whatever it was she would do it unwillingly, obstinately, as if she were working in a field; what she did would be emptied away like a painfully-filled basket, and her time would be spilled away with it' (216). As Ingelbein indicates, Larkin felt peripheral during the early 1940s since 'Larkin was a young artistic intellectual cut off from the war effort, sexually insecure and ill at ease with certain manifestations of wartime English patriotism' (90). Although many celebrated the war with a fervour that eluded Larkin, his responses stand at a crossroads amid a larger set of experiences and events, where past and present collide, both fragile and torpid, outcomes uncertain, meaning contestable. Clearly, the past led to war and might be therefore regarded as suspect, another direction is required in future to transcend any such conditions of impasse and misdirection, perhaps a new beginning. However, as Larkin senses at the time with a marked fragility and hostility, the 1940s as a decade – with all its contingencies, indeterminacy and paradox – have damaged the nation leaving it facing the Cold War with its potentially destructive tribulations – without time to heal, reflect or recuperate resources. The curious equivocation of the proto-Larkin, balancing the heroic and the antipathetic, indicates key aesthetic and cultural coordinates for Britain in the latter half of the 1940s. When considered in retrospect, the war necessarily looms large; a sense of its enormity, its violence, its injustice and the impossibility of unpacking and resolving its influence.

As Kristin Bluemel indicates, Stevie Smith was employed for thirty years as secretary to the two 'baronet publishers Sir Neville Pearson and Sir Frank Newnes' (62) at Newnes Publishing Company based at 8-11 Southampton Street, off the Strand in London, where the Blitz caused significant disruption. Her second and third novels chronologically frame the war, both its imminence, and the aftermath and associated memories. *Over the Frontier* (1938) is a melancholic and complex fantasy full of intrigue and in surreal fashion captures the obsessions and fears of the 1930s. The protagonist, Pompey Casmilus (modelled on the author), depressed by a hapless love affair, leaves for what Bluemel describes as 'the fantastic but seemingly real Schloss Tilssenon' (32) on the northern German border to recuperate. In *Women's Fiction of the Second World War*, Gill Plain observes that it 'presents a striking and intensely pessimistic indictment of the impulse to war' (68). Pompey's first-person, often surreal, narrative interrogates and undermines nationalism (of both countries), posing the difficult question of how much freedom might be lost in order to oppose fascism in 'an effort to imagine an Englishness strong enough to withstand the Fascist threat' (29). Seduced by German militarism, as many were (like Larkin's father), Pompey ends up in uniform and concludes of her comrades, 'they are cruel and barbaric and ruthless to hold at all costs, at any cost whatsoever of pain and suffering to other people, the power of their privilege' (270). Few saw fascism and its possibilities quite as starkly, but as Plain observes in her extensive analysis of this book the focus is on individual culpability since the author 'identifies the forces of chaos and evil as internal rather than external' (1996: 69).

In *The Holiday* (1949) Smith describes the 1930s and 1940s as having been 'the times of a black split heart [...]. This was the false-simple way of the Nazis driving at the democracies, which are still too much split and dark [...]' (143-4). Plain notes how long Smith struggled to get the novel published but observes that 'it is perhaps not surprising that this account of post-traumatic stress and inchoate grief was judged unwelcome fare by wartime publishers' (2009: 172) This created a lag between writing and publication that was achieved only, as Plain reveals, 'after she had replaced all war references with the nebulous concept of "post war"' (172). According to Bluemel the English and their country are greatly diminished in this novel (49-50), particularly the less affluent, suburban middle classes of which protagonist, Celia, is in essence a part of despite her resistance to their values. Celia's ambition to write 'something that is truly noble' seems out of joint with the times which 'are wrong, they are certainly wrong, at least in the West they are wrong' (53) and records, as Florian Niedlich observes, 'a dismal time of suspension, marked by paralysis, corruption and, above all, uncertainty' (73). Lee Rourke suggests Smith's last novel 'is also fiercely political and can be read as a post-colonial, post-war critique' (n.pag). Although the war has ended, anxieties have not and one character is reduced to tears 'because she had anxious news of her daughter Dinah serving with the A.T.S. in Palestine' (173). Celia's clique discuss decolonization, the antipathy towards the English in former colonies (125) and specifically the situation in India; the protests of Gandhi and the Congress Party (127). When the radio news intrudes on Celia's world, it tells her, '5,000 people are now known to have lost their lives in the Bengal Hindoo-Moslem riots' (182). For Niedlich the novel is marked by fragmentation (68-9) and mirrors a sense of the fracturing social and geopolitical certainties of the late 1940s for which the war was a catalyst. As Plain makes clear, Smith was 'unusual in her attempt to make explicit the pain of war' (2009: 172) but *The Holiday* succeeds in representing its aftermath, too. In *Literature of the 1940s* Plain describes it as a narrative that 'configures war's end as a void – a gap, a chasm, a desire for oblivion – characterised by lack of purpose and confusion' (185).

Waugh time

A vital context of situating this decade is that of class and social change, particularly the fortunes of the aristocracy. As Elizabeth Maslen indicates, a 'growing unease about tradition and the old hierarchies was fairly common as the war progressed [...]' (629). Evelyn Waugh's *Put Out More Flags* (1942) is dedicated to Randolph Churchill (a military comrade of the author's) and, as recorded in a 'Preface' dated 1966, was written after a period of 'two years of military service [when] I had been entirely divorced from writing' (7). The narrative features warfare on various fronts, including the one at home, and the realization that there was a serious challenge to the status quo is reflected in the opening of the novel which incorporates the public declaration of war itself as a pivotal moment in the lives of various characters:

> In the week which preceded the outbreak of the Second World War – days of surmise and apprehension which cannot, without irony, be called the last days of peace – and on the Sunday morning when all doubts were finally resolved and misconceptions corrected [...]. (11)

Basil Seal lodges with his sister, Barbara, who struggles to maintain her 200-year-old country manor house at Malfrey, her servants abandoning her for better-paid work:

> An hour later the remaining three housemaids had appeared with prim expressions of face.
> 'Edith and Olive and me have talked it over and we want to go and make aeroplanes. They say they are taking on girls at Brakemore's.'
> 'You'll find it terribly hard work, you know.'
> 'Oh no, it's not the work, madam. It's the Birmingham women. The way they leave their rooms.'
> 'It's all very strange for them at first. We must do all we can to help. As soon as they settle down and get used to our ways ... ' but she saw it was hopeless while she spoke.
> 'They say they want girls at Brakemore's,' said the maids. (13–14)

Here are encapsulated many of the tensions of the war economy and the aspirational spirit of change the conflict appears to unleash, economically and socially, an overturning. Initially, the old order cleaves to coordinates that are falling apart, as we see with Basil's mother listening to the declaration of war, still dependent on her man-servant, judging the world on experiences of the First World War, memories of which haunt the first sections of the narrative to comic effect:

> 'Shall I remove the radio, my lady?'
> 'Yes, by all means. He spoke very well, very well indeed.'
> 'It's all very sad, my lady.'
> 'Very sad for the Germans, Anderson.'

> It was quite true, thought Lady Seal; Neville Chamberlain had spoken surprisingly well. She had never liked him very much, neither him nor his brother – if anything she had preferred the brother – but they were comfortable drab fellows both of them. However, he had spoken very creditably that morning, as though he were fully alive to his responsibilities. She would ask him to luncheon. But perhaps he would be busy; the most improbable people were busy in wartime, she remembered. (20)

This is a world about to be plunged into vertiginous upheavals, all the snobbish certainties disturbed, but still open to comic exploitation by her son, improbably and unscrupulously busy. Basil develops a 'racket' by volunteering as the billeting officer who rehomes problem children, Waugh mirroring the utopian spirit of evacuation and the class antagonism it continued to suffer from at times. Basil takes cheques for not burdening the upper crust with the worst of the children, Doris, Marlene and Micky. Basil shifts from this racket to counter-intelligence, betraying his homosexual acquaintance, the half-Jewish intellectual Ambrose Silk who works at the Ministry of Information, and who writes about his lost love, a Brownshirt named Hans (an echo of Isherwood), but persuaded to omit Hans by Basil, the latter condemns his work. Ironically given Ambrose's acute fears about his fate if invasion ensues, his publisher is imprisoned as a Nazi sympathizer, so Ambrose flees to neutral Ireland disguised as a Jesuit. The narrative moves slowly from a series of comic vignettes that echo the pre-war partying of Waugh's earlier fiction (including some of the same characters) to Basil's gradual darkly comic realization, that 'There's only one serious occupation for a chap now, that's killing Germans. I have an idea I shall rather enjoy it' (255) when he joins a Special Forces commando unit.

Waugh himself seems to have hoped for the opportunity to distinguish himself militarily in a way that made those ranked above and below him somewhat nervous. His conservatism and nostalgia for the past is conveyed by *Brideshead Revisited* (1945) that is one of his best remembered books but was identified by many as out of step with the times. Nevertheless, the novel's 'Prologue' begins in Scotland in 1944, with thirty-nine-year-old Captain Charles Ryder and his men in C Company facing boredom, disillusionment and the pettiness of finicky superior officers and army discipline generally, but – unbeknown to all – about to move south. As Waugh reflected in his diary on 21 May, also unaware of the upcoming invasion of Europe, he was 'in alternate despondency and exultation about the book' (566), adding on 6 June, 'This morning the waiter told me the Second Front had opened. I sat down early to work and wrote a fine passage of Lord Marchmain's death agonies' (567). By 24 June he noted his full draft of the novel was complete (568). Ironically, in this prologue Ryder is acutely aware of their proximity to a lunatic asylum, one that implies a broader and more fundamental craziness in the world-at-large:

> As we marched past the men used to shout greetings to them through the railings – 'Keep a bed warm for me, chum. I shan't be long' – but Hooper, my newest-joined platoon commander, grudged them their life of privilege: 'Hitler would put them in a gas chamber,' he said; 'I reckon we can learn a thing or two from him.' (8)

Ryder reflects, 'Hooper became a symbol to me of Young England, so that whenever I read some public utterance proclaiming what Youth demanded in the Future and what the world owed to Youth, I would test these general statements by substituting "Hooper" and seeing if they still seemed as plausible' (12). Essentially, Ryder regards this lower class and uncomplaining young man a harbinger of things to come, representing both uncomfortable change and the next generation, elements that would feature prominently in the post-war environment. In the 'Epilogue' also set in 1944, arriving at Brideshead, Ryder visits Nanny Watkins, who is full of tales of the Blitz and its bombing (302). The first edition of the book ends with a locationary note 'CHAGFORD, *February-June, 1944*' (304) which reflects the period of composition Waugh spent at a military camp awaiting orders as the conflict raged. By the time of *The Loved One* (1948), set in America, the war seems long over, since Waugh renders it mostly a matter of memory, decried by Aimée the beautician, who recalls with distaste her customers' obsession in a beauty salon during the war years with pattern-bombing, most especially Mrs Komstock whose 'nephew who was high in indoctrination' (92). The wife of Aimée's employer refuses to listen to the radio beyond the news which has reflected Cold War fears: '"Turn it off," said Mrs Joyboy. "Well, he says there'll be war again this year"' (113). However, ironically the poems of the protagonist, Dennis, and their very success are imbued with the previous conflict since

> They had taken their shapes in frigid war-time railway journeys – the racks piled high with equipment, the dimmed lights falling on a dozen laps, the faces above invisible, cigarette-smoke mixing with frosty breath; the unexplained stops, the stations dark as the empty footways. He had written them in Nissen huts and in spring evenings, on a bare heath, a mile from the airfield, and on the metal benches of transport planes. (84–5)

Such snatched moments in the inconvenient martial settings of a modern war, often spent in transit, mirror Waugh's life and experiences during the period when he wrote *Brideshead Revisited*, its nostalgia framed by sour reflections upon military life, whose patterns were a retrospective coordinate for so many during the rest of the decade.

Waugh was far from the only backwards looking prominent literary personage of the time. Hewison quotes T. S. Eliot's fears for the future: 'The true purpose of education is to preserve the class and to select the elite' (1995: 53). While these views may have been widely shared, the result of victory in the war was a General Election in which the majority of voters clearly distrusted Churchill's will to follow through on the Beveridge Report. In its wake, Attlee's Labour government was able to bring about significant change in access to higher education. As Angus Calder (1997: 585) reports one in seven children were going to university in 1950 compared to one in sixteen before the war. Such changes during the decade could, however, have little effect on the writers active within it, like Waugh and others, who were necessarily raised in the pre-war world with all the experiences that entailed.

From the ranks

Born in 1911, and with three 1930s novels behind him, Gerald Kersh was publishing short stories in mainstream periodicals and newspapers (which featured fiction in this period) when the war started. While posher writers tended to contribute to the war effort via the Ministry of Information, the BBC or the secret service, Kersh joined the Coldstream Guards:

> I had pipe dreams of myself on active service – a hero, battered and magnificent, rallying a last desperate handful of exalted men and achieving glory on the field. Such things do happen, after all. But not to me. My Army career was remarkable inglorious. The only scars I have to show are surgeon's scars. After a couple of operations on my legs it was established that, as a soldier, I was fit for nothing but spud-bashing, floor swabbing and latrine cleaning. [...] Blasted into Category C, unfit for service overseas, I pelted the enemy with paper and slung ink at him. It was all I could do. (1946: 62)

Initially these efforts resulted in a series of short journalistic sketches published anonymously in the *Daily Herald*. When these were gathered as *Private Life of a Private* in 1941 and submitted for approval to the Director of Public Relations at the War Office, Kersh was asked to write a pamphlet on infantry training, and was transferred to the reserve to do it. While His Majesty's Stationery Office didn't take the product forward, Kersh was allowed to expand it and submit it to Heinemann and the result, *They Die With Their Boots Clean* (1941), became 'one of the best-selling books of the war' (63). According to Andrew Sinclair, Kersh's book is 'a stark view of the war at last written from the ranks' (106). The 'at last' is telling. According to Angus Calder in *The People's War* in June 1941 there were two and a quarter million infantrymen, but very few were actively fighting, most were stuck in isolated camps in Britain while 662,000 RAF and 395,000 Navy men were actively engaged in the conflict (249), or, as Kersh puts it in *Clean, Bright and Slightly Oiled*: 'The Army was in the shadow just then. Nobody wanted to have anything to do with the old-fashioned foot-slogger. It was half-believed that the Army was not necessary, and that only the Air Force and the Navy really mattered' (62).

They Die With their Boots Clean is a book about army training presided over by the charismatic one-eyed Sergeant Nelson. Rawlinson describes it as 'bellicose' (148) as the raw recruits are turned into finished products (soldiers), but there is no actual fighting or violence, just the coming together of largely working-class men from across the country meeting regimental height and size requirements. The first chapter makes very clear their diversity of background (different accents are heavily represented). It is a group portrait of England's indomitable fighting men: the Yorkshireman; the cynical Cockney; the fly Brummie; the fairground boxer from Stoke who is all endurance but no skill; Old Silence, the atheist, who dies on marriage leave; the schoolmaster who will become an officer; Thurstan, the raw Geordie who can barely express himself; the anonymous narrator who evaluates them all and tries to describe the cocktail: 'Dash of ferocious Britain, spot of aromatic Asia, jigger of crazy Celt, splash of gentle and murderous Saxon, tinge of iron Roman, shot of haughty Norman, drip of fierce Norse – the elements, even when they are blended to neutrality, give birth to something queerly individual' (37). The last chapter becomes somewhat sentimental over the career soldier but an epilogue returns to Sergeant Nelson in a pub talking, in his distinctive informal way, about discipline and makes clear how unimpressed he would be to find out someone had written literature about basic training.

On the back of this popular success, Kersh wrote *The Nine Lives of Bill Nelson* (1942) in which the Sergeant Nelson appears to have died in an air raid while on leave and various characters, mostly other NCOs, tell stories about him which account for his losing an eye at Dunkirk while trying to rescue a refugee orphan and cumulatively illustrate the resoluteness of the man and the ruthlessness of the enemy, before discovering accounts of his demise to have been premature. These two books were published together as *Sergeant Nelson of the Guards* which was published in the United States in 1945.

Kersh wrote other short novels during the war, with very different tones. *The Dead Look On* (1943) is an account of a Nazi massacre a fictional Czech village, Dudicka, dedicated to the victims of Lidice. The narrative is brutally efficient and shockingly grim, 'an awesome graphic parable' according to St John (301). It is so downbeat it is surprising to learn Kersh made efforts to turn it into a play, though possibly for radio (1946: 76). But the grimness is justified. Within the context of 1942, when it was written, *The Dead Look On* is simultaneously an attempt to make 'a far-away country of which we know little', according to Chamberlain, human and worth fighting for and to identify the pitiless nature of the enemy.

Brain and Ten Fingers (1943) is about a group of Jugoslavian resistance (the dedication is careful not to identify them with either royalist guerrillas or communist partisans) who are pursued after a raid and reduced to ten. The narrative is mostly told by Andrej, a boy in the group, who is too naive to know the worst of what happened when their village was attacked, but other characters have their own chapters, including Klemen the Fool, the group's emerging leader. A raging torrent has washed out a bridge that they need to cross to escape their pursuers. Klemen is the Brain that solves the problem, even though Tomaz, his stepbrother is washed away: 'I saw his head, like a potato in a boiling saucepan. Then that was gone, and that was the end of Tomaz, who was just about everything I ever loved on the face of the earth' (60–1). It is clear from the memoir *Clean, Bright and Slightly Oiled* that Kersh observed a (dry) training exercise in bridge building that inspired this sequence and was fascinated to see from where leadership emerged (72–3).

In *Faces in a Dusty Picture* (1944) written in 1943, according to Rawlinson's *British Writing of the Second World War*, 'the ideals of instrumental community are the mainstay' (113). It tells the story of a desert war battle, a modest victory against the Italians, from privates to general. The violence is matter-of-fact, the casualties random:

> A Bren-gunner sucking a small, downy moustache, sees men moving on the Italian side and fires a couple of short bursts at them: he will never know whether he has hit them or missed them. In point of fact he has killed one man and wounded two; thus shedding human blood for the first time in his life. At home, he works as a sandwich cutter in a ham-and-beef shop. (116)

Rawlinson is near the mark. The war has to be fought, but the consequences were borne by individuals. Veterans wrote to Kersh praising his description of a sandstorm, though he had never been near North Africa (1946: 90) and American reviews of the 1945 United States edition assume he fought there with the Coldstream Guards.

Another writer from the ranks makes a useful point of comparison. Born in London in 1912, as James McLaren Ross, Julian Maclaren-Ross partly grew up in the south of France, returned to Britain as his family's money dried up and lived on the south coast around Brighton, working as a vacuum-cleaner salesman. Already working on radio adaptations, he met old colonials fallen on hard times and with a fine ear for language wrote and adapted their anecdotes into short stories like 'Bit of a Smash in Madras' that launched him in *Horizon* in 1940 before he was called up into the army.

Maclaren-Ross's ear for speech also served him well in recording his army experiences in the short stories that appeared in many magazine, miscellanies and anthologies during the war years, and which were collected and published as *The Stuff to Give the Troops* (1944). By the time the collection emerged, its author was out of the army. The title was already ironic in that the author's lean reportage of disorganization, miscommunication, accidental death, incompetence (not sparing himself), squalor and stalled romance was in no way a recruiting manual, much as it may have amused soldiers who knew the truth of it. A knee injury rendered Maclaren-Ross unfit for active service, but proving it became a Kafkaesque nightmare ('I Had to Go Sick'). Deciding unilaterally that he was not being used to the best advantage Maclaren-Ross deserted, was arrested, was threatened with court martial, spent time in a psychiatric unit and was finally invalided out. This traumatic time is recounted in Paul Willetts's biography of the author but is never fully played out in his writing – unlike most of the other events in his life (though the court martial is mentioned in his 1946 memoir of Alun Lewis).

Becoming a conspicuous fixture in Soho pubs, Maclaren-Ross lived out the 1940s producing two more books of short stories titled *Better Than a Kick in the Pants* (1945) and *The Nine Men of Soho* (1946), a novella about the South of France in the 1930s he named *Bitten by the Tarantula* (1946), and a novel. *Of Love and Hunger* (1947) recycles his time on the South Coast selling vacuum cleaners adding an adulterous romance and an epilogue with the protagonist, Fanshawe, as a Captain in the army. The novel is told in frank dialogue and lean prose from the first-person narrator. Maclaren-Ross gives Fanshawe a backstory in Madras which is revealed in brief, italicized memories and produces a bravura sequence when the narrator experiences a recurrence of malarial fever. The novel was largely successfully reviewed but Maclaren-Ross's post-army hand-to-mouth existence meant he was always trying to get advances from publishers and did not always deliver if he did. In consequence *Of Love and Hunger*'s publisher Allan Wingate was small, with little in the way of advertising budget, and there was not a substantial print run to sell. Ironically, two years later, Allan Wingate was reprinting Norman Mailer's war novel *The Naked and the Dead* eight times. Maclaren-Ross was to remain stalled in the 'promising' category and seldom appears in summaries of the decade, publishing little substantial in the fifteen years that remained to him other than informative, but partial, memoirs.

Maclaren-Ross has numerous similarities with Kersh; both cultivated an image, both spoke French but lacked university education and both may have felt less British than those around them – Maclaren-Ross's parents were born in Canada and India, his mother having Anglo-Indian parentage (though this may have been concealed from him), while Kersh's father was born in Poland. Both thrived when writing about army life, both exploited the short story market of the war years, each publishing three collections of stories previously published in periodicals. In fact, Kersh's later Heinemann collections share out between them (and add to) the contents of his 1943 *Selected Stories* published by Staples and Staples. This is again indicative of the demand for reading material in the period and the short print runs due to paper rationing (see above).

Where Maclaren-Ross carried the burden of living up to the potential seen by most reviewers, Kersh was declared the literary discovery of the war quite early. In February 1943 John Brophy announced:

> Whether or not war poets are in short supply, the war has produced one outstanding prose writer, a novelist with a sharp and distinct individuality of his own who nevertheless contrives to express a considerable amount of those common national characteristics we lump together as British. […] He is that rare combination, a master craftsman with the popular touch; he can satisfy highbrow and lowbrow alike. (*Sunday Graphic*, cited in Duncan 2017: 7)

This was not quite true. Kersh was not among those contributing to the highbrow literary journals and magazines such as *Horizon*. To a significant extent he didn't need them – he was writing radio comedy for the BBC, commentaries for documentary films, weekly 2,000-word articles for *The People* under a byline, and later articles under his own name and was working on film scripts for stage and film star and radio broadcaster, Leslie Howard. Kersh had been attached to the Army Film Unit but was unable to actually join it because he failed Officer Training in 1943, despite the fact he was doing the job. *Clean Bright and Slightly Oiled*'s 'To Whom It May Concern' preface claims to be a partial memoir of the last six years with other instalments to come, and in it Kersh addresses this issue and why he refused to go through with his application earlier in the war when the process was much easier: 'As soon as I put a pip on my shoulder I set myself socially apart from the ordinary man in uniform' (61). Ultimately, becoming an officer is about class.

The first story of Maclaren-Ross's *The Stuff to Give the Troops*, 'The Tape', uses the voice of a working-class soldier to describe a fellow recruit who is unwilling officer material:

> I'm just an ordinary type of bloke, myself, but Phil was educated. Been to college and everything. He talked pound-noteish, but not in a way to get on your wick, like Weston, who was in for a commission and treated you like you didnt even exist. Old Phil werent like that. Mucked in like the rest of us. He was a socialist, see? That's why he wouldnt put in for a pip. [sic] (7)

Phil is pressured by his girlfriend and ranking officers to seek promotion but, on principle, won't face the barrier it will put between him and men like the narrator, Ford, since the separation of NCOs and privates is enforced due to the need for 'discipline'. Phil changes his outlook and, without his influence, Ford drinks too much, is caught coming late back to the camp and punches another NCO. Maclaren-Ross is well positioned to inhabit this awkward boundary, having been raised on a private income but reduced to attending the Labour Exchange in Brighton before the war. His 1946 article 'Second Lieutenant Lewis' highlights the same problem in recounting his brief acquaintance with another writer who felt the problem keenly; '"I'm not certain I shouldn't have stayed in the ranks," Lewis said, "I thought as an officer I'd be able to do something for the men. But one's more helpless than ever"' (407).

The division between officers and men is fundamental to the problems Kersh sees in the other writers' attempts to accurately represent army life, arguing in *Clean, Bright and Slightly Oiled* that:

> The truest kind of reporting comes out of the experiences of men involved in the little problems of their fellow-men. Our intellectuals are not so involved: the ordinary British soldier won't let them be, because he doesn't like them. So the intellectual footslogger-faute-de-mieux frequently finds himself back in the cafés, discharged because of neuroses; or on his backside at a Company Office Desk, where he spends his days in clerical work and his nights in introspection: a

misfit with a mission, itching to tell the world the sufferings of the plain man in uniform.

Much he knows of the plain man! (20)

It may or may not have been intentional, but a lot of what Kersh describes here applies accurately to Maclaren-Ross's experiences, such as those described in 'Are You Happy in Your Work' where he is clerk to a unit's second-in-command and finds the working-class runners assigned to him largely a pain. In the same disingenuous plain-speaking mode Kersh names four 'progressive editors of high-priced highbrow anthologies' whose ideas of the common soldier he finds wanting.

In 1944, Kersh and the army parted company. Through commercial film connections Kersh acquired an American War Correspondent pass, took unauthorized passage on a flight to Normandy and broke various regulations to get himself to Paris shortly after its liberation. The chapter 'Bits out of my French Diary' makes it seem something of a reckless and wilful escapade, though the articles in *The People* indicate he looked up a Jewish family living in Paris, but not that they were his aunt and cousins (see Duncan 2017: 11). Kersh would later work on the script for an incomplete film documentary (*German Concentration Camps Factual Survey*) and be exasperated by contemporary soft-pedalling of German guilt on the one hand and disbelief of the facts on the other.

This post-war angst comes through in Kersh's late 1940s novels, when the increasing availability of paper hade made full-length works viable again. The first, *Prelude to a Certain Midnight* (1947), is detective fiction, sort of, in that it deals with the pre-war murder of a ten-year-old girl from the perspective of its post-war aftermath. But the reader does learn the identity of a pre-war child killer, unlike the eccentric amateur sleuth Asta Thundersley or the professional Detective Inspector Turpin. The grim parade of suspects from Soho drinking and writing circles is at once satirical and a tortured examination of the urgent question, 'who enables murderers?' The answer is that those who allow themselves to be bullied empower the bully to take their 'experiments' one step further. Asta Thundersley at least identifies the enabler: 'the submissive Catchy, who said that she only wanted to make men happy, [who] made happy only those men who needed victims, willing victims' (202). The actual murderer is discovered by the eccentric investigator's peripatetic sister, who leaves the country rather than attempt to prove it – an indictment of those who know where the guilt lies but won't, for their own convenience, commit to bringing it home. If one understands this narrative in the context of post-war Germany and Cold War 'practicalities' it hits much harder when a character reiterates: 'It is all the same sort of thing. Maidanek, Belsen, Auschwitz, Sonia Sabbatini – the difference is only a matter of scale and legality' (203).

Song of the Flea (1948) returns to the seedy London underworld of Kersh's pre-war success *Night and the City*; wherein the aspiring writer protagonist, Pym, negotiates cheap bedsits, conniving crooks and con-men, dodgy publishers, various theatrical types, straight-talking women and female fantasists. The protagonist's financial difficulties are not unlike those of Maclaren-Ross's contemporaneous *Of Love and Hunger* in its obsession with pounds, shillings and pence. The anonymous 1948 TLS reviewer shrewdly suggests the 1930s setting may mean some earlier material is being recycled and goes on to identify that: 'if people are soft-hearted in this world they often do more harm than good; and, in establishing this thesis, Mr Kersh draws on his picturesque and convincing knowledge of human vileness in a manner which is both entertaining and instructive.' It is all too easily forgotten how novels like those of Maclaren-Ross and Kersh challenged ideas of what was acceptable subject matter.

Kersh's *The Thousand Deaths of Mr Small* published in America in 1950 and the UK in 1951 takes this further. It is a troubling combination of the self-loathing of a man working in advertising and his recollections of his parents who he blames (and sometimes forgives) for his psychology even as he indulges its flaws. The parental domestic strife is very funny, the self-loathing not at all and the parallel narrative of dynamic entrepreneur Solly Schwartz, who once looked up to the narrator's father, erupts unpredictably at various points. Kersh is certainly trying to push the barriers in what is and is not acceptable in *Mr Small* with what one American reviewer calls his 'emetic vocabulary' and another 'catalogues of loathing and revulsion as have rarely been seen in print'. For example:

> Now, since he lacks [his father] I. Small's knack of talking himself into great expectations, having more objectivity in his little finger than that old fool had in his body, he knows himself for what he is – a sort of bifurcated turd, a dropping cursed with consciousness, afflicted with a sentience so that he can smell himself, worse luck; dropped with strain and pain out of one bloody hole to go in shame and pain into another, into the dirt, where lies his grubby little destiny. (237)

This too is the 1940s, not just a decade of courage and victory but one that was angst-ridden and traumatized by the awareness of the depths of human weakness even as technological capability reached new heights. It was also the decade in which the term 'existentialism' was coined and thrived.

Kersh helpfully signs his books with where they were written and had clearly become a tax exile from the British Welfare State relocating to the United States by 1950, where he would work for many American magazines, and write deeply British London-set novels such as *Fowlers End* (1957) and *The Angel and the Cuckoo* (1966). He has not been without admirers, but tends to be a writer's writer, sidelined by most literary critics. Why? Leaving the country is not such a great career move for literary reputation, and Kersh's work was simply too popular to be well regarded by highbrow criticism of the time, often being associated with the less reputable genres of crime and comedy. In short, Kersh has not been regarded as officer material.

Yet the lens of the 1940s shows Kersh reflecting the decade without the distractions of his works in the surrounding decades. His novels show the rallying of the early 1940s, consciousness of the need for collective effort to engage with the war, then, in the post-war novels a traumatized self-examination of where the war came from and a measure of self-disgust. Kersh's output also reflects the shape of the literary decade; its extraordinary productivity, and successes, but, also its post-war re-evaluation, and a relative lack of recognition beyond its end.

The 1940s: A literary decade

The collection opens with Ashley Maher's Literary History of the 1940s which surveys critical approaches to the decade and the way recent critics have redefined it in terms of continuities rather than divisions, identifying Intermodernism, Late Modernism and 'mid-century' as appropriate designations. The survey engages with the writings of George Orwell, Christopher Isherwood, Virginia Woolf, Elizabeth Bowen, Patrick Hamilton, Roger Mais and Victor Reid in considering significant contexts of the decade, including the importance of the short story form, Mass Observation, the Beveridge report, austerity and Empire.

Philip Tew's chapter considers a range of examples of the literature of the Blitz and also private authorial reactions to these events, assessing the experiences so reflected, and whether such narratives contributed to, drew upon or contested the myth of the Blitz that was being inculcated both officially and in more indirect fashion. His analysis and contextualization consider works by Phyllis Bottome, Elizabeth Bowen, Henry Green, Graham Greene, Patrick Hamilton, James Hanley, Norah Hoult, Daphne du Maurier, Winifred Peck, Jocelyn Playfair, Noel Streatfeild and Virginia Woolf. The texts considered reflect the experience and concerns of civilians in wartime, from fears to actuality to propaganda.

In her recent *British Literature and Culture in Second World Wartime* (2020) Beryl Pong describes the literal suppression, both culturally and politically, of people's doubts and their terror at the air raids, pointing out that 'where the state discouraged non-fiction from articulating such negative sentiments, the creative licenses of fiction enabled the expression of a wider range of emotions and psychological states, including fear and dread, as well as suspicion and scepticism about the People's War' (56). This is reflected in the literary responses, both contemporaneous and in the immediate post-war period, that are examined here, before the Cold War and the beginnings of the arms race replaced that fear and trauma with even grimmer possibilities.

In 'Genteel Bohemia: Capable Women in Women's Fiction of the 1940s,' Deborah Philips considers women's participation in the war effort, and looks at the fight by many to continue in such roles after the war despite official and de facto opposition mostly from men. As she argues, 'That "pride in work" and a sense of frustration with the "confines of home" resonate throughout women's fiction written over the period of the 1940s' (93) even when the fiction ostensibly represents earlier periods. Philips offers an account of Stella Gibbons's *Ticky* (1943), demonstrating its contemporaneity despite a Victorian setting, focusing on gender and class, and especially the nineteenth-century debate over the nature of the female mind. Analysis of Nancy Mitford's bestseller, *The Pursuit of Love* (1945), set in the interwar period, shows how its narrative centres on a generational divide in world views, tinged with both nostalgia and a validation of more modern mores. Jean Rhys's *Good Morning Midnight* (1939) charts the aftermath of the era of the Bright Young Things with bleak humour and an enduring sense of ironic comedy. The 1940s fiction of Monica Dickens is also considered, particularly *Flowers on the Grass* (1949) that Philips reads in terms of 'a post-war state of the nation novel' (99), in which the various women characters that Bohemian artist and widower Daniel encounters represent a range of versions of post-war femininity. Mary Renault's *The Friendly Young Ladies* (1944) is set on a houseboat on the outskirts of London in 1937, with Leo (Leonora) nursing the ill and dying and showing show Elsie, her younger seventeen-year-old sister, womanhood not dependent on men. Daphne du Maurier's *The Parasites* (1949) concerns three gifted, and yet aimless siblings, whose bohemian and artistic parents have left them incapable of survival in any conventional sense. Together they represent a past world, their impulses anachronistic, out of time, doomed to relative failure. As Philips suggests it 'is an awkward and ambiguous novel [...] recognising that theirs is a bohemian culture which has no place in the post-war world' (105). Philips's chapter charts the ambiguous and belated presence of bohemianism and women writers and characters determined to recast their social and cultural presence.

Chris Hopkins's 'The ship and the nation' analyses the wartime naval novels by Anthony Thorne and J.P.W. Mallalieu, looking in depth at how education and training initiatives in the Royal Navy allowed the mixing of classes to go on in a way that produced novels with a documentary edge, changed attitudes and contributed to the sense of the conflict being a 'People's War' despite governmental suppression of discussion of post-war change. Close analysis of these texts shows them explicitly challenging conventional representation of class attitudes and allegiances in the preparation for and prosecution of naval warfare. Hopkins goes on to discuss the later success of Nicholas Monsarrat's *The Cruel Sea* (1951) which indicates more conservative attitudes re-establishing themselves, claiming the victory and marking the divide between the decades.

Karen Schaller's 'Feeling Political: Elizabeth Bowen in the 1940s' looks in depth at Elizabeth Bowen's 1940s short stories which have often played second fiddle to her 1948 novel *The Heat of the Day*. Carefully positioning her chapter in the context of burgeoning academic interest in this once neglected writer, Schaller argues for the importance of feeling in Bowen's works and demonstrates it in the wartime and immediate post-war settings of 'I Hear You Say So', 'Unwelcome Idea' and 'Careless Talk'. With reference to the Ministry of Information archive, Schaller shows Bowen's liveness to the value of feeling as being the essence of morale and how Bowen's broadcasting and writing works to channel the daily frustrations of rationing not against the government that imposed it but against the enemy that necessitated it. It is in the details that we see the nuances of feeling in the 1940s heightened by the conflict and the gear-grinding change to its aftermath and Bowen's knowing literary exploitation of dialogue and reaction that is the very opposite of careless talk.

In 'The Life of Animals: George Orwell's Fiction in the 1940s' Tamás Bényei contextualizes the writer's landmark texts of the decade with reference to 'Revenge Is Sour', a journalistic piece reflecting on a visit to a prisoner-of-war camp in Southern Germany, Hannah Arendt's notion of the banality of evil and the idea of revenge. This illustrates Orwell's obsession with how power functions, drawing on thinkers including Arendt, Isaiah Berlin, Friedrich Hayek and others, against his idea of Englishness. Next, the analysis considers the ideological and aesthetic dimensions of *Animal Farm* (1945) especially its 'performative speech acts'. In his reading, threat and convoluted jargon are used to silence the animals, masking the pigs' perversion of the concept of equality, in which Animalism becomes first seven commandments, and later the famous maxim of Orwell's text: 'Four legs good, two legs bad' (21). Bényei describes how this perversion of language accords with political practices and results in 'ways in which plain narrative style is contaminated by what is happening to language within the narrated world' (171) and outlines the intricacies of this animal fable, with terms drawn from Giorgio Agamben: *bios* for a full life (humans and eventually pigs) and *zoē* or bare life (all other animals). The account of *Nineteen Eighty-Four* focuses on how Orwell exploits the novel form to undermine narrative and thereby magnify Winston Smith's sense of dislocation in Oceania where the Party has eliminated most of the private realm upon which humanistic 'novelistic discourse' (176) depends and replaced it with anti-novels written at the Ministry of Truth in Newspeak. For Bényei the protagonist's glass paperweight offers 'a looking glass through which Winston sees, opaquely' (182) Orwell's images of an imperial subjugation of otherness and the suppression of human multiplicity.

Charlotte Charteris's chapter, 'Purposes of Love: Rethinking intimacy in the 1940s', explores bodies, intimacy, trauma and healing in the context of Mass Observation's 1949 'Little Kinsey' report serialized in the *Sunday Pictorial*. Focusing on topics of repression, rebellion and reconnection this chapter illustrates how some novels of the decade both enabled and prefigured the report's findings. The central figure is Mary Renault, later associated with historical novels but shown here writing about contemporary issues of gender and sexuality with remarkable poise. Introduced with reference to Renault's debut *Purposes of Love* (1939), the chapter focuses on repressed adolescents in works by Jocelyn Brooke, Francis King and Denton Welch, rebellious women in novels by Renault, Nancy Mitford and Barbara Comyns, and the recovering ex-serviceman in Monica Dickens, Henry Green and Renault. Using texts from across the decade this chapter addresses contemporary considerations of sexuality, intimacy and trauma.

Rebecca Dyer's 'Masters and Servants, Class, and the Colonies in Graham Greene's 1940s Fiction' begins with the author's reflection on the historical nature of being in household service and considers those servants found in other 1940s texts, particularly P. G. Wodehouse's fiction, Ivy Compton-Burnett's *Manservant and Maidservant* (1947) and Robin Maugham's *The Servant* (1948), all written during a period when the number of servants radically declined in Britain and Europe. In a European setting, Greene revisited his 1936 story 'The Basement Room' when writing the screenplay for its 1948 adaptation as *The Fallen Idol*, about a boy and the family butler, Baines, who charms him with tales of his time in colonial Africa but, as the film title indicates, also introduces him to disturbing elements of the adult world. The subsequent focus of the essay explores Greene's direct representation of Africa via *Journey Without Maps* (1936), a nonfiction travel narrative, and *The Heart of the Matter* (1948), a novel with semi-autobiographical elements, set in an unnamed colony based on Sierra Leone, where Greene was posted from 1942 to 1943. The protagonist Major Scobie juggles a dependent relation with his servant, Ali, marriage, an affair and his role as police commissioner. Dyer argues 'servants and sex workers are the most prominent African characters in the novel' (195) and are highly significant in plot terms though often neglected in criticism. Dyer details Greene's enigmatic portrayal of ethnicity and class in colonized Africa where the locals service the imperial middle class and, while noting his approval of Imperial values, suggests Greene's interest in the paradoxes of human interaction 'might be read as a re-envisioning of Conrad's frame narrative in *Heart of Darkness*' (208).

Andrea Hammel's chapter considers the work of ex-patriate German and Austrian writers in Britain from the bestselling author of the 1930s, Stefan Zweig, to those struggling to adapt as German first-language writers landing in the UK, focusing on Robert Neumann, Hilde Spiel, Hermynia Zur Mühlen and Anna Gmeyner (aka Anna Reiner). Hammel considers their struggles to adapt to becoming writers in English and English writers and their attempts to not simply make a home and living but to influence through their writing the post-war reconstruction of their former homelands. Such writers in exile are often doubly excluded, falling outside of the category of British writing yet no longer fully belonging to their own culture, and their contributions have previously received little attention.

Glyn White's 'Un-British: The Transatlantic Crime Film Connection' addresses cultural responses to the crime genre and its perceived contribution to the Americanization of British culture within the context of the dominance of Hollywood in British cinemas. In 1939 James Hadley Chase's American-set gangster novel *No Orchids for Miss Blandish* dominated the bestsellers, provoking Orwell's objections in the essay 'Raffles and Miss Blandish' (1944). The 1948 movie adaptation of this novel which features a bizarre, coercive, class-crossing love affair and an ersatz American setting became a particular lightning rod for critical ire. British-set films featuring urban black market racketeers known as 'spivs' could also expect rough treatment from film critics including the Boulting brothers' 1947 film of Graham Greene's *Brighton Rock* (1938). This was only one of nine adaptations of Greene's work in the decade. His collaboration with Carol Reed, *The Third Man* (1949), about an

American wartime racketeer, neatly sidestepped critical concerns about the representation of crime in Britain with its Viennese setting. The adaptation of Gerald Kersh's novel *Night and the City* (1938) in 1950 on location in Britain with imported American stars and an American director, Jules Dassin, avoiding the House Un-American Activities Committee effectively brought the spiv cycle to an end. The film found no favour with British critics of the time who, despite a decade which may be seen as the high point of British cinema, could not happily acknowledge the transatlantic power shift which meant, as White suggests, 'British attitudes could no longer be imposed on the world and American dominance previously seen in the film industry would extend exponentially into other areas' (296–97).

Cumulatively, these chapters offer an overview of the fiction of the 1940s (albeit, by its nature, a partial one) alongside salient features of the decade's wider literary culture, exploring experiences of war and its aftermath and various records of often conflicting feelings of fear and anxiety, belonging and not belonging, liberation and constraint, and certainty and uncertainty in a time of unprecedented social and political change and re-evaluation.

Note

1 For examples consult either the National Archives at: https://www.nationalarchives.gov.uk/theartofwar/prop/home_front/; or the online 1940s Society at: http://www.1940.co.uk/

Works cited

Anon. 'Comment'. *Horizon*, February 1940: 69.
Bates, H. E. *The Modern Short Story: A Critical Survey*. London: T. Nelson & Sons, 1941.
Bluemel, Kristin. *George Orwell and the Radical Eccentrics: Intermodernism in Literary London*. Houndsmill, Basingstoke and New York: Palgrave Macmillan, 2004.
Calder, Angus. *The People's War: Britain 1939-45*. London: Pimlico, 1997 [1969].
Cull, Nicholas John. *Selling War: The British Propaganda Campaign against American 'Neutrality' in World War II*. Oxford: Oxford University Press, 1995.
Duncan, Paul. 'Introduction: One Murder Makes Many'. In *Prelude to a Certain Midnight*. London: London Classics, 2017: 7–26.
Feigel, Lara. *The Love-charm of Bombs: Restless Lives in the Second World War*. London: Bloomsbury, 2013.

Harris, Jose. 'War and Social History: Britain and the Home Front during the Second World War'. *Contemporary European History* 1 (1), March 1992: 17–35.
Hewison, Robert. *Under Siege: Literary Life in London 1939-45*. London: Weidenfeld & Nicolson, 1977.
Hewison, Robert. *In Anger: Culture in the Cold War 1945-60*. London: Methuen, 1988.
Hewison, Robert. *Culture and Consensus: England, Art and Politics since 1940*. London: Methuen, 1995.
Hillard, Christopher. *To Exercise Our Talents: The Democratization of Writing in Britain*. Cambridge, MA: Harvard University Press, 2006.
Hillary, Richard. *The Last Enemy*. London: Macmillan, 1942.
Hirsch, Pam. 'Authorship and Propaganda: Phyllis Bottome and the Making of The Mortal Storm (1940)'. *Historical Journal of Film, Radio and Television* 32 (1), 2012: 57–72.
Holland, Steve. *The Mushroom Jungle: A History of Postwar Paperback Publishing*. Westbury (Wilts): Zeon, 1993.
Howard, Alexander Josef. *The Place of the Poet: An Examination of the Evocation of Space and Place in the* Oeuvre *of Philip Larkin*. [Doctoral thesis in English Literature.] Edinburgh: University of Edinburgh, 2018.
Ingelbein, Raphaël. 'A Girl in the Forties: Larkin and the Politics of World War Two'. *Critical Survey* 13 (1), 2001: 80–93.
Kersh, Gerald. *I Got References*. London: Michael Joseph, 1939.
Kersh, Gerald. *Private Life of a Private*. Paul Duncan (ed.), Greater Coventry: Wordsmith Solutions, 2020 [1941].
Kersh, Gerald. *They Die with Their Boots Clean*. London: Heinemann, 1941.
Kersh, Gerald. *The Nine Lives of Bill Nelson*. London: Heinemann, 1942.
Kersh, Gerald. *The Dead Look On*. London: Right Book Club, 1944 [1943].
Kersh, Gerald. *Brain and Ten Fingers*. London: William Heinemann, 1943.
Kersh, Gerald. *Faces in a Dusty Picture*. Kingswood: The World's Work, 1944.
Kersh, Gerald. *Sergeant Nelson of the Guards*. London: Faber & Faber, 2013 [1945].
Kersh, Gerald. *Clean, Bright and Slightly Oiled*. London: William Heinemann, 1946.
Kersh, Gerald. *I Got References*. London: William Heinemann, 1947.
Kersh, Gerald. *Prelude to a Certain Midnight*. London: London Classics, 2017 [1947].
Kersh, Gerald. *The Song of the Flea*. London: Faber & Faber, 2013 [1948].
Kersh, Gerald. *The Thousand Deaths of Mr Small*. London: Faber & Faber, 2013 [1951].
Larkin, Philip. *A Girl in Winter*. London and Boston: Faber and Faber, 1975 [1947].
Larkin, Philip. *Collected Poems*. Anthony Thwaite (ed.). New York: Farrar, Straus and Giroux, 2004 [1988].
Lowe, Peter. 'Resistance and Rebuilding: The Wartime Writings of George Orwell and Albert Camus'. *English Studies* 90 (3), 2009: 305–27.
Maclaren-Ross, Julian. *The Stuff to Give the Troops: Twenty-five Tales of Army Life*. London: Jonathan Cape, 1944.
Maclaren-Ross, Julian. *Of Love and Hunger*. London: Penguin, 2002 [1947].

Maclaren-Ross, Julian. *Collected Memoirs*. London: Black Spring, 2004.

Mackay, Robert. *Half the Battle: Civilian Morale in Britain during the Second World War*. Manchester: Manchester University Press, 2002.

Maslen, Elizabeth. 'Women Writers in World War II'. *Literature Compass* 3 (3), 2006: 625–35.

Mayne, Joan Sheila. *The Novels and the Poetry of Philip Larkin*. [MA thesis in English]. Hull: Hull University, 1962.

Mengham, Rod. 'British Fiction of the War'. In Marina Mackay (ed.), *The Cambridge Companion to the Literature of World War II*. Cambridge: Cambridge University Press, 2009: 26–42.

Niedlich, Florian. '"The Times are the Times of a Black Split Heart": The "Post-War" in Stevie Smith's *The Holiday*'. *AAA: Arbeiten aus Anglistik und Amerikanistik* 35 (1), 2010: 61–74.

Orwell, George, *Nineteen Eighty-Four*. London: Secker & Warburg, 1949.

Piette, Adam. 'Childhood Wiped Out: Larkin, His Father, and the Bombing of Coventry'. *English* 62 (238), August 2013: 230–47.

Plain, Gill. *Women's Fiction of the Second World War; Gender, Power and Resistance*. Edinburgh: Edinburgh University Press, 1996.

Plain, Gill. 'Women Writers and the War'. In Marina McKay (ed.), *The Cambridge Companion to the Literature of the Second World War*. Cambridge: Cambridge University Press, 2009: 165–78.

Plain, Gill. *Literature of the 1940s: War, Postwar and 'Peace'*. Edinburgh: Edinburgh University Press, 2013.

Pong, Beryl. *British Literature in Second World Wartime: For the Duration*. Oxford: Oxford University Press, 2020.

Priestley, J. B. 'We've known them and laughed at them, these fussy little steamers'. ['Postscript', BBC Radio Broadcast]. *Speakola*. Undated [orig. 5 June 1940]: n.pag; https://speakola.com/ideas/jb-priestley-the-little-steamer-dunkirk-1940

Rawlinson, Mark. *British Writing of the Second World War*. Oxford: Clarendon, 2000.

Ross, Alan. *The Forties: A Period Piece*. London: Weidenfeld & Nicolson, 1950.

Rourke, Lee. 'The Beautiful Melancholy of Stevie Smith'. *The Guardian*. 9 January 2008: n.pag; https://www.theguardian.com/books/booksblog/2008/jan/09/thebeautifulmelancholyofst.

Sinclair, Andrew. *War Like a Wasp: The Lost Decade of the 'Forties*. London: Hamish Hamilton, 1989.

Smith, Stevie. *Over the Frontier*. London: Virago, 1980 [1938].

Smith, Stevie. *The Holiday*. London: Virago, 1979 [1949].

St. John, John. *William Heinemann: A Century of Publishing 1890-1990*. London: Heinemann, 1990.

Waugh, Evelyn. *Put Out More Flags*. London: Chapman & Hall, 1967 [1942].

Waugh, Evelyn. *Brideshead Revisited: The Sacred and Profane Memories of Captain Charles Ryder*. London: Chapman & Hall, 1945.

Waugh, Evelyn. *The Loved One: An Anglo-American Tragedy*. Boston: Little, Brown, 1977 [1948].
Waugh, Evelyn. *The Diaries of Evelyn Waugh*. Michael Davie (ed.). London: Book Club Associates, 1976.
Whittington, Ian. *Writing the Radio War: Literature, Politics, and the BBC, 1939-1945*. Edinburgh: Edinburgh University Press, 2018.
Willetts, Paul. *Fear and Loathing in Fitzrovia*. Stockport: Dewi Lewis [revised edition] 2013.

1

Their Finest Hour? A Literary History of the 1940s

Ashley Maher

From the outset of the 1940s, George Orwell was certain that the future would present no surprises to the discerning writer. In the 8 June 1940 instalment of his war diary, he describes a prescience among the British literary community that far exceeded political leaders' own insight. To poet Stephen Spender's query, 'Don't you feel that any time during the past ten years you have been able to foretell events better than, say, the Cabinet?' Orwell voiced his agreement:

> where I feel that people like us understand the situation better than so-called experts is not in any power to foretell specific events, but in the power to grasp what *kind* of world we are living in. At any rate, I have known since about 1931 [...] that the future must be catastrophic. I could not say exactly what wars and revolutions would happen, but they never surprised me when they came. (345)

In such a way, he anticipated Stalinist purges, for he 'could feel it in [Russian] literature' (346). Through Orwell's assertion that a delay had arisen between mid-century authors' grasp of politics and that of the so-called experts, he affirms literature as a medium that registers historical change before it materializes.

The upset temporality that Orwell describes – a new manifestation of the literary avant-garde – challenges the very idea of a decisive, collectively experienced historical break. That he voiced such a sentiment in the midst of the Second World War is still more significant. As twentieth-century Anglo-American history has traditionally been schematized and taught, the year 1945 carves the century in two, though recent work in mid-century studies has begun to upend that bisecting periodization. In *British Fiction after Modernism: The Novel at Mid-Century*, a foundational collection for the then-emergent literary field, Lyndsey Stonebridge and Marina MacKay explain why using 1945 as a divider is unhelpful for studying this work: 'the fact that the term "postwar" has come to mean so many things suggests that a literary history of breakthroughs and ruptures is never going to work particularly well for this period' (2). Instead, they characterize mid-century fiction as 'a literature of continuities and transitions between the earlier and later parts of the century'; in short, literary scholars' and historians' use of 1945 as a pivot or break has blinded critics not only to the contemporary experience of history but also to the value of this writing for reconstructing twentieth-century British literary trajectories (2). More recently, Gill Plain has called 1945 an 'arbitrary caesura' for British fiction, noting that despite the 'many "1940s"' that scholars have chronicled, this 'multiplicity' has been 'most often distilled into the crude division of 1945 and after' (2013: 1). She similarly notes that, while the Second World War has finally received its critical due through 'an explosion of new writing', the post-war period remains underexplored (2018: 2). This scholarly reconnection of wartime to post-war Britain enables critics to recapture the complex understanding and experience of historical events that Orwell communicates in his response to Spender: crisis and its resolution are not so neatly defined.

As I will argue, this decade – perhaps more than any other in the twentieth century – exposes the folly of sharp divisions, historical and literary historical. Indeed, it is the ambiguity, contradictions and extremes of this decade, along with its authors' lack of consensus or common purpose, that have left it largely neglected. While it lacks the recognition afforded to decades such as the 1930s, the period's critical value lies *in* its nebulousness. Up to now, most critical energies have been channelled towards exposing the porousness of boundaries between war and peace, in light of the intense focus on post-war rebuilding early in the war and the uncertainty generated by the Cold War in the latter 1940s. Richard Bessel and Dirk Schumann accordingly emphasize 'the shock of the mass violence' that carried across the decade, 'during which time more people were killed by their fellow human beings than ever before in the history of humankind' (4, 1). In addition to contesting the 1945 division in order to reach new understandings of wartime fiction, scholars have revisited the decade to challenge fundamental critical narratives about postcolonialism, modernism and postmodernism. For this reason, I will examine 1940s divisions and continuities from three angles: historically, through the blurring of war and peacetime and self and state; geographically, through migration and the dissolution of empire, amid changing formations of British identity and literature; and literary historically, through the co-existence of late modernism, realism and incipient postmodernism. After demonstrating why critics of twentieth-century British literature have increasingly turned to 1940s fiction, I'll conclude by surveying the imaginative return that later authors made to the decade. While scholars have been slow to recognize the literary historical significance of this period, the 1940s have always loomed large for writers of British fiction.

Unsettled temporalities

Before the Second World War even began, authors said their goodbyes to an older world, all while evaluating whether the global order – and they themselves – had already irrevocably changed. Adam Piette calls the travel writing of the late 1930s 'a journey to a war, exploring border psychoses in a world both psychoanalytic and political, the Fascist enemy fabulously internalised' (2004: 418), while Steve Ellis expands E. M. Forster's notion of the '1939 state' to reconstruct 'the climate of anxiety, suspense and speculation' that developed following the Munich crisis and during the 'phoney war' (1). To demonstrate how British authors assessed the moral compromises war would require, Ellis cites Forster: 'if Fascism wins we are done for, and [...] we must become Fascist to win' (3). This fight against fascism was, of course, nothing new to 1939. The Spanish Civil War, seen as a proxy conflict for an unavoidable world war, provided governmental officials and scientists a glimpse of the extensive civilian casualties they could expect from aerial bombardment (5). Alongside these official predictions, the pre-war fiction of authors like Orwell and Christopher Isherwood portrays a Europe where anticipated conflict transforms everyday life in unsettling ways. In Orwell's *Coming Up for Air* (1939), insurance salesman George 'Tubby' Bowling seeks relief from intrusive visions of a war to come – an unprecedentedly modern conflict waged by 'stream-lined men who think in slogans and talk in bullets' – through revisiting the country setting of his youth, only to witness that symbol of peace succumb to friendly fire (188). After Bowling observes that the town 'seemed to be creeping with [bombing planes]' (224) and muses that when war 'starts it won't surprise us any more than a shower of rain' (234), he witnesses his first bombing raid of the still-undeclared war, as RAF pilots mistakenly attack the town while performing 'a bit of bombing practice' (263). Though Bowling recognizes that war has already come to destroy the 'privateness of all those lives' (268), Orwell's novel concludes with Bowling pondering what he sees as the much more relevant continuity of his marital conflict, a diminished vision of the future that chimes with the ending of Isherwood's *Goodbye to Berlin* (1939). After documenting the gradual entry of Nazi violence and ideology into everyday German life, the British narrator's conclusion is tinged with nostalgia as well as anticipation, as he leaves the documentary present to review this prewar moment from the future:

> I catch sight of my face in the mirror of a shop, and am shocked to see that I am smiling [...]. The trams [...] and the people on the pavement, and the teacosy dome of the Nollendorfplatz station have an air of curious familiarity, of striking resemblance to something one remembers as normal and pleasant in the past – like a very good photograph. (207)

As the narrator closes by observing, 'No. Even now I can't altogether believe that any of this has really happened ....,' Isherwood collapses the 'Today' of the Berlin moment into the 'now' of his post-Berlin life (207). His photographic narration changes this early 1930s scene from menacing to 'normal and pleasant' through changing temporal perspective, even as the sketches that comprise the longer work are arranged out of chronological order to emphasize the political violence creeping into his private life.

Isherwood's narrator has the privilege to leave Germany when danger arises, but we see a different sort of temporal and geographic distance from war in Virginia Woolf's final novel, *Between the Acts* (1941), built around a village pageant that enacts its creator's vision of the long march of English history. Though war had gone from anticipated crisis to present reality, Woolf's narrative addresses it indirectly, through a summertime day on the cusp of the war's outbreak, thus providing what Plain calls 'a test case for the concept of "war writing"' (2018: 16). Indeed, Maroula Joannou argues that 'war is the key structuring absence that dominates *Between the Acts*, much as the First World War had dominated *Jacob's Room* in 1922': the pageant stands in for an 'embattled Britain' just as Jacob had stood in for a generation of lost men (736). As the play concludes with the audience members forced to study themselves uncomfortably in a series of reflective objects, Woolf resists any too-easy formulations of collective identity.

Twelve passing planes drown out the speaker's words after the pageant's end, and the ominous drone of aircraft similarly prompts Woolf to reflect on conflicts both internal and international in her 1940 essay 'Thoughts on Peace in an Air Raid'. 'Let us think', Woolf urges readers, 'what we can do to create the only efficient air-raid shelter while the guns on the hill go pop pop pop and the searchlights finger the clouds and now and then, sometimes close at hand, sometimes far away a bomb drops' (n.pag). Developing her ideas from *Three Guineas*, Woolf describes women's fight against sexism as a contribution they make to the fight against fascism: 'Let us try to drag up into consciousness the subconscious Hitlerism that holds us down. It is the desire for aggression; the desire to dominate and enslave.' Woolf identifies a fascist spirit within British leaders and homes that must be conquered to secure peace, even as she describes lying in bed counting the 'seconds of suspense' during which 'all thinking stopped.'

As Woolf shows through dramatizing how her thought processes were transformed by air raids, the Blitz marked an unprecedented erasure of the boundary between British civilians and combatants. In her critical survey of wartime citizenship, Sonya O. Rose records that, until the last full year of war, there were more fatalities among those on the home front than in the military (1). For this reason, Bessel and Schumann contend that women in the 1940s were impacted by war violence at a level never before seen (9). This erasure of the gendered lines of wartime produced an altered sense of self and the domestic sphere. As Piette notes, the Second World War was remarkable for its 'power to displace and unsettle, its violent dismantling of ordinary ideas of home and private life' (1995: 7). Indeed, Karen Schneider has exposed the 'sex-gender-war matrix' (16) through revealing how international conflict was described using 'explicitly sexual rhetoric' such that war plots and 'the plot of heterosexual romance' were increasingly inseparable (12). Even after the conflict ended, memoirist and pacifist Vera Brittain felt the peace was fragile and criticized Churchill's victory speech, for he 'introduced no phrase of constructive hope for a better society which renounces war' (qtd. Kynaston, 7).

The scepticism authors expressed towards national feeling used to compel war participation points to something important about the Second World War in British cultural history: the careful tending and rewriting of the war's memory. In the decades following the conflict, historian Angus Calder deflated the mythology surrounding the so-called People's War, writing in his most famous text, 'If a mythical version of the war still holds sway in school textbooks and television documentaries, every person who lived through those years knows that those parts of the myth which concern his or her own activities are false' (15). Indeed, Mark Rawlinson asserts that the war was fought with a focus on how later generations would interpret British exploits; it existed not as present but as the past of the future (2000: 2). In this, Churchill's framing of the war was not so removed from 'Hitler's millennial rhetoric', revealed in his famous pronouncement on how history would immortalize the war: 'if the British Empire and its Commonwealth last for a thousand years, men will say, "This was their finest hour" ' (2). As Rose argues in *Which People's War?*, the mythology of common sacrifice obscured the very real class and gendered divisions that persisted. Poet and novelist Sylvia Townsend Warner denounced the demands put on working-class Britons, as they were effectively made unarmed defenders of the home front:

> The people of London and the industrial areas have been told that they will be manning the front line in the present stage of the Battle of Britain .... It is an army without weapons, without training, without professional traditions, without structure or hierarchy. It is not even a levée [sic] en masse. It is a restèe [sic] en masse, an army that cannot retreat. (Qtd. Joannou 735)

Townsend Warner suggests that the blurring of civilian and combatant identities made it easy to seek the ultimate sacrifice from the working class. Though it was the leftist *Tribune* in which a '"people's war" was first called for by name', just days into the war the Ministry of Information described this idea as key for ensuring citizen compliance, as Rawlinson explains: 'The people should be told this is a civilians' war, or a People's War, and therefore that they are to be taken into the Government's confidence as never before' (2000: 141). Rawlinson concludes of this governmental branding, 'Rallying to a People's War meant consenting to increasingly centralized social and economic direction' (141). While this mobilized working class may have lacked 'training' as well as 'structure or hierarchy', their efforts effectively propped up a highly stratified war machine.

As the demands for national unity seemingly dissolved boundaries between citizens, authors faced an unwilling sacrifice of individual thought to group consciousness. Though Elizabeth Bowen worked for the Ministry of Information, her wartime writing reflects her unease with state institutions and collectivity and registers a perceived loss of individual identity. In the postscript to her much-lauded *The Demon Lover and Other Stories* (1945), Bowen calls this short fiction 'sparks from experience – an experience not necessarily my own' and describes the varied stories as a way to account for the 'many lives' she lived in wartime (217). 'It seems to me that during the war the overcharged subconsciousnesses of everybody flowed and merged,' she recalls from the perspective of October 1944, 'It is because the general subconsciousness saturates these stories that they have nothing to do with me' (217). In her switch from 'subconsciousnesses of everybody' to 'the general subconsciousness', Bowen attributes authorship of these stories to a collective body of thought and experience. Yet she describes this as intensely discomfiting, for the dissolution of physical walls between citizens precipitated a figurative collapse: 'I felt one with, and just like, everybody else. Sometimes I hardly knew where I stopped and someone else began [...]. Walls went down, and we felt, if not knew, each other' (217–18). Under the pressure of the Blitz, knowing yields to common feeling and individual authorship yields to literary and cultural meaning understood only after the fact. She muses that 'all wartime writing' may be 'resistance writing', and attention to 'personal life' through reading and writing an attempt to keep war from 'annihilat[ing]' it (220): to the war effort British fiction contributed 'saving illusory worlds' (221).

Bowen's understanding of the cultural value of fiction points to a larger blossoming of the short story during the conflict. Already 'the child of the twentieth century' (1945: 310), 'the short story is the ideal prose medium for wartime creative writing', Bowen pronounced in 'The Short Story in England' (314). While 'the discontinuities of life in wartime' present a major challenge to novel-writing – much wartime fiction arrives only after the fact – the short story 'gains rather than loses by being close up to what is immediately happening' (315). Bowen's shrewd assessment aligns with her own writing experience. With the unique temporality of the short story comes the ability to capture the upset temporality of the Second World War. 'These are between-time stories,' she writes of the pieces that comprise *The Demon Lover*, 'mostly reactions from, or intermissions between, major events. They show a levelled-down time, when a bomb on your house was as inexpedient but not more abnormal than a cold in your head' (1945: 222). She ascribes to this short fiction a documentary value that matched or even exceeded its artistic merit. Indeed, short story writer and novelist Angus Wilson identified the Blitz as one of the transformative literary and historical events of the twentieth century; it is 'there with the trenches of the First World War as an extraordinary revelation of English behaviour and feeling' (7). While Bowen mourned the loss of individual identity to collective consciousness, that permeability is to be celebrated in her stories: 'They are the particular. But through the particular, in war-time, I felt the high-voltage current of the general pass' (1945: 224).

In Bowen's collection, one of the most powerful expressions of the pressure of wartime on individual consciousness is a story set in neutral Ireland, which allowed the Anglo-Irish Bowen to show that war is every bit a state of mind as a problem of geography for Blitzed civilians. In 'Sunday Afternoon', Henry Russel prepares to return to London, as friends pry him for a sanitized account of the war over tea. The narrator describes the house and Irish countryside as false shelter from that war: lilac forms a 'barrier' and the group sit on the 'sheltered edge of the lawn', where they assume 'an air of being secluded behind glass' (616). Irish insularity extends to a denial of the value or even possibility of wartime literature. After Henry acknowledges that '"[o]ne's feelings seem to have no language for anything so preposterous"' (617) as the Blitz, another guest pronounces, '"this outrage is *not* important. There is no place for it in human experience [...]. It will have no literature'" (618). Yet that is precisely the reason Maria, the hostess's young niece, seeks to travel to the war zone: this experience "'is not in history yet'" (620). Her wristwatch, which appears early in the story, assumes new significance as Henry realizes the 'importance of time' to Maria: it is counting the minutes until he leaves for London, even after he admits "'I still want the past'" and internally 'protested against the return to the zone of death' (621).

With Henry's departure, a crisis of meaningful time merges with a crisis of meaningful identity. Before, he ponders his nonexistence, reflecting on what would have happened had he not been away when his flat was bombed, and a friend ventures, "'I wonder how much of you *has* been blown to blazes'" (620). That figurative loss of identity collides with the loss of individuality under the wartime state. After Maria expresses her intention to journey to England to experience the conflict firsthand, Henry warns, "'when you come away from here, no one will care any more that you are Maria. You will no longer be Maria, as a matter of fact [...]. You may think action is better – but who will care for you when you only act? You will have an identity number, but no identity'" (622). Outward action in wartime hides an inward emptiness; one has only the marker of individuality assigned by the state: 'an identity number, but no identity'. While Henry first formulates an alternative story in which wartime violence stamps out his existence, he ultimately recognizes that his survival has been only physical, and he anticipates Maria's own loss: "'You'll come round my door in London – with your little new number chained to your wrist'" (622). As he does so, he overturns the certainties and consolations of wartime solidarity, as peddled by British propaganda. "'[W]ith nothing left but our brute courage", Henry reflects, "we shall be nothing but brutes'" (621).

The 'general subconsciousness' of civilian life that Bowen captured emerged amid wider mid-century efforts to record the experiences and reactions of the masses. Founded in 1937 with the aim of producing 'an anthropology of ourselves', the social research organization Mass-Observation enlisted diarists to document everyday life and deployed 'investigators' to chronicle the speech and behaviour of Britons across classes and regions, yielding an archive of in-the-moment attitudes, against tightly controlled, official versions of a war seen from the perspective of future generations.[1] The rise of Mass-Observation coincided with a new drive to represent collectivity in fiction, not only in the documentary mode that Bowen describes, but also in an effort to envision political formations that had not yet come into existence. Robert L. Caserio underscores '[h]ow the novelistic and governmental models of collective life play into each other, or against each other' in this period; formulating a newly collective existence was a matter of pursuing new literary as well as governmental forms (205). The novel thus became a key site for seeking alternative models of British identity while scrutinizing the contemporary state of the nation.

Nowhere does the war weigh heavier on fictional communities than the boarding houses that feature strongly in the period's literature. These shared spaces – and the conflicts and corruptions they host – not only reflect the scarcity of suitable wartime housing but also expose the totalitarian elements that enter the national body. Bringing together an assortment of Britons while simultaneously eliminating the possibility of private life, these fictional dwellings allow tyrants (in all guises) to flourish. In Patrick Hamilton's *The Slaves of Solitude* (1947) the Rosamund Tea Rooms (now occupied by lodgers) is not merely a microcosm of the larger war; the conflict itself comes to be understood in terms of personal alliances and grievances. In his morning newspaper, boarding-house bully Mr Thwaites

> intermittently saw things about what he called his 'friends' – saw, for example, that our friends the Russians had retreated in a certain sector, that our friends the Italians were undergoing bombardment, that Friend Rommel had done this, and that Friend Montgomery had done that, that Friend Churchill was to broadcast next week, that Friend Woolton was further tampering with 'the nation's larder', that Friend Bevin had issued a fresh decree in regard to man-power, and so on and so forth. (69–70)

Thwaites's use of 'friends' makes no distinction between friend and foe, and he is himself a fascist sympathizer and 'tyrant' (34): 'Mr. Thwaites had since 1939 slowly learned to swallow the disgrace of Hitler, of whom he had been from the beginning, and still secretly remained, a hot disciple' (13). In this war of talk, he manipulates language as he manipulates his fellow boarders; there are no illusions of solidarity in this novel. Comic as Thwaites is – Terry Eagleton calls Hamilton's novels 'sub-Dickensian' – the boarding house reflects the very real degradations of wartime collective life. Matched by Hamilton's omniscient narrator, strict governmental surveillance invades private life, and wartime propaganda morphs into flurries of notices enforcing strict rules of behaviour: 'Experienced guests were aware that to take the smallest step in an original or unusual direction would be to provoke a sharp note within twenty-four hours at the outside, and they had therefore, for the most part, abandoned originality' (5). Such a loss of individuality and privacy chimes with Bowen's London, though Hamilton draws out the isolation of this wartime experience, for boarders are 'prisoners […] in their cells' (10) and 'lonely […] in [their] own' country (22).

Feeling overwhelmed by intrusive wartime speech further resonates with the lost opportunities for private thought that Orwell notes in the numerous British writers employed by governmental institutions. 'To compose a propaganda pamphlet or a radio feature needs just as much work as to write something you believe in, with the difference that the finished product is worthless,' he declared in 'As I Please' in October 1944, 'I could give a whole list of writers of promise or performance who are now being squeezed dry in some official job or another' (254). As Frank Shovlin explains, amid this perceived danger to authorship came the challenge of disseminating literature in an era of paper shortages – and after the government banned new journals in May 1940 (100). With the psychological and material pressures of war, many feared for the end of the little magazine and others like Wyndham Lewis perceived that literature itself was in danger of disappearance.

Nonetheless, the future-oriented war effort engendered a degree of optimism, and the circulation of plans for reconstructing Britain – literally and figuratively – blurred the boundary between war and post-war. William Beveridge's much-studied blueprint for a welfare state provided a justification for the war to citizens on the home front and abroad. As Kelly M. Rich underlines, the fact that his 1942 report sold 635,000 copies signals 'its timeliness as, strangely enough, a summary of what Britain had been fighting for all along' (1185). Yet, as Plain indicates, public interest in post-war planning faded (2013: 12), and following the 1945 election of a Labour government, Orwell remarked that 'the mood of the country seems to be less revolutionary, less Utopian, even less hopeful, than it was in 1940 or 1942' (qtd. Kynaston, 80). The creation of the welfare state was not so much a sharp pivot, more what Caserio calls 'a compromise among the pre-war ideological divisions' (205). After Churchill's infamous Gestapo speech, his daughter, Sarah Oliver, counselled him on Labour's appeal by explaining that there had already been a socialism of sorts, under his direction: 'Socialism as practised in the war, did no one any harm, and quite a lot of people good. The children of this country have never been so well fed or healthy, what milk there was, was shared equally [...] there is no doubt that this common sharing and feeling of sacrifice was one of the strongest bonds that unified us' (1621).

Though conservative author Evelyn Waugh lambasted what he perceived as social levelling following Labour's election, Orwell warned in 1945 that the Cold War threatened to erase any post-war gains. In 'You and the Atom Bomb', he argues that 'The great age of democracy and of national self-determination was the age of the musket and the rifle', but the atomic age promised to be an undemocratic one, for periods 'in which the dominant weapon is expensive or difficult to make will tend to be ages of despotism' (904); ultimately, this was 'a "peace that is no peace"' (907). As a result, the Cold War yielded an even more unsettled experience of time than the Second World War. 'Mid-century British fiction [...] unfolds within the ambiguous space between imminent doom and compromised futurity,' Allan Hepburn argues, 'Above all, atomic age fiction treats catastrophe as a set of variations wrought upon the future' (369). Whereas Churchill asked Britons to imagine the wartime present from the perspective of the future, the Cold War threatened to eliminate that future.

Yet, even as citizens kept their eyes on global powers, they were consumed by the mundane reality of austerity. Because rationing continued until 1954 – and new items were added after the war – victory did not radically change their day-to-day lives. 'Believe us, this is worse than the war!' Isherwood's friends declared in response to the rationing of fuel in the winter of 1947, during his first visit since moving to the United States in January 1939; he concluded from their testimony that their post-war condition 'couldn't by any stretch of the imagination be viewed as a challenge to self-sacrifice or an inspiration to patriotism; it was merely hell' (qtd. Kynaston 191). This tension between valorized and meaningless deprivation provides the irony for the opening of Muriel Spark's *The Girls of Slender Means* (1963): 'Long ago in 1945 all the nice people in England were poor, allowing for exceptions' (7). Even in later British fiction, the imaginative return to wartime captured not so much Britain's 'finest hour' as interminability and privation.[2]

Unsettled geographies

Given the entrapment, paralysis and diminished horizons that typify representations of the Second World War and the ensuing period of austerity, we can productively read this fiction in relation to the mobility of authors themselves and the body of writing that captured in fine detail the dissolution of the British Empire. Indeed, one of the most influential accounts of mid-century British literature concerns the shifting boundaries of the national imagination. In *A Shrinking Island*, Jed Esty argues against equating 'geopolitical and aesthetic decline' (15) as he establishes a 'late-imperial dialectic of lost universalism and restored particularity' (5). Through analysing the narrowing span of British identity, Esty locates an 'anthropological turn' whereby 'English intellectuals translated the end of empire into a resurgent concept of national culture' (2), with links to broader documentary efforts like Mass-Observation (44).

While the story of shifting national and imperial affiliations and migration at the end of empire is now a familiar one, the diminution that Esty pinpoints was for some apparent only in retrospect. Plain establishes that strong imperial ties were seen as crucial to the war effort, and policymakers of all stripes believed that Britain would maintain its world power status (2018: 9), as Bill Schwarz attests: 'Amongst the British political class at the end of the war there was perhaps not a single figure who anticipated the speed and thoroughness of the collapse of Britain's world-system' (7). Churchill was a prime example. In an April 1944 speech to the House of Commons, he looks forward to strengthening the empire while creating with the United States and 'our great Russian Ally' a 'world order to keep peace' (79). Marvelling at Commonwealth unity – apart from the 'one lamentable exception' of Ireland (76) – he asks, 'What is this miracle, for it is nothing less, that called men from the uttermost ends of the earth, some riding twenty days before they could reach their recruiting centres, some armies having to sail 14,000 miles across the seas before they reached the battlefield?' (77). In Churchill's telling, geography presents no challenge to 'union in freedom' (77), and that unity would only strengthen through advances in air travel (78–79). '[M]ysterious natural forces' thus promised to hold the empire together: 'amid the wreck of empires, states, nations, and institutions of every kind, we find the British Commonwealth and Empire more strongly united than ever before' (77).

Churchill's insistence that the British Empire would emerge from war with an ironclad bond led Jamaican author Roger Mais to denounce the new constitution for Jamaica, which led to his six-month imprisonment on sedition charges. In 'Now We Know', published in the 11 July 1944 edition of *Public Opinion*, Mais contrasts the promises of greater self-governance with 'the real official policy', best seen in Churchill's rhetoric: 'Time and again he has avowed in open parliament that, in so many words, what we are fighting for is that England might retain her exclusive prerogative to the conquest and enslavement of other nations' (n.pag). Young colonials consequently sacrificed their lives for such outrages as 'That the sun may never set upon the insolence and arrogance of one race towards all others' and 'That we may take pride if we are no more than the great hunks of red meat upon which the noble Lion feeds that he might have the great sinews and the fierce blood and the mighty roar to affright his enemies' (n.pag). As Mais protests, the British had exacted complicity with the machinery of empire through instilling false patriotism.

Upon travelling to England during and after the war, many West Indians encountered the illusoriness of the inclusive British identity that colonial classrooms and cinemas peddled. 'Yes, it is wonderful to be British – until one comes to Britain,' the narrator of E. R. Braithwaite's autobiographical novel observes (35). Mais and Braithwaite were among the Windrush generation, named after the former German ship that brought hundreds of West Indian immigrants to London in June 1948 – a media event at the time and the symbolic beginning of a wave of post-war migration. Yet this narrative has sometimes erased the earlier presence of migrants and their long-time contribution to British fiction. James Procter likens the use of 1948 in accounts of black British literature to the use of 1945 by mid-century historians and literary critics, noting that 'The 1940s mark a "caesura" in histories of both British and black British writing, where the end of the Second World War (1945) and the arrival of the Empire Windrush (1948) typically divide the decade around inaugural moments of absolute beginning' (117). What's more, this Windrush dating effectively casts black British writing as belated and isolates it from wider literary historical accounts of the war and its aftermath: 'as discrete symbolic moments, "1945" and "1948" tend to separate out British and black Atlantic literary production at the midcentury, where at best the latter comes after, as part of a staggered, supplementary visitation from the outside' (117). More than simply reductive, these two dividers have obscured the importance of West Indian authors to wartime and post-war British fiction.

In response, scholars such as Alison Donnell, Glyne Griffith and Peter Kalliney offer powerful accounts of the generative literary exchanges between metropolitan and late colonial authors, particularly through such institutions as the BBC. Jamaican poet and playwright Una Marson, the first black woman to work for the broadcasting company, steered programming for West Indian audiences as part of the BBC Empire Service. Beyond her work on the wartime programme *Calling the West Indies*, she helped create the famed *Caribbean Voices* literary programme that provided exposure for a range of authors living in Britain and the Caribbean.[3] Sam Selvon, John Figueroa and George Lamming made a name for themselves on the programme, through submitting work and by reading on air. While *Caribbean Voices* was broadcast overseas, its authors moved on to other programming, and the BBC led West Indian authors to collaborate with literary figures such as T. S. Eliot, George Orwell, Mulk Raj Anand, Stephen Spender, John Lehmann and William Empson. Kalliney argues that, by doing so, these West Indian authors adapted modernist aesthetic autonomy 'to insist that the world of the imagination […] should not be diminished by the types of racial discrimination so prevalent elsewhere' (10), and they transformed the BBC – a tool for 'a culturally integrated British Empire' (4) – into a mouthpiece 'to subtly criticize, and sometimes brazenly denounce, British imperialism' (5).

The BBC was in turn linked to a network of Caribbean and British little magazines that carried this work, and *Caribbean Voices* presenter Andrew Salkey later released two influential collections of short stories. Among the pieces in his *West Indian Stories* are Roger Mais's 'Blackout' and Victor Reid's 'Waterfront Bar', both of which appeared in a 1948 issue of *Life and Letters* that featured a selection of West Indian writing by the likes of George Lamming and Edgar Mittelholzer.⁴ We might productively read Mais's 'Blackout', set in a West Indies city, alongside Bowen's stories of Blitzed London, as he presents a chance wartime encounter between an American woman and a local man. In this collision of very different perspectives – precipitated by a war that brought Americans to bases established on Jamaica and other British Caribbean islands – the woman's unease in this setting allows Mais to explore unjust systems of power in the larger Black Atlantic. The young man approaches her for a light at a shadowy bus stop, for '[t]he city was in partial blackout' through 'the wartime policy of conserving electricity', and she is initially taken by the 'novelty' of the situation: 'In her country it is not every night that a white woman would be likely to be thus nonchalantly approached by a black man [...]. She seemed to remember that any sort of adventure could happen to you in one of these tropical islands of the West Indies' (161). As their conversation progresses, he challenges her unspoken assumptions about how black men should behave – '"This isn't America [...] In this country there are only men and women. You'll learn about that if you stop here long enough"' – and the parts told from her point of view confirm her willingness to envision violence against him, had they been in another geographic sphere: 'In America, they lynched them for less than that, she thought' (163). Yet her 'supreme confidence' is ultimately 'shaken', and against her segregationist upbringing, she recognizes his manner towards her as one 'without the interruption of artificial barriers [...] as between man and woman; any man, any woman' (164).

Much as Mais stages an unlikely wartime meeting whose intimacy unsettles American white supremacist norms, so too does Reid's 'Waterfront Bar' portray the Kingston waterfront as a site of transnational encounter, among the cultural diversity of the West Indies. Starting with three washerwomen, the story builds as new arrivals add to its layered dialogue. The reader is reminded of a longer history of migration with a 'quarter-Chinese girl' who enters the bar, though the conflict again turns on a group of Americans, whose ethnic and racial norms are exposed in this West Indian locale (166). As the oilboat-men debate a Southerner's refusal to sail with a black man in a position of responsibility, one uses slurs to declare that he "'[p]ersonally [...] wouldn't kiss'" a black or Jewish person, precipitating this exchange:

> 'Listen, punk, Christ was a Jew and Solomon was a coloured guy, see?'
> 'Yeah, does that make me kiss 'em?'
> 'Listen, punk, a guy named Hitler – '
> 'Pipe down, mugs, you're in a foreign port.' (168)

The biblical references bring new resonance to one washerwoman's drunken repetition of 'Wash me in the blood of the lamb', before the slang-filled argument over the man's disavowal of cross-ethnic and cross-racial intimacy pivots to a timely concern – the war being fought against an anti-Semitic dictator (167). That challenge to view American prejudice as tantamount to Nazi ideology ends, however, with the reminder that they are 'in a foreign port'; they are called to awareness of their uncertain standing in this British colonial space.

West Indian literature has thus been understood as a product of unsettled geographies and migration in the 1940s, though we should not see that movement as unidirectional. Likewise, one of the biggest events for South Asian literature in English was not an arrival but a departure from London. Mulk Raj Anand – a BBC collaborator and an anti-imperialist writer integrated into diverse literary circles, whose first novel featured a preface by Forster – spent two decades in England before returning to India the year it won its independence (Kalliney 10). Yet, despite the shifting boundaries of British literature's geographic imagination, the violence and forced migration that followed British officials' division of the Indian subcontinent in 1947 ultimately yielded an image of stark borders. To the spatial metaphors of expansion, paralysis and contraction – the Atlantic voyages, the Blitz entrapment and the 'shrinking island' – that defined the mid-century came Partition, testifying to the folly of imposed spatial division.

Unsettled literary histories

As Kalliney reveals, late colonial authors entered British literary circles at a time when the future of British writing seemed uncertain. Few high modernists survived the 1940s: by the conflict's end, Virginia Woolf and James Joyce had died, and Ezra Pound was in American custody, following his wartime broadcasts in fascist Italy. However, before Woolf died, she herself anticipated that the post-war novel would be radically transformed. 'If the pressure of the income tax continues, classes will disappear,' she declares in a paper delivered to the Workers' Educational Association in May 1940, and so too would the educational inequalities that led British literature to be produced by the privileged (1948: 150). This would mean 'the end of the novel, as we know it' (151). Yet the standard of British literature would only improve. 'The novel of a classless and towerless world should be a better novel than the old novel,' Woolf avows, for the social world captured in that novel would comprise 'people who have had a chance to develop their humour, their gifts, their tastes' (151).

Wartime enthusiasm for political reform similarly promised an expropriation of literary capital, for Woolf announces that '[l]iterature is no one's private ground' but 'common ground' (154). That sentiment aligns with literary histories of the 1940s, which often note the blurring of such divides as public and private, as well as elite, middlebrow and popular. Kristin Bluemel proposes the term 'intermodernism' to conceptualize this in-between writing of the 1930s and 1940s and identifies three key elements in these texts: 'cultural features (intermodernists typically represent working-class and working middle-class cultures); political features (intermodernists are often politically radical, "radically eccentric"); and literary features (intermodernists are committed to non-canonical, even "middlebrow" or "mass" genres)' (1). Given mid-century authors' strong interest in film and radio, intermodernism likewise embraces cross-media exchange (4).

While Bluemel uses 'intermodernism' to capture 'an ideology' as well as a 'period and style', 'late modernism' has held significant explanatory power for other scholars as they turn from modernism's beginnings to its endings (5). Advanced by Fredric Jameson, the term 'late modernism' has come to designate several different groups of writers and phenomena.[5] Tyrus Miller's influential *Late Modernism* has theorized it as an interwar development, with figures like Djuna Barnes and Samuel Beckett representing a 'satiric and parodic' late modernism (19) that marks 'a closure of the horizon of the future' (13), while Esty's *A Shrinking Island* is primarily concerned with the late career of British modernists as they negotiate 'the cultural transition between empire and welfare state' (3). MacKay's *Modernism and World War II* similarly considers the transformation of modernism under the pressure of mid-century history, though she attends to the ways in which 'the consensus politics of the Second World War' launched 'acutely self-aware literary forms'; her late modernism is characterized by 'its critical national consciousness, its scrutiny of the links between creative and economic privilege and its rehabilitation of the private life against abuses of collective power' (14). Kalliney notes a tendency among these late modernist critics to document British fiction's narrowing geographic and temporal outlook, as authors envisioned 'a more imaginatively limited, culturally bounded future for modernist culture', yet his account of modernism in the mid-century records an attempt 'to reinvent anglophone modernism as a truly global enterprise' (11). Establishing 'late colonial and early postcolonial intellectuals as the self-nominated heirs and most incisive readers of high modernism', he provides a largely unacknowledged mid-century link between high modernism and the postcolonial writing of the latter twentieth century (37).

Other critics have questioned whether modernism is indeed the right term of analysis for 1940s fiction. '"[M]odernism" is a distraction' for this decade, Plain argues, and critics who insist on its use threaten to erase 'the very diverse voices and literary developments of the period' (2013: 5). For her, 'The 1940s do not tell a story of modernism or postmodernism; they are uncannily familiar, and yet impossibly different' (34). An alternative term that has come into favour is, simply, 'mid-century', though Stonebridge and MacKay maintain that one cannot interpret mid-century novels adequately without reference to modernism, for these authors not only acted as 'modernism's first readers' (5) but also went about 'self-consciously rewriting' it (7): 'Modernism lingered in the literary imagination as, sometimes ironically, sometimes peevishly, mid-century writing reacted to its influence by adapting some of its elements to new political and fictional ends' and thus 'late modernism continues to splinter into the gritty concerns of mid-century writing' (2). Mid-century in this way designates not just the flexibility of the period's stylistic commitments but also the mutability of modernism itself.

As this range of scholarship demonstrates, the 1940s do not display a singular literary tendency but rather have critical value precisely because of the varied responses the decade generated – both to fictional form and to the historical pressures of world war and empire, linked as they are. Yet just as striking is the propensity of British authors to revisit this unsettled decade in their fiction. We can thus regard the 1940s as a crucible for British literature, not only a period of great change and self-reflection but also a set of ideas and provocations to which authors return. Its unresolved crises of style and national identity have made it a key point of reference for the British literary and political imagination.

The centrality of the Second World War to British national identity is evident in MacKay's description of the Blitz and Dunkirk as 'nostalgia magnets', remarkable because they are not moments of triumph but 'moments of national vulnerability' (2007: 2). In Colin MacInnes's *Absolute Beginners* (1959), his teenage protagonist actively resists that nostalgia, as youth culture provides an alternative to older generations' attempts to enshrine a national narrative anchored by the People's

War and the welfare state. Though his mother calls him 'Blitz Baby' because of his birth in an air raid shelter, the unnamed narrator refuses this retrospective personal and national identity (37). To his older brother's proclamation that "'The war [...] was Britain's finest hour'", the narrator retorts, "'All of you oldies certainly seem to try to keep it well in mind, because every time I open a newspaper, or pick up a paperback, or go to the Odeon, I hear nothing but war, war, war. You pensioners certainly seem to love that old, old struggle'" (41). While the narrator resists retrospection and MacInnes documents the absolutely modern, including events like the Notting Hill riots that unfolded while composing the text, other novelists used the 1940s as a setting to generate the same 'acutely self-aware literary forms' and 'critical national consciousness' that MacKay deems fundamental to 1940s fiction. The solidarity and sacrifice at the heart of official accounts of the war are thus transformed into meditations on personal and political guilt in Spark's *The Girls of Slender Means* (1963), Kazuo Ishiguro's *The Remains of the Day* (1989) and Ian McEwan's *Atonement* (2001).[6] Even future fiction returns to the Second World War. Bletchley Park alumnus Angus Wilson approaches that period by inventing a third world war in *The Old Men at the Zoo* (1961). Though many have read it through the lens of the Cold War, the novel is 'a study of 1938-42' according to Waugh, one that captures its 'wildly exaggerated notions of the impending disaster' – namely an eminent Nazi takeover of Britain (574). Whereas Churchill urged Britons to imagine the war through the eyes of grateful future generations, Wilson – prone to seeing, as Kynaston indicates, 'the British as self-congratulatory, smug victors in the war' (524) – projects that war onto the future, though the story he imagines is one of complicity and defeat. By erasing Britain's 'finest hour' via an imagined invasion, Wilson's novel demonstrates the liberties that the decade's upset temporalities and geographies granted British fiction. The history of the 1940s thus opens itself to being written and rewritten.

Notes

1. Nonetheless, as Rawlinson underlines, 'By the early 1940s, M[ass]-O[bservation] had become an unofficial branch of the Coalition Government's growing intelligence and publicity machine for imagining the postwar world' (2018: 144).
2. For the 'generative side' of austerity for British authors, see Marina MacKay's 'Slender Means: The Novel in the Age of Austerity' (51).
3. See Alison Donnell's 'Rescripting Anglophone Women's Literary History: Gender, Genre, and Lost Caribbean Voices' (2015).

4 As the all-male cast of *West Indian Stories* indicates, women's contributions to *Caribbean Voices* and literary magazines have often been left out of the canon that emerged, given the dominant narrative of (mostly male) migration. See Donnell (2015).
5 See Thomas S. Davis's 'Late Modernism: British Literature at Midcentury' (327).
6 For the war's lingering presence in these and other works of post-war fiction, see the coda of MacKay's *Modernism and World War II* (2007).

Works cited

Bessel, Richard, and Dirk Schumann. 'Introduction: Violence, Normality, and the Construction of Postwar Europe'. In Richard Bessel and Dirk Schumann (eds.), *Life after Death: Approaches to a Cultural and Social History of Europe During the 1940s and 1950s*. Cambridge: Cambridge University Press, 2003: 1–13.

Bluemel, Kristin. 'Introduction: What is Intermodernism?' In Kristin Bluemel (ed.), *Intermodernism: Literary Culture in Mid-Twentieth-Century Britain*. Edinburgh: Edinburgh University Press, 2009: 1–18.

Bowen, Elizabeth. 'Postscript by the Author'. In *The Demon Lover and Other Stories*. London: Jonathan Cape, 1945: 216–24.

Bowen, Elizabeth. 'The Short Story in England'. In Allan Hepburn (ed.), *People, Places, Things: Essays by Elizabeth Bowen*. Edinburgh: Edinburgh University Press, 2008: 310–15.

Bowen, Elizabeth. 'Sunday Afternoon'. In *The Collected Stories of Elizabeth Bowen*. New York: Vintage Books, 1982: 616–22.

Braithwaite, E. R. *To Sir, With Love*. London: Vintage, 2005.

Calder, Angus. *The People's War: Britain 1939-1945*. London: Jonathan Cape, 1969.

Caserio, Robert L. *The Cambridge Introduction to British Fiction, 1900-1950*. Cambridge: Cambridge University Press, 2019.

Churchill, Winston. 'Spirit of the Empire'. In *The Dawn of Liberation, 1945*. New York: Rosetta Books, 2013: 71–9.

Davis, Thomas S. 'Late Modernism: British Literature at Midcentury'. *Literature Compass* 9 (4), 2012: 326–37.

Donnell, Alison. 'Rescripting Anglophone Women's Literary History: Gender, Genre, and Lost Caribbean Voices'. In J. Dillon Brown and Leah Reade Rosenberg (eds.), *Beyond Windrush: Rethinking Postwar Anglophone Caribbean Literature*. Jackson: University of Mississippi Press, 2015: 79–96.

Eagleton, Terry. 'First-Class Fellow Traveller'. *LRB*, 2 December 1993, https://www.lrb.co.uk/the-paper/v15/n23/terry-eagleton/first-class-fellow-traveller.

Ellis, Steve. *British Writers and the Approach of World War II*. Cambridge: Cambridge University Press, 2014.

Esty, Jed. *A Shrinking Island: Modernism and National Culture in England*. Princeton: Princeton University Press, 2004.

Griffith, Glyne. *The BBC and the Development of Anglophone Caribbean Literature, 1943–1958*. Basingstoke: Palgrave Macmillan, 2016.

Hamilton, Patrick. *The Slaves of Solitude*. New York: NYRB, 2007.

Hepburn, Allan. 'The Future and the End: Imagining Catastrophe'. In Gill Plain (ed.), *British Literature in Transition, 1940–1960: Postwar*. Cambridge: Cambridge University Press, 2018: 369–84.

Isherwood, Christopher. *Goodbye to Berlin*. In *The Berlin Stories*. New York: New Directions, 1963.

Joannou, Maroula. '"Our Time": Sylvia Townsend Warner, Virginia Woolf and the 1940s'. *Literature Compass* 11 (12), 2014: 732–44.

Kalliney, Peter. *Commonwealth of Letters: British Literary Culture and the Emergence of Postcolonial Aesthetics*. Oxford: Oxford University Press, 2013.

Kynaston, David. *Austerity Britain, 1945-1951*. London: Bloomsbury, 2007.

MacInnes, Colin. *Absolute Beginners*. London: Allison & Busby, 2011.

MacKay, Marina. *Modernism and World War II*. Cambridge: Cambridge University Press, 2007.

MacKay, Marina. 'Slender Means: The Novel in the Age of Austerity'. In Gill Plain (ed.), *British Literature in Transition, 1940–1960: Postwar*. Cambridge: Cambridge University Press, 2018: 37–51.

Mais, Roger. 'Blackout'. *Life & Letters* 59, November 1948: 161–4.

Mais, Roger. 'Now We Know'. Typescript. From UWI Mona Library Digital Collections, *Roger Mais Collection*. http://contentdm64srv.uwimona.edu.jm/cdm/ref/collection/RogerMS/id/1575 (accessed 29 June 2020).

Miller, Tyrus. *Late Modernism: Politics, Fiction, and the Arts Between the World Wars*. Berkeley: University of California Press, 1999.

Oliver, Sarah. 'Sarah Oliver to Winston S. Churchill (Churchill papers, 1/387)'. 5 June 1945. In Martin Gilbert and Larry P. Arnn (eds.), *The Churchill Documents: The Shadows of Victory January–July 1945*. Hillsdale: C & T Publications Limited, 2018: 1620–2.

Orwell, George. 'As I Please'. *Tribune*, 13 October 1944. In Sonia Orwell and Ian Angus (eds.), *The Collected Essays, Journalism, and Letters of George Orwell*, vol. 3. London: Secker & Warburg, 1968: 252–5.

Orwell, George. *Coming Up for Air*. San Diego: Harvest, 1950.

Orwell, George. 'War-time Diary: 8 June 1940'. In Sonia Orwell and Ian Angus (eds.), *The Collected Essays, Journalism, and Letters of George Orwell*, vol. 3. London: Secker & Warburg, 1968: 345–6.

Orwell, George. 'You and the Atom Bomb'. In *Essays*. New York: Alfred A. Knopf, 2002: 903–7.

Piette, Adam. *Imagination at War: British Fiction and Poetry 1939–1945*. London: Macmillan, 1995.

Piette, Adam. 'World War II: Contested Europe'. In Laura Marcus and Peter Nicholls (eds.), *The Cambridge History of Twentieth-Century English Literature*. Cambridge: Cambridge University Press, 2004: 417–35.

Plain, Gill. 'Introduction'. In Gill Plain (ed.), *British Literature in Transition, 1940-1960: Postwar*. Cambridge: Cambridge University Press, 2018: 1–29.

Plain, Gill. *Literature of the 1940s: War, Postwar and 'Peace'*. Edinburgh: Edinburgh University Press, 2013.

Procter, James. 'Wireless Writing, the Second World War and the West Indian Literary Imagination'. In Gill Plain (ed.), *British Literature in Transition, 1940-1960: Postwar*. Cambridge: Cambridge University Press, 2018: 117–35.

Rawlinson, Mark. *British Writing of the Second World War*. Oxford: Oxford University Press, 2000.

Rawlinson, Mark. 'Narrating Transitions to Peace: Fiction and Film after War'. In Gill Plain (ed.), *British Literature in Transition, 1940-1960: Postwar*. Cambridge: Cambridge University Press, 2018: 143–60.

Reid, Victor. 'Waterfront Bar'. *Life & Letters* 59, November 1948: 165–8.

Rich, Kelly M. '"Nowhere's Safe": Ruinous Reconstruction in Muriel Spark's *The Girls of Slender Means*'. *ELH* 83 (4), 2016: 1185–209.

Rose, Sonya O. *Which People's War?: National Identity and Citizenship in Wartime Britain 1939-1945*. Oxford: Oxford University Press, 2003.

Schneider, Karen. *Loving Arms: British Women Writing the Second World War*. Lexington: University Press of Kentucky, 1997.

Schwarz, Bill. 'Introduction: Crossing the Seas'. In Bill Schwarz (ed.), *West Indian Intellectuals in Britain*. Manchester: Manchester University Press, 2003: 1–30.

Shovlin, Frank. *The Irish Literary Periodical 1923-58*. Oxford: Oxford University Press, 2004.

Spark, Muriel. *The Girls of Slender Means*. New York: New Directions, 1998.

Stonebridge, Lyndsey and Marina MacKay. 'Introduction: British Fiction after Modernism'. In Marina MacKay and Lyndsey Stonebridge (eds.), *British Fiction after Modernism: The Novel at Mid-Century*. Basingstoke: Palgrave Macmillan, 2007: 1–16.

Waugh, Evelyn. 'To the Editor of *the Spectator*'. In Mark Amory (ed.), *The Letters of Evelyn Waugh*. Boston: Ticknor & Fields, 1980: 573–5.

Wilson, Angus. 'Introduction'. In *The Collected Stories of Elizabeth Bowen*. New York: Vintage Books, 1982: 7–11.

Woolf, Virginia. 'The Leaning Tower'. In *The Moment and Other Essays*. New York: Harcourt Brace, 1948: 128–54.

Woolf, Virginia. 'Thoughts on Peace in an Air Raid'. *The New Republic*, 21 October 1940. https://newrepublic.com/article/113653/thoughts-peace-air-raid.

2

British Blitz Fiction of the 1940s: Another Finest Hour, Myth or Propaganda?

Philip Tew

'I have nothing to offer but blood, toil, tears, and sweat. We have before us an ordeal of the most grievous kind. We have before us many, many months of struggle and suffering.'

Winston Churchill, 13 May 1940

In this chapter, selected key fictional accounts of the Blitz will be considered as well as occasional extracts from other sources such as diaries and interviews (of literary figures of the period); such fiction will include: Phyllis Bottome's *London Pride* (1941); Elizabeth Bowen's *The Heat of the Day* (1949); Daphne du Maurier's *Frenchman's Creek* (1941) and 'The Birds'; Henry Green's *Caught* (1943); Graham Greene's *The Ministry of Fear* (1943) and *The End of the Affair* (1951); Patrick Hamilton's *The Slaves of Solitude* (1947); James Hanley's *No Directions* (1943); Norah Hoult's *There Were No Windows* (1944); Winifred Peck's *Housebound* (1942); Jocelyn Playfair's *A House in the Country* (1944); Noel Streatfeild's *Saplings* (1945) and Virginia Woolf's *Between the Acts* (1941). In some 1940s Blitz fiction, cities become killing grounds haunted by a multifaceted spectre of fear, death and other curious passions while in others the Blitz is a backdrop, events intruding from London on a seemingly otherwise undisturbed Home Front full of evacuees and the Home Guard. These novels chart radically disturbed landscapes permeated by variously bravery, cowardice, foolhardiness, fortitude or impetuosity and other qualities that constitute trauma fiction in the sense defined by Ingrida Žindžiuvienė: 'The term "trauma novel" refers to a work of fiction that represents an emotional and/or cognitive response to profound loss, disaster, disruption, or devastations on the individual or collective level' (66). The following analysis will draw in passing upon trauma theory from other critics in this field such as Jeffrey C. Alexander, Ruth Leys and Neil J. Smelser. Other secondary criticism featured about literature in this period and its sociocultural and historical milieu includes: Angus Calder's *The Myth of the Blitz* (1991); Juliet Gardiner's *The Blitz: The British under Attack* (2010) and N. Reeve and Rod Mengham's *The Fiction of the 1940s: Stories of Survival* (2001). This chapter will explore how writers incorporated the effects of the Blitz into their work, and consider variously the personal, social and physical impact on their lives and the areas affected, and awareness of such events of those outside the immediate zone of terror and destruction. Such narratives often incorporate and interrogate a deep trauma engendered by this serial bombardment and the very unpredictability of aerial targeting, particularly of residential urban areas both in London and other British cities. A key issue is how much the myth of the Blitz is reflected by certain writers named above as another 'finest hour' of the Second World War alongside the Battle of Britain.

Clearly the Blitz echoed headline events and anxieties of the 1930s, especially the bombing of Guernica, a type of attack long feared in pre-war Britain.[1] In *The Oaken Heart* (1941) Margery Allingham describes early air raid precautions in rural Essex, evoking thoughts of Spain and China. She indicates: 'we had no illusions whatever about the value of the aeroplane as an offensive weapon' (33). As Geoffrey Field reports, in 1939 'military expert Basil Liddell-Hart suggested that a conflict could result in 250,000 dead and injured in Britain in the first week' (12).[2] Field adds that 'A 1938 report presented to the Ministry of Health by a group of psychiatrists forecasts that millions of people would be afflicted by varying degrees of neurosis and panic' (13) and that central planning was haphazard with most areas lacking sufficient bomb shelters as the cost 'was considered prohibitive and there were additional concerns that large communal shelters might become incubators of political disaffection and defeatism' (13). As Allingham records: 'We expected London to be razed in a week, and I know my own private fear was the idiotic notion that a terrorised city population would spread out like rings in a puddle all over the Home Counties, bringing fear and quarrels and chaos with it' (40). Certainly, in passing the Emergency Powers (Defence) (No. 2) Act, 1940, on 22 May the government extended laws adopted the previous September specifically to provide central control over many areas of public life, and writing for publication in October 1940 W. Ivor Jennings explained, this 'gave a much wider power over labour than' (133) its predecessor and 'enable[d] criminal justice to be administered by special courts in war zones, and to enable offences against the Defence Regulations to be punished in special courts' (133). Jennings regarded the changes as partly a preparation for invasion when 'the whole judicial system, like the whole administrative system, would break down in the invaded areas and for wide areas outside' (133).³ In practice, catastrophic breakdown of society did not occur. Instead, the public response became a foundation stone of Britain's image of itself in wartime.

William Cederwell explores the myth of the Blitz, consisting of the people 'taking it' and facing this menace collectively, as represented by the iconic photograph taken by Herbert Mason of 'St Paul's Cathedral, miraculously still standing, after the air raid of 29 December 1940, a night so bad it became known as the Second Fire of London' (1).⁴ Petra Rau observes another recurrent feature of the narrative of the Second World War Britain in cultural accounts of the 1940s:

> One of the clichés of the myth of the Blitz is that Londoners carried on regardless: anything else would have been an acknowledgement of suffering and defeat. The incongruity – some might say the absurdity – of maintaining a mundane routine in the face of catastrophe became a collective coping strategy, officially encouraged and publicly extolled. In this myth, the strangeness of war seems to have consolidated familiar national virtues rather than resulted in collective trauma. (31)

The predominance of the Blitz and its intense focus upon London, in 1940 and 1941 in particular, is key to the myth Rau identifies of stoicism and the apparent refusal of the traumatic. Yet, many had been reluctant about a potential war in 1938-9, as reflected by the mother's words on her son's sixth birthday in Phyllis Bottome's novel *London Pride* (1941): "'War!" he heard his mother repeat to herself, while glancing at a placard he could not read, "Well – I should 'ave thought, once bitten twice shy myself – but that's men all over'" (14). A bestseller in America, this author was employed by the Ministry of Information. Her Cockney children are bombed and injured, but survive. The narrator observes in the text that only 'Later – when the Prime Minister said what he thought of the City – Londoners could not help adding to their accustomed stoicism a faint flavour of pride' (60). Already in November 1941, the myth of the Blitz already well established, an American edition – illustrated sentimentally by Rafaello Busoni who drew stoic Cockney infants – had already been published by Little, Brown and Company in Boston. Field insists that in reality a more varied and fractured set of social relations characterized the reality of these times:

> Against the standard images of altruism and solidarity must also be set contrary evidence of division and selfishness. There were plenty of rows, fights, petty thefts, and arguments about noise and space in public shelters. Vandalism, especially by gangs of youths, became a serious problem in many districts, as did petty pilfering and opportunistic looting. (19)

Significantly, in analysing Green's *Caught* Marina MacKay, for instance, casts doubt on the novel's apparent, but superficial effacement of class differences (99–100), finding in the end only 'Green's bogus classlessness [...]' (103). Calder in considering the overarching myth cites the GPO Film Unit's *The First Days* (1939) as evidence that 'By the time war broke out in September 1939 the myth of the Blitz had been all but scripted' (195), a quasi-official narrative supplemented by others made by those involved in the same unit. Calder adds that

> In so far as the Myth of the Blitz did not evolve spontaneously (and I have argued that in great part it did), it was a propaganda construct directed at American opinion as at, British, developed by American news journalists in association with British propagandists and newsmen – and was all the more strongly accepted by Britons because American voices proclaimed it. (212)

He describes various contributions in terms of radio broadcasts and photography, but states 'the most important figure in its dissemination was Edward R. Murrow' (212).[5] His style was vivid and compelling, as on 21 September 1940:

> Straight in front of me now you'll hear two sounds in just a moment. There they are. That was the explosion overhead, not the guns themselves. I should think in a few minutes there may be a bit of shrapnel around here. Coming in, moving a little closer all the while, the plane is still very high and it's quite clear that he's not coming in for his bombing run. (n.pag)

Certainly, Murrow's live broadcasts had much impact. The focus of the GPO film cited above on London is telling, since as Cederwell argues, in supplying so 'much striking imagery' (2), London displaced the suffering endured elsewhere in areas including provincial cities, towns and in the countryside itself, and its Blitz spirit obscured countervailing views, far less positive ones (4). However, its impact was undeniable and, as Calder details, the worst raid on London on 10 May 1941 killed 1,436, seriously injured 1,792 and 'A third of the streets of Greater London were left impassable. All but one of the main railway stations were blocked for weeks. Brown smoke blotted out the sun' (37). Indeed, Murrow focused largely on London in his broadcasts. Clearly, the populace both British and American soon became familiar with the effects of an enemy dropping high explosives and incendiary canisters.[6] It seems conceivable that any apparent myth was in fact an extension of what Jeffrey C. Alexander describes: 'Cultural trauma occurs when members of a collectivity feel they have been subjected to a horrendous event that leaves indelible marks upon their group consciousness, marking their memories forever and changing their future identity in fundamental and irrevocable ways' (1).

As Cederwell states reading increased in importance during the war, since 'National expenditure on books increased from £9 million in 1939 to £23 million in 1945, and the city's literary magazines, such as *Horizon* and *Penguin New Writing*, tapped into this voracious new appetite for reading and writing' of which in 1942, fiction comprised 10 per cent (8), so at least for a minority of wartime readers literature and fiction conveyed much about the war itself and the Blitz in particular. In light of the above contexts, this chapter will survey, analyse and review primarily fictional narratives of the Blitz composed during the 1940s, considering six fictional texts which deal with such events and experiences contemporaneously (published by 1943) and six more retrospective narratives written and produced between 1944 and 1951. Seemingly straightforward, nevertheless the terms *the Blitz* and *Blitz Fiction* are, like so many others, freighted with various meanings and debates. Earlier in May the British Army had evacuated from Dunkirk and the French government had surrendered in June 1940. For Basil Woon in *Hell Came To London* (1941) this attack on the Home Front is simply 'the story of the "Blitzkrieg" that failed: the first fourteen days of the bombing of London by Germany, written while the bombs were falling' (vii). There were other surprising strategic dimensions. According to Peter Crisp 'before Hitler could invade, he first had to win control of the air' (iv), so the London attacks were actually unhelpful in that strategy, diverting aircraft from more strategically useful raids. In analysing the attacks from a strategic planning perspective, Williamson Murray says:

> German planners had to decide whether the *Luftwaffe* should deliver the weight of its attack against a specific segment of British industry such as aircraft factories, or against a system of interrelated industries such Britain's import and distribution network, or even in a blow aimed at breaking the morale of the British population. The bombing offensive against London, referred to as the Blitz, attempted to achieve all three strategies, none of which proved decisive. (54)[7]

More broadly conceived, as Juliet Gardiner explains, the term 'the Blitz' was adopted for 'the almost continual bombardment of the British Isles that stated on 7 September 1940 and continued with little relief until 10 May 1941' (xiv). As she reports Hermann Göring claimed this was retaliatory, responding to British bombing of Berlin (7). These attacks had been preceded by other smaller raids, testing Britain's defences, attempting to degrade its ability to wage war (particularly targeting aerodromes), and as part of a blockade on supplies and food, from August mostly using night-time attacks. Mass Observation diarist Nina Masel records the end of the first raids in Stepney 'Every Street was damaged, bombs everywhere. Smoke and flames streaming from the docks. Shouting, finding relatives, chaos' (10), and she describes a 'mass hysteria' (Crisp 10). As Nicholas John Cull notes, on that very day: 'The War Cabinet issued the "invasion imminent" signal and then waited' (97), but Cull adds that Churchill was convinced this would bring the Americans into the war (97–8).

Living in Sussex in the flight path from France to London, on that first day Virginia Woolf records in her diary, 'An air raid in progress. Planes zooming. No, that one's gone over, very quick & loud. [...] More planes over the house, going I suppose to London, which is raided every night' (315–16), along with which came 'A sense of invasion [...]' (319), the absence of which she records severally (321), before noting on 15th November, 'Coventry almost destroyed' (339).[8] Marina MacKay notes that later Woolf would suffer directly in several ways, for

> Having lost her London residence in the Blitz, and hearing nightly the planes passing over her home in vulnerable Sussex, Woolf knew at first hand that modernist homelessness could become more than a metaphor. The ruining of the home might come, if not from Nazi bombs, from the accelerated social change that would follow a military victory. This is perhaps why *Between the Acts* is so obsessively ethnographic, with a long view of history that looks as far back at the Domesday Book and the last invasion of 'English' soil. (39)

Woolf's draft novel was completed in 1941 (the author not entirely happy with her work) and is set significantly 'on a June day in 1939' (94) a few months before war was declared. After the pageant with its flow of British Imperial history, the local vicar, Mr Streatfield, delivers a rambling speech, which is interrupted with a vision of technological modernity, one rendered radically ambivalent by a reader's sense of this novel being written at a time that both anticipates and incorporates the Blitz: 'Twelve aeroplanes in perfect formation like a flight of wild duck came overhead. *That* was the music. The audience gaped; the audience gazed. Then zoom became drone. The planes had passed' (225). Earlier Giles is absorbed by 'his vision of Europe, bristling with guns, poised with planes. At any moment guns would rake that land into furrows; planes splinter Bolney Minster into smithereens and blast the Folly' (66–7) and angered at the indifference of 'old fogies' (66). Giles's 'blood-stained tennis shoes' (205) evoke acts of fatal violence. Clearly, Blitz fiction may not reflect literally upon events taken directly from the Blitz itself, but may merely incorporate various elements, even if just psychological effects or the vicarious impact on evacuees, for instance.

As Crisp reports in Coventry in the aftermath of its bombing: 'The overwhelmingly dominant feeling on Friday was the feeling of utter helplessness. The tremendous impact of the previous night had left people practically speechless in many cases. And it made them feel impotent' (22). For many such as Mass Observation diarist Nita Marcus, writing from a vantage point in Lewisham, the initial mass raid initiated a strong sense of being at war:

> We have started using the phrase 'since the war started,' meaning since Saturday afternoon when the great raid set the whole skyline ablaze; & all the hill tops here (which gives a fine view of the Thames & dockside & half of London) were covered with sightseers between the first raid & the second. Bombs first dropped in the district on Friday, just a few [...]. (Crisp 11)

In London, after initial reluctance during the first week of attacks, the authorities acceded to the public's demand that tube stations be used as shelters, as Field reports allowing people in after 16:00 (15). In describing the effects of the Blitz, most diarists observe how space is literally transformed, often with buildings or people obliterated, the domestic transformed into sites of public significance, no longer private and associated with transformation, fear and trauma:

Subsequently other cities, including Belfast, Birmingham, Bristol, Exeter, Glasgow, Hull and Liverpool, suffered often intense aerial attacks. The so-called Baedeker Blitz would follow in 1942. Hence for several years, initially unprepared civilians effectively found themselves on a new front-line or Home Front. They would continue to do so later in the war with the V1 and V2 attacks.[9] Perhaps the reason for the focus on 1940–1 can be attributed to the many contemporaneous reports, perhaps most notably *Front Line: 1940–1942: The Official Story of the Civil Defence of Britain* (1942), a book of dramatic black-and-white photographs and copy about the bombings 'Issued for the Ministry of Home Security by the Ministry of Information' (3), which serves as official propaganda. The three sections detailed on the contents page are 'The Onslaught on London' (4), 'The Ordeal of the Provinces' (4) and 'The Army of Civil Defence' (5), and throughout its unrelenting emphasis is on the spirited endurance and stoicism of the populace, the methodical organization of those working to protect and administer to those attacked. Rather than be guided solely by chronology and location, given the carnage continued, it seems logical to include later attacks in a more broadly conceived category of Blitz or bombing fiction, particularly when human suffering, death and trauma characterize such narratives. This would include the aforementioned Baedeker Blitz (initially a response to the devastating raid by RAF planes on Lubeck),[10] which in a strict sense lasted from 23 April to late May 1942, but Bath, Canterbury, Chelmsford, Cheltenham, Cowes, Exeter, Grimsby, Hastings, Ipswich, Kings Lynn, Lincoln, Maidstone Norwich, Poole, Sunderland, Weston-super-Mare, York and various other towns were targeted in raids that went on for two years beyond the initial attacks. One might also consider the V-1 and V-2 rocket attacks, the so-called Vengeance weapons (*Vergeltungswaffen*) which greatly affected those on the Home Front.[11]

My next example of this fictional sub-genre, discussed briefly, is an historical romance, *Frenchman's Creek* (1941), by Daphne du Maurier, and, as Jenny Hartley indicates, was published 'when the threat of invasion was still strong' (149). It was composed as the Blitz took place overhead, after its author, as Jane Dunn explains, 'moved as a paying guest into a beautiful Lutyens house, in Langley End near Hitchen owned by Christopher and Paddy Puxley' (242), with du Maurier later having an affair with the former (243–4). As Dunn says:

> Daphne could still watch a formation of twenty German bombers on their way to bomb Luton, only eight miles away, and see the beauty of them rather than the deadly menace they embodied. To Angela [du Maurier] in Torosay, she wrote dreamily: 'It really was rather an exquisite sight, so remote and unreal, those silvery creatures like humming birds above us at twenty thousand feet, whilst above them circled their own protective fighters.' (245)

Later Daphne moved her family back to Cornwall, leaving her husband behind in military service (248). The menacing element Dunn refers to above together with Du Maurier's metaphor of the planes akin to birds makes its way into her later novella, 'The Birds' which was made famous by Hitchcock's film adaptation. The protagonist of Du Maurier's narrative, Nat Hocken, significantly has 'a wartime disability' (1) and later he discovers the attacks are widespread with a National Emergency proclaimed (23). As Mary Ellen Bellanca observes, 'Du Maurier's "Birds" can be contextualized historically as a post-World War II dystopia in which attacks from the air destroy civilization throughout the British Isles, if not the wider world. [...] The birds are a cultural text, a projection and symbol of human terrors and our vulnerability to forces from which our social machinery is inadequate to protect us' (27). They also incorporate Du Maurier's wartime metaphor for Luftwaffe planes, which Belanca describes as the story's 'most salient cultural backdrop is Britain's recent experience of World war II [...]. [R]eminiscent of German air raids' (31). Later, Nat realizes why the radio plays only light music, 'He knew the reason. The usual programs had been abandoned. This only happened at exceptional times. Elections and such. He tried to remember if it had happened in the war, during the heavy raids on London' (22–23). By the end Nat and his family face this apocalypse alone, when as Bellanca notes, 'Their fate, ambiguously unspecified, nonetheless appears grimly certain' (29). The Blitz element of Du Maurier's *Frenchman's Creek* is residual: the protagonist, Dona, has fled from London accompanied as a mother by her two children (thus evoking wartime evacuation), away from a turbulence that is only hinted, having undertaken a journey and escape that structures the novel.

Other Blitz novels more inclined towards pastoral realism feature the countryside or the suburbs, as either a contrast to the city's bombing or a site of retreat and evacuation. Jocelyn Playfair's *A House in the Country* (1944) commences at the Fall of Tobruk in 1942, a military disaster that might indicate potential defeat. The widowed, upper-middle-class protagonist, Cressida Chance, struggles without servants to maintain life (as did the novelist herself) with her country house, Brede Manor, full of paying guests and what Victoria Stewart calls 'a disparate community of evacuees and refugees' (2006: 113), one a European, Tori. The English country house is adapted to exigencies of war, a fundamental transformation which occurs in Evelyn Waugh's *Brideshead Revisited* (1944). On several levels Playfair's narrative accords with Žindžiuvienė's notion that 'In the trauma novel, the reconstruction of massive trauma becomes a process of restatement, during which the response to the work of fiction contains both, a personal and transpersonal dimension' (65). Playfair's narrative opens with Charles Valery, who is in love with Cressida (165–6), badly burned after an enemy attack upon a ship (1–2), this first brief chapter introducing his reflections and fears while drifting injured in a lifeboat, his fate uncertain, a focus of further chapters. One of Cressida's guests, her spinster aunt Miss Ambleside, reflects on the bombing of the capital:

> After all, these new tremendous raids we were making would upset the Germans a good deal. But, on the other hand, it would be very trying if they stimulated the Germans into sending several thousand bombers over London, where one had lately begun to live quite a normal life again. Miss Ambleside's life in London had never been far from normal. During the blitz she had done a great deal of visiting in the country. (96)

This contrasts with Charles's observations as he travels by train after his rescue and return to England, noting the effects of war and the Blitz in particular:

> Charles could not have said in so many words what it was he had expected to find in England. Perhaps he had not quite imagined that the entire countryside would be a blackened ruin, that people would be picking their way nervously

between yawning bomb craters and darting into underground holes as soon as daylight began to fade. Perhaps he had not quite expected to see on every face the hard lines of heroism and stark, but controlled, fear. (235)

Ironically even in the countryside the aunt's anticipated German retaliation does happen, when later, a nearby village, Brede Somervel, suffers a single raid while Cressida is fire-watching, so far a precautionary ritual she has mostly enjoyed. The first real raid occurs after several hundred 'sirens without bombs, and once three bombs, without sirens, had fallen on a field of clover at midnight' (112). After the single death of an old woman in a makeshift shelter (123), 'everyone was for a time intensely conscious of being alive, less ready to grumble about trivialities, but readier to enjoy the simple pleasures of routine that usually passed unremarked. There was, until the return of peace dulled it, a sense of active friendliness, of affection, between the little collection of people who had escaped death together' (130–1).

Another tangential Blitz fiction with a suburban focus is Winifred Peck's *House-Bound*, its narrative focus almost exclusively on upper-middle-class Edinburgh, but the Blitz permeates its interstices, recurring periodically as a conversational topic or implied effects. Initially, Rose Fairlaw seeks servants at an agency for her large, ramshackle Victorian house. Later she is resigned to failure: 'Only what hope was there with girl's streaming away from service into the Services, and the Government caring nothing about the servant problem, and worse than nothing?' (6). This mirrors practical difficulties for such households, as Lucy Lethbridge details: 'Following the introduction of conscription for women in 1941, employers of domestic servants were required, if they wanted to keep them, to submit a written justification to the Ministry of Labour' (253). Rose is haunted by her own apparent cowardice and not being actively involved in the war effort. She struggles to maintain her large home, and deal with 'her own dark, difficult Flora [...]' (3), a wayward daughter fathered by a sailor she married in the last war (who later died). The women's relationship is conflictual, the child moody and fractious. An American soldier, Major Hosmer, assists by listening to Flora, to whom he seems attracted, while discussing her neuroses, presumably the result in part of her experiences in London in the Blitz. Meanwhile, Rose attempts her household duties with limited help:

> And yet during the bitter January of 1942, while bad news fell daily on her ears as certainly as the sound of good housewives scraping snow from their pavements in the black dawn, it seemed absurd to wash and sweep and polish

rooms, as if they had any conceivable importance in the scheme of a nightmare existence. (87)

Eventually, as Lethbridge notes, she is aided by 'the former upper-servant Mrs Childe, who undertakes to train Rose in everything needed to make her a "passable lower servant"' (258). According to Terence Handley MacMath the American major acts as a symbol and 'a catalyst for change throughout the novel' (n.pag). The larger national conflict is juxtaposed with her domestic struggle highlighting realities that persisted, framing people's lives, troubling them existentially. Significantly, when Rose tidies Flora's room:

> When the war began Flora at once elected to go off to a Red Cross unit in the South, and until Mickie only too soon gained his wings, life was at last tolerable again. Poor, poor, Flora! Rose pitied her child, and reproached herself vehemently, as she dusted the little china ornaments and old treasured scent bottles which made Flora seem a vulnerable, pitiful child again. (80)

The war and the bombings evoke a sense of vulnerability and threaten an infantilization of the individual (implied in the very smallness of the objects, while 'treasured' hints at adventures and fairy tales), and clearly this affects Flora who finally accuses the major of conspiring with her mother. He responds, his vocabulary echoing Rose's thoughts: "'You're talking like a child. You know the very great admiration and respect I have for you, but you also know perfectly well that as a psychiatrist I have to view your character from the angle of your friends and relations'" (219). Christine Harding notes 'the strong, snobbish class system in force at the time' (n.pag), which contrasts the so-called Blitz spirit. Finally, while Rose is away at Flora's nuptials, her daughter marrying the major, Rose's house is destroyed by a random bomb. When her stepbrother, Mickie, is killed on active military service, Flora seems more distraught than even her mother, because Flora realizes she hadn't articulated her love for him. As Michael Morpurgo observed to Harriett Gilber on Radio 4 there is 'at the heart of the story tragedy' (n.pag). Her mother indicates the underlying reality where even in wartime: "'Families don't talk about their love for each other, do they?" she said steadily. "Mickie was very proud of all you did in the blitz, dearest. 'Flora's a great girl,' he said, I remember'" (272). Gradually reconciled with her daughter, despite gloomy war news, Rose anticipates wider changes, reflecting on the fading residue of a Victorian past 'What matter if a world of the privileged and idle and cultured passed away?' (294). Such egalitarianism that some identified in the Blitz has perhaps even marginally permeated her upper-middle-class consciousness.

An evacuee himself, in 1968 B. S. Johnson reflected on wartime evacuation: 'Thirteen million people were in evacuation areas, eighteen million in reception, and fourteen million in neutral areas' (11), with children made a priority. He records, 'The first evacuees moved out of the cities on the morning of Friday 1 September 1939: by the evening of the 3rd, a few hours after war had been officially declared, 1,473,391 people had been placed in reception areas. Most of these were children [...]' (13). Noel Streatfeild's *Saplings* (1945) mixes pastoral with glimpses of urban destruction and incorporates these culturally central figures of the Blitz, the young evacuees. As Jacqueline Kyte observes of Streatfeild's novel: '*Saplings* is hard-hitting, drawing explicitly on her experience as an A.R.P. Warden, her work running a regular canteen service for people in the Deptford shelters and her mobile W.V.S. canteen that took tea, cocoa and buns through the blasted streets of South London' (51). Hartley reflects, 'Some novelists saw their function as straightforwardly as historians of the scene. Noel Streatfeild's wartime diary records 'an interesting argument about the place of the novelist in the world. I stood up for their value as historians of the age' (9). The narrative opens with a child-centred scene of affluent and idyllic bourgeois security, Tuesday, Laurel, Tony and Kim are on a month's holiday in Eastbourne waiting for their parents to join them. Their parental separation creates a range of symptoms which contrast the stoical working-class brothers, Albert and Ernie Parker, whom Kyte regards as typical of another strand of evacuation experience, partly a matter of class:

> They represent the experience of many children who took part in the first wave of evacuation – that it was short-lived. Parents quickly took their children back to London, feeling guilt at abandoning them to the hands of strangers, unable to overcome their own sense of loss, compounded by the children's homesickness and by the false alarm of the phoney war. [...] Albert Parker is a foil to the sensitive Wiltshire children; he is physically reckless and emotionally detached from his own parents. (54)

On their return the Wiltshire children find Albert's first-hand account of the bombing grimly compelling, with images of barely covered bodies, after which compulsive violence emerges, with them attacking an old cottage in 'an orgy of smashing. All the pent-up excitement of the world around them came out. All the whispers and grown-up waiting for something to happen. All the disbelief in the ordinary world. Nothing was left. Everything that could be torn down or smashed was ruined' (132). This microcosm of destruction contrasts emotionally Tony's subsequent despairing response to news of a specific death by a bomb, their father killed in their London home, after which as Hartley details the susceptibly 'bad' mother: 'goes downhill [...] and becomes an alcoholic with a weakness for American soldiers' (112). Much earlier the father appealed for self-discipline and purpose in highly suggestive terms:

> 'I want you to see yourselves as part of the nation. Everybody's on the move and practically nobody wants to be. [...] And children are being sent away from danger. What's making all this possible without much excitement? Because nearly everybody, including the children, are doing what they have to do without fuss.' (59)

His appeal is to a Britishness that for Kyte is part of 'the stiff-upper-lip attitude and emotional restraint that underpinned so much propaganda' (57), with an underlying sense of sacrifice. However, the various responses among the siblings are traumatized, particularly Tony who, haunted by an image of his father buried alive, rebelliously returns to London, unable to accept his father's demise. He digs in the wreckage with his hands. 'The wind was blowing and somewhere something swung against a broken lead pipe. To his distorted imagination, listening for just that sound, it was tapping from below ground' (144). Confronted by a warden, Tony retreats, denying knowledge of the inhabitants, wretched and sullen.

In contrast to such historically centred realism in a pastoral register, another category of novels share what Nil Santiáñez labels *catastrophic modernism* (232) [italics in original], where 'The modernism of catastrophic modernist works is, therefore, a function of the horror that they depict' and 'seeks to transfer the destructive effects of catastrophes to the readers' understanding and affectivity' (232). First, James Hanley's *No Direction* is a surreal, fragmentary and periodically impressionistic narrative, its aesthetic coordinates attuned to an insistent underlying theme of a painterly consciousness. As Michael Neil Hallam details, Hanley moved to London in 1939 seeking 'to foster links with BBC radio, to which he was frequently submitting fiction in the hope it would be adapted for broadcast' (31) and in Chelsea 'he observed the aerial bombardment of London at very close quarters' (31). The novel includes familiar tropes of the blackout and the ARP (Air Raid Precautions) warden, yet its opening is stark, drawing on the immediacy of the author's own experiences: 'After the deluge of sound ceased, after the wind passed, the sailor fell, was sick. They were in a desert of air' (9). Jean-Christophe Murat insists the novel 'is strongly indebted to the then fashionable rhetoric and imagery of Apocalyptic poetry; it is therefore a period piece in that respect, emphasising linguistic and formal experimentation to the point of artificiality' (n.pag). Its sense of chaos and fear is compelling, charting the effects of the bombing on one local area. Reluctantly the house's various inhabitants retreat to a large cellar for safety. For Hallam the author seeks to incorporate in the '"tragic"' (9) aspects of these attacks an authenticity or avant-garde realism:

> Yet, there are discernible tensions in *No Directions* between such truth-telling impulses and the formal innovations through which the text stages its representation of such exceptional events. Hanley was not alone in struggling to find a mode of expression – a 'terror language' – appropriate for capturing what he perceived as the 'immensity' of the Blitz [...]. (10)

The narrative revolves around both residents of and visitors to a boarding house in Chelsea, including Mr Johns, a sailor so drunk he is uncertain where he is, and Clement Stevens, a reclusive painter, and his wife, Lena. The sailor's utter confusion suggests a traumatic symptomology, since, as Ruth Leys observes, 'for Freud traumatic memory is inherently unstable or mutable owing to the role of unconscious motives that confer meaning on it' (20). None of the characters has any clear trajectory in life. Moreover, as Murat says, 'The loss of bearings that explicitly affects the drunken sailor upon entering a strange blacked-out building at night is matched by the reader's initial puzzlement at having to grope his or her way through an unlit text' (n.pag). The war transforms domesticity, and relationships themselves, in what Hallam calls 'the new hyper-sensitivity to sound that seems an inevitable concomitant to being bombed' (43). Nevertheless, as Alan Munton notes, 'War is a social activity' (1), and so is enduring it. Lena suffers from breast cancer which her spouse believes to be cancer of the heart, coexisting in their room which remains 'a riot of canvases' (26). She meets her doctor during the blackout, and later takes a walk where she encounters an unfinished bridge 'that began on stone foundations and ended in space, a half-arch, it wasn't really a bridge, it was a gesture [...]' (68), a stark image of incompletion, of provisionality. As John Fordham suggests the narrative is 'an indication that not all wartime stories were concerned with morale boosting or military heroism' (227). Events are tortuous, and intersecting. They include the surprise arrival of Elia Downs, a former artist's model seeking Clem, diverted by an unwanted sexual encounter with the sailor. The reverberations of a raid on the nerves of various characters differ wildly. For Elia they are challenging, her words curt, enigmatic: '"The bombers," she said, suddenly cold all over, they made her feel like that, a cosmic coldness, mysterious, terrifying' (52). Inner feelings emerge, both surprising, and unexpected. As Hallam observes, 'the novel's emphasis [is] on the friction of new inter-class and inter-generational relations and the tentative, sometimes arduous interdependence the air-raids enforced' (32), although, as Fordham notes, still 'the class lines are clearly delineated' (229). Periodically, the logic is almost one of panic and incoherence, and Hallam suggests:

> Several of the characters, not least the sailor, are in a sort of fugue or hallucinatory semi-trance, yet the narrative insists on representing their imaginative responses without explanatory verbs like 'imagined' or 'believed', indeed sometimes without explanatory pronouns or even transitional words like 'and' or 'then'. This gives the prose a jagged, chopped-up rhythm and much of the characters' speech and internal monologues are similarly staccato [...]. (34)

For Meg Jensen this would reflect the impact of the Blitz since: 'The post-traumatic writer, therefore, may be attracted to autobiographical fiction as a form of life story telling that allows them to express feelings without being forced to attribute meaning to them and also engages the "dilemma of representation" that mimics their psychic state' (705), part of what Munton calls '"Experienced" or "felt" novels [which] possess a sense of immediacy that brings with it fictional authority' (10). Clem clambers to a roof during the height of the raid where he perceives a savage beauty, and finally on his descent, he encounters a horse that was 'first demented and now calm, it would go where he went' (138), and for Munton 'The artist has mastered a natural force, and that is his true purpose, not to welcome destruction' (43). Subsequently, in a quasi-bathetic moment, the inhabitants of the house discover the sailor has died. Their lives have been reconfigured, not consciously, for as Rod Mengham explains the image represents 'a recognition of the role of the subconscious in coming to grips with' – or 'taking in – the Blitz: with a situation in which the conventional means of imaginatively organising space and time no longer apply' (132), a reality marked paradoxically by the very absence 'of a perspective that would impose order on this array of details [...]' (131).

A subdued sense of catastrophe subtends Graham Greene's only contemporaneous account of the Blitz, *The Ministry of Fear*. Its narrative is in part a dark, quasi-Gothic thriller, telling of a convicted, but subsequently released, murderer, Arthur Rowe. The narrative was written initially, as Richard Greene indicates, in Freetown while Greene was posted in Sierra Leone (111). As Nicolas Tredell notes the protagonist previously 'administer[ed] a lethal dose of hyoscine to his terminally ill wife, Alice' (n.pag). After release from an asylum Rowe 'lived in Guildford Street. A bomb early in the blitz had fallen in the middle of the street and blasted both sides, but Rowe stayed on' (14). Haunted by both his past and a sense of disengagement from the war effort, improbably he encounters a fifth columnist, a lodger new to his digs, who tries to kill Rowe to retrieve a cake the latter has won at a local fête aided by a fortune teller, Mrs Bellairs, who mistakes him for a member of a German spy network. Such complications seem bizarre, incongruous, but a raid intrudes, ironically saving Rowe through a direct hit, by killing his assailant. Shell-shocked, he tries to fathom what he has encountered by employing investigative agent, Mr Rennit and his assistant, Jones. The bombing is part of what Victoria Stewart calls 'the auditory uncanny' (2004: 66), and serves to radically disarrange the city for the amnesiac Rowe, yet curiously he adapts: 'Now in the strange, torn landscape where London shops were reduced to a stone ground-plan like those of Pompeii he moved with familiarity; he was part of this destruction as he was no longer part of the past [...]' (39). For Greene war here is replete with contradiction and mystery, its trauma inherent in what Stewart details: 'the time-lag which often occurs between hearing and understanding in *The Ministry of Fear*, or between cause and effect, is therefore related to the kind of delayed comprehension that is found in *Caught*' (2004: 66), a novel by Henry Green considered below. As Damon Marcel DeCoste indicates in contrast to the prevailing threat of violence the fête has offered the illusion of pastoral utopia (435) echoing Rowe's rereading of two Dickens novels encountered in childhood. And yet as DeCoste suggests equally he 'welcomes the violence of the blitz, as it quite forcibly eradicates that present life he, burdened with dreams idyllic past, cannot abide [...]' (437). His amnesia thrusts him into a demi-monde of intrigue where, as Tredell observes, London becomes 'a place where the predictable and the improbable, waking consciousness and dream, the real and the surreal mix and merge [...]' (n.pag), and not the 'realist mode' (231) that Nil Santiáñez assigns to the novel, which is both ambivalently asserted and subverted throughout. At a séance, Rowe witnesses the apparently fatal stabbing of Mr Cost, after which he becomes the prime suspect, seeking respite in a shelter, where he speaks to his dead mother: "'I'm wanted for a murder I didn't do. People want to kill me because I know too much. I'm hiding underground, and up above the Germans are methodically smashing London to bits all round me'" (71). For Rau the private and public both coalesce:

> the uncanny effects of war and their fictional representation in the 1940s, with intellectual uncertainty about the shifting or collapsing boundaries between otherwise distinct categories of the strange and the familiar, the past and the present, the other and the self, the enemy and the ally. (32)

Another oddly decentred Blitz narrative is Graham Greene's retrospective account, *The End of the Affair*, which focuses on three central characters: civil servant, Henry Miles and his wife, Sarah Miles, and writer Maurice Bendrix, with wartime seen from the perspectives of both the protagonist as a writer and the author, Greene. Bendrix and Sarah are lovers and, as Lawrence Phillips notes, 'The affair encompasses the entire period of the war' (24). The novel opens:

> A story has no beginning or end; arbitrarily one chooses that moment of experience from which to look back or from which to look ahead. I say 'one chooses' with the inaccurate pride of a professional [...] but do I in fact of my own will choose that black wet January night on the Common in 1946, the sight of Henry Miles slanting across the wide river of rain, or did these images choose me? (7)

Greene's convoluted narrative draws upon his actual affair with Lady Catherine Watson and his experiences when his home at 14 Clapham Common Northside was bombed. However, for most of the novel conflict serves as a muted backdrop to a curiously passionless affair that ends so painfully and later restarts, prior to which 'The bombs between those daylight raids and the V1s of 1944 kept their own convenient nocturnal habits, but so often it was only in the mornings that I could see Sarah [...]' (34). As Ronald G. Walker notes direct dramatic presentation of these events that constitute the affair 'occupy a total of approximately 27.6 pages, or about 14.4 percent of the text' (225). Greene evokes what Michael Gorra describes as 'an apparently old-fashioned novel of adultery in a world where such infidelity no longer seems a matter of overwhelming importance' (120). The Blitz as processed by both writers, Greene and his fictional alter-ego, Bendrix, has subsumed any such normative values. As Ruth Leys indicates trauma can be phased and cumulative: 'Freud stressed the role of a post-traumatic "incubation," or latency period of psychic elaboration, in ways that made the traumatic experience irreducible to the idea of a purely physiological causal sequence' (19). Intense personal catastrophe undermines Bendrix, who agonizes over Sarah having ended their liaison, the war hardly seeming to trouble his consciousness, while ironically he finds himself impelled toward action ironically by her husband's doubts. So directed, Bendrix pursues his ex-lover for evidence of a new affair (aided by Parkis, a detective). The new attachment transpires to be simply her seeking spiritual guidance from a secularist, Richard Smythe, given she is uncomfortable with her newly discovered faith. Later, as Walker notes, Bendrix's renewal of their tryst occurs 'when his romantic passion for Sarah turns to jealousy and pettiness' (235), a visceral degradation. Ironically after a V1 appears to have killed Bendrix, Sarah's prayer for a miracle seems to result in his survival, which, as Walker comments, 'necessitates their separation' (237). It also inculcates in Sarah a new belief in God. Although for Gorra 'Erotic experience has brought her to a knowledge of the divine and even into a state of grace' (110), one might alternatively identify the intensity of even apparently casual human interactions under conditions of extreme stress, including the traumatic experience of the V1 raid with the narrative's segue towards its potentially preternatural resolution. Greene uses a chronological and experiential compression that conjoins the different periods and allows an avoidance of what Richard Creese labels 'chronological confusion' by distinguishing the three interrelated timeframes, unifying the war experience within an overwhelming sense of loss (4).

Arguably the full catastrophic intensity in literal and emotional (psycho-sexual) terms of the Blitz is also conveyed in Henry Green's *Caught* (1943), a narrative haunted by what Geoffrey Easeman calls the certainty of death anticipated (140), which relates experiences of the author (real name, Henry Yorke) as a member of the London Auxiliary Fire Service (AFS) in which he served in 1940 at the height of the bombing. Ironically the novel opens in the 'Phoney War', which for Lyndsey Stonebridge is an 'irreal space' (1998: 27; 2001: 49), and where as Nicholas S. Shepley comments 'everyday existence is charged with the apprehension and frustration of waiting for an attack that never seems to arrive' (187). Green's alter ego, the partially deaf, upper-class protagonist Richard Roe, goes from initial training by Fireman Instructor Arthur Pye, a permanent fireman, to service during a cataclysmic raid on the docks. As Rod Mengham explains Green's protagonist 'is in the habit of retailing the myth of catastrophe in the hope of having it explained away', of which 'wishful thinking' (1980: 117) Ilse, a Swedish woman, disabuses him. Roe later visits his evacuated son, Christopher, on a furlough after a concussive head injury. The first section circuitously retells how Christopher has been abducted from a store by Pye's sister, subsequently incarcerated in an asylum for her transgression. The act is both tinged with trauma and inflicts yet more, as does the war by stealth. Much later, the convalescing Roe tells his sister-in-law, Dy, an account where, as Munton explains, 'Green ingeniously splits this Blitz story between Roe's awkwardly told version, and a parenthetical omniscient narration written in vivid literary prose' (46). Unlike the auditory effects that dominate most accounts of such events, in contrast Green emphasizes the visual with layered details so that in one description 'colors abound. Pinks, blacks, and greens are supplemented by vibrant rainbows, mushrooms and fox-dyes' (108), a feature that recurs. As

Rex Ferguson demonstrates the technique of direct visual representation is rare because of a traumatic gap (103-4), and such a use of intense and 'destructively loud colors' (111) is broadly hallucinatory (110-11). The narrative charts both sex and compulsive desires, punctuated by various affairs such as Richard's with Hilly. As Pye comments to Richard toward the novel's end after reluctantly seeing a psychologist, "'Skirt, eh? Well that's sent many a good man off his nut'" (154), evoking perhaps an illusory guilt of incestuous sex with his sister, a subtext that resurfaces. However, as John Russell records, 'Pye's psychological guilt obviates the necessity of his having actually committed incest' (154) since his desire condemns and subverts him. Richard encounters an exotic repulsion in his relentless pursuit of passion, for when '[H]e leaned over, in pitch dark, and kissed Hilly on the mouth. Her lips' answer, he felt, was of opened figs, wet at dead of night in a hothouse' (106), both luxurious and traumatic. Pye is both undermined by AFS politics, gossip and sexual compulsion. Such incongruities permeate the text multiply, and, as Stonebridge notes:

> Fascinated by the misheard, the unspoken and the oblique (his word), Green is a trauma writer not before but very much of his time. [...] It is precisely what cannot be consciously realized in wartime that attracts Green; and it is from the wounds in time and experience – anxiety, death and sex – that his writing draws its understated power. (1998: 26; 2001: 48)

After enumerating several deaths of colleagues which upsets his sister-in-law (173), Roe admits to Dy that "'only the point about a blitz is this, there's always something you can't describe, and it's not the blitz alone that's true of'" (175) events being in excess of both comprehension and apprehension, a traumatic gap between experience and recollection. Haunted by his past Pye cannot adapt, and, as Stonebridge suggests, 'Pye, is subject to traumatic memory images which shatter meaning and identity by bringing desire and anxiety together' (1998: 35; 2001: 57), a conjunction he cannot resolve or mediate. Roe co-opts these potentially undermining elements through a different, less mundane sensibility. For Roe such experiences are retrospectively more 'literary' or filmic since 'Then afterwards, when you go over it, everything seems unreal [...]' (170). As Leslie Brunetta concludes, 'Green's blitz isn't a scene of spiritual triumph. The men turn out to be neither heroes nor cowards. Some are killed – but out of sight. There are no thrilling rescues, no last words' (123). Finally, Green's narrative is firmly anti-heroic, marked by undercurrents of despair and anguish, but its acute spatial awareness of the phenomenological exteriority of self for Warwick Smith responds precisely to 'technology of warfare' (20).

Elizabeth Bowen also gleaned material from her war work. As Emma Zimmerman notes, she 'directly witnessed the uncanniness of wartime whilst patrolling London's blitzed streets as an Air Raid Precautions warden' (43). Later in the war Elizabeth lived in County Cork, working as an agent, supporting at least obliquely the British Government's war effort.[12] Espionage and its impulses permeate her retrospective wartime novel, *The Heat of the Day*, which initially features an open-air concert in central London and subtly references the sky above by which bombs will be delivered to the city, emphasizing by implication both the randomness of attack and the utter vulnerability of these city-dwellers. In this scene, as Claire Seiler observes, 'As the narrative literalizes the public metaphor of the theater of war, it adopts the lexicon of conflict' (131). With the Blitz '[T]he dead, from mortuaries, from under cataracts of rubble, made their anonymous presence – not as today's dead but as yesterday's living – felt through London' (91), so that a transformation occurred in the people's psyche whereby 'The wall between the living and the living became less solid as the wall between the living and the dead thinned. In that September transparency people became transparent, only to be located by the just darker flicker of their hearts' (92). Bowen foregrounds conditions that subtly confirm Neil J. Smelser's observation: 'the status of trauma as trauma is dependent on the sociocultural context of the affected society at the time the historical event or situation arises. A society emerging from a major war [...] is more trauma prone than others' (36). London has emerged from an attack on a daily basis. In the novel, the initial Blitz has passed, but the catastrophic after-effects initiate a scenario of vulnerability and doubt in which widowed protagonist, Stella Rodney, is stalked and cornered in her borrowed flat by Harrison, seemingly either a spiv or secret service agent (or, just possibly both). He claims to be monitoring her fascist-inclined lover, Robert Kelway, revealing the latter as a traitor and foreign spy. As Megan Faragher explains: 'Harrison's sexual desire for Stella taints the credibility of this information, as it also takes the form of blackmail' (58), and in the uncertainties of war the coordinates of certainty remain nomadic, nebulous. While puzzling over an Irish inheritance, her son, Roderick finds his visit unsettling since on a mundane level he is unfamiliar with her surroundings; according to Smith the pair 'are suspended in a present without personal meaning – echoed by the sofa without environment – because their psychic connection with the past has been severed' (8), such changes in spatial awareness accelerated by war conditions (19). Indeed, for Gill Plain the novel focuses 'upon the contradictory presence of nothingness' (1996: 167).

Robert's curiously ambivalent character mirrors his stunted, perverse bourgeois origins in 'Holmdene' in Sussex, which Stella visits, where, first, his mother seeks to diminish her presence, and second, Robert compares memories of adolescence to his current life, the latter found empty, fraudulent. Curiously, such negations seem contemporaneously ineffective, only residually disturbing the psyche. Jessica Gildersleeve quotes the draft preface to Bowen's *The Last September*, where she details the creative sensibilities central to fiction and even her excisions reaffirm the spectral and traumatic qualities of the past:

> Sensation accumulates ~~where it is least sought, meaning flows in where we had imagined none, one is drawn by the mysterious hauntedness of a period not understood in its own time~~, retrospectively, where we were blind to any. One is captured by the mysterious the imperious hauntedness of a period not understood in its own time. (Qtd. Gildersleeve 15) [deletions in original]

Retrospection is key to a new apprehension, and for Gildersleeve 'In *The Heat of the Day*, it is the unknown, and the effect of the unknown, that the narrative seeks to elucidate and construct' by purveying 'the traumatic unknown' (147) as an 'aftershock from, the traumatic event of war' (148). As Phillips indicates, 'Stella's affair with Robert starts during the 1941 Blitz, and the conclusion of the novel brings us to the first V1 raids of 1944' (19), both suggestive coordinates of a troubled affair, but only understood as such retrospectively. Although her relationship with Harrison seems tentative, very possibly manipulative on his part, always potentially a matter of a bluff that she might call (42), as Phillips says, 'He is the ultimate urban stranger whom Stella continually struggles to place and categorize' (18). Stella is undermined by her uncertainties about Robert, which she hides from him. Ironically, Stella's characteristic reserve is a consequence of her clandestine war work whereby 'The habit of guardedness was growing on her as on many other people, reinforcing what was in her an existing bent' (26). Yet while first meeting Harrison any such provisionality dissolves with Stella's habitual actions, 'she took up the receiver with the unfumbling sureness of one who answers the telephone at any, even the deepest, hour of the night' (44), a subtle sign of her own inner certainty, even though the unknown remains elusive, unknowable, as is the final cause of Robert's death. As Faragher concludes: 'Bowen's fiction, with its incorporation of obfuscation and masking, aestheticizes the crisis that comes from a truth that is inaccessible' (64), written from the perspective of what Seiler conceives as a 'midcentury imaginary' (130) that allows a reconsideration of the myth of the Blitz, as much as for Phillips, Robert has rejected 'the myth of triumph associated with' Dunkirk (20) on his path to disillusionment.

Another most striking Blitz novel focusing on trauma is *There Were No Windows* by Dublin-born Anglo-Irish writer Norah Hoult, a harrowing narrative intense in its depiction of the initially unnamed, aged, and utterly confused female protagonist, Claire Temple. A former suffragette (276), she is both literally and symbolically vulnerable, eventually so convinced her cook is attempting to poison her she takes her lunch to the police who comically regard it as evidence of the deprivations of rationing (272–3).[13] Her existence is underpinned by the past, its certainties being obliterated by the present conflict. Her dementia increases as the war continues, events largely beyond her comprehension, with Hoult's third-person narrative generally following but not coterminous with Claire's consciousness, as at the opening when she distractedly calls for her Irish cook after 'a sudden loud explosion' (3) which intensifies her anxieties:

> What was that noise, cook?
> Kathleen's face appeared at the bottom of the staircase. 'Ah, it was nothing, nothing but a time bomb going off. It was streets away from here. Aren't you making your bed?'
> She went down the stairs eagerly. 'A time bomb? Is that a new kind of bomb? Do you suppose anyone was hurt?' (4)

The scenario is underpinned implicitly by the paucity of servants (a recurrent wartime theme), explicitly by Claire's infantile state of consciousness, her growing sense of isolation, lapses of memory (due to dementia) and her fear of incarceration, periodically threatened by Kathleen. Hence, as Jeanette King says, 'Claire becomes increasingly disoriented' (51). For King 'the blackout reflects the terror and inner darkness experienced by Claire Temple under the onslaught of dementia' (44) and as King concludes, speaking to Mrs White, a part-time help, Kathleen relates her mistress' madness with earlier promiscuity (44), suggesting: '"That's makes it all the more terrible, the way she's bent on disgracing herself in every possible way. Didn't you hear her yourself admit that that same sister wouldn't speak to her because of her wickedness and disgracing the family?"' (56). Both servants remain implacably unaware of Claire's literary success; specifically, Kathleen fails utterly to comprehend the context of Claire's earlier Bohemian upper-class life. King details the Shakespearean qualities, an explicit allusion when the servants conspire to pilfer her possessions: 'You've plotted together to rob me. Before you hand me over stripped and naked. King Lear's daughters over again' (299). This intimates a tragic dimension to Claire's fate, with the Blitz as a catalyst, mirroring the inner chaos and conflict. As Anne Cunningham suggests of the author's post-war collection that Hoult through her 'reductionist' style sustains an ability to distil character in a very few sentences, a compacted realism of nuances and unspoken implications, adding intriguingly, 'The history books tell us that in the aftermath of World War II the gaps between the social classes were narrowed. Norah Hoult's fiction tells us quite the opposite' (n.pag). This awareness permeates Hoult's earlier novel, and perhaps the most interesting commentary found at several levels of narrative both implicitly and explicitly is the failure of any genuine reconciliation or understanding between the classes despite the conflict. In this context Claire confides in a stranger, an air-raid warden, about her life, knowing Henry James and deviating from her origins:

> 'I do bore people so. It's difficult to explain, but if I'd remained in my own class and married suitably, a country squire, like my sister did, and not mixed myself up with artists, and been an artist myself, well, then, I should not have been left like Cardinal Wolsey, given over in my old age. Only he said it about serving God, didn't he?'
> There was a pause. Mr Mills then said: 'You mean toffs stick together?'
> 'How clever you are. That's just what I do mean,' said Mrs Temple delighted. (244)

The continuing class differences are confirmed by a scene in a local pub, where Claire's ongoing snobbery is evident, the locals reacting to the 'sort of general benediction' (172) she offers on leaving: '"After the ruddy war, people who think they own the ruddy earth will have to get off, see. And the quicker, the better"' (172). As Katherine E. Fisher observes of Claire: 'She roams the city, wondering why she sees no familiar faces and why certain landmarks are absent; she is disoriented by the blackout, ignores the air-raid sirens, and confuses the current war with the previous one' (137), yet her very disorientation links the two conflicts, inextricably matching the one bellicose disaster with the next in the reader's mind. For Claire unhappiness and loneliness outweigh any personal fear (124); she loses her way not just because of her fragility (108) and senescence, but because of the reiteration and deepening of disaster.

Set in the winter of 1943, Patrick Hamilton's *The Slaves of Solitude* (1947) is also darkly comic, focusing on the evacuee inhabitants of a boarding house, the Rosamund Tea Rooms, in Thames Lockdon (for which read Henley-on-Thames) where their interactions make their lives seem stultifying. The period is bleak as is the setting: 'The conditions were those of intense war, intense winter, and intensest blackout in the month of December' (1). Enduring what Thierry Labica labels an 'anguished insomnia' (76), Miss Roach, a thirty-nine-year-old spinster, has been bombed out of her room in Kensington, but commutes daily to her publishing house job in London. She feels this survival conveys a certain status as indicated in the reaction of her companion, an American, Lieutenant

Dayton Pike: 'He said he guessed that must have been pretty tough, and he looked at her with considerable awe and naïvety. She felt a sudden, delightful, modest, gin and French pride in her experience as a 1940s Londoner' (29). In contrast, despite the apparent safety, dull suburban evenings bring mealtimes and the unsubtle mockery of a grotesque and quasi-Dickensian villain, Mr Thwaites, Nazi sympathizer and bore, encountered 'in this dead-and-alive dining-room, of this dead-and-alive house, of this this dead-and-alive street, of this dead-and-alive little town' (157). David Lodge describes his 'tireless malice and negative energy' (n.pag) that animates his verbal bullying and his attempts to humiliate Miss Roach, and as Lodge indicates, in doing so Thwaites tortures the English language 'making remarks in a ghastly idiolect full of phoney archaism, stage dialect, threadbare cliché and proverbial bromides' (n.pag).[14] As Labica observes, 'He totally ignores the Cooperative principle as the matrix of interaction,' annexing the common space (78). Curiously both Bowen and Hamilton similarly relate a middle-class male affinity with fascism, but in *Slaves of Solitude* this is far more fervent than resigned. 'Mr Thwaites had since 1939 slowly learned to swallow the disgrace of Hitler, of whom he had been from the beginning, and still secretly remained, a hot disciple' (13). German-born Vicki Kugelmann, who takes a room after befriending Miss Roach, acts as a catalyst, eventually winning over her American, Lieutenant Pike, to whom both are attracted. As Munton concludes, 'Hamilton has recorded the minute details of social inhibition and the subtle destructiveness of private languages [...]' (53), with Hamilton making his reader aware that despite the war the pettiness and inconsequentiality of life continues. Miss Roach reacts with a pervasive snobbery toward another American accompanied by two shop assistants, clearly of a lower class, embarrassing her.

Such fictional details draw upon the presence of American forces, whose active involvement had long been a key objective of the British government and broadcasters such as Morrow, occurring with rapidity after the Japanese attack on Pearl Harbor. Eventually planning and training commenced for D-Day, whose consequences included a military advance toward Mr Thwaite's friends in Germany and the end of the V-1 and V-2 rocket attacks as the production sites were seized. At the same time German cities were subjected to bombing raids by day (by Americans) and at night (by other allies including the British) delivering far more destructive payloads than those suffered during the Blitz, ironically realizing pre-war British fears about the destructiveness of air warfare. After Germany surrendered unconditionally, what followed was the destruction of Hiroshima and Nagasaki by the Americans, initiating a new dimension to aerial warfare, compared to which even the Blitz pales to insignificance and which would later be further magnified by the application of German expertise in rocketry.

Notes

1. As Robert Mackay indicates the 'devastating potential' (19) of air attacks had been equally proven by the British on Kurdish tribesmen in 1932 in northern Iraq; the Italians in 1935–6 on Abyssinian armies; and the Japanese in 1937 on cities in China (19). He reports, 'By 1937 the Committee of Imperial Defence [...] was forecasting 1,800,000 casualties in the first two months, one third of them killed' (20).
2. Angus Calder summarizes thus: 'Between the wars official circles in Britain had been obsessed with the role of the bomber in war. As early as 1925, British Air Staff was predicting that casualties in London alone in a new war would begin at the rate of 5,000 on the first day and settle down at 2,500 a day. It predicted a collapse of morale and added that there was no possible defence against this sort of attack' (59).
3. As any criminal offence could be adjudicated in a special court and might be subject to a sentence of death, Jennings regarded the law as conferring 'therefore, a wide and dangerous power, and it is a great pity that the House of Commons did not insist on the insertion of additional precaution' (134). Of these powers, after listening to a résumé on the BBC, Margery Allingham wrote in *Oaken Heart*, 'A conquered country could not give up much more of its freedom' (192).
4. Nicholas John Cull indicates the narrative was efficacious in a transformation of perspectives: 'As the second Fire of London raged, it seemed natural for "purgatorial fire" to be the dominant metaphor in both British literature and American reportage. The formula of national death and glorious resurrection promised much for the British cause in America. It side-stepped doubts over the historical unworthiness of Britain, no longer needed to deny its heritage of imperialism, debt, defaulting, and appeasement' (99).
5. Interestingly, as Calder notes, 'Murrow's wife, Janet, actually took a job at the MoI' (212). Calder adds 'He and Janet were frequent guests at 10 Downing Street [...]' (213).
6. Calder reports that very early in the war entirely before the Blitz: 'A small British Library of Information already existed in New York. In 1939 a secret government inquiry was set up to devise a more ambitious policy. This was done on the basis of "direct and detailed consultation" with Edward R. Murrow, the London-based European director of the Columbian Broadcasting Service' (211). As MacKay indicates Murrow referred specifically in August 1940 to 'a people's war' (22).
7. Failures in intelligence were also critical in the air battle, for, as Murray argues, 'the Germans misjudged their opponents. In a study dated July 16, *Luftwaffe* intelligence estimated the "Hurricane" and "Spitfire" well below their actual performance

capabilities, making no mention of Britain's radar-controlled air defense system, and ended on the optimistic note that "the *Luftwaffe*, unlike the RAF, will be in a position in every respect to achieve a decisive effect this year'" (47). Göring also made the unfathomable decision to suspend 'the promising attacks on [...] 'radar installations' (50).

8   Coventry, as Calder points out, was 'a key centre of war production [...]' (36). On 20 May 1940 Woolf records in her diary: 'Last night Churchill asked us to reflect, when being bombed, that we were at least drawing fire from the soldiers for once' (285). As Rebecca Beatrice Brooks observes Woolf and her husband (alongside Churchill) were on the Nazi 1940 *Sonderfahndungsliste G.B.* [Special Search List G.B.] compiled by Walter Schellenberg (222), comprising details of 2,820 individuals to be arrested and potentially executed (n.pag). Both of the Woolfs were to be referred to the RSHA (Reich Main Security Office) VI G, a group that organized the liquidation of 'undesirables.'

9   Gill Plain describes a 'sting in the war's tail was the onset of rocket attacks in June 1944, returning London to a state of threat all the harder to bear for its arbitrariness and military futility' (2013, 11).

10 The term was initiated in a *Daily Mail* report on 29 April, derived from a comment made at a Press Conference for Foreign Correspondents in Berlin by Baron Gustav Braun von Stumm, a temporary spokesman for the German Foreign Office.

11 The latter attacks commenced on 13 June 1944, and ceased only a month before the European war ended, when the remaining launch site in the Low Countries was overrun on 29 March 1945. V-1s were known colloquially as buzz bombs, or doodlebugs.

12 Megan Faragher details some of her intelligence work (50–1), especially with regard to reactions to Churchill's speech in 1940 regarding 'the neutrality policy of Ireland and the refusal to leave ports open to British fleets [...]' (50).

13 The story is based upon the final years of writer, Violet Hunt (1862–1942), formerly a literary hostess, lover of H. G. Wells and the married Ford Madox Ford; she lived in Campden Hill Road, Kensington, throughout the Blitz until her death of pneumonia.

14 Labica details how Thwaites 'paternalistic authoritarianism' (76) is set amidst dialogue that mirrors the repetitive and intensely manic qualities of Blitz discourse (77) which was identified by Mass Observation researchers (and that also featured in Hanley's novel).

Works cited

Alexander, Jeffrey C. 'Toward a Theory of Cultural Trauma'. In Jeffrey C. Alexander et. al. (eds.), *Cultural Trauma and Collective Identity*. Berkeley and London: University of California Press, 2004: 1–30.

Allingham, Margery. *The Oaken Heart*. London: Michael Joseph, 1941.

Anon. *Frontline: 1940–194: The Official A Story of the Civil Defence of Britain*. London: His Majesty's Stationery Office, 1942.

Bellanca, Mary Ellen. 'The Monstrosity of Predation in Daphne du Maurier's "The Birds"'. *ISLE: Interdisciplinary Studies in Literature and Environment* 18 (1), Winter 2011: 26–46.

Bottome, Phyllis. *The Mortal Storm*. London: Faber and Faber, 1937.

Bottome, Phyllis. *London Pride*. London: Faber and Faber, 1941.

Bottome, Phyllis. *London Pride*. Boston: Little, Brown, 1941.

Bowen, Elizabeth. *The Heat of the Day*. Harmondsworth and New York: Penguin, 1962 [1949].

Brooks, Rebecca Beatrice. 'Virginia Woolf and Hitler's Blacklist'. *The Virginia Woolf Blog*. 22 January 2012: n.pag; http://virginiawoolfblog.com/virginia-woolf-and-hitlers-blacklist/

Brunetta, Leslie. 'England's Finest Hour: And Henry Green's Caught'. *The Sewanee Review* 100 (1), Winter 1992: 112–23.

Calder, Angus. *The Myth of the Blitz*. London: Pimlico, 1992 [1991].

Cederwell, William. *Reading London in Wartime: Blitz, the People and Propaganda in 1940s Literature*. New York and London: Routledge, 2018.

Creese, Richard. 'Abstracting and Recording Narration in *The Good Soldier* and *The End of the Affair*'. *The Journal of Narrative Technique* 16 (1), Winter 1986: 1–14.

Crisp, Peter. *The Blitz*. [Mass Observation Teaching Booklet No.1] Sussex: University of Sussex Library, 1987.

Cull, Nicholas John. *Selling War: The British Propaganda Campaign Against American 'Neutrality' in World War II*. New York and Oxford: Oxford University Press, 1995.

Cunningham, Anne. 'Fine Forgotten Writer Worthy of Renaissance'. *Independent.ie*. 9 April 2018: n.pag; https://www.independent.ie/entertainment/books/book-reviews/fine-forgotten-writer-worthy-of-renaissance-36783656.html.

DeCoste, Damon Marcel. 'Modernism's Shell-Shocked History: Amnesia, Repetition, and the War in Graham Greene's *The Ministry of Fear*'. *Twentieth Century Literature* 45 (4), Winter 1999: 428–51.

Du Maurier, Daphne. *Frenchman's Creek*. London: Gollancz, 1941.

Du Maurier, Daphne. *The Birds and Other Stories*. London: Virago, 2014 [1952].

Dunn, Jane. *Daphne Du Maurier and Her Sisters: The Hidden Lives of Piffy, Bird and Bing*. London: HarperPress, 2013.

Easeman, Geoffrey. *War and the Writing of Henry Green*. Doctoral thesis, University of Leicester, May 2001.

Faragher, Megan. 'The Form of Modernist Propaganda in Elizabeth Bowen's *The Heat of the Day*'. *Textual Practice* 27 (1), 2013: 49–68.

Ferguson, Rex. 'Blind Noise and Deaf Visions: Henry Green's *Caught*, Synaesthesia and the Blitz'. *Journal of Modern Literature* 33 (1), December 2009: 102–16

Field, Geoffrey. 'Nights Underground in Darkest London: The Blitz, 1940–1941'. *International Labor and Working-Class History* 62, Fall 2002: 11–49.

Fisher, Katherine E. *Writing (in) the Spaces of the Blitz: Spatial Myths and Memory in Wartime British Literature*. Doctor of Philosophy (English Language and Literature), Michigan: University of Michigan, 2014; https://deepblue.lib.umich.edu›bitstream›handle›kefisher_1.

Fordham, John. *James Hanley: Modernism and the Working Class*. Doctoral Thesis. London: Middlesex University, September 1997.

Gardiner, Juliet. *The Blitz: The British Under Attack*. London: HarperPress, 2010.

Gilbert, Harriett. 'Michael Morpurgo & Sara Maitland'. *Good Read: BBC Radio 4*. 7 October 2011: n.pag; https://www.bbc.co.uk/programmes/b015ck9n.

Gildersleeve, Jessica. *Elizabeth Bowen and the Writing of Trauma*. Doctor of Philosophy, Bristol: University of Bristol, November 2009.

Gorra, Michael. 'On *The End of the Affair*'. *Southwest Review* 89 (1), 2004: 109–25.

Green, Henry. *Caught*. Introd. James Woods. New York: New York Review Books, 2016 [1943].

Greene, Graham. *The Ministry of Fear: An Entertainment*. London: Heinemann, 1960 [1943].

Greene, Graham. *The End of the Affair*. London and New York: Penguin, 1975 [1951].

Greene, Richard (ed.). *Graham Greene: A Life in Letters*. London: Little, Brown, 2007.

Hallam, Michael Neil. *Avant-garde Realism: James Hanley, Patrick Hamilton and the Lost Years of the 1940s*. Doctoral thesis [DPhil]; Brighton: University of Sussex, 2011; http://sro.sussex.ac.uk/id/eprint/7573/.

Hamilton, Patrick. *The Slaves of Solitude*. Oxford and New York: Oxford University Press, 1982 [1947].

Hanley, James. *No Directions*. London: André Deutsch, 1990 [1943].

Harding, Christine. 'Do You Clean Vegetables With Soap?' *The Book Trunk*. 6 June 2012: n.pag; http://chriscross-thebooktrunk.blogspot.com/2012/06/do-you-clean-vegetables-with-soap.html.

Hartley, Jenny. *Millions Like Us: British Women's Fiction of the Second World War*. London: Virago, 1997.

Hillard, Christopher. *To Exercise Our Talents: The Democratization of Writing in Britain*. Cambridge, MA: Harvard University Press, 2006.

Hoult, Norah. *There Were No Windows*. London: Persephone Books, 2005 [1944].

Jennings, W. Ivor. 'The Emergency Powers (Defence) (No. 2) Act, 1940'. *The Modern Law Review* 4 (2), October 1940: 132–6.

Jensen, Meg. 'Post-traumatic Memory Projects: Autobiographical Fiction and Counter-monuments'. *Textual Practice* 28 (4), June 2014: 701–25.

Johnson, B. S. 'Introduction'. In *The Evacuees*. London: Victor Gollancz, 1969: 9–20.

King, Jeanette. *Discourses of Ageing in Fiction and Feminism: The Invisible Woman*. Houndsmill, Basingstoke and New York: Palgrave Macmillan, 2013.

Kyte, Jacqueline. *Literary Representations of Safety in British Fiction of the Long Decade 1939–1950*. PhD Thesis, English and Humanities, London: Birkbeck, University of London, 2016.

Labica, Thierry. 'War, Conversation, and Context in Patrick Hamilton's *The Slaves of Solitude*'. *Connotations: A Journal for Critical Debate* 12 (1), 2002/2003: 72–82.
Lethbridge, Lucy. *Servants: A Downstairs View of Twentieth-century Britain*. London: Bloomsbury, 2013.
Leys, Ruth. *Trauma: A Genealogy*. Chicago: Chicago University Press, 2000.
Lodge, David. 'Boarding-house Blues'. *The Guardian* 17, February 2007: n.pag; https://www.theguardian.com/books/2007/feb/17/fiction.featuresreviews3
Mackay, Marina. *Modernism and World War II*. Cambridge: Cambridge University Press, 2007.
Mackay, Robert. *Half the Battle: Civilian Morale in Britain During the Second World War*. Manchester: Manchester University Press, 2002.
MacMath, Terence Handley. 'Reading Groups: Learning a Woman's Work in Wartime'. *Church Times*. 4 February 2009: n.pag; https://www.churchtimes.co.uk/articles/2009/6-february/books-arts/book-reviews/reading-groups-learning-a-woman-s-work-in-wartime.
Mengham, Rod. *The Idiom of the Time: The Writings of Henry Green*. Doctoral thesis, University of Edinburgh, 1980.
Mengham, Rod. 'Broken Glass'. In Rod Mengham and N. H. Reeve (eds.), *The Fiction of the 1940s: Stories of Survival*. Basingstoke and New York: Palgrave, 2001: 124–33.
Munton, Alan. *English Fiction of the Second World War*. London: Faber & Faber, 1989.
Murat, Jean-Christophe. 'City of Wars: the Representation of Wartime London in Two Novels of the 1940s: James Hanley's *No Directions* and Patrick Hamilton's *The Slaves of Solitude*'. *Caliban: French Journal of English Studies* 25, 2009: n.pag; https://journals.openedition.org/caliban/1652.
Murray, Williamson. *Strategy for Defeat: The Luftwaffe 1913–1945*. Air University, Maxwell Air Base, Alabama: Air University Press, January 1983; https://archive.org/details/DTIC_ADA421966.
Murrow, Edward R. '1940. Edward R. Murrow from a Rooftop during the London Blitz'. *Bill Downs, War Correspondent* [website]. 14 September 2015: n.pag; https://www.billdownscbs.com/2015/09/1940-edward-r-murrow-from-london.html
Peck, Winifred. *House-Bound*. London: Persephone Books, 2007 [1942].
Phillips, Lawrence. *London Narratives: Post-War Fiction and the City*. London: Continuum, 2006.
Plain, Gill. *Women's Fiction and the Second World War: Gender, Power and Resistance*. Edinburgh: Edinburgh University Press, 1996.
Plain, Gill. *Literature of the 1940s: War, Postwar and 'Peace'*. Edinburgh: Edinburgh University Press, 2013.
Playfair, Jocelyn. *A House in the Country*. London: Persephone Books, 2002 [1944].
Rau, Petra. 'The Common Frontier: Fictions of Alterity in Elizabeth Bowen's *The Heat of the Day* and Graham Greene's *The Ministry of Fear*'. *Language & History* 14 (1), May 2005: 31–55.

Russell, John. *Henry Green: Nine Novels and an Unpacked Bag.* New Brunswick, New Jersey: Rutgers University Press, 1960.

Santiáñez, Nil. 'Aerial Bombing and Catastrophic Modernism'. *Neohelicon* 45, 2018: 229–48.

Schellenberg, Walter. *Sonderfahndungsliste G.B.* [Special Search List G.B.]; https://digitalcollections.hoover.org/images/Collections/…A1…/DA585.A1_G37_V.pdf

Seiler, Claire. 'At Midcentury: Elizabeth Bowen's *The Heat of the Day*'. *Modernism/modernity* 21 (91), January 2014: 125–45. https://www.press.jhu.edu/journals/modernismmodernity

Shepley, Nicholas S. *Henry Green: An Oblique Approach to the Everyday.* Doctoral thesis; University College London, 2010.

Smelser, Neil J. 'Psychological Trauma and Cultural Trauma'. In Jeffrey C. Alexander et. al. (eds.), *Cultural Trauma and Collective Identity.* Berkeley and London: University of California Press, 2004: 31–59.

Smith, Warwick. *War and Space in English Fiction, 1940–1950.* Sussex: University of Sussex, DPhil (English), January 2016.

Stewart, Victoria. 'The Auditory Uncanny in Wartime London: Graham Greene's *The Ministry of Fear*'. *Textual Practice* 18 (1), 2004: 65–81.

Stewart, Victoria. *Narratives of Memory: British Writing of the 1940s.* Basingstoke and New York: Palgrave Macmillan, 2006.

Stonebridge, Lyndsey. 'Bombs and Roses: The Writing of Anxiety in Henry Green's *Caught*'. *Diacritics, Special Issue: Trauma and Psychoanalysis* 28 (4), Winter 1998: 25–43; later version: in Rod Mengham and N. H. Reeve (eds.), *The Fiction of the 1940s: Stories of Survival.* Houndsmill, Basingstoke: Palgrave, 2001: 46–69.

Streatfeild, Noel. *Saplings.* London: Persephone, 2000 [1945].

Tredell, Nicolas. 'Graham Greene: *The Ministry of Fear* – 1943'. *London Fictions.* N.D.' N pag.; https://www.londonfictions.com/graham-greene-the-ministry-of-fear.html.

Walker, Ronald G. 'World without End: An Approach to Narrative Structure in Greene's *The End of the Affair*'. *Texas Studies in Language and Literature* 26 (2), Summer 1984: 218–41.

Waugh, Evelyn. *Brideshead Revisited, The Sacred & Profane Memories of Captain Charles Ryder.* London: Chapman and Hall, 1944.

Woolf, Virginia. *The Diary of Virginia Woolf.* Anne Oliver Bell. London and New York: Penguin, 1985 [1984].

Woolf, Virginia. *Between the Acts.* London: Hogarth Press, 1965 [1941].

Woon, Basil. *Hell Came to London: Reportage of the Blitz During 14 Days.* London: Peter Davies, 1941.

Yogerst, Chris. 'Searching for Common Ground: Hollywood Prior to the Senate Investigation on Motion Picture Propaganda, 1935–1941'. *Historical Journal of Film, Radio and Television* 39 (4), 2019: 725–48.

Zimmerman, Emma. 'A "Tottering Lace-like Architecture of Ruins": The Wartime Home in Elizabeth Bowen's *The Heat of the Day*'. *Literary Geographies* 1 (1), 2015: 42–61.

Žindžiuvienė, Ingrida. 'Elements of Trauma Fiction in the 9/11 Novel'. *British and American Studies*, Timisoara 19 (19), 2013: 65–75.

3

Genteel Bohemia: Capable Women in Women's Fiction of the 1940s

Deborah Philips

In May 1940 Deborah Mitford wrote from the family home to her sister Jessica in America (in a missive later featured in a volume of such sisterly letters she edited):

> You do sound to be having a lucky time. It's all right here at least more or less. [...] I have got very what Stiegson [a governess] would call 'keen on the garden' isn't it extraorder [sic], in fact I'm going to lunch with Aunt Sport [Dorothy] tomorrow to get more plants [...].
> I think Bobo [Unity] is a bit better but I don't know. All outsiders think she is, but she is certainly very odd. Things like this happen – Colonel Buxton came here this morning & she dashed at him thinking he was the Dean & he looked rather surprised when she kissed him. (157)

Their life as a family was in fact very far from being as settled as she suggests. Six months earlier 'Bobo', their sister Unity, a great admirer of Hitler, had shot herself in the head at the declaration of war on Germany and suffered severe brain damage from which she would never recover. Deborah had had to deal with collecting the injured Unity from Switzerland and was now living with her warring parents and her much damaged sister. Jessica herself was not having a very 'lucky time' either, having eloped to Spain with her cousin, the couple had moved to America, where she was now eking out a living as a shop worker.[1] Their elder sister Nancy was working as a nurse in London and had suffered two miscarriages. Diana's husband, the Nazi sympathizer and leader of the British Union of Fascists, Oswald Mosley, was in prison, and she too was about to be interned (in part because of Nancy's testimony against her). The Mitford family embodied the political tensions that had played out in the build-up to war, with Diana and Unity embracing fascism (literally so, in the case of Diana's marriage to Mosley), Jessica's membership of the Communist Party and Nancy and Deborah's horror at Unity and Diana's support for Hitler. While the Mitfords offer an extreme familial example of the divergent positions of the period, Deborah Mitford's spirit of cheery positivity at a time of personal and political crisis is typical not only of the letters that the Mitford sisters wrote to one another but is a tone found across women's writing throughout the decade of the 1940s. That spirit is evident in fiction written during the period of the Second World War and survives into its aftermath; it is a mode of women's writing that Gill Plain has suggested is marked by a 'refusal of seriousness' (2013a: 240). The decade of the 1940s is, of course, bifurcated by the end of the Second World War and the conflict transformed women's experience of family, marriage and work. The demand for wartime workers had opened up previously unimagined possibilities for women from a range of classes, particularly those not previously expected to enter employment; unprecedented numbers of women were recruited into the work force and the armed services in roles that had once been barred to them. In 1945 the Ministry of Information provided some indication of the numbers of women employed over the course of the war and outlines the range of work they had undertaken (albeit while suggesting that it took more women than it did men to do these jobs). Women played a significant part in freeing men for the forces or for work in heavy industry.

> In 1943, 40 per cent of the employees in the aircraft industry were women [...]. In the engineering and allied industries the corresponding figures are 35 per cent [...]. About half of all workers in the chemical and explosives industry are women.
>
> In the munitions industries, including shipbuilding and heavy engineering, one worker in every three is a woman.
>
> In agriculture and horticulture the introduction of 117,000 women has freed nearly 100,000 men; while 160,000 women have replaced 184,000 men in the various transport services.
>
> Between June 1939 and June 1944 there was a net addition of 1,345,000 women in the munitions industries, 792,000 in the basic industries and 523,000 women in the Auxiliary Services and whole-time Civil Defence. (Ministry of Information 14)

The independence, skills and capabilities that many women had learned during wartime would not end with the war; despite the withdrawal of support for women workers, women did not lightly give up on the economic and social autonomy that many had experienced for the first time. Two years into the aftermath of the war in 1947, six million women continued to work. In the introduction to their collection of oral histories from women who had been through the First and

Second World Wars Gail Brayborn and Penny Summerfield write of the ways in which many women had felt war to be a liberation from pre-war expectations of femininity:

> Women's pride in their work comes through very strongly in their testimony and so too does the sense of freedom many felt when comparing their war work with the confines of home or a typical 'woman's' job. In both wars there were women who felt that they had been 'let out of the cage' even when they were critical of the pay and conditions they had to put up with, and the way that men reacted to them. (1)

That 'pride in work' and a sense of frustration with the 'confines of home' resonate throughout women's fiction written over the period of the 1940s.

Stuart Laing has suggested that the cultural position of the novel in 1945 was 'insecure': 'Publishing conditions (as well as time constraints, on writers, of wartime activities, military and civilian) had discouraged the production of extended works of fiction during the war; poems, short stories and documentary reportage were preferred forms' (236). This may have been the case for 'literary' fiction, and for fiction written by men,[2] but, as Plain points out, throughout the war: 'familiar forms [...] remained popular. Most of the pre-eminent writers of the interwar period – Margery Allingham, Agatha Christie, Gladys Mitchell – wrote prolifically during the war years' (2013a: 237). There was a considerable, and well-documented, appetite for fiction throughout and after the war despite the strictures of paper rationing and of time; McAleer refers to 'the tremendous demand created by the reading boom during the Second World War' (67). Christina Foyle, then working in her father's bookshop Foyles,[3] saw the war as providing opportunities for publishers and booksellers: 'The blacking out of street lighting, the reduction in transport facilities, and the long hours of waiting in involved in civil defence duties, all favoured the habit of reading' (qtd. Holman 27). According to McAleer public libraries 'recorded peak levels of usage' across the country throughout the war (50). Publishers reported increases in book sales, and consumer expenditure was marked by 'a striking increase in the expenditure on books' (qtd. Holman 273). Light fiction, genre and romance novels were particularly popular, as the bestseller lists and library records for the war years demonstrate (see Bloom, 358). In 1939, *The Publishers' Circular* reported that 'the great British book-buying public are [...] choosing the lighter books these dark days' (qtd. McAleer 73). Jan Struther's *Mrs Miniver*,[4] based on columns she had written for *The Times* and published in book form in 1939, was among those 'lighter books' and, with its success, established a prototype for the resiliently patriotic, resourceful and practical English heroine. As Alison Light points out, Struthers's *Times* columns ran between 1937 and 1939 and the published text, unlike the 1942 film, is set not in wartime itself, but during the 'phoney' war (114); aspects of *Mrs Miniver* are nonetheless to be found in many women's novels written during the war and after.

Many women novelists of the period evade any direct engagement with the war or with wartime work, often setting their narratives back in a pre-war period, as in Mary Renault's *The Friendly Young Ladies* (1944), or, as in the case of Stella Gibbons's[5] novel *Ticky* (1943), making use of the genre of historical fiction. Nonetheless, the effects are there to be read; the experience of war necessarily permeates women's writing of the period, as Plain has argued: 'Texts bore the imprint of conflict even as they consciously turned from its direct representation. Writing became a mode of resistance and release [...]' (2013a: 233). Writing was also a means of holding on to the sense of possibilities that the war had opened up for women and of asserting their capabilities in the new landscape of the post-war world.

Gibbons' *Ticky* displaces the contemporary experience of the army into the Victorian period and, despite its trappings of Victoriana, written in 1943, inevitably it carries traces of the current war. The novel is dedicated to '198380 and the rest of the British Army', which indicated the army number of Gibbon's husband Allan Webb (see Oliver 176). Set in the base of the 'First Bloods', an élite army regiment, this is an ostensibly all-male world, as Captain Gabriel Venner explains (with his pronounced lisp) to the new recruit Barry: 'Stwictly forbidden to admit a wife or child to the Club on pain of shootin'. Against the wules you see' (14). Nonetheless, women do intrude into this privileged masculine world; it is Queen Victoria who rules over the club, examining its accounts every month. The headmaster, Dr Pressure, has a lovely daughter, Beatrice, who is the object of desire for the lovelorn Captain Gabriel. Dr Pressure himself harbours guilty feelings for a 'young person' with whom he 'had passed the nights [...] and the days correcting her grammar, for she was not a lady' (35).

Gender and class tensions emerge forcibly as the privileged guardsmen attempt a land grab on an area that serves as a recreation ground for their manservants. This is the Pleasure Garden, presided over by the redoubtable Mrs Sawyer and her daughter Philly; it is a carnivalesque and chaotic space in which the rigid masculine codes of the Club and the regiment are unsettled in the presence of femininity. As the men on both sides engage in increasingly preposterous disputes, it is the women who resolve the situation. Mrs Lovecombe, the 'young person' of Dr Pressure's past (and, it transpires, mother of Beatrice), has emerged from a bohemian affair with Dr Pressure and reinvented herself as the elegant headmistress of a school in Belgrave Square, and she returns to puncture his intellectual pretensions and moral hypocrisy. While Dr Pressure insists that 'the female mind is incapable of finding any subject of interest that does not touch upon infants or dress' (130), Mrs Lovecombe teaches her young 'ladies' History and Philosophy, it is her keen intelligence which brings Dr Pressure to heel and the narrative to a happy conclusion in a flurry of weddings. The women of the novel prove to be much more competent at negotiation than the men, and less prone to fantasy. In the finale, nuptial celebrations unite the Club and the Pleasure Ground, 'two banquets over-flowed into one another's territories and mingled' (208), in a magical resolution of class and gender difference. As Gibbons's biographer, Reggie Oliver, points out, this is a fairy tale, but it carries with it a sharp critique of rigid masculinity:

> Underneath all this airy fantasy lurks an unmistakeable strain of serious mockery at all-male societies, and their divisive, competitive aspects, and this is what gives *Ticky* its backbone. It is the women in the book who are instrumental in crossing the social boundaries and making peace [...]. (179)

Nancy Mitford's *The Pursuit of Love* (1945) has that same air of 'serious mockery' and shows women, if not 'making peace', then certainly crossing social boundaries. Published in 1945, the novel begins in the pre-war world of the narrator's childhood. The narrative opens with a litany of disasters befalling the seven children of the aristocratic Radlett family; what could be read as forms of trauma in any other hands are here told for comic effect. A near-drowning, a ten-year-old suicide bid (over the death of a dog), Uncle Matthew's beating and hunting of his children are briskly recounted; the narrator commenting crisply, 'It was great fun' (11). It is that determined optimism and a refusal to be cowed which carries the narrator, Fanny, throughout the novel and its representation of the war.

Fanny is detached from the family (unlike Nancy Mitford herself) as a cousin who observes the eccentric Radletts with a cool, but affectionate, eye. She has been abandoned by her parents; her mother is known as 'The Bolter', who felt herself to be 'too beautiful and too gay to be burdened with a child at the age of nineteen' (Mitford 7), her father is now on his fifth wife. Both parents are irresponsible figures who belong to the past, and much like Evelyn Waugh[6] characters, who represent, to adopt Waugh's observation in *Put Out More Flags* (1942), 'a forgotten cove, where the wreckage of the roaring-twenties [...] lay beached, dry and battered' (40). In Mitford's novel, when Fanny's mother finally appears, towards the end, she is a relic from another era: 'She was curiously dated in her manner, and seemed still to be living in the 1920's. It was as though [...] she had pickled herself [...] ignoring the fact that the world was changing and that she was withering fast' (195). It is the unglamorous Aunt Emily who provides the 'solid, sustaining, though on the face of it, uninteresting, relationship that is motherhood as its best' (26). Aunt Emily provides a 'calm and happy' household, which is valued more than the extravagant but inappropriate presents sent by the narrator's absent parents. As her Aunt indicates, Fanny is in a perilous financial position, her inheritance at risk from her father's vagaries, unlike her privileged cousins '"the modern world being what it is, she may have to earn her own living"' (37). Fanny is not judgemental about the Radlett children's excesses of sentimental feeling (especially for animals), nor is she moralistic about her parents' behaviour, but she is critical of their inclination to get by on charm and privilege: 'while they bridged gulfs of ignorance with their charm and high spirits, they never acquired any habit of concentration, they were incapable of solid hard work. [...] [T]hey completely lacked any form of mental discipline' (37). Such a lack of 'discipline' becomes ever more apparent and its consequences more serious as the narrative unfolds (for which, see below).

Linda, the Radlett sister closest in age to Fanny, is compared from childhood with Fanny's mother; she shares her beauty, her romantic intensity and her riding skills and will eventually emulate her as a 'Bolter'. It is Linda who is 'entranced' by the glamour and brilliance of the house party brought to enliven the dull Radlett family ball by the decadent, but charming, Lord Merlin, while the narrator aligns herself with the sensible Aunt Emily and sternly refuses a bohemianism that she associates with the generation of her parents: 'I did not aspire to this. I saw that they were admirable, but they were far removed from me and my orbit, belonging more to that of my parents; my back had been turned towards them from the day Aunt Emily had taken me home and there was no return [...]' (53).

Plain rightly suggests that the novel is poised between a nostalgic 'evocation of a lost world' and 'the complex depiction of a changing society', an ambivalence that is acted out in the relationship between Fanny and Linda. Plain argues that 'from the intersecting lives of these two women there emerges an unresolved tension between a celebrated romanticism and a validated modernity' (2013b: 165). In Mitford's novel that tension is evident in the marital choices each makes; the narrator marries the 'kindly scholarly' academic Alfred and finds with him a 'refuge from the storms and puzzles of life which I had always wanted' (92); a validation of sober respectability. Fanny, unlike Linda, refuses the extremes of politics and emotion, while Linda rushes to embrace them; Fanny faces the future with a pragmatic sensibleness that is more fitted to the post-war reconstruction than Linda's wayward romanticism. Linda is fuelled by an emotional intensity that belongs to the pre-war period rather than to the present conjuncture. She embarks upon two reckless marriages each of which represents the extremes of the pre-war political context (and of the Mitford family itself); as Plain points out 'it is almost impossible to write the 1930s without simultaneously inscribing the seeds of the Second World War' (2013b: 162). Linda's first marriage is to the dull Tony, whom she had mistakenly assumed to be part of Lord Merlin's world of 'smart bohemianism' (98); it transpires that he is a mercantile Tory who admires Hitler (although it is not his politics that are the main reason for Linda's disenchantment). She is completely disinterested in her daughter and leaves her without any regret. Her second husband is the handsome Communist sympathizer Christian, who (like Jessica Mitford's first husband) enlists for the International Brigades in the Spanish Civil War. Linda is ill equipped for the exigencies of war, she has no education or training and her lack of skills renders her 'hopeless' at the welfare work that is all she is vaguely qualified to undertake. Christian leaves her for the practical Lavender who had 'trained as a nurse and as a welfare worker' (139). It is no longer acceptable for women to get by on charm and beauty; as Linda's final lover tells her: '"Everybody is getting more serious, that's the way things are going"' (154). Linda is 'enveloped in the present, in her own detached and futureless life' (173), her passions belong to the past and she will not survive to the end of the war. Linda does live through an air raid bombing and survives a bombing. Ironically, it is not the war which kills her but childbirth, so finally her mode of being is 'futureless'. The responsibilities of parenting, war work and the post-war reconstruction require 'mental discipline'; it is the sensible Fanny, as Aunt Emily had done for her, who will raise Linda's second child and so secure the future.

Jean Rhys's heroines are rather more dour than the Mitford sisters or the Radlett family, but they do share their spirit of resilience. *Good Morning, Midnight*, first published in 1939, follows Sasha through the fringes of a sordid and fading bohemia from London to Paris in a reversal of Rhys's 1931 novel *After Leaving Mr Mackenzie* which took the protagonist Julia from Paris to London. Set in 1937, 'Sasha' is an invented persona who is revisiting the city she last saw in the 1920s, in the aftermath of the First World War. Rhys's narrative begins with Sasha's low expectations both of Paris and of her life, and significantly her hotel is located in a literal and metaphorical dead end: 'What they call an impasse' (9). Nonetheless, she comments, 'I have arranged my little life' (9). Like Julia, Sasha is mourning a marriage and a lost child; it is also suggested that she is recovering from a suicide attempt.

Sasha, like the Bolter, is reprising the past of 1920s Paris, she dyes her hair 'blond cendré' (the Bolter has a canary-coloured bob), and revisits the Bohemian haunts of her youth, the Dôme, the nightclubs of Montparnasse, an artist's studio. However, the Paris Bohemia of the 1920s is now tatty and sleazy; the music is old, the décor faded and 'dirty' (77). Sasha is playing out a parody of bohemian life, buying a painting, shopping for clothes and drinking in bars. However, she is constantly aware of her lack of money, and that what money she has is not her own. The Frenchman who picks Sasha up in the street compliments her by underestimating her age but situates her as one of the bright young things of the inter-war period. '"All you young women," he says, "dance too much. [...] Ah, what will happen to this after-war generation? [...] What will happen? Mad for pleasure ...."' (75). Sasha is, however, far more self-aware than the Bolter; 'I don't deceive myself' (89). There is a strong sense of impending disaster throughout the novel, not only for Sasha, but for Paris and for Europe. When Sasha remarks 'But people are doing crazy things all over the place. The war is over. No more war – never, never, never. Après la guerre, there'll be a good time everywhere ....' (96), it is with a hysterical insistence that betrays a real fear.

While Sasha's situation is dire, she nonetheless maintains a caustic wit; *Good Morning, Midnight* may be grim, but it is also bleakly funny. Elaine Savory has pointed to 'the subversive comedy of the novel' (117); such subversion derives from the constant thread in the novel that Sasha is far more resourceful than she will admit. Unlike her friend Paulette who is 'regretful, fatalistic' (113), Sasha has some hope for the future. While the traumas of her past continuously erupt in her thoughts she resolutely refuses to dwell on them. She continues to wait 'for the door that will open, the thing that is bound to happen ....' (83), even if that 'thing' proves to be a loveless encounter. Savory argues that:

> The mocking, ironic first-person narrative voice of the protagonist, Sasha Jansen, is the source of the novel's almost unbearable tension between humour and tragedy, between a bitterly mocking critique of society and a devastating and enervating spiritual chaos. (119)

The term 'spiritual chaos' is not entirely fair to Sasha, while she comes perilously close (at several points) to disaster, she does in the end survive. Like the Mitford sisters, it is the ability to find comedy in the direst of circumstances that keeps her going, as Savory acknowledges: 'It is that desire to laugh which saves Sasha's life over and over again' (120). While the joyless sexual encounter which ends the novel is abject, it is Sasha's choice, she looks her partner straight in the eye and refuses to be a victim. Lorna Sage has written of *Good Morning, Midnight* that it is a novel of fractured reflections: 'In *Good Morning, Midnight* time passes on the hard surfaces of the [...] Paris cafés, where shadows of past selves and spectres of future ones jostle with one's present image on the same glassy plane' (49). The novel's form and that of Sasha herself are similarly fractured, as if both are poised between a past that is disappearing and a future that is frightening.

Monica Dickens's semi-autobiographical work presents a persona of a practical and capable young woman, who is very unlike Sasha, but who nonetheless shares the same wry 'desire to laugh'. She will turn her hands to whatever work is required; in her 1939 memoir *One Pair of Hands* Dickens describes her experiences as a maid and cook, she writes of nursing in *One Pair of Feet* (1942) and in the 1943 novel *The Fancy* she details her work in an aircraft factory. D. J. Taylor points to the pride in work shared by the factory women of the novel, but suggests that their opportunities and influence are limited:

> The female operatives of *The Fancy* are [...] pleased to be 'doing their bit', and proud of their ability to undertake men's work, but they are aware that the real decisions are still being made by the male-dominated works committee: the best they can hope for is a sort of uneasy patronage. (240)

Dickens's 1949 novel *Flowers on the Grass*, however, is structured around a range of women characters who hope for considerably more than 'uneasy patronage' and who will not accept that the 'real decisions' should be automatically made by men. This book represents a post-war state of the nation novel, structured as a picaresque narrative in which the central figure, Daniel, links together a set of stories, most centred around a woman. These interlocking narratives allow for a journey through characters and places in an unsettled post-war world of rentals and cheap lodgings, in which Daniel encounters a range of different modes of contemporary femininity. Daniel is a Bohemian spirit, an artist with a damaged past, although that damage is not directly connected to the war but caused by the sudden death of his wife. The novel begins with a domestic rural idyll, in which Daniel's wife Jane is entirely supportive and caring of him. Jane's is a self-sacrificing femininity which is hardly plausible in the post-war context, and hence Jane dies suddenly in an accident with an electric kettle, a demise that is both banal and appropriately domestic. Her final thoughts are for her husband.

Daniel moves on to a boarding house, where the chambermaid Doris proves to be ingenious in sheltering the impoverished Daniel and his dog from the landlady. She has a fiancé who is in a wheelchair (from a childhood illness rather than any war injury); it is Doris who is saving her wages for the wedding, and who 'would have to go on working after they were married' (61). Despite these plans it transpires that Doris harbours romantic feelings for Daniel, but there is a clearly delineated class difference, and Daniel must move on. His next landlady is 'Momma', a Jewish matriarch who takes in lodgers to keep the family finances stable. Her sons are South London spivs, dealing in the consumer goods that were hard to come by in the age of austerity: 'wireless and television sets, gramophones, cameras, typewriters, chocolate, rolls of silk and boxes of nylons' (69). While the family live on the edge of chaos and criminality, it is Momma who keeps them together and on an even keel.

The only possibility of a romantic resolution for Daniel is with his next landlady, Valerie, a beautiful widow with a young son, who is both class and age appropriate. Like Aunt Emily in *The Pursuit of Love*, according to Dickens's narrator Valerie is a calm and capable presence, 'her first-aid box, which was as neat and well-equipped as her work-basket, her kitchen and her wardrobe' (115). It is made clear that Valerie is one among many war widows who is having to adjust and to earn her own living through letting out rooms. In her marriage Valerie was, like Jane, a traditional and supporting wife: 'She was wholly feminine, utterly dependent. Marriage to Philip had been her refuge as well as her joy. [...]. Since then, the years had made her more independent' (116). The loss of her much-loved husband 'killed in the last month of the war' (116) had forced her into a hard-won independence. At dinner at the Savoy, she encounters young women who evoke her pre-war self: 'Harmless, amiable girls [...]. Girls who thought this was all of life [...]' (141). The war had demonstrated that for good or ill, there was far more to life for women and that it was no longer appropriate to simply be 'harmless and aimiable'.

Daniel is characterized as charming but irresponsible, he refuses to make plans, to be 'pinned down' and demonstrates 'a complete disregard for butter and cheese rationing' (95). Despite coming close, Valerie cannot in the end bring herself to marry him. Like Jane, every woman Daniel encounters copes with the damage that has been done to men, although that is rarely directly associated with the war itself. All the episodes concerned with men reveal that they are incapacitated or ineffectual; Geoffrey is an epileptic, Ossie, Daniel's loyal friend, is luckless in love, Momma's sons might skirt close to the edge of criminality but are invariably incompetent in their illicit endeavours, and George the lorry driver suffers from an ulcer brought on by a nervous disposition. The women characters are determined to have their own financial resources and exhibit the resolve to find their own futures; the schoolgirl Pamela is disillusioned by the pretensions of her progressive school, she 'wanted so much to learn, so that she could have job and be independent in the world. [...] [S]he must be able to get away and change her name and earn her own living as soon as she was grown up' (194). Dickens devotes an entire chapter to 'The Nurses', which figures stand as an embodiment of post-war responsible femininity and citizenship (see Philips and Haywood 1998), a woman with training and an independent income. The women who tend Daniel's broken leg have a passionate vocation, but they are also notably practical, brisk and efficient in their servicing of the new National Health hospital. All the women in the novel are more successful than the male characters in their adaptation to the post-war conditions, some more so than others, but without fail all show themselves to be more competent and capable than any of the men, especially the seductive and wayward Daniel who is repeatedly rescued by the kindness of strange women.

The women of *The Friendly Young Ladies* (1944) are also more able than their male counterparts. Mary Renault was still working as a nurse when, as she records in a later afterword, the novel, 'my third, was written in the pauses of full-time hospital nursing. [...] I was seeing again terribly ill and dying and bereaved people, and [...] as well, young men suddenly disabled for months or years, often for life, facing their future without complaint' (310). None of these injured and dying people feature in her novel; although written and published in the midst of war it is set in the pre-war period and creates a semi-rural idyll in which women are in charge of their lives. It opens with the young heroine Elsie suffocated by her conventional life with her parents in rural Cornwall, who escapes to find her sister, Leo, living in happy harmony on a houseboat with the beautiful Helen. The reader and Elsie gradually come to realize that this relationship is more than 'friendly'. Both Leo and Helen are entirely independent both emotionally and financially; Leo makes her living by writing Western novellas, a defiantly 'unfeminine' genre, while Helen is an illustrator, working in the masculine field of technical illustration.[7] While aware of the absurdity of her own metier, Leo takes pride in her writing, and defends her work vigorously to her would-be suitor Joe, a 'serious' novelist who is clearly a nascent Angry Young Man. All the men in the novel, like Dr Pressure, harbour intellectual pretensions which are both unwarranted and result in damage. As with Pamela in Dickens's *Flowers in the Grass*, Elsie is emotionally abused by a man who uses his professional position (as respectively teacher and doctor) to prey upon her. Elsie had been seduced by the bohemian and Freudian affectations of Peter, fulfilling her unrequited crush, but disillusioned, comes to recognize that there is a future for her that consists of work and independence and that men are not entirely to be trusted. Plain identifies a bleak comedy in *The Friendly Young Ladies*: 'Renault's acutely observed account of one man's determination to reassert heterosexual authority in the face of two women's happy indifference is simultaneously comic and bleak, and indicates the extent to which desire remained a battlefield within women's writing' (2013a: 239). But the men ultimately fail to assert their authority; the relationship between Helen and Leo is the one relationship in the novel which is not embattled. The novel is not solely Leo's story; it is also that of her younger sister Elsie. Between them, Helen and Leo show Elsie a different way of being a woman; the novel begins with Elsie 'incapable of following her [Leo's] example as she would have been of soaring through the air' (1). By the end of the novel she is planning on taking a secretarial course and moving to London (albeit with her parents). Peter Wolfe, writing in 1969, in the very early years of the Women's Liberation Movement, suggests that the ending of the novel leaves Elsie 'to a fate worse than the one she had before' (58), but that is surely to deny that Elsie now has choices that she did not have previously. The friendly young ladies have shown her that there is a world beyond family and marriage.

Daphne du Maurier's *The Parasites* (1949) is a novel concerned with a family of artistically gifted siblings. Du Maurier takes the critique of bohemianism found in Mitford even further; here the bohemian life is not only irresponsible, but shown to be actively destructive. The novel opens with a strongly worded epigraph from the *Encyclopaedia Britannica*: 'Parasites affect their hosts by feeding upon their living tissues or cells, and the intensity of the effect upon the hosts ranges from the slightest local injury to complete destruction' (7). Maria is a beautiful actress, her 'brother' Niall a brilliant musician who aspires to write symphonies but who turns his talents to 'catchpenny tunes' (16). Celia, unlike her handsome siblings, is 'a stout, heavy little girl' (18) and the only biological child of their parents' marriage. Celia has a gift for drawing but, assuming responsibility for their ailing father, gives up art school and does not pursue a publisher's interest in her work. Celia is the only one who is prepared to take care of Maria's children and their father. Thus her talent is sacrificed to the intensity of the family dynamic.

Like the Radlett family, the Delaneys have relied upon an inheritance of charm and good looks, which represents an artistic, rather than an aristocratic, heritage. It is Charles, Maria's apparently dull and conventional husband, who calls them out on their privilege: '"You are doubly, triply parasitic; first, because you've traded ever since childhood on that seed of talent you had the luck to inherit from your fantastic forbears; secondly, because you've none of you done a stroke of ordinary honest work in your lives but batten on us, the fool public [...]"' (13). Their father is an opera singer, Maria's mother a 'Viennese actress', his second wife, and Niall's birth mother (his biological father is unknown but rumoured to be a pianist), is a dancer (seemingly in the Isadora Duncan mode). Their artistic milieu belongs to a past pan-European world guided by the aesthetic values of music and theatre, a bohemian world in which the young Delaneys spent their childhood. The parental generation were young adults in the First World War, their children have grown up in the interwar period, trailing in the wake of their theatrical parents across Europe, an upbringing which makes them 'cosmopolitan in outlook, belonging to no particular country' (19). Ironically, it will be that rootlessness that will finally condemn them. The only constant parental presence in the novel is Truda, the dancer's dresser, who has cared for Niall as a baby and who becomes a surrogate mother to them all. With no extended family beyond their parents, little formal education and only each other for company, they become a tightly bonded group. They are so close that, as du Maurier's editor, Sheila Hodges, has noted, the narrative voice repeatedly refers to a collective 'we', without any indication of whose point of view this represents (26). Such a communal 'we' is claustrophobic, but nevertheless each of the Delaney children is unable to survive without the others. They do not want to accept adulthood, and already express a melancholy nostalgia for their childhood while they are still children: 'There will never be a photograph of this, thought Niall, of the five of us together, round the table, holding the moment, smiling and being happy' (70). The 'happy' moment is abruptly shattered when Niall's mother dies in an appropriately bohemian fall from a clifftop, like Isadora Duncan, strangled by her own scarf. The children are separated, while their father takes up residence in a house in London, in the (then) bohemian neighbourhood of St John's Wood.

The Delaney family history is part of a vanished world of glamour and plenty which would acquire specific resonance in a post-war context of rationing:

> We ate creamed chicken, we ate meringues, we ate chocolate éclairs and we drank champagne. [...]
> We were all lovely, we were all clever [...]. Pappy smiled down at us, approving, a glass of champagne in one hand [...].
> There was no yesterday and no to-morrow; fear had been slung aside, and shame forgotten. We were all together [...]. It was a game that we played, a game that we understood. (50)

'Tomorrow' must nonetheless intrude, as the novel moves on from the Delaney's childhood memories into much bleaker territory. Both Niall and Maria attempt to perform adulthood, Niall tries to emulate his parent's bohemianism with a Parisian affair with an older woman, Maria marries the 'county' aristocrat Charles. But the contemporary world and the demands of marriage, family and responsibility can never compare with the glamour, excitement and intensity of the period of their childhoods. Light's chapter on Du Maurier in her study of interwar conservatism and femininity is titled 'Daphne du Maurier's romance with the past', in which she argues that:

> Pastness in all its forms, personal, biographical and national captured her imagination and there is much in du Maurier's writing to suggest hers is a romantic Toryism, one which invokes the past as a nobler, loftier place where it was possible to live a more expansive and exciting life. (156)

The Delaney family do indeed lead an 'expansive and exciting life', but the 'noble' and 'lofty' artistry of the parents is debased in the next generation, as their father ruefully notes, they are reliant on the family name, just as their father has predicted: "'The name alone will carry them through, if nothing else does. They've got the spark all right, but possibly nothing more than the spark'" (75). Niall's musicianship does not have the practiced dedication of his father, he produces only 'pitiful cheap nonsense' (16); Maria is described by her husband as a "'just a hotpotch of every character you've ever acted'" (14), her skill at mimicry a marker of her lack of substance.[8] She is much more concerned with the parts that she plays than she is with her husband and children, her relationships with them filtered through theatrical roles she has assumed. Like Linda in *The Pursuit of Love*, Maria takes little interest in her children, leaving their care largely to Celia, both she and Niall are uncomfortable in the world of nannies, teas and the children's 'plastic toys', and impatient with the contemporary and ordinary demands of family life.

Niall and Maria have a passionate connection which, as they were brought up together so closely, has suggestions of incest, although they are not biological siblings. Moreover, as Julie Myerson points out, it is a relationship that is childlike in its intensity, but which cannot become an adult relationship, despite the fact that they are not directly related:

> Here are a girl and a boy who grow up as siblings but are not blood related – whose bond is intense, passionate, unstoppable. They understand each other intuitively, like twins, but the love itself is immature, hopeless and selfish, irresponsible even, leaving no room for others. It's the story of two people who spend their lives both in thrall to and in denial of this central passionate relationship. (168)

It is that 'selfishness' and 'irresponsibility' which denies Niall and Maria any future together; the careless romance of their parents belongs to an older generation. While the relationship between Niall and Maria initially recalls *Wuthering Heights*, as Myerson observes, in its narrative of the powerful passion between two unrelated children brought up together as siblings, by the end *The Parasites* their relationship is more resonant of *The Mill on the Floss*. There is a strong implication that Niall deliberately crashes the boat, a recognition that both he and his relationship with Maria belong to the world of the past and that their way of being can no longer be sustained. Niall retreats into childhood, unable to deal with modernity, while leaving his sisters to face uncertainty: 'Maria and Charles had to make up their minds about the future. Celia had to make up her mind about herself. The problem "What now?" stared them in the face' (346). Niall is not prepared to confront that future. It is Truda, the one constant of their childhood, whom Niall recalls at the end of the novel, in an elegiac illusion of safety: 'the sea itself was calm and comforting, even as Truda had been long ago. The sea was another Truda, upon which he could cast himself when the time came, without anguish, without fear' (350). *The Parasites* is an awkward and ambiguous novel, which relishes the intensity and glamour of its protagonists while simultaneously recognizing that theirs is a bohemian culture which has no place in the post-war world. It is more nostalgic and regretful than either *The Pursuit of Love* or *Good Morning, Midnight* in its relegation of bohemianism to the past, but it shares with them a fractured narrative that shifts between the comic and the tragic, unable to reconcile nostalgia with the demands of the present.

What all these novels considered above share, whether written by 'popular', 'literary' or 'middlebrow' writers, is a sense that women find themselves in a world in which the standards of etiquette and comfort which they had once expected no longer applied, coupled with some recognition that there are opportunities to be grasped in the period of post-war reconstruction. Bohemianism seems to offer a way of life that refuses gender conventions and the strictures of family life. The heroines of these novels may launch themselves into bohemian lives and flirt with the possibilities that it offers them, but finally they retreat from Bohemia and choose instead to face the new world with a pragmatic, if fragile, optimism. They may be tempted by bohemianism as a rejection of the constraints of the domestic and conventional femininity, but, finally, Bohemia comes to signify a pre-war hedonism and lack of responsibility, as in the case of Fanny's parents and the prodigals Daniel and Niall. Figures such as the 'Bolter' are the '*Glamorous Outcasts*' of Elizabeth Wilson's title (2000), but by the 1940s this is a glamour that belongs firmly to the past. The charm of the outcast has faded, their marginalized status confirmed, and, as Wilson suggests, 'the arrival of the fully fledged welfare state was a threat' (227). As Plain argues, the new generation of young women are equipping themselves to be the good citizens of the war and the post-war reconstruction: 'Young women [...] were left to negotiate a hybrid identity, combining a residual and powerfully symbolic domesticity with an emergent modernity that made them newly minted citizens and a previously untapped labour force for the warfare state' (2019: 18). That 'emergent modernity' expresses itself in a disdain for the conventions of pre-war femininity and marriage; the middle-class women who write and populate women's fiction across the decade of the 1940s clearly articulate a frustration with the restricted expectations for women and are in search of new modes of contemporary womanhood.

Virginia Nicholson concludes her study of those involved in British Bohemianism in 1939, and her final chapter is elegiac:

> Bohemia didn't end with the Second World War, though many people said it did. With the formation of the Arts Council in 1946, and the foundation of the welfare State, some of the struggle was removed, and with it the sacrifice. For those who had survived the times of hardship, and got through the war, their personal Bohemia seemed a bitter-sweet memory, like the passing of youth. (281)

That bitter-sweetness is evident in the tragi-comic tone of so many of these novels. Their heroines do finally eschew bohemianism, but not without considerable regret. Wilson has also argued that 'bohemian nostalgia is partly a lament for lost youth, since it was above all the young who flocked to bohemia' (9). The nostalgia in these novels is in part for a childhood in which it was possible to be irresponsible, but the irresponsibility of the parental generation is regularly called to account, Bohemia is shown to be a place that is not conducive to bringing up the next generation, especially in wartime. Keith Waterhouse was among those who claimed that Bohemia had died with the end of the war, writing in 1955:

> Bohemianism is obviously finished. There may be some isolated cases – the odd chap in the attic – but on the whole much of the struggle has been removed from the artistic career. Nobody in his sane mind and with a reasonably balanced budget would fling himself into a total *décadence* or *Sturm und Drang* [...]. (Qtd. Wilson 227)

Bohemianism was not 'obviously finished' in 1945, there were more than a few odd men and women pursuing unconventional lives in attics throughout the 1940s, and in the late 1940s and the 1950s Bohemia would flourish in London's Soho and Fitzrovia. Nonetheless, the women protagonists in these narratives are largely shown as finally shying away from the '*décadence*' and '*Sturm und Drang*' of pre-war bohemia, while, like Fanny and Celia, maintaining a great affection, and some admiration, for those who embrace it. Those characters who cannot adjust their intensity to the new world order, such as Linda of *The Pursuit of Love* and Niall of *The Parasites*, are, however, destined not to survive.

Very few of these novels directly address the war (Mitford is an exception) or their writers' own experience of war, but clearly its impact is evident; the seriousness of wartime has intruded too much and cannot be evaded totally. It serves as a constant backdrop to these narratives. What Light calls Mrs Miniver's 'stable civilian life' (148) has been permanently disrupted; by the time the film of *Mrs Miniver* came out Mrs Miniver's cheerful resilience was already under considerable strain, as Light puts it: 'In retrospect Struthers's breezy optimism reads like self-delusion [...]. [T]hat calm optimism had already been tried and tested by the Blitz and the Battle of Britain' (153). By 1945, in the aftermath of war, this sanguinity is even further strained, but it does persist in a form of wry resignation, calm still, but far less optimistic. The 'breezy optimism' of Jan Struther is maintained as a tone in women's fiction well beyond 1942, it is there in Nancy Mitford's *The Pursuit of Love* (which echoes Deborah Mitford's 1940 letter to their sister Jessica), it continues in Monica Dickens's work, and can be read in Rhys and du Maurier. The cheerful register is not, however, consistent, even in those writers whose tone is predominately comic, such as Mitford, Gibbons and Dickens there are element of a bleak darkness.

Many of the writers of the late 1940s had experienced two world wars and had seen women's relationships to work and family being radically transformed. The war had also challenged conventional morality, as Wilson explained: 'Total war was a situation in which many normal social conventions were suspended, and even if they were replaced with new rules and regulations, there were bohemian aspects to wartime, a relaxation in sexual behaviour [...]' (79). 'Total war' also had a direct impact on the family; sons and husbands had been lost and injured, young men and women bombed, households destroyed. There are new widows in the post-war landscape, women such as Valerie, who have lost their previous life of domestic femininity and who must now make their own way both economically and emotionally. There are also new nurses who learned their skills during wartime, and women such as Leo and Helen who are exploring new kinds of work that would once have been closed to them. The world of post-war Britain is one of rationing and austerity in which irresponsibility ceases to be charming. The new welfare state and the National Health Service require professionalism and dedication from the women who now work there. Fanny's regret at the Radlett family's lack of 'mental discipline' is widespread; competence and practicality have become expected qualities in heroines by the late 1940s.

While Bohemianism might remain alluring and attractive in part, like Valerie, the post-war women depicted in these novels are too practical to give themselves up to it entirely, opting instead for some form of genteel independence. This is not quite the 'conservative modernity' of the novels of Light's study of the inter-war period, although many of women's novels of the 1940s do carry traces of what Light labels Mrs Miniver's 'crisp commonsense' (118). The modernity of the 1930s was a very different prospect from that of the 1940s. From 1945 'modernity' was a 'brave new world' of reconstruction and the building of the welfare state and a reconfiguration of the nation under a Labour government which would see the decade out.

There is a strong sense in these novels across the range of women writers of the need for independence, particularly financial, and a pride in newly acquired competencies. Plain has argued that the 'refusal of seriousness' in women's writing of the Second World War is a form of 'fatalism' (2013b: 240). However, the recurrent tone of comic resilience does not entirely refuse seriousness or hope. In Mitford's narrative Linda is 'possessed by a calm and happy fatalism' (178), but Fanny is not, and it is the sensible Fanny in Mitford's novel who represents the future for post-war femininity. The competence shown by women characters from Struther's Mrs Miniver to du Maurier's Celia and Mitford's Fanny suggests more than a fatalistic approach to war – but rather a determination to keep going and to survive. They may, like Jean Rhys' heroines, find themselves in desperate circumstances, but, like the Mitford sisters, they keep calm and carry on. In the words of the Ministry of Information: 'The women of Britain know about war. So do many of the children, because when war came to Britain it was total' (Ministry of Information 78). In the Second World War, women of Britain did not say 'Go' to their men folk as they were instructed to in the first war but were active participatory agents. Women characters in the novels of the 1940s do not forget that agency and are determined to hold on to it at the end of conflict. Their 'refusal of seriousness' is a means of coping with the responsibilities of war time and with a future as post-war citizens.

Notes

1. Jessica had also lost her daughter to the measles epidemic the year before.
2. The only woman writer cited in Laing's account of the novel of the 1940s is Elizabeth Bowen (239). There is no woman contributor to Sinfield's 1983 edited collection *Society and Literature 1945–1970*; the entire index references only

twenty-five women writers, largely represented by Doris Lessing, Iris Murdoch and Elizabeth Bowen throughout.
3   Christina Foyle would become manager of Foyles Bookshop in 1945.
4   *Mrs Miniver*, 1942 (dir. William Wyler), has been credited with boosting support for America's intervention in the war.
5   Stella Gibbons is more widely known for the 1932 *Cold Comfort Farm*, but she claimed *Ticky* as her own favourite among her novels.
6   Nancy Mitford and Waugh were friends, regularly writing to one another, see: Mitford, Nancy. *A Talent to Annoy: Essays, Journalism and Reviews 1929–71*. London: Capuchin Classics, 2013.
7   Wolfe mistakenly characterizes Helen as a nurse, a more traditionally 'feminine' profession.
8   The 'actress' as an inauthentic figure is a familiar trope in post-war fiction of the 1940s and 1950s; see Philips 2014: 29.

Works cited

Bloom, Clive. *Bestsellers: Popular Fiction since 1900*. Houndmills, Basingstoke: Palgrave Macmillan, 2008.
Brayborn, Gail and Penny Summerfield. *Out of the Cage: Women's Experiences in Two World Wars*. London: Pandora Press, 1987.
Dickens, Monica. *Flowers in the Grass*. London: The Book Club, 1950.
du Maurier, Daphne. *The Parasites*. London: Victor Gollancz, 1949.
Gibbons, Stella. *Ticky*. London: Longmans, 1943.
Hodges, Sheila. 'Editing Daphne du Maurier'. In Helen Taylor (ed.), *The Daphne du Maurier Companion*. London: Virago, 2007: 25–43.
Holman, Valerie. *Print for Victory: Book Publishing in England 1939–1945*. London: The British Library, 2008.
Laing, Stuart. 'Novels and the Novel'. In Alan Sinfield (ed.), *Society and Literature 1945–1970*. London: Methuen, 1983: 235–59.
McAleer, Joseph. *Popular Reading and Publishing in Britain 1914–1950*. Oxford: Oxford University Press, 1992.
Ministry of Information. *What Britain Has Done 1939–1945*. London: Atlantic Books, 2007 [1945].
Mitford, Nancy. *The Pursuit of Love*. Harmondsworth: Penguin Books. 1949.
Mosley, Charlotte (ed.). *Letters Between Six Sisters*. London: Harper Perennial, 2008.
Myerson, Julie. '*The Parasites*'. In Helen Taylor (ed.), *The Daphne du Maurier Companion*. London: Virago, 2007: 156–60.
Nicholson, Virginia. *Among the Bohemians: Experiments in Living 1900–1939*. London: Viking, 2002.

Oliver, Reggie. *Out of the Woodshed: The Life of Stella Gibbons*. London: Bloomsbury, 1998.

Philips, Deborah and Ian Haywood. *Brave New Causes: Women in Post-war Fictions*. London: Leicester University Press, 1998.

Philips, Deborah. *Women's Fiction 1945-Today: Writing Romance*. London: Bloomsbury, 2014.

Plain, Gill. 'Women's Writing in the Second World War'. In Maroula Joannou (ed.), *The History of British Women's Writing 1925–1945*. Houndmills, Basingstoke: Palgrave Macmillan, 2013a: 233–49.

Plain, Gill. *Literature of the 1940s: War, Post-war and 'Peace'*. Edinburgh: Edinburgh University Press, 2013b.

Plain, Gill. 'Introduction'. In Gill Plain (ed.), *British Literature in Transition, 1940–1960: Post-war*. Cambridge: Cambridge University Press, 2019: 1–35.

Renault, Mary. *The Friendly Young Ladies*. London: Virago, 1984 [1944].

Rhys, Jean. *Good Morning, Midnight*. Harmondsworth: Penguin, 1969.

Sage, Lorna. *Women in the House of Fiction: Post-war Women Novelists*. Houndsmill, Basingstoke: Macmillan Press, 1992.

Savory, Elaine. *Jean Rhys*. Cambridge: Cambridge University Press, 1998.

Sinfield, Alan (ed.). *Society and Literature 1945–1983*. London: Methuen, 1983.

Taylor, D. J. *After the War: The Novel and England since 1945*. London: Chatto & Windus, 1993.

Waugh, Evelyn. *Put Out More Flags*. London: Penguin Books, 2011 [1942].

Wilson, Elizabeth. *Bohemians: The Glamorous Outcasts*. London: I.B. Tauris, 2000.

Wolfe, Peter. *Mary Renault*. New York: Twayne Publishers, 1969.

4

The Ship and the Nation: Royal Navy Novels and the People's War 1939–45

Chris Hopkins

There has been considerable work by historians on the concept of 'the people's war', and much work by film historians on the contribution of cinema to that idea (see bibliography). The best-known historical work is Angus Calder's *The People's War: Britain 1939–1945*, which aims to 'describe, as accurately as possible, the effect of the war on civilian life' (15). Featuring a great range of topics, including culture, Calder argued that 'the people increasingly led itself […] the war was fought with the willing brains and hearts of the most vigorous elements in the community […] who worked more and more consciously towards a transformed post-war world' (18), although he was pessimistic about the degree of post-war transformation. There have been a number of more specialized historical studies of the Ministry of Information and service and civilian morale, while for film historians, a key question is how film genres and individual films tried to adapt in order to present their versions of 'the people's war'; and, in *This is England*, Neil Rattigan says:

> The propaganda films of the people's war, in which all classes[…] unite for the common good, had to evolve from a set of practices and a set of assumptions […] in which the notion of the upper and middle classes having anything in common were hardly considered. (97)

The iconoclastic historian David Edgerton is thus somewhat of an outlier in arguing that two linked ideas about the British experience of the war represent false starting points. It was not particularly 'a people's war' – a term he says was rarely used (Calder indeed does not trace its wartime usage). Nor, says Edgerton, was wartime change well explained by the 'left's story of Blitz to Beveridge': on the contrary he argues that Britain was, and continued to be, not a welfare but principally a 'warfare state' (1, 4, 123, 152, 294–5). He does, however, admit that *narratives* about the growth of democratization did emerge during the war (7, n. 8). As Ian McLaine's discussion in *Ministry of Morale* makes evident, ideas about socially progressive war aims roused great public interest from 1941 onwards, as Ministry of Information records attest. However, as he also makes clear, the Ministry of Information (MoI) found itself in an odd position, trapped between much public opinion and the different views taken by a powerful section of its political leadership: 'How was it to buoy up the post-war aspirations of the nation, while simultaneously bowing to the Prime Minister's desire for silence on the subject?' (171). Nevertheless, the MoI was not the only political arena, and I will argue that the idea of 'the people's war' was a strong factor in wartime British popular culture and that while its presence in film has been widely explored, its influence in popular reading has been largely neglected. There is only one literary study which sees 'the people's war' as a key factor in wartime writing – and that has not had the influence it deserves. In Alan Munton's *English Fiction of the Second World War* (1989), he correctly claims his is the first substantial study of Second World War fiction. Early in the book, he explains that faced with a multiplicity of material he has 'confronted the chaos by using one main category, the historian's term "the People's War"' (1). His first chapter 'Fiction and the People's War', as well as others, develops this theme. However, with a few exceptions, his main focus is not on popular fiction but on what were by that stage more-or-less canonical 'literary' works (many actively hostile to the idea of 'the people's war', and quite a few published long after 1945). Thus Munton focuses on wartime and post-war novels by Elizabeth Bowen (9, 30), Henry Green (44–5), Graham Greene (33), Anthony Powell (74–5), C. P. Snow (74–5) and Evelyn Waugh (74–5, 83–5). Popular texts do have some place in his book – there is brief discussion of Jack Lindsay's *Beyond Terror: a Novel of the Battle of Crete* (1943) and Alexander Baron's excellent people's war novel, *From the City, From the Plough* (1949), and of Nicholas Monsarrat's *The Cruel Sea* (1951) at greater length. I want to build on these important foundations a more substantial study of the significance of popular narratives published during the war itself, and which served, now often forgotten, as channels for the public discussion of the purpose of the war and of hopes for the post-war world. This chapter focuses on novels/documentaries about the Royal Navy because there seems to have been a specific subgenre of Royal Naval writing which especially promoted 'people's war' sentiment and discussion.[1]

Work by historians other than Edgerton certainly reinforces the idea that democratization was a key narrative, if a contested one, within government, government agencies and the armed services.[2] S. P. Mackenzie traces the struggle between the Army Education Corps and some senior army officers from 1940 on, with one set of progressive officer-educators who, wishing to develop a politically aware citizen-army, were often locked into quite public controversy with those in the army hierarchy and Parliament who regarded any such programme as tantamount to subversion. In many respects the progressive voices in the Army Education Corps won, with the crucial support of one of the two most senior army officers, the Adjutant-General Sir Ronald Adam, who had ultimate responsibility for army welfare and education (the so-called radical general) (see Broad 2013). He implemented the idea that a nation fighting for democracy should have an army made up of informed citizens who knew what they were fighting for and why, and who had fora in which to discuss their views and the possible shape of the post-victory world. After 1941 and up until 1945 British soldiers were expected to take part in weekly lectures and discussion groups, based on the pamphlets produced in huge imprints by the Army Bureau of Current Affairs (ABCA). The pamphlets, intended to provide up-to-date material for the junior officers whose duty it was to give the lectures and lead discussions, alternated between a focus on the military situation and a focus on broader current affairs, and included several discussing post-war reconstruction.[3] The RAF adopted similar activities after 1943.

The Royal Navy was not keen on this idea, and it was the only service where resistance from senior officers prevented the development of 'citizenship education' until late in the war (see MacKenzie 1992: 227–8; Prysor: 431–2). Admiral Sir John Cunningham (C-in-C Mediterranean Fleet since December 1943) was still arguing in late 1944, according to MacKenzie, that 'junior officers were not capable of keeping control of discussions which might well touch on social and political questions – "whence it is but a short step to criticism of politicians, of authority in general, and finally of naval authority in particular"' (1992: 226).[4] As recorded by Glyn Prysor, one destroyer commander recalled with distaste his encounter in 1944 with a citizenship training course: 'its […] whole tenor was socialist, run by the ABCA, who might have been better employed in the front line. We were encouraged to start "discussion groups" in our ships […] I doubt if many active ships did anything about it. I certainly didn't' (431–2).[5] Nevertheless, in wartime popular fiction and documentary writing *about* the Royal Navy, there was a notable interest in ideas of the Navy as democratic and meritocratic, and in the social organization on naval ships themselves as a possible lesson for post-war Britain. This body of texts has been little explored by literary critics or historians, though comparable film-texts have been studied – as we shall see, fiction/non-fiction showed a tendency to hybridize, as Jonathan

Rayner argues was also the case with many naval films, which he categorizes as 'documentary features'. The one exception among historians is Brian Lavery who in his book on wartime Royal Naval officers briefly identified a group of books dealing particularly with the experience of Commissioned Warrants. Commissioned Warrants were ordinary seamen who had been selected during basic training as having officer potential but had to serve at least three months at sea 'below decks' before taking up their officer training place at a shore establishment (2012: 31–7). Lavery observes that 'One side effect of the CW scheme was to expose the rich and exotic culture of the lower deck to a large number of articulate and well-educated people, and to produce a small but significant body of literature on the seaman's life' (2008: 147). Starting from this helpful insight, further analysis of these neglected texts suggests that some popular wartime writing, engaged thoroughly with the idea of the 'people's war' (if with some difficulties of class perspective) and that a widely read patriotic literature about the 'Senior Service' had a perhaps unexpected political potential to contribute to attitudes underpinning the post-war settlement in 1945.

Wartime public interest in the Navy in general is not surprising. While acknowledging the rivalry of the RAF, many wartime books saw the Navy as the traditional defender of British freedom, and (more-or-less) official publications supported this perspective (see Stubbs, 181). It is important to note the range of popular texts written about the Navy during the entire war.[6] Valerie Holman in her work on wartime-publishing refers to keenness from the Ministry of Information to ensure that books on selected topics, including the Navy, reached wider audiences through being sold at lower than commercial prices (100). *The Royal Navy Today*, which had no named author, was published by Odhams in April 1942, sponsored by the Admiralty, and makes strong links between the Navy and ideas of freedom and democracy. Holman notes that Odhams requested enough extra paper for *The Royal Navy Today* to print 125,000 copies, so they were anticipating a large readership (85). The Foreword by A. V. Alexander develops the theme of freedom: he argues that Trafalgar and Jutland 'laid the foundations of the defeat of the enemies of liberty […] as our victories in the Atlantic and the Mediterranean are doing in this'. Strikingly, he says that 'this book gives a general picture of the lives of the men who fight in this *democratic* and disciplined organisation. I hope all who read it may capture a glimpse of the spirit alive in the Royal Navy today' (3). It is notable that A. V. Alexander endorses the book: he had been appointed First Lord of the Admiralty in May 1940 as part of Churchill's reorganization of the coalition government, and, while it is natural enough that he should introduce the text, his representation of the Navy as democratic is also pertinent to his position as the first Labour/ Co-Operative MP First Lord, and to his presentation of the war as progressive.[7] *The Royal Navy Today*'s main text develops the relationship between tradition and democracy, stressing that all classes contribute equally, and that the Navy is meritocratic:

> [The ship's company] [...] come from very different walks of life, particularly in these days. As they march down to their new home from the barracks to the dockyard, a man who used to own a Rolls and a large house in the country may be marching next to a man who was born and brought up in the circus.
> Any man even if he has not been noted in the first place as a potential officer may, if he shows keenness and the necessary qualities, be recommended at any time by his Commanding Officer for a commission.
> Every man in the ship, whatever his rank, if he has a grievance [...] is entitled to be seen by the Captain ... there is no Service in which the relations between officer and man are more human or more satisfactory for both parties. (5, 116, 21)

Of course, one of the book's intentions is to interest readers in the Navy in general and in joining the Service in particular, but this is framed in terms of a shared experience which will unite people with different origins (avoiding the exoticism of the circus performer for a factory or shop worker might have been more effective, but perhaps would have raised the issue of class difference too boldly). One might not think that the recognition of leadership qualities wherever found was a radical policy, but this was a recent possibility: as indicated in Chris Howard Bailey's book, up until the outbreak of war most naval officers came from a narrow upper-middle-class background and often through a specialized naval education which required family funding from childhood (122–4).

In addition to these more-or-less-official publications, there was a large range of other popular publications about the Navy. There were the 'Famous Hurricane ninepennies' pamphlets, which included Captain Frank Shaw's *The Convoy Goes Through* (1942), and medium-length booklets by Cassell, the format in which Nicholas Monsarrat's three accounts of naval life as a corvette lieutenant were first published (*H.M. Corvette*, 1943, *East Coast Corvette*, 1943, *Corvette Command*, 1944), before being reissued in one volume as *Three Corvettes* in 1945. There were also full-length hardbacks such as Anthony Thorne's *I'm a Stranger Here Myself* (Heinemann, 1943), 'Tackline's' *Holiday Sailor* (Hollis and Carter, 1944), J.P.W. Mallalieu's *Very Ordinary Seaman* (Gollancz, 1944) and Lieutenant John Davies's *Lower Deck* (MacMillan, 1945), as well as one by a civilian, C. S. Forester's *The Ship* (Michael Joseph, 1943).

This chapter will focus on two wartime novels about life on Royal Navy ships which stress certain kinds of (markedly male) equality as superior to peacetime class-divisions: Anthony Thorne's *I'm a Stranger Here Myself* (1943) and J.P.W. Mallalieu's *Very Ordinary Seaman* (1944). These examples suggest that popular fiction accounts of the experiences of naval crews were seen as entirely appropriate foci for discussions of the relationship between 'warfare state' and 'welfare state', the character of English society and its potential for radical post-war reconstruction. It is no co-incidence that both novels have among their chief protagonists Commissioned Warrants, or CWs. Both authors were, once promoted through this route, members of the RNVR (Royal Naval Volunteer Reserve) and thus by definition 'citizen sailors', rather than professional naval officers. There were five editions of *Very Ordinary Seaman* published by Gollancz before 1945, and it prominently reproduced on its dust-wrapper part of a *Daily Mail* review by Peter Quennell which proclaimed it 'the most interesting modern war book that has so far reached me'. An hour-long abridgement was broadcast by the BBC Home Service on 13 October 1944.

Thorne's *I'm a Stranger Here Myself* has a diary form which, while implying that these events are in the past, also often records the day in a continuous present, frequently mixing anticipations and expected future memories, and leading to a complex temporality. The first entry thus opens with the first-person narrator joining a new mess (mess P9) aboard his new ship:

> Seven sailors are shouting with laughter, and it's as though the light above them had blazed up suddenly and left the rest of the mess-deck in shadow ... I can stand in obscurity and look at the seven. Just as I wanted it to be when I came to join them.
>
> I wouldn't have wanted to see them singly, at first, as separate human beings. I wouldn't have wanted anything better than to find seven men laughing and know that in a little while I'd be the eighth.
>
> I shall remember this moment always, it will go on happening. I have dropped my kitbag and hammock on the deck. (1)

There is an emphasis first on the men in the mess as a group, and a desire on the part of the narrator not to be noticed as an intruding individual stranger. The group of seven is highlighted ('blazed up'; 'obscurity'), almost as if they are in a painting using *chiaroscuro*, and the group is instantly given the status by the narrator of an artistic image which will retain a lasting meaning beyond that of the ephemeral. This effect of instantly achieved special status is strongly reinforced by the temporal switches: this image is what the narrator wanted to see before he arrived, he recalls it for a second time as soon as he has seen it for the first time, and he is sure that he will always remember the image as eternally present in several senses.

One notes too that this epiphany is constructed from what in most respects looks like an everyday language of observation which, despite its power to heighten the moment, is not visibly striving for effect. In fact, immediately after this opening passage, there is a partial reality check which continues the theme of group solidarity, but also de-sentimentalizes the idea to a degree:

> These are the men with whom in the weeks to come I shall live in sticky intimacy. We shall eat, wash, curse, gossip, sleep and wake together, and we may drown together. At all events, we shall know each other's habits only too well. We may grow to hate one another, and even now I can imagine it. (1)

The so-far nameless narrator (eventually to be individualized by the mess as 'Thorney') is clearly entering a world which is new to him, and there are from early on hints that his interest in the inter-relationships of individuals and groups springs from his sense that he has a concealed difference: 'Now I must speak to them, and I expect I shall be awkward and jaunty because I don't wish to betray myself' (1). The cover of the 1945 paperback continental edition published by Zephyr Books – 'not to be introduced into the British Empire or USA' – gave the game away on the dust-wrapper front flap: 'the author is an ordinary seaman in for a commission', but the original Heinemann edition did not explicitly name 'Thorney's' in-between status until page 185 (of a 188-page novel).

Nevertheless, there are many earlier clues to a difference in status. Thorney's early faith in his mess-mates is buoyed up by the fact that they deliberately make no fuss about his possible differences. He is grateful that the mess-leader Stripey (a nick-name deriving from his good-conduct stripes) is from the beginning 'conventionally hostile' and that he helps – the narrator thinks: 'Now be careful, Stripey. Favour me in nothing, or you will add to the barriers that I have to pass' (3). Eating some dubious leftovers, Thorney feels that he is being accepted as 'a newcomer to the mess who doesn't care what he shoves down his throat, though he has a blasted college voice and hands that aren't yet a sailor's' (2–3). However, everyday life throws up many challenges: Thorney is puzzled by a word he doesn't recognize when soon after his arrival there is a 'crisis' as Stripey demands that he contribute his 'noods'. Thorney then realizes that each seaman is meant to add to the display of 'pictures of naked or semi-naked women' on the mess walls and ceiling (17). Luckily, 'culture' comes to his rescue, when he remembers that he has an arts magazine containing two photographs or 'Artistic studies'; nevertheless, he fears that 'my noods have let me down badly. They have something which I am afraid will be mistaken for Class' (18).

Equally, Thorney has trouble with some of the physical labour, and early on pulls his shoulder: 'The others know, when we are lifting bombs together, that I am not doing my share of work, and it makes me furious: but although I have said nothing, they know the reason' (29). His mess-mates' concealed knowledge may be of his injury or of his class-background, but either way they show the admirable quality of comradeship by saying nothing. In many respects, Thorney's situation resembles that of some inter-war upper-middle-class writers who wanted to express class solidarity by joining in with the workers (see, for example, the tragic-comic class-sensibilities of Christopher Isherwood's protagonist in his 'fictional memoir', *Lions and Shadows* from 1938), but the wartime context of necessity and his participation in an institution make it less personal and more practicable: the class gap is here represented as something which can be partially bridged, with mutual effort.

The men are curious though and while the unpopular Olsen tries to force a confession of what Thorney is doing in the Navy as a rating – '"Come on now, spill it"' (41) – others are gentler. Eventually, 'they ask me the question which I have so often dreaded':

> 'What did you do in Civvy Street, Thorney? What were you before you joined the bloody navy?'
>
> Olsen is staring at me. Stripey looks up. Whiskers leans over the table to hear. Knocker and Bungy pause with wet plates in their hands. Whacker Payne opens an eye …
>
> 'I was a writer.'
>
> And then, realising that for sailors a 'writer' is a clerk, or an accountant, I add, for I don't want to tell these men anything but the truth:
>
> 'A writer of stories.'
>
> There is a startled pause. Nothing hostile about it: they are just working that out. You buy stories at a shop: they come from a firm. It's difficult to think of somebody sitting down to write them …
>
> 'What kind of stories, Thorney? Crime or Spicy?'
>
> Well, Crime or Spicy, take your choice. There's evidently no alternative. (45–6)

Here Thorney becomes the unwilling centre of attention. He is anxious that the men will not understand his answer, correctly, in that for them the idea of authorship as a job is unfamiliar, but once they have absorbed this novelty, they are able to fit him quite readily into a familiar genre schema – he must write one of the two fiction genres they know – thriller or pornography. Thus, once again class difference is negotiated, and the scene ends with renewed solidarity as the sailor Whiskers offers to lend Thorney his current risqué book, *Fig Leaves Forbidden*. This title (I take it to be invented) perhaps also reinforces the idea that among true comrades there should be nothing hidden – a theme already invoked by Thorney when he thinks that he must tell these men only the truth, even when it draws attention to his differences. There is a perhaps surprising amount of reference to reading to pass the time, but there is also a running gag about Thorney being more prone to reading than others. Whiskers notes that Thorney 'is terrible with books' (45), and he is indeed trying to read Conrad's *Typhoon* (1902), but 'for some reason' (13) has not yet found the peace to do so. Thorney's ease with literacy makes him both useful and an outsider. Like Larry Meath in Walter Greenwood's *Love on the Dole* (1933), he becomes a scribe:

> I am one of those Chinese who sit at street corners waiting for clients with a brush and a bottle of ink. I am a professional letter-writer [...] Hell's bells, why on earth didn't I tell them that in private life I was an acrobat? [...] Knocker White is breathing down the back of my neck, a photograph in his hand. Whiskers edges towards me with a writing pad [...]. (64, 66)

He cannot help but notice that from his perspective the written language of the sailors has its limitations – Nobby Clark is stuck with a letter he is writing to his wife and after three lines can only think of concluding, 'I wish you was here.' Since the ship is at sea on active service, Thorney quite reasonably queries this, '"But you don't do you? You wish you were there." Nobby says, "Now you've messed me up proper"' and Thorney has to help further with a now co-produced letter:

> We start to catalogue the charms of Gladys Clark [...] and using I'm afraid a number of horrid clichés: but these I think she will forgive, may even like them and out of it all some sort of feeling does emerge. (66)

Clearly, there are comic possibilities here, drawing on age-old literary assumptions about a hierarchy of articulacy in the alleged language-competence of different classes. This seems potentially at odds with the admiration Thorney expresses for the ratings and his urge to gain full membership of the group, though perhaps this is best thought of as a pastoral effect – they are simpler but nobler than the more sophisticated man who observes them. Equally, Thorney applies the scrutiny afforded by his middling position to the officer-class which he is destined to join. Bungy Williams wonders whether the officers really enjoy their shore leave. Thorney thinks their 'pleasures are organised and follow an easy, well-known pattern' and his imagination of their composite conversations ashore suggests that he is just as critical of officer-class inarticulacy and cliché:

> 'Your war going well?'
> 'How are things back at home?'
> 'What about a game of golf this afternoon?'
> 'Make a fourth at bridge?'
> 'Do you know Rodney?'
> 'Have you met Blake?' (83)

The last two questions are, of course, naval jokes, since the names could be first names or surnames, but are also the names of distinguished eighteenth-century and seventeenth-century admirals, as well as of past and contemporary capital ships.

Thorney is very aware of the danger of his sense of solidarity being seen as sentimental rather than real; in a letter to his wife he does describe sailors as 'simple and sentimental', but then thinks that 'he should have qualified it' (170, 173). Indeed, his own method of representing the qualities of the lower deck as a whole is foreshadowed in the opening page of the novel: he represents the crew as ideal before showing their lapses. After a long period of slow-convoy escort-duty, the much-praised comradeship of the mess deteriorates: '"It's just as well that we have not far to go. Another week and there'd be murder on the mess deck. The surrounding tables have already sent several casualties to sick bay"' (176). Even his particular mate, Knocker, falls out with Thorney and for the first time his long unmentioned CW status is held against him:

> He thinks me aloof, bored, superior [...] 'Never mind Thorney, not much longer to go before you're an officer [...] in a few months time you'll have more gold braid than that. And nice sheets to sleep in. And lovely grub. As for us, we'll get no promotion this side of the –.' (178)

The allusion at the end is to the song Bungy Williams was singing in the very first diary entry of the novel:

> Officers don't bother me – not much –
> Officers don't worry me –
> For we'll get no promotion
> This side of the ocean. (5)

Of course, this had a strong relevance to Thorney's CW status at that point too, but no one commented on it, even though his appearance may have sparked off the choice of these particular lines from verse four of what was an army song, often known as 'Bless 'Em All'.[8] Thorney is hurt because there is some truth in the accusation, but disgusted because it is a breaking of the voluntary social contract he has valued:

> His tactics sicken me. He is constantly reminding me of something that I'm trying to forget – that in a little while I shall sell them all for a mess of pottage with a little chopped parsley on the top of it. (178)

Nevertheless, the final part of the novel returns to the initial sense that the lower deck is a uniquely sociable society, and a possible model for other societies. Thorney knows that his lower deck experience is coming to an end and feels it intensely: 'there is nothing like them I have ever known or am ever going to experience again [...] something has happened inside me and I feel a love of them and cannot speak' (183–4).

J.P.W. Mallalieu's *Very Ordinary Seaman* (1944) also uses a CW as a centre of consciousness, though the narration is third person. The novel begins by focusing on Williams as an individual as he leaves home to join-up, and his social status is quickly established: he has flat in London and a housekeeper, has been to a school with an OTC (Officer Training Corps), and is a journalist on a daily newspaper. He has volunteered for the Navy because of his negative OTC experiences and because of what he has heard about the 'stupidity' of army life. He 'had heard the Navy was different' (8) and is sent off with other volunteers to a shore-training establishment. The diverse origins of the group are stressed, immediately suggesting a 'people's war' theme: one has been in a City bank, one in the merchant navy, one a printer's apprentice, one a car assembly-line worker and so on. The representation of their speech suggests class and regional differences, as do political discussions. The focus thus markedly shifts to the group of men rather than Williams individually, though the novel retains a sense throughout that his perspective is aligned with that of the impersonal narrator – partly through the familiar device of a shared 'normative' Standard English, indicating a shared 'educated' class position. As in Thorne's novel, however, there is also a theme about how knowledge is not the possession of one class and that the more 'educated' often need help: 'They took pity on someone [Williams] who was so obviously helpless. Real work, putting studs in boots, folding clothes, using an iron ... an office worker could not be expected to know about these things' (57). In return, Williams, like Thorney, can share his literacy – 'they asked him things – how to spell words or translate French tags which were always cropping up in letters from girl-friends' (57).

There is an emphasis, as in Thorne's novel, on life in the Navy being meritocratic and democratic, and as actively promoting the development of equality from the bottom up, if often via considerable conflict. At the beginning of training each class has two class-leaders appointed. Though these leaders have no rank, they are asked to lead their class who are asked to help them through co-operation (standard pronunciation seems to help you to be picked for this role). Each class, mirroring mess arrangements on board ship, has to provide 'cooks' who fetch food from the galley and serve it. Since the first new 'cooks' take advantage of their position, leading to radical inequalities (large plates for some, no meal at all for others), this soon leads to argument among the hungry trainees:

> 'I'm going to take darn good care I get a big breakfast this morning. I'd nothing at supper last night.'
> 'Look lads, let's stop this. There's enough to go round if we share it out equally.'
> 'Why the 'ell should we share it out equally? Everyone else pinches as much as they can when they're cooks. [...] What makes you think that the rest will stop swiping if one does?'
> 'I don't know that they will. But we can try.' (37)

This issue is resolved by the class-leaders who create a system whereby four permanent cooks are appointed who in return for fair distribution are excused hut-cleaning duties which are done instead by classmates. The discussion of the problem quoted above makes this sound like a microeconomic rehearsal of behaviours which can also be related to the macroeconomic picture – making these domestic naval arrangements a possible model for the nation. There is, though, a clear sense that the class-hierarchy is sustained – the more regional and working-class accents need to be educated by the more middle-class voices. But there is also a sense that this wartime service which in principle requires equality of sacrifice offers a potential improvement on pre-war social organization, suggesting the common sense of applying this equal distribution more widely. It is notable how relatively small a part officers play in either Thorne's or Mallalieu's stories: they make some appearances, but in the main our perspective is from the lower-deck society of ratings, petty officers and chief petty officers, who maintain their own social order. Mallalieu writes that the lower deck

> were prepared to admire any officer who showed that he knew his job [and] at sea there was much less consciousness of distinction [...] than there is between manager and workers in a factory. But in matters of duty the three badge A.B.s [Able Seamen] and the great majority of other ratings looked on officers just

as schoolboys look on schoolmasters [...] They were on the other side of the fence. (122)

The social hierarchy on ship is superior to that on land, but we are invited to admire the 'people' rather than the leaders. Lessons about social equality are drawn from other social problems – including theft and shirking. On the latter topic, the CPO supports the arguments put forward by Redfern and Williams: "'You work together a little more [...] you'll get the ruddy work done a sight sooner'" (55). Again, this sounds as if has resonances for nation as well as ship. The men, while not losing their individual characteristics, do become more co-operative, especially once on board ship and even more so after sustained action on an Arctic convoy.

As in *I'm a Stranger Here Myself*, the CWs feel a particularly intense, nostalgic, loyalty to the community of the lower deck as their departure from the ship and towards a different class-experience grows closer:

> Their first thought was thankfulness [...] they only wanted to go home. But then they thought of the ship. They had a right on that mess deck [...] as soon as they left, they would be outside of its community [...] It was amazing how attractive [the destroyer] seemed, the farther they got away from her. (274, 275)

Despite indications that naval life may offer lessons for a better (male) English social organization, both novels also see the sailors as practising a kind of equality rather than being articulate political theorists. There are a range of political discussions in both books. On one occasion Thorne's sailors (drunkenly) invoke revolution but then move to the political right. Whacker Payne starts it all by blaming his many misfortunes on the system:

> 'Just wait till after the war, mates. I'm going to start a revolution!' Revolution? Well, there's a thing to say. And what's your opinion mate? There is obviously a political discussion to follow. I've heard it many times, but I sit down to listen.
>
> At the moment the sailors are, I know, influenced by shore propaganda. Afloat, they are not in the least politically minded – the Rights of Man are the rights of Sailors. They've only personal grievances, their world is bounded by port and starboard, stem and stern. If they're subversive, it's in some sort of naval tradition [...]
>
> In any case sailors have no time for Socialism. Their most Bolshevik utterance could be followed by a vote for the Tories. They have never forgiven and never will forgive the Labour Government of Ramsay MacDonald for whittling down the British Navy [...] Already I can hear Whacker saying how much he admires Anthony Eden. (25-6)

I take it that the 'shore propaganda' is current discussion of post-war reconstruction. However, its influence seems shallow and quickly shifts to an apparently explicit rejection of progressive party politics. This may partly continue Thorney's position as intermediary observing the noble innocence of his messmates, whose political understanding is neither deep-rooted nor stable. Curiously, and perhaps specifically because of this passage, which might be seen as portraying the sailors as patriotic working-class Tories, there was a new edition of the novel published in 1945 by the Right Book Club – possibly before the July elections. Presumably, Anthony Thorne must have given permission for this new edition, though whether for primarily commercial or political reasons we do not know, since there is no Right Book Club Archive in which to search for correspondence, as Terence Rodgers points out (1–15). Rodgers also helpfully characterizes the Right Book Club as representing an aspect of the 'conservative modernism' first identified by Alison Light, 'a Conservatism, in the words of one RBC author [William Teeling] in which "tradition should [...] be able to blend with Modernity"' (2003: 3).⁹ The Right Book Club's founder, Christina Foyle, herself said that the purpose of the Club was to counteract 'the murderous embrace of the extremes' and in Rodgers's summary 'to foster a renewed interest in democracy among the ordinary public' (2). It may be that Thorne was not himself a leftist, though the character Thorney recalling peacetime reflects guiltily that while he was 'writing a book, there was war in Spain' (74). The novel nevertheless still seems to belong to a group of texts which promote the Navy as an exemplar of the people's war in that class co-operation and the deep virtues of ordinary people (or men, anyway) are seen as a key to war-time and perhaps post-war society.

There is lower-deck discussion of the post-war. Thorne's novel is set on an AMC (armed merchant cruiser – a passenger-liner lightly armed and transferred into Royal Navy service), which for much of the novel acts as a convoy escort but is also used as a troop-ship to deliver 'pongos' (Navy slang for soldiers) to overseas theatres.¹⁰ The sailors are tolerant but superior to the 'pongos', and they somewhat unexpectedly worry about the post-war impact of the soldiers' unnatural life. One of Thorney's duties is to clean some of the lavatories (a duty he notably prefers to cleaning the officer's mess). He notes that there are always solemn discussions going on: 'In the Seamen's Starboard Lavatory there is always a Brains Trust' (162). He records a few discussions in the form of a dialogue:

> [Lavatory] No. 5: But what's going to happen to them pongos after the war? What do they do when there's nobody's guts to rip out?

> No. 3: You mean them as they've taught to use nine-inch knives? [...]
> No. 2: I'll tell you what'll happen to them, mates. When the war ends, they'll have to be postmen and bakers and porters again. They'll have to live nice and quiet and peaceful again, and if they do anything they didn't ought, the law'll be down on them.'
> No. 5: [...] Poor ruddy pongos! There's many of them as hasn't had time to learn any other trade but killing. They haven't been postmen and bakers and porters. They haven't even that to go back to. (163)

There were genuine worries towards the end of the war that ex-servicemen might be prone to violence and find it difficult to settle back into post-war civil society.[11] But how should we read this dialogue? It may make the point that the sailors are (in their own view) better models for post-war society, or as so often in this novel may display their noble innocence through a pastoral effect, making fun of them while also admiring them. Thorney has himself consciously raised the issue of the post-war a few pages earlier, though he seems to conclude that in simply asking the question he has shown his outsider status:

> And, as usual, I have started an argument [...] I had merely asked Bungy Williams what he wanted to do when he left the Navy. In retrospect it seems like a silly newspaper question, but at the time I genuinely wanted to know. Not one of them could give me a reasoned answer, I realise, for not one of them will have considered post-war conditions ashore. They are not politically minded: they are sailors. They will answer from their imaginations, and that is good enough for me. I like to know what a man wants, not what he thinks he can get. (150)

Specific political ambitions seem suspect in Thorney's view – about material acquisition as much as authentic need – but again a pastoral move puts sailors outside that kind of corruption. However, the clearest answer comes from Knocker White and focuses on a decent life for all: he says he would like "'a Nice Young Lady [...] and a house and a garden and a motor-cycle and a daughter'" in preference to a son in case he becomes a 'ruddy matelot', though another sailor says it could be worse – he could grow into a 'perishing pongo' (150). Knocker's vision of post-war Britain seems pacific enough, with a high value put on material well-being for the ordinary family – not too modest a wish given some pre-war working-class living conditions.

Despite the reluctance to espouse shore politics, Thorney believes that he has learnt some powerful lessons. His situation on the ship is odd, as is pointed out to him in a rare conversation with an officer early on. Thorney is the only CW on board where there might more usually be two or three on a warship. The officer worries that his learning experience will not be that good: "'I think you'd have been better off on a destroyer [...] here, the routine is a mixture of Royal Navy and Merchant Service' (42). Still, the officer, keeping morale up, concludes that, 'actually, I think you should learn a lot'" (42). Thorney feels by the end of the novel that this is true, and even in his immediate response to the officer, he shows what he is learning:

> His voice is charming. But it is a voice that I know, and it does not reach the inside of my head. I am still listening, I suppose, to the Welshman, the Cockney, the Yorkshireman. These are the voices that I hear most [...] I am an Ordinary Seaman. I have a broom in one hand and a sponge in the other, orb and sceptre of lowliness. (42–3)

Thorney has, for the moment, gone over to the lower deck, and regards himself as having learnt something of the utmost value.

The political content of *Very Ordinary Seaman* is in some ways more explicit, though it too registers sailors who do not engage deeply with politics and, in its representation of class co-operation, does not avoid some curious clashes in class- perspectives. Some sailors claim political allegiances, but as with Whacker in Thorne's novel, their actual engagement does not seem deep-rooted. Price is, like Whacker, constantly 'dripping' (moaning) and sometimes his complaints adopt a political dimension:

> 'Oi'm a Communist,' he would say. 'Oi don't think Jerry's so bad. There's a lot over 'ere who are as bad, anyway. Look at this blasted Government. They just represent vested interests. They're not put there by the people – not by us blokes who 'ave to fight their basstud war, anyway. We were too young to vote when the last General Election was on. But we're not too young to foight, not bleeding loikely. (59)

This is a curious mixture. The idea that the wartime Coalition Government represents vested interests is certainly arguable – most key roles were held by Conservatives (Churchill notably was simultaneously Prime Minister, Minister for Defence and First Lord of the Treasury, while Eden was Foreign Secretary), but Labour held some significant posts (Herbert Morrison was Home Secretary and Ernest Bevin Minister of Labour and National Service, while Clement Atlee was Deputy Prime Minister). Of course, Price as a Communist might be suggesting that Labour as a social democratic party represents the status quo just as much as the Conservatives. Nevertheless, his assertion that this is as bad as Nazism might seem to most ill-founded. On the other hand, his point about a mismatch between being eligible to fight and to vote has more secure foundations. First, since the 1940 elections were not held due to the outbreak of war, the last election before the war had been held in 1935, when the National Government was elected and many young men now of fighting age were certainly too young to vote. Second, while eighteen-year-olds were adults when it came to military service, they could not vote until they were twenty-one (eighteen-year-olds had to wait until 1970 to get the vote in Britain).

These issues might receive sympathy from some readers. The hostile passage which follows and firmly places Price's declamation is, however, particularly interesting in terms of the politics of this novel. A speaker who is not explicitly named questions Price:

'What constituency do you live in?'
Price did not know.
'Well, who's your M.P.?'
He did not know.
'Well, if you don't take enough interest in politics even to know your M.P., how the hell do you expect to get a decent Government?'
'Oh, shut your flicking mouth.'
'Is that the way they teach you to argue in the Communist party?' (59)

The speaker clearly puts Price in his place, exposing his political ignorance of democratic procedures and implying that his claimed Communist allegiance is not based in real commitment (in fact Price is treated by his interlocutor, as Mackenzie indicates, exactly as the kind of 'slick disgruntled mess desk politician' whom the naval authorities feared might exploit citizenship education) (1992: 227, n. 6).[12] But one notices, again, the part played by language variety in establishing a hierarchy: the Standard speaker trumps the Midlands speaker. Moreover, the lack of an assigned speaker (and speech attribution) has a curious effect. A reader would usually identify the speaker by looking for the most recently named character with whom the speech is consistent. In this case that points to the voice at the opening of this self-contained section, which is most obviously read as an impersonal narrator. This implies an identity between the narrator and the speaker, suggesting that this self-confident character is Williams, and emphasizing forcibly at this point the novel's general sense that the CW character is also an intellectual superior. The fact that he is also of higher-class status sits uncomfortably with the novel's positive sense of social mixing as a virtue. It may be that the interchange points out that complaining is in itself not necessarily a political act and that not all working-class characters are admirable. Equally, the scene may point out that the novel is supportive of 'real' democracy, and, indeed, may show its allegiance to the Labour Party and its distrust of Communism.

After prolonged action in the second half of the novel, having suffered a number of fatalities, Williams feels that they have achieved real unity: 'the nearness of death had welded them in fellowship [...] the *Marsden* was no longer merely a ship. She was a community' (272). As in Thorne's novel, community is experienced most intensely in combat and then again as the CWs are taken off the ship (their focal points dominating the narratives' concluding moments) and head for the different experience of officer-training ashore: 'it was amazing how attractive she [the ship] seemed, the farther they got away from her' (275). Both novels end with codas which articulate apparently final perspectives on the two CWs' experiences. There are similarities but also differences in how these are handled.

Thorne's postscript takes the form of a one-page letter 'To a Friend who Made Enquiries'. The enquiry is about the loss of a mutual friend on his former AMC, which is recorded 'in the bare and official statement' as 'bombed and a total loss' (187). But Thorne (or Thorney?) feels sure he can fill in the details of this loss from his experience:

> I know in my heart that she will have gone down in a blaze of fury, barking and spitting like the battleship she was not [...]. But her crew I seem to see everywhere I look [...] Stripey, Curly, Knocker [...]. Sometimes they salute me and walk on, and sometimes, crossly, they interest themselves in a passing motor-car. They don't realise how well I know them and that we were once mates [...] for mine were all the sailors in the world, all the sailors that ever were or will be. (188)

Despite the power of this feeling and Thorney's earlier antidotes to sentimentality, this seems sentimentalizing and generalizing in its move from experience of specific individuals to their resurrection as eternal types.

J.P.W. Mallalieu's postscript is crisper in its interpretation of its narrative. First, this is clearly the 'Author's Postscript' rather than being merged into the viewpoint of the novel's narrator. Second, it articulates very explicitly an interpretation firmly located in contemporary history

> You landsmen may be finding wartime life uncomfortable – worse than uncomfortable when the blitz is on. But it's never so bad as wartime life on a destroyer. I have tried both [...]. But don't think of sailors as heroes, either. They are

not heroes – not in any storybook sense. They 'drip' […] [but] we feel instinctively that there is not room in the world both for us and for the Nazis.

We have no illusions about our country or about the war. We do not believe that Britain will be part of a new world, fit for heroes to live in, when the war is won. We only hope that by defeating the Nazis we will prevent it from becoming a worse place.

But for all that, we are learning about a new world. The lower deck is not a competitive organisation. Seamen are not honoured because they get more for themselves than the rest of their messmates. They are not taught or forced to fight against each other. They learn to live in a community, sharing equally its terrors and its happiness. […] They learn to help each other […] we do not want to surrender this fellowship when at last we come home; and if we find competition, inequality, and uncertainty of livelihood in the post-war world, we may no longer content ourselves with 'dripping.'

We have learned to *fight*, landsmen. (277)

The linking of the destroyer experience to the key 'people's war' experience of the Blitz is important in seeing both as equal contributions, as is the explicit sense of the war against fascism. As for Thorne, there is a wish to avoid sentimentality – in this case unrealistic hero-worship and political utopianism (Lloyd George's First World War promise, of which Churchill had a particular dislike, is specifically disavowed). Nevertheless, there are high post-war expectations that the spirit of equality and social security which the author sees in the Service will be reproduced in post-war Britain.

Both novels were widely reviewed in 1944 and many reviews praised their authenticity and attributed this to direct experience of the lower deck in wartime: 'Mr Thorne has cast in fiction his own experience as an Ordinary Seaman' (H.R.G.W 1943: 2). L. P. Hartley in *The Sketch*, however, strongly objected to the repetitive swearing and saw it as undermining clarity of meaning:

> Automatic bad language, if neither picturesque nor funny […] is very boring to listen to. Instead of adding something to language […] it weakens and detracts and after a time begins to have an ugly life of its own, which, like a parasite, preys on the meaning of what is being said. Undoubtedly an effect of realism is obtained […] but is that effect worth it at the expense of so much monotony? (1944: 244)

Other reviewers picked out clearly the people's war motif in *Very Ordinary Seaman*. These include Peter Quennell, whose *Daily Mail* review was quoted on the dust-wrappers to later editions:

> He tells us, simply and modestly, something that we ought to know – what it feels like to be precipitated from the calm of a sedentary job into the hurly-burly of life on a destroyer's lower deck; how men respond to their first experience of

action [...] how the members of a ship's company merge into a corporate whole [...] it suggests the more moving sequences of Noel Coward's film, with none of its sentimental and slightly stagey touches. (2)

The review notably picks out Williams's experience as central (strictly speaking we see the adaptations made by men from other backgrounds too). It also invokes as a comparison a film which was materially supported by the Ministry of Information and which is firmly regarded as a (peculiar) part of the people's war – *In Which We Serve* (1942) which was directed by Noel Coward and David Lean for Two Cities Films, – where the crew, with its diverse class origins, is also bonded by their shared experience.[13] Quennell ends his review by stressing that the cross-class bonding of Mallalieu's crew also extends to the novel's reader: 'We learn to recognise, and as we recognise, we also learn to like them.' The novelist Elizabeth Bowen in *The Tatler* also clearly identifies the motif. Though drawing on the dust-wrapper blurb, she also supplies her own acute reading of the text. Bowen says that the six ratings we have followed all the way from training 'are of all types and from all sorts of homes':

> [they] strictly [...] do not change: they become themselves. At the start, these six are [...] the products of a competitive society, from which they have carried over acquired prejudices, habits, catchwords, animosities and fears. Their idea of freedom [...] has been to get the best they can, and the most they can for themselves. (86)

This starting point they eventually exchange for the 'co-operative life of the Service [...] how it makes them and what is shown before *Very Ordinary Seaman* reaches its end.' L. P. Hartley picks out the theme too, emphasizing its force by comparing *Very Ordinary Seaman* to C. S. Forester's *The Ship* (1943), and correctly noting very different conceptions of social co-operation in the two naval novels:

> the two books have the like intention – to show how the individual lives of men may be merged in a common effort. But the method employed in each case is different. Mr Forester gives us a gallery of portraits, carefully framed and separated from each other, whereas Mr Mallalieu from the start throws his men into a crucible and welds them together. (244)

Where Forester has a highly individualist sense of his ship's crew each doing their duty in their own allotted (and often claustrophobic) space, Mallalieu's crew has a highly social identity, and this is their strength. Hartley does also see, despite his distaste, that the swearing is partly a device which contributes to the egalitarian vision: 'there is no doubt that mechanical, unimaginative bad language is a great leveller. Talking alike makes men seem alike' (in this respect swearing may partly redress the assumptions about hierarchies of speech varieties). Overall, Hartley says that the novel's 'sense of solidarity is memorable and touching'. The *Chelmsford Chronicle* makes a similar point about *I'm a Stranger Here Myself* and stresses some democratic aspects of the narration: '[it] hardly ever rises above the ordinary in manner, but it is based on a fundamental love of the sailors who are described [...] these men are "reported" by their comrade Thorney, who, an ordinary seamen, himself tells the story'; it is perhaps no co-incidence that the same column also reviews positively *Education in Transition – a Sociological Study of the Impact of War on English Education 1939–43* (Kegan Paul, 1943), observing that its author, H. C. Dent, 'believes that the English people desire a great and trenchant advance in all departments of national life' (Looker 1944: 3).

As it turned out, another wartime naval writer rather eclipsed these two novels and other memories of the British naval war with a post-war bestseller, *The Cruel Sea*. Wartime RNVR Lieutenant-Commander Nicholas Monsarrat's novel was published by Cassell in 1951, and its reach increased by the very successful 1953 film, made at Ealing Studios and directed by Charles Frend. The novel has many of the features of a 'people's war' novel in being about 'hostilities only' sailors from varied origins and seeing strength in this social variety. However, despite Monsarrat's pre-war left-wing sympathies (which he said were especially inspired by the Invergordon Mutiny of 1931), his novel was much more a view from the bridge than a history from the lower deck, though there is much about how the officers look after the ratings and a good deal of comic material derived from the ratings' perspectives on life. Munton observes that 'the novel is not illiberal, but numerous details show how it was possible to forget wartime ways of thinking [...] and transform them into something less generous' (78). It may be significant that, unlike Mallalieu and Thorne, Monsarrat was commissioned directly into the RNVR: he never served below decks.

The tendency towards a view from the bridge was there already in Monsarrat's three wartime novellas. In *H.M. Corvette* (1942) the 'Hostilities Only' sailors' social range is noted: '[they] ranged from van-boy to statistical accountant' (1945: 17).[14] Nevertheless, the dominant focal point is from above:

> Of course, there were defaulters – leave-breakers, losers of property by negligence, ratings who (in the Coxswain's magic phrase) 'tried to poke bravado at their superiors'; but they were never a daily routine, and only on very rare occasions did the full force of the First Lieutenant's Gestapo have to function. (107)

In the concluding chapter of the second volume, *East Coast Corvette* (1943), the officer-narrator spends some time describing 'What Sailors Think and Say', but notably speaks *for* them. There are familiar statements on political (dis) engagement and knowledge: 'This ship was at sea when the Beveridge Report was published in the newspapers: as a result not one rating in ten has any idea of its scope, not one in fifty a detailed knowledge of its provisions' (167–8). Still, it is said that there is a general progressive hope among the sailors that the 1930s will never return, and a brief quotation of a sailor's words:

> What will it be like after the war? [...] Perhaps things will be much the same, possibly a little better: there is sure to be unemployment and uncertainty still, but the readiness with which enormous grants for war-expenditure are authorised gives some promise that money may be found [...] for peace-time schemes to relieve this sort of distress. There will be more education available – 'more of an equal chance for everybody'. (168)

In the third volume, *Corvette Command* (1944), Monsarrat specifically parodies the idea that the Navy is a democracy:

> To H., a friend [...] who wrote inquiring (with an eye to my peace-time interests) whether true democracy reigned on board:
>
> 'Certainly it does,' I replied, 'and not only democracy but fully centralised democracy at that [...]. A select committee sits at the back of the bridge, debating my helm-orders and countermanding any of them which appear to conflict with public welfare. Whether we go to sea or not is determined by popular vote'. (201)

This acknowledges the strong wartime association of the Navy with the democratic, but also clearly feels that the officers/upper classes must in reality lead. The bridge may have (in this instance) a progressive commander – 'are we going to do better this time?' he asks, contemplating the post-war (265) – but he speaks *en haut en bas*.

The social exclusivity of the bridge is reduced in *The Cruel Sea* by the ordinary origins of the Corvette captain, Lieutenant-Commander George Ericson (RNR), and by the lack of social capital and confidence of his two junior officers, Lockhart and Ferraby. However, one notes that *The Cruel Sea* includes near its conclusion an extended critical representation of citizenship education in action on a frigate (HMS *Saltash*, the ship which Ericsson commands after the sinking of his corvette, *Compass Rose*). Set in 1945, the scene mirrors the actual late naval introduction of the approaches pioneered in the army from 1941 onwards, including the use of ABCA materials. The junior officer Vincent has just concluded a lecture on war aims to ratings:

> He shut his note-book with an unconvincing snap, and put on top of it the *Army Bureau of Current Affairs* booklet [...]. The serried eyes looked back at him unblinkingly [...]. They were the eyes of men attending a compulsory lecture on British War Aims. As on so many previous occasions, thought Vincent, the heady magic of ABCA had not worked [...]. A better world, thought Vincent – how could he sum it up in terms which would mean something to a second-class stoker who had been a boiler-maker's apprentice before the war? He knew in his own mind what it involved – the Four Freedoms, the rule of law, an end to tyranny, the overthrow of evil; but he had listed all these things in the course of his lecture [...] and clearly it had meant absolutely nothing'. (2009: 427–8)

Vincent strongly believes in the justice of British War Aims and the Beveridge Plan, and that they herald a more just post-war society in Britain and across the world, but he has no faith that he can communicate 'this crucial question' to the ordinary man.

As Monsarrat's novels suggest, there were clearly different conceptions of the ordinary seaman's capacity, of the depth of class-difference, of the 'people's war' itself, and of its potential for real post-war social change. But some of the widely read naval novels breathed new life into the ancient political metaphor of the 'ship of state', promoted the virtues of the 'ordinary' man and developed interesting hybrid forms of documentary and the novel which made claims of authenticity and relevance on their readers. Soon after July 1945, as S. P. MacKenzie records, many Conservative politicians began blaming the influence of the ABCA on service personnel for Churchill's defeat and the Labour victory. MacKenzie argues that this was to overrate the influence of the ABCA and the impact of military votes, and that there was undoubtedly a decisive swing towards Labour among civilian voters too, attributable to the 'massive changes war brought about in people's lives', which had 'helped alter their socio-political attitudes and assumptions' (1992: 187, 174–90). It seems clear that ABCA itself was part of a range of official programmes which promoted ideas broadly associated with the 'people's war', including the MoI's sponsorship of films such as *In Which We Serve*. Less explored are works of popular fiction/documentary which are also contributions to 'the people's war', and which themselves frequently run into difficulties in dealing with deep-rooted assumptions about class and hierarchy. Curiously, Mallalieu's novel was produced under circumstances which mirror the paradoxical relationship of the wartime government to the 'people's war' –

an idea which it both sponsored and feared. For, as Mallalieu recalls in his autobiography, though the novel was made possible by immediate Royal Naval patronage, the patron was unsure in the end about the novel's overall effect:

> I requested two months' leave to write a third book [...]. I found that I had been appointed Commander's Messenger which meant that for eight hours a day, five days a week, I sat in Commander Reid's outer office, facing a blank wall and typing myself dry. There was no question of hanging about waiting for inspiration. There were no pauses for artistic temperament. I was under 'naval discipline'. I wrote. 'Just one thing,' said Commander Reid. 'I hope this book's going to be broadly favourable to the Navy. Not a whitewash but not a hatchet job either.' [...] I wrote of the slow realisation that, in the navy at least, individuals of different classes and upbringing could remain individuals and yet merge together into one society, a ship's company working for what was recognisably the common good. Differences of rank, some inequality in the share of material comfort, did not divide because we knew that metaphorically as well as literally we were in the same boat. (203–4)

Mallalieu sent the top copy to Gollancz and the carbon to Commander Reid:

> What I got, within two days, was a sharp letter from Commander Reid. 'You said your book would be broadly favourable to the Navy. It isn't.'
> Two days later he wrote again. 'Sorry. I've read it all again and think it's fine.' (1983: 203–4)

Mallalieu's clarity about how he read his own book is evident. The partial commitment of some institutions of the wartime state to a range of ideas and sentiments linked to the notion of a 'people's war' is reflected here in the uncertain response of Commander Reid, a particular reader. But that uncertainty may also reflect the difficulties and contradictions which even authors sympathetic to post-war social reform had in finding new and (somewhat) more inclusive ways of representing class in Britain through focussing on the lower deck. Nevertheless, some works of popular fiction made a distinctive, if voluntary and unofficial, contribution to the people's war and to tentative ideas of a new post-war Britain.

Notes

1   This is despite Neil Rattigan's conclusion that the Navy was the service least 'amenable' to 'democratisation' and his not wholly accurate sense that there was there 'no opportunity to rise from the ranks' (2001: 77–8).

2   See Ian McLaine (1979) and also Hopkins (2012).
3   These pamphlets were published by the Directorate of Army Education as a consolidated edition in 1944, with 'appendices of documents of post-war reconstruction', probably in a large edition, judging by the number still available for sale.
4   Citing letter from Cunningham (8/12/1944), to Sir Henry Markham (Secretary of the Admiralty).
5   Citing Alec Dennis, from material in the IWM archives, However, Pryor also cites more positive responses to citizenship education on some ships – see 420–3.
6   Though Elizabeth Bowen felt that 'Novels about the Navy have been surprisingly few' (*The Tatler*, 19 April 1944: 86), a view echoed by the *Birmingham Daily Gazette*: 'Less has been written about the Navy than any other service in this war' (11 April 1944: 2).
7   Alexander had been First Lord of the Admiralty in the Labour government of June 1929 to August 1931. His reappointment under wartime conditions was surely a gesture towards the representative nature of the new government. Churchill referred to Alexander as his 'favourite socialist'. See Alexander's *Oxford Dictionary of National Biography* entry and also John Tilley's 1995 biography.
8   Song with a complex authorship (four writers shared the royalties). It perhaps dated to 1917, but was first recorded by George Formby in 1940 on Regal 78 record MR3394 (see http://www.traditionalmusic.co.uk/song-midis/Bless_em_All_British_Army_WWII.htm and http://www.fredgodfreysongs.ca/Songs/Bless_em_all.htm). There were numerous variations in the lyrics. My father sang a version he had learnt in the British Army around 1942.
9   Citing William Teeling's *Why Britain Prospers* (Right Book Club, London, 1938: 19).
10 *OED* lists the word's first usage in this sense as 1890, and suggests it may derive from a Yombi word for the lowland gorilla.
11 See Alan Allport (2009), Chapter 1, especially 'Prologue': 1–12.
12 Citing communication from Commodore (D) Western Approaches to C-in-C Western Approaches, 31 July 1944.
13 The periodical *Britannia and Eve* also made the comparison with the same film, 1 July 1944: 41.
14 Page references are to the collected three wartime novellas, published as *Three Corvettes* in 1945.

Works cited

Aldgate, Anthony and Jeffrey Richards. *Britain Can Take It: British Cinema in the Second World War*. London: I.B. Tauris, 2007.

Allen, Trevor. 'Books'. *Britannia and Eve*, 7 January 1944: 43.

Allport, Alan. *Demobbed – Coming Home After the Second World War*. Yale: Yale University Press, 2009.

Bailey, Chris Howard (ed.) *The Life and Times of Admiral Sir Frank Twiss: Social Change in the Royal Navy 1924-1970*. Stroud: Royal Naval Museum Publications/Sutton Publishing, 1996.

Bowen, Elizabeth. 'With Silent Friends'. *The Tatler*, 19 April 1944: 86.

Broad, Roger. *The Radical General: Sir Ronald Adam and Britain's New Model Army 1941-1946*. London: The History Press, 2013.

Calder, Angus. *The People's War: Britain 1939-1945*. London: Pimlico, 2008 [1969].

Chapman, James. *The British at War: Cinema, State and Propaganda 1939-1945*. London: I.B. Tauris, 1998.

Davies, Lieutenant John. *Lower Deck*. London: MacMillan, 1945.

Edgerton, David. *Warfare State, Britain's War Machine: Weapons, Resources and Experts in the Second World War*. Harmondsworth: Penguin, 2012.

Fred Godfrey Songs; http://www.fredgodfreysongs.ca/Songs/Bless_em_all.htm.

Forester, C. S. *The Ship*. London: Michael Joseph, 1943.

Hartley, L. P. 'Literary Lounger' column. *The Sketch*, 3 May 1944: 244.

Holman, Valerie. *Print for Victory: Book Publishing in England 1939-1945*. London: The British Library, 2008.

Hopkins, Chris. 'The Army of the Unemployed: Walter Greenwood's Wartime Novel and the Reconstruction of Britain'. *Keywords - A Journal of Cultural Materialism* 10, October 2012: 103-24.

Howell, David. 'A.V. Alexander, Early Alexander of Hillsborough'. In *Oxford Dictionary of National Biography* online. Oxford: Oxford University Press, 2008.

H. R. G. W. 'Ships and Men at War'. *Birmingham Daily Post*, 21 December 1943: 2.

Lavery, Brian. *Hostilities Only: Training the Wartime Royal Navy*. London: Conway Maritime Books, 2004.

Lavery, Brian. *In Which They Served - the Royal Navy Officer Experience in the Second World War*. London: Conway Maritime Books, 2008.

Lavery, Brian. *All Hands: The Lower Deck of the Royal Navy since 1939*. London: Conway Maritime Books, 2012.

Light, Alison. *Forever England: Femininity, Literature and Conservatism Between the Wars*. London: Routledge, 1991.

Looker, Samuel. 'Books'. *The Chelmsford Chronicle*, 25 February 1944: 3.

MacKenzie, S. P. *Politics and Military Morale: Current Affairs and Citizenship Education in the British Army 1914-1950*. Oxford: Clarendon Press, 1992.

MacKenzie, S. P. *British War Films 1939-45*. London: Continuum, 2001.

Mallalieu, J.P.W. *Very Ordinary Seaman*. London: Gollancz, 1944.

Mallalieu, J.P.W. *On Larkhill*. London: Allison & Busby, 1983.

McLaine, Ian. *Ministry of Morale: Home Front Morale and the Ministry of Information in World War II*. London: Allen & Unwin, 1979.

Monsarrat, Nicholas. *H.M. Corvette*. London: Cassell, 1943.

Monsarrat, Nicholas. *East Coast Corvette*. London: Cassell, 1943.

Monsarrat, Nicholas. *Corvette Command*. London: Cassell, 1944.

Monsarrat, Nicholas. *Three Corvettes*. London: Cassell, 1945.
Monsarrat, Nicholas. *The Cruel Sea*. London: Cassell, 1951.
Munton, Alan. *English Fiction of the Second World War*. London: Faber and Faber, 1989.
Murphy, Robert. *British Cinema and the Second World War*. London: Continuum, 2001.
Prysor, Glyn. *Citizen Sailors: The Royal Navy in the Second World War*. Harmondsworth: Penguin, 2012.
Quennell, Peter. *Daily Mail*, 15 April 1944: 2.
Rattigan, Neil. *This is England: British Film and the People's War, 1939–1945*. London: Associated University Presses, 2001.
Rayner, Jonathan. *The Naval War Film: Genre, History, National Cinema*. Manchester: Manchester University Press, 2007.
'Rod'. *The Traditional Music Library*, British Army World War Two page; http://www.traditionalmusic.co.uk/song-midis/Bless_em_All_British_Army_WWII.htm.
Rodgers, Terrence. 'The Right Book Club: Text Wars, Modernity and Cultural Politics in the Late Thirties'. *Literature & History*, third series 12 (2), 2003: 1–15.
Shaw, Frank, *The Convoy Goes Through*. London: W.H. Allen, 1942.
Stubbs, Bernard. *The Navy at War*. London: Faber and Faber, 1941.
'Tackline'. In *Holiday Sailor*. London: Hollis and Carter, 1944.
The Royal Navy Today. London: Odhams, 1942.
Thorne, Anthony. *I'm a Stranger Here Myself*. London: Heinemann, 1943.
Tilley, John. *Churchill's Favourite Socialist – a Life of A.V. Alexander*. Manchester: Holyoake Press, 1995.

5

Feeling Political: Elizabeth Bowen in the 1940s

Karen Schaller

They'd much better not feel at all till they feel normal. The first thing must be, to get everything organized.

Bowen, 'I Hear You Say So' (850)

In Elizabeth Bowen's 1945 short story 'I Hear You Say So', a nightingale sings into a warm London night a week after VE day. Its song shapes the narrative: rather than contract around a single set of characters, or plot, the text alights momentarily, in turn, on those who hear the nightingale's song.[1] First Violet, who mistakes it for a wireless broadcast, and her army friend Fred who believes it must really be a thrush. Then a family of two sisters, their children, and one of their husbands, who, recently returned from the war, tries to tell them about nightingales singing on the Front. But his stories are drowned out by Kathleen's insensitivity: 'It's all one to me what I hear now, I tell you frankly, provided it isn't a siren' (849). Friends Naomi and Mary, prompted by Naomi's revelation that nightingales listen, question each other's secrets and disclosures while the bird sings. And recent widow Ursula is woken, by the nightingale, from the sleepwalking induced by the telegram of her husband's death. In the silence after the nightingale's 'last note dropped', she remembers 'disjected lines of poetry, invocations' (852). Looking down at the carpet on which she has awoken, she wonders if there is a secret in its pattern: 'Naturally', the narrator tells us, 'it was too dark to see' (852). What we are left with is a text whose shape is determined by the effects of listening: speculations, suspicions, losses, reminiscences, anxieties and pleasures felt by those who hear the nightingale's song.

Bowen's story signals the kinds of 'listening in' that Allan Hepburn attributes to her work in the 1940s: 'like other Londoners who lived through the Blitz, she was attuned to the changes wrought by radio as a mechanism for disseminating news and culture' (2010: 11). But what does 'I Hear You Say So' tune into?

Hepburn notes that what resonated with Bowen about radio was its 'emotive effect' (11). Later, in her 1969 review of Angus Calder's *The People's War*, she would remark that during the war, '[i]n the main, the voice was mightier than the pen. Sound made for community of sensation, was emotive (which was required)' (Lee 1986: 184). Given the frequency with which the nightingale in 'I Hear You Say So' calls to other transmission technologies – telegrams, sirens, floodlights – the story extends 'emotive effect' beyond radio into the full theatre of technological transmissions defining war life. More notably, however, it suspects the nightingale itself as being one of these technologies, one that does not simply transmit but effects questions of feeling. The nightingale's song does, indeed, make 'for community of sensation', but that community is not passive, nor unaware of how such transmissions might make them feel: the listeners in Bowen's story are agents, in their own ways – they ignore, they interrogate, they interrupt, they interpret. Indeed, we should be careful not to confuse that community with a public ignorant of the use of transmissions to organize their feelings, especially given Naomi's objections to the nightingale's song:

> Apart from anything, it's too soon. Much too soon, after a war like this. Even Victory's nearly been too much. There ought not to have been a nightingale in the same week. The important thing is that people should go carefully. They'd much better not feel at all till they feel normal. The first thing must be, to get everything organized. (850)

Here, the public organization of personal feeling is considered so ordinary that even the possibility that a nightingale's song has been orchestrated does not feel, to Naomi, extraordinary. Yet, in collecting its 'figures of listeners' (850), the nightingale's centralizing affects should not be mistaken as endorsement for a spirit of collectivity, nor for the consolatory promise of normalcy: what makes Ursula feel 'profound happiness' (852) is also – as for the unnamed man who 'could not outdistance [its] throbs' (848) – an inescapable threat.

Recently, Sinéad Sturgeon has argued that the nightingale's song 'projects a fragile and evocative symbol of hope for the renewal of a war-ravaged world' (92). For Sturgeon, Bowen's representation of the natural world in her war stories neutralizes the political concerns of the human world, realigning us with nature: 'this engagement with the natural world as ontological other sidesteps geopolitical borders and long-standing vexatious questions of national identities to put new emphasis on ecological relations' (91). Those relations, as figured in the nightingale, 'promise a restoration of harmonious relations between the human and the natural world' (92). As Sturgeon points out, however, that possibility 'remains qualified' by the final line of the story (93). I am less inclined to read the nightingale's song as a sign of nature's force but, rather, as a destabilization of the boundary between the natural and political worlds. By figuring the nightingale's song as a transmission, one that has the capacity to reorganize the lives, feelings, and indeed subjectivities of those who hear it, the story signals, instead, to the capacity we have to engage what seems most natural as a technology of war. That includes the feelings we think of as our own, and the subjectivity they supposedly sign. At the end of the story, the scrap of poetry Ursula remembers is from Keats's 'Ode to a Nightingale': '*I cannot see what flowers are at my feet*' (852). The intertextuality here should disturb any recourse to a natural world to which one might return. As a poem preoccupied with the relation between the 'I' and the feelings that confirm its presence, Keats's fascination with subjectivity is, also, a historical artefact in Bowen's world: 'disjected', Keats's invocation is dismembered. As Lis Christensen notes, the story reverses the movement of Keats poem: 'In the Ode, it is the bird that moves […]. In Bowen's story the nightingale – or, rather, its song – remains in the same place' (2001: 19). In these movements we should, however, also read a reversal of the version of subjectivity for which Keats's nightingale sings: rather than confirm the 'I' desired by a romantic subjectivity, its emotive effects are simultaneously centralizing and decentring (see Bennett and Royle 156).

In this chapter I situate Bowen, in the 1940s, as a writer who was acutely preoccupied with feeling. This was a career-long interest of hers: throughout the 1920s and 1930s she had already attributed to cinema, to lighting and, indeed, to the short story itself the significance of sensation, feeling, and emotion. My contention in this chapter, then, is that her interest in the 'emotive effects' of the 1940s should be read not as an inaugural interest but as a refined attunement that takes on particular kinds of valance, registering a critical awareness of, and orientation to, the official uses of feeling. Although criticism on her work from the period has tended to focus on her 1948 novel *The Heat of the Day*, I am primarily interested in how the mediations of feeling at work in 'I Hear You Say So' can direct us to an earlier concern in her short stories and essays with official interest in the public's feelings. Beginning with an overview of developments in recent Bowen scholarship to situate her work in the 1940s, I provide a brief discussion of how developments in the past few years speak to Bowen's status and ways of reading her now, and how this relates to my own approach to Bowen. I then identify what she was working on in the 1940s, highlighting recently collected material before turning to her stories 'Unwelcome Idea' (1940) and 'Careless Talk' (1941). My method throughout this chapter is to pay close attention to selected writing to show how it engages with the politics of feeling at work in the textual cultures developed by the Ministry of Information. My interest in how Bowen was tuning into the political uses of feeling represents a departure from existing scholarship: while other readers of her stories are correct to note that her writing is sensitive to how life in the period felt, her representations *of* these feelings should not be conflated with a psychological realism. By putting her writing in dialogue with the cultures of feeling being actively produced and shaped by the Ministry of Information, her representations of feeling from the period should be understood as textual strategies alert to the government's interest in the political uses of, and for, feeling. This contention is, in part, an address to some of the ways *The Heat of the Day* has been read recently, particularly the tendency to engage the novel's love plot to preserve a distinction between private and public, personal and collective, by reading the novel as one in which love is either made political by the war, or war is seen as a political outcome of internal conflict. While we might now readily deconstruct the discourses of feeling underpinning Hermione Lee's ascription, in 1999, of the novel as a 'woman's view of a male world of intelligence' (168), we can see their persistence in recent appraisals of the novel as one in which its political critique is perceived to lie in an opposition between the historical and personal, political and subjective. Ana Ashraf, for example, writes that the *Heat of the Day* 'reveals the inadequacies of institutionalized mechanisms for the corroboration of stories' (121), while Annette Oxindine argues that the novel's instabilities are countered by feelings of regeneration: she reads *The Heat of the Day* as articulating a 'salvific turn' that 'resists dissolution' (200). As I go on to show, however, by the time Bowen wrote *The Heat of the Day* no feeling should be either distinguished from the public realm, or considered recuperable to a private terrain. As Bennett and Royle argue, '*The Heat of the Day* relentlessly picks up, picks at, undoes assumptions of personal identity, and thus undoes the values of all constructions of the individual, social, political, erotic and ethical on which they rest' (1995: 89). The work I look at adds feeling to this list.

Bowen is no longer a neglected writer, and her current critical status is indebted to several major late-twentieth and early-twenty-first-century critical interventions by critics such as Maud Ellmann, Phyllis Lassner, Bennett and Royle, Neil Corcoran, renée c. hoogland, Lis Christensen and Heather Bryant Jordan, as well as biographers Victoria Glendinning and Hermione Lee.[2] Following these, there has been a substantial growth in Bowen studies: Allan Hepburn has continued to add to the Bowen oeuvre available to her scholars through his four edited collections of materials from archives held at the Harry Ransom Centre;

Patricia Laurence has published a new biography (2019); Bowen's *Collected Stories* has been reissued with a new introduction by John Banville (2019); the Elizabeth Bowen Society was formed in 2017 and has subsequently established and published three editions of *Elizabeth Bowen Review* and held two conferences; and Jessica Gildersleeve and Patricia Smith published *Elizabeth Bowen: Theory, Thought and Things* (2019), the most recent study dedicated to Bowen's work. While too numerous to count, individual chapters and articles on Bowen, as well as doctoral theses, have proliferated far beyond what was available when I first began reading her in 2007. While Bowen scholarship is still characterized by debates about categorization, periodization, identity and ideological frames, recent work suggests a renewed critical desire to recognize how her writing frays at both the efficacy of such approaches and the divergences so often effected by critical friction between them. Indeed, Gildersleeve and Smith position the work in their edited collection as a commitment to Bowen's language, writing and thinking as points of difficulty unresolvable by recourse to the categories or historical trajectories underpinning our critical narratives about twentieth-century literature. Given my own interest in Bowen's theorizations of affect, and the short story, it is promising, too, how many of Gildersleeve and Smith's contributors attend to Bowen's short stories, and/or her preoccupations with feeling: Aimee Gasston reads Bowen's use of fashioning in her short fiction; renée c. hoogland her queer adolescent structures of feeling; Ulrika Maude Bowen's sentient objects and Laurie Johnson the inter-objectivity of Bowen's Blitz stories. Phyllis Lassner once remarked that the short stories tend to be treated as 'glosses' on the novels' concerns (xi). This is beginning to change, but we should notice that critical attention to the short fiction still tends to contract around those written 1941-5 and collected in *The Demon Lover and Other Stories* (1945), particularly 'The Happy Autumn Fields', 'The Demon Lover' and 'Mysterious Kôr'.[3] Although this concentration lends scholars of the period the advantage of a critical corpus on a short story oeuvre that remains otherwise understudied, it does also mean that at times critics have attributed aesthetic and theoretical preoccupations visible across her oeuvre to the effects of the war alone. That said, Bowen's writing from the first part of the 1940s has played a substantial role in her critical revival: writing in the New England Review in 2003, Ellmann remarked that the 'most fecund area of Bowen scholarship at present focuses on her writings of World War II, and belongs to a wider reconsideration of the cultural implications of the Blitz' (156).[4]

This scholarship continues to be dominated by *The Heat of the Day*, the *Demon Lover* stories mentioned above, and a few others, most notably 'Look at all those Roses' and 'Summer Night', both published in her fourth short story collection *Look at All Those Roses* (1941). Critical analyses of the stories tend to assert the effects of the war on her literary formations of subjectivity, and most contextualize the feelings circulating in these as unique to the war, and specific to the effects of trauma and witnessing; this also means that these stories tend to be engaged to endorse a literary trajectory in her own work that substantiates a shift from a late modernist, to post-modernist, sensibility. Despite the range and variation in her short story oeuvre from the period, the complexity of their representations is often subsumed either within the concerns of the few noted, or – to use Lassner's word – as 'glosses' to *The Heat of the Day*. But, as with all of Bowen's work, her stories from the period betray neat categorizations, and have lent themselves as much to the 'uncertain I' that Neil Corcoran attributes to the war's obliteration of self (168), as they do hoogland's more consolatory interpretation that the stories 'defend against disintegration' (110). My approach is somewhat different: rather than historicize Bowen's inventions of feeling by locating the origin of their radicality in the war, I see these in continuation with, rather than diverging from, the preoccupation already established in her earliest work with how fiction can theorize feeling. This approach extends Bennett and Royle's interest in Bowen's dissolutions (1995). But I am also indebted to Ellmann's study *Elizabeth Bowen: The Shadow across the Page*, which shows us how Bowen 'thinks in fiction […] ideas are inseparable from her objects, settings, plots, and characters, and from the oddities of her unnerving syntax' (7). Bowen's fiction is also thinking about feeling. Consider, for example, her 1944 broadcast and essay 'Panorama of the Novel' featured in Hepburn (2010: 135–44).[5] Applying a near-surgical precision to the thinking about feeling shaping literature from 1918 to the 1940s, it reveals a critical acuity to literary representations of, and aesthetics about, emotion. Bowen appraises the aesthetics of those 'schooled in the rigours of objectivity', such as H. G. Wells, Arnold Bennett and Somerset Maugham, as unaffected by the feeling of their climate: 'They had learned – and, consequently, felt reassured – that nothing in human experience was without precedent […]. Not that they did not feel the impact of the war, but they had already succeeded in not entertaining any feeling that could not be reported' (136). Woolf, Richardson, Joyce and Lawrence 'emphasise interior being rather than the exterior forces that motivate feeling and knowledge' (137). And in those works, written after 1930, 'religious and political sentiments have contributed equally to make the English novel dynamic and to rescue it from the psychological cramp that threatened to overtake it towards the end of the preceding decade' (142). Bowen's orientation to feeling, here, exemplifies her alertness, at mid-century, to a history of thinking about feeling inflecting these literary, critical and aesthetic inheritances. How, we might wonder, would she situate her own writing? She doesn't say, of course – but between her assessment of the writers represented by Wells, and those represented by Woolf, we should recognize an aesthetic that untethers emotion from experience merely to be reported or limited to subjectivity and interior being. As I have argued elsewhere, Bowen's career as a writer not only coincided with cultural preoccupations with, and interests in, the proliferation of theories of self and feeling in psychoanalysis and sexology, but was contemporaneous with, and critically oriented to, literary contributions to this thinking (see Schaller 2013). In her 1940s fiction, then, we find a writer who is not only informed by the history of dialogues about feeling circulating in the historical, intellectual and cultural climates in which she had been writing for two decades, but one who thinking theoretically about this through her fiction. By the 1940s her writing was thinking, very carefully, about the politics, and political uses, of feeling.

While more than a few critics have lamented that Bowen wrote only the one novel, throughout the 1940s Bowen produced a remarkable amount of writing. Although *Collected Stories* (first published by Jonathan Cape in 1980) included twenty-eight from the period, Hepburn's 2008 edition of archival materials discovers six more, including one published as part of an appeal for the Yugoslav Relief Society in 1946. Despite these additions to her oeuvre, the pattern of the decade remains unchanged: she wrote most of her short stories from the period by its midpoint, after which her short story writing waned. Throughout, Bowen also wrote a great deal for broadcast, ranging from pieces about literary figures, to book reviews, and reflections on writing for the BBC Third Programme, Home Service, and Overseas Services for China and the Pacific (Hepburn 2010: 344–78). She also dedicated tremendous energy to non-fiction: in 1942 she published her history of her family, and family home, *Bowen's Court*; her memoir of early childhood *Seven Winters*; and *English Novelists*, a collection of literary criticism. Hepburn points out that by the mid-1940s, her output, though impressive, was also a source of anxiety:

> Throughout the 1940s, her reputation grew further because of unstinting hard work: she wrote essays for money; she wrote in aid of charities. She wrote to pay for repairs to the house on Clarence Terrace, which was twice damaged by bombs during the war. Her output of short stories and non-fiction was prodigious, but she scarcely had time for novels. Solicited from all sides, she hired a secretary to deal with business correspondence. Secretarial help alone could not stem the tide of queries and demands. On 3 July 1946, Spencer Curtis Brown, Bowen's

literary agent since 1927, advised her to direct all business, not just negotiations for books, through his office. Requests for articles, broadcasts, and adaptations, he proposed, could be handled by his staff. He played on Bowen's worries about sacrificing fiction-writing to energy- dispersing non-fiction. (2008: 5)

Hepburn also discovers essays about London: 'Regent's Park and St. John's Wood' (commissioned for a book about London); 'Calico Windows', which was part of a 1944 fundraising publication for the Soho Hospital and takes its title from the practice of covering blown-out windows with fabric; and 'Britain in Autumn', which, as I discuss later, was an early version of what would eventually be published as 'London, 1940' in *Collected Impressions* (1950). After the war, Bowen's essays addressed how to resume life at 'home'. In 'Opening of the House', she writes: 'But what about us – about the sensations and problems involved in our coming back? The return, however calmly one tries to take it, cannot but be in the nature of ordeal. How can it not drag things up?' (Hepburn 2010: 133). Post-war, Bowen travelled widely as a journalist and literary figure, reporting on the 1946 Paris Peace Conference for the *Cork Examiner* and lecturing as part of the British Council's work in Austria, Hungary, Czechoslovakia and West Germany. These trips gave rise to a number of essays and broadcasts.

Bowen was actively involved with the war effort as an Air Raid Precautions warden. Hepburn quotes a 1959 interview with Bowen to indicate her attitude towards civil responsibility: 'Just as in an air raid, if you were a warden, which I was, you stump up and down the streets making a clatter with the boots you were wearing, knowing you can't prevent a bomb falling, but thinking, "At any rate I'm taking part in this, I may be doing some good"' (2008: 12). And, as is vividly documented by existing scholarship on Bowen's life and work – especially criticism on *The Heat of the Day* – during this time Bowen volunteered to work for the Ministry of Information, reporting on Ireland. While she was open about this work, Hepburn shows her employment with the ministry didn't end with peace, and may not have been limited to reports on Ireland as has usually been assumed by her readers:

> While writing dispatches about the [Paris] conference, Bowen may also have been gathering intelligence. Bowen never made a secret of being employed by the Ministry of Information in the early part of the war. She casually mentions her work for the government in various publicity notices, and articles in *Collected Impressions* are identified as Ministry of Information contributions. Critics have commented at length about these activities in 1940–2 [...] Tax records, however, reveal that the Ministry of Information also paid Bowen between 1944 and

1947. In 1944-5, she earned £115 from the Ministry. The next year, she earned £117.12.0. At the end of her employment in 1946-7, she received a mere £21.3.0 (HRC 12.5-6). Whereas intelligence-gathering in 1940-2 took her to Eire, the nature of her work between 1944 and 1947 remains unspecified. (13)

Documenting Ireland's neutrality and public attitudes during the war put Bowen in a unique position to understand the ways in which the British government was actively monitoring and administering climates of feeling throughout the decade.[6] Indeed her writing about Ireland following her 1940 and 1941 trips to Dublin for the Ministry evidences a very careful attention to feelings: in 'Eire', her 1941 essay for *The Spectator*, Bowen describes Irish neutrality as 'inflammatory' to a Britain 'with not much idle angry feeling to spare' (1986: 30). The essay works, in many ways, to broker feeling for a country perceived, she writes, as 'passively hostile' in its neutrality, and portrayed by the British press with an attention to the 'unfeeling ostentation' of 'the blaze of Dublin city lights' and 'hams, steaks and butter given luscious prominence by journalists' (30). She intimates that such British reports are, themselves, small acts of aggression, and Bowen's remarks on the irresponsibility of these journalists imply her own to be an adjudication. Neutrality might be a difficult position to understand, she admits, but it should not be conflated with being unaffected, and she points to the censorship which allows 'freedom of public speech, but no freedom of reporting' (32). The official position of what she terms a 'dispassionate press' makes for 'the sense of a ban on *feeling*' (33). Yet, she reassures her readers, that does not negate the compassion of the Irish, who feel for the British on the Home Front a 'horror and pity that are a good deal more than perfunctory' (33). Eire, she asserts, *is* experiencing shortage and insecurity: '[e]verywhere there is sombreness, and anxiety' (34). Bowen's report on feeling is not mere documentation. In it she explicitly articulates, and performs, the political significance of what is felt, and how such feeling is handled, for Anglo-Irish relations: 'Time and tact, on which there are many demands already, must go to disposing of rumours hostile to this' (31).

Tact is a key preoccupation in Bowen's 1940 story 'Unwelcome Idea' (1999: 573-7), in which two women meet after shopping on a tram in Dublin.[7] While the text's attention to their parcels might appear trivial, these textures contextualize the political charge of the story's atmosphere. Miss Kevin, who, with a 'virgin detachment', has 'kept thumbing her sales parcels', finally undoes one: '"Listen"', she says, '"isn't this a pretty delaine?"' (575). In feeling the fabric, Miss Kevin's touch locates the story: 'She runs the end of a fold between her finger and thumb. "It drapes sweetly. I've enough for a dress and a bolero. It's French: they say we won't get any more now"' (575). The war's impressions on Miss Kevin and Mrs Kearney – that they won't get French delaine, or 'that Coty scent' anymore (575) – is both tactful, in its recognition that neutrality does not mean being untouched, and also, potentially, tactless in these characters' limited apprehension of the feeling of war. Written the year before 'Eire', that essay's understanding of tact is something 'Unwelcome Idea' appears to still be grappling with. Indeed, the ending, in which Miss Kevin and Mrs Kearney depart with promises of 'Happy days to us all' (577), suggests comfort and cheer, yet ends with a bizarre image of Mrs Kearney, hands too full to hold her periodical as she prepares to descend: 'Mrs. Kearney, near the top of the stairs, is preparing to bite on the magazine. "Go on!" she says. "I'll be seeing you before then"' (577). Uncomfortably loaded, the phrase threatens to detonate the cheerful resolution with which the story ends.

'Unwelcome Idea' suggests a national character apprehensive about how, or what, to feel – speculation about how to act, and what to do in case of evacuation or invasion forms most of Mrs Kearney and Miss Kevin's conversation, while the authorities remain an unspecified 'they'. But it also registers a population under intense observation. Indeed the narrative perspective is capable of both sweeping comprehension and minute detection. The text opens, as if like a search light, by panning the landscape and villas of Dublin bay, observing that 'in the distance, floating across the bay, buildings glitter out of the heat-haze on the neck to Howth' (573). Nothing escapes this attention, not even 'an inner door left open [that] lets you see a flash of sea through a house' (573). Sharpening with a telescopic focus from the 'point' at which 'you see the whole bay open' the text searches out the tiniest of sensory details: '[h]ousewives with burnt bare arms' (573), ladies who 'squeezed between the kerb and the shops' (573), and even children that 'by themselves curl their toes in their plimsoles' (574). Two pages are spent securing the movements of Dublin's population, no matter how big or small, before turning to the ladies' conversation. How might her readers have received this story's attentions? If, on the one hand, it represents Ireland to English readers as a nation that does not grasp the feeling of war, it also represents Ireland as a territory that is far from neutral. Omniscience here functions as a form of surveillance: someone is listening in. Someone is watching. But are 'they' an authority to be trusted? While Bowen's story is about the climate of feeling in Ireland, it's also a representation of the intensity of official interest in that feeling. We might read the detonative effect of that final line as a charge, to her readers, to take notice, themselves, of the extent to which their own sentiments, and senses, are under scrutiny. The image of a magazine is, we should note, a repetition of Mrs Kearney's introduction when, 'in a slither of rather ungirt parcels, including a dress-box, with a magazine held firmly between her teeth, she clutches her way up the stairs to the top' (574). Reading it twice over, the image is explosive in its intimations of weaponization in the textual culture she holds in her mouth.

The next year, in October of 1941, *The New Yorker* published Bowen's story about four friends meeting up for lunch at a restaurant in London. Joanna, who lives in the country after her London house was bombed, has come back to London for the first time in four months to visit. Originally titled 'Everything's Frightfully Interesting', the story was published four years later in *The Demon Lover and Other Stories* under a new name: 'Careless Talk'. Yet it does not need its reference to the 'Careless Talk Costs Lives' propaganda campaign of the period to signal its engagement with life in England during the war. Only four pages long, the narrative is saturated with the kinds of detail that characterized life on the Home Front. References to evacuees, foreign strangers and bombed houses share the page with off-hand comments about cigarettes obtained on the black market – '"I just got twenty out of my hairdresser,"' says Mary (752) –, the rationing of butter such that a 'shilling sized portion' is 'spread tenderly' (752) and, of course, the value of three eggs brought from the country and left with the waiter for safekeeping. It's a story that voices its attunement to the lived reality it represents, and indeed its use of voice and tone to do so is notable.

Hepburn attributes to 'Careless Talk' a combination of 'social banter and wartime news in a swirl of voices so dense that information pertinent to the Allied cause – evacuees in the country, the Poles and the Free French in London – mingles with harmless chatter about eggs and good restaurants. No talk can be too careful, especially in the charged atmosphere of war' (2010: 3–4). Stephania Porcelli uses the story to show how *The Heat of The Day* refers to the Ministry of Information's propaganda posters, arguing that printed propaganda 'play a major role in Bowen's representation of wartime London' (108). According to Patrick Deer, the speakers of Bowen's story 'inhabit a cheerful, self-censoring vacancy, deriving an erotic buzz from their proximity to power, but robbed of any substantive communication by their shallow coded exchanges' (182). Celine Magot also focuses on talk to suggest that food shortages infer a 'word shortage' that charges the story's chatter with the threat of annihilation: 'Existential anguish is expressed through the constant tension between abundance and lack—concerning not only the food supply in a context of shortage, but more interestingly the abundance of words resulting in a lack of meaning and loss of substance' (2). These readings show how Bowen's writing registered the official practices shaping the public's attention and conduct. If, for example, we hadn't already suspected the work of a censor in the text's frequent use of ellipses and dashes, we are reminded to by the repetition, throughout the story, of Mary's last name: 'Dash'. We might notice its resemblance to the Ministry of Information's use of troping, as, for example, in the July 1940 government announcement in *Picture Post* calling for the silence of Mr Secrecy Hush Hush, Mr Knowall, Miss Leaky Mouth, Miss Teacup Whisper, Mr Pride in Prophecy, and Mr Glumpot.[8]

Censorship in 'Careless Talk' takes the form of self-censoring, and the talk in the story is as much about what they stop themselves from saying, as what is actually said. Of course, that was the point of the campaign – to administer talk and eliminate the spread of damaging rumours. But the story also suggests that this culture is producing new identities, new divisions and new alliances: every time Joanna engages her old friends in meaningful conversation, she is interrupted (or they are, by one another). The censor is not an external agent, here, but one of them – indeed all of them, except Joanna. The cheerfully – or we might say, carefully – care-less talk makes Joanna feel like a foreigner even while it promises belonging to a collective identity through mutual effort. That 'swirl' of talk is her immersion in a culture, and practice, of double-talk that speaks while appearing to say nothing. Yet it's also a realization that these cultures are actively shaping, re-narrativizing and indeed re-writing the 'people' of the People's War and using feeling to do so. As historian Joanna Fox has pointed out, this particular propaganda campaign produced a tense public atmosphere by making people feel like no one could be trusted, and 'ran the risk of disrupting the wartime master narrative of the "People's War"' (936). Feeling was crucial to the campaign: Fox remarks that it actively promoted a culture of 'distrust, suspicion, and fear, where such aspects of "ordinary" life as conversational gossip were presented as dangerous [it] cast the entire population as potential suspects who lacked discipline, and whose words and private thoughts required control' (937). Feelings were seen by the government as volatile, and as a real threat. But the government was not only transmitting, through its propaganda, messages about how to feel: it was actively gauging, shaping, monitoring and recalibrating how it managed morale, mood and feeling. In 1940 the ministry established a Home Intelligence Division with a former BBC producer, as Fox explains, in order to 'provide a basis for publicity [and] to provide an assessment of home morale' (940). Daily reports telephoned in by a network of Regional Information Officers offered excerpts from things they'd overheard at work, during their commute, or in pubs 'to report the feelings of those with whom they came into contact' (941).⁹ But Fox also fingers surveys undertaken by the BBC in Listener, 'postal censors', and Mass Observation, and we might think back to that image of the magazine in 'Unwelcome Idea': another means of 'assessment' was textual culture itself. This alters our sense of the flow of information effected by the period's textual cultures – they were not simply administering the public through passive consumption, but by getting people to participate in documenting themselves. Throughout these reports we can see an acute anxiety about feeling, and its potential to disrupt official business. Such findings were instrumental in the development of the careless talk campaign, which intentionally altered the tone of propaganda from 'comfort' to 'command'. Unlike earlier propaganda, which was about boosting morale, Fox points out that the tactics of the careless talk materials were designed to compel behaviours by producing feelings of shame, guilt and condemnation as an intentional means of disciplining the public (943).¹⁰ Writing in 2012, Fox notices that the campaign has received relatively little scholarly attention. Although often understood in our popular imaginary as a campaign about information, or about knowledge – what you are allowed or not allowed to say, what is frivolous detail or what might be damaging intelligence – her account is suggestive of the extent to which this aspect of the period's textual culture was primarily concerned with constructing particular kinds of feeling as a means of public control. However, we can also use these materials to notice that it worked by representing, to the public, how one's feelings, themselves, operated as signs of a patriotic citizen on the Home Front, or an enemy within. As Fox records, on July 12, 1940, Minister of Information Duff Cooper named this threat in *The Times*: 'Those who spread doom and despondency do definite harm: they are hurting the cause, they are delaying the victory; they are *enemies* – unintentional enemies probably – *but enemies of our side*' (944). Indeed, only a month earlier, on 4 June, the MoI's Home Morale Emergency Committee issued a report to the Policy Committee identifying five 'menaces to public calm', three of which were fear, suspicion and class feeling (957).¹¹

This allows us to situate 'Everything's Frightfully Interesting'/Careless Talk' as a text in which there is *no* frivolous detail, or vacant conversation. Language is not evacuated of meaning, so much as charged with the official effects of these campaigns. In Mary Dash's bright tones, we should hear the public performance of the kinds of feeling meant to secure one as, personally, part of the careful collective working to achieve British victory, in a climate of emotional regulation, policing, and discipline. Cheerfulness was an officially acceptable feeling – the Home Security League in Southampton, for example, described their mandate as helping to 'maintain a high standard of public morale by personal cheerfulness and by killing rumours' (Fox: 940). Indeed, in one of their earliest posters, the MoI officially recognized cheerfulness as a patriotic feeling: 'YOUR COURAGE, YOUR CHEERFULNESS, YOUR RESOLUTION – WILL BRING US VICTORY.'[12] Here, as Fox explains, affect is crucial to the ways in which citizenship was being rewritten and narrativized at the intersection of individual and collective, personal and public feeling, not simply to orient the public towards a collective feeling, but to actively create in their imaginations the feeling that there *was* such a 'people's community' (946) to which one might be oriented, and belong. We might, borrowing Sara Ahmed's observations about the way propaganda sticks feelings together in order to imagine the coherence of a national body, notice that the commas work here to bring into association feelings that appear to be of different orders: the feminine, and personal, is brought into alignment with national valour (2004). Such language also works through its repetitions of a 'you' that culminates in an 'us' with which subjects can identify and align. Yet in the dash, whose punctuation keeps apart, even as it joins, we might also read the persistence of an awkward division between 'you' and 'us' in these early attempts to reconfigure public perceptions of national belonging, and responsibility. Imagination was not just affected by the war, then, but was a front line for the Ministry of Information, who wanted the public to re-imagine the front as not a foreign location but a territory at home consisting of restaurants, cafes, homes, and even the feelings and responses of the British public. As Fox details, these campaigns actively worked to cultivate in the individual a form of citizenship that imagined everyone as on the front line because *anyone* could be an enemy, even oneself, if they deviated from officially acceptable feelings (946).[13] But advances on this front are not limited to the enemy bombs; for, as Fox demonstrates, what worried the ministry about the effectiveness of this project was that the government was being imagined by the public as rather uncomfortably like the enemy. By empowering the public to be suspicious, these campaigns risked subjecting the authorities' organization of public sentiment to the same scrutiny. Far from forge a coherent 'we', the 'your' and 'us' of these campaigns risked eliding distinctions between a fascist enemy and an authoritarian state. By recognizing how intentionally multi-valanced the Ministry of Information's campaigns were, we can recognize in Bowen's story both a representation of the lived realities of this reshaping of personal feelings as a territory of war *and* a performance of these tactics and the tensions they produced. In her post-script to *The Demon Lover and Other Stories*, Bowen wrote, 'I see war (or should I say I feel war?) more as a territory than as a page of history' (1986: 95). Territory, in this sense, is not only geographical or temporal, but personal: human subjectivity is, itself, a front.

We might think differently, then, about the harmless chatter, and the things – those apparently trivial details – Bowen's story takes as its object, especially the eggs that open and close the story. Feelings of care and suspicion gather around these. These are not just eggs, but objects of intense feeling:

> 'How good, how kind, *how* thoughtful!' said Mary Dash. 'I can't tell you what a difference they will make! And you brought them like this all the way from Shepton Mallet in the train?' She looked helpless. 'Where do you think I had better put them? This table's going to be terribly small for four, and *think*, if one of Eric Farnham's sweeping gesticulations ... ' She signalled a waiter. 'I want these put somewhere for me till the end of lunch. *Carefully*,' she added. 'They are three eggs.' (750)

By delaying their identification while Mary Dash effuses for eight lines about the as-yet-unnamed objects, the text does not simply represent Mary's feelings about the eggs, but makes them objects of our attention too, orienting us, and instructing us, as Mary instructs the waiter, to see them as objects of care. Throughout, the eggs are never far from Mary's attention, or the readers: her speculations about the suspicious attention they might attract keeps them on our radar. The story closes with further iterations of the proximity between suspicion and care. In the final lines she wonders where they've been put by the waiter to whom she entrusted their safe-keeping: 'I don't know how I'd feel if I lost three eggs' (754). Certainly, Mary's remark recognizes the reality of rationing: when available, egg rations could be as low as one fresh egg per adult per week. But her revelation about what she wants to use them for seems, given this reality, remarkably careless: 'all the time we've been talking I've been thinking up a new omelette I want to make' (754). We might see in Mary's remark tinder for the volatility of 'class feeling' recorded as a menace to public calm in the MoI's Home Morale Emergency Committee reports. But we can also see that the story's attention to eggs is not merely representing them as objects of feeling, but as objects whose meaning is changed because of the feelings produced by their rationing. Because food was such a sore spot for the British public, those feelings were especially subject to scrutiny and management by the government. Food resources needed to be very carefully organized, making the way people felt and imagined food, eating and rationing another major threat to security. We can see this in the Food Control Committee Records and the Kitchen Front

Broadcasts.[14] The focus on Britain's kitchens reminds us that the front line the public was being encouraged to imagine was not simply a public territory but also a domestic one. Daily 'Kitchen Front' broadcasts produced by the Ministry of Food's Public Relations branch gave cookery instructions (especially important given things like powdered milk and powdered eggs) and recipes specially tailored to rationing. But these were also instructing the public about how to feel about these foods and their administration. Given the volume of material in this archive, the Ministry of Food was dedicating considerable resource to this aspect of its Public Relations work. Consider, for example, their broadcasts on household (powdered) milk, designed to tackle the kinds of discontents worried about in the careless talk campaign:

> Good morning. I've had a lot of letters telling me what a hardship it is to have only two pints of milk a week, which is the allowance for ordinary consumers at the moment. Well believe me, I know from personal experience what it means, and I don't like it any more than you do. This morning I'm going to answer some of your questions. (MAF 102/7: 9)

The broadcast goes on to explain why, despite the growth in milk production, rations still prioritize some consumers: women who have had, or are about to have, babies; children; and invalids. Public suspicions about the necessity for 'priority consumers' are allayed by emphasizing that these policies are neither new nor unexamined:

> That has been the policy of the Government since 1940; and they have the experts behind them. Only a week or so ago the government asked the medical and scientific experts to look once again at the allowances we give to these priority consumers. And the experts, far from recommending any reduction, said that the allowances are as low as they can be. (MAF 102/7: 9)

We can see here that the government was tracking the public feelings that rationing affected – suspicion, hostility, doubt – and managing these with emotional instruction under the guise of public education. Public suspicions about abuses of the policy are answered with a sense of scale, and reassurance:

> Well, some abuse is inevitable in a big scheme of this sort – that must be admitted – but the Ministry of Food doesn't think there's a great deal and certainly not sufficient to justify our altering the scheme [...] the selfish people who take a mean advantage of the system are not many in proportion. But these abuses do worry the Ministry and we're always trying to make the scheme more watertight without penalising those who really deserve the extra. (MAF 102/7: 9)

That last line is worth noticing. It is not simply a reassurance to stave off disaffection: it is also reminding the public that abuses won't go unnoticed. Yet it does so in a way that carefully manages the public spirit. The broadcast could have said that the government is watching out for abusers and will punish them. But it doesn't. Instead, the Ministry of Food is 'worried' by abuse. This is a subtle but powerful way of reimagining a political and government body from the sort of impersonal institution that an individual might feel able to cheat and instead constructing them in the listeners' imagination as a caring and protective body, one that is looking out for – rather than watching – the public. Given the fragility of trust and morale, it is a politic use of language.

As a writer for broadcast in the period, Bowen had first-hand experience of these textual strategies. In Hepburn's editorial notes on Bowen's essay 'Britain in Autumn' (which would later become 'London, 1940'), he catalogues the cuts made by the censor. These can be read as evidence of what Bowen was not allowed to represent: but they can also be read as evidence of what she knew passed official review. What is also notable are Bowen's own cuts when she later revised the essay. Although 'London, 1940' ends with the oft-quoted statement that 'we have no feeling to spare' (52), this earlier version does not allow the reader to assume this means there is no feeling, nor that war has traumatized the capacity *to* feel. Instead, Bowen represents the British as angered, a public outraged by the enemy:

> One thing absorbs us – anger. This anger varies over the face of Britain [...]. This anger has lost us our native fat: the moral muscles stand out in everyone. And this anger acts like a weight in the base: it keeps us upright. Also, it keeps us calm. There is no question of you controlling such anger; such anger controls you. You do not spend anger like this in small change. It is the complete corrective for 'big' talk. By day, we neighbours discuss our own little angles on the nuisance – but its implications we store up. There occur some flare-ups of irritability, but as a general rule we are less cross [...] We need all we have: save everything, most of all nerves. Collectively, the outcome of all this is a complete slump in the feeling of competition. In brief, since this Britain became a garrison she ceased to be a competitive society. (2008: 52)

The rest of the essay offers a detailed representation of that collectivity as a natural quality of British culture and character. Anger, here, is a centralizing emotion, one that smooths out differences, or petty disputes, and provides purpose and stability. Anger is represented as a major feeling that is powerful, when regulated and trained – together – on a common enemy. Look as well at that construction of feeling as a resource: 'we need all we have: save everything'. This sits personal and public feeling as, like iron, food and fabric, something with which one should not be wasteful. We might also notice how autonomy is being reimagined as an obstacle to responsible citizenship: the force with which 'such anger controls you' is not a sign of one's instability, but the opposite – it secures participation in *might*, that is, in the power and strength of a nation. Importantly, this form of imagining a relationship between feeling and national belonging constructs a sense of identity that is more than a spirit, or nationality. It is the sign of a national body – the 'outraged we' – that has the capacity to be affected. Feelings of personal violation and responsibility work, as Ahmed indicates in her work on discourses of British nationalism, to produce 'a group of subjects who can identify themselves with the injured nation in this performance of personal injury' (2). It is the same kind of strategy we can see in the worried 'we' of the Kitchen Front Broadcasts, which invites care for a nation being drained of its affective resources by those who abuse the system. But the agency of anger does more than imagine this national body: it signifies, and signs, a natural authority and moral justice rather than authoritarianism. Feeling British, in this sense, is preserved from accusations of the kinds of national feeling mobilized by the authoritarian regimes of the enemy.

Given the extent to which the Ministry of Information archives identify resentment, frustration or anger with government policies as a threat to stability and safety, here we have a representation of what looks like a very politic way of rewriting feelings of discontent into a new narrative about a unified public citizenry harnessing even the resources of their psyche towards the war effort, and doing so in a manner that presents personal complicity with the centralizing of affect as, itself, a sign of patriotism. Indeed, earlier in the essay Bowen asserts that '[h]ow you feel is your own fight' (50). The best we can surmise about the essay's context, given the Covid-19 lockdown in the winter of 2020 curtailing visits to archives, is that, following Hepburn's observation that 'Britain in Autumn' appears to address an American audience, it would have been seen and administered by the Ministry of Information as a piece of propaganda. Hepburn points out that in the essay Bowen compares the junction between Oxford Street and Hyde Park with that of Fifth Avenue and Central Park. But we should also notice that she writes, '[e]ven in Britain it was Thanksgiving Time' (50). While Hepburn does not identify this as part of Bowen's paid work with the Ministry of Information, its tone and content are very similar, in this version, to the kinds of essays she wrote about Ireland under her relationship with the MoI. If that is the case, then feeling, in this context, would need to work both as an appeal to an American sensibility, and as the right kind of performance of a British national identity whose injuries, on the Home Front, are neither destabilizing nor weakening. Given the timing of the piece, we might read this as a deft use of political tact in order to align an American audience with a moral outrage they hadn't yet decided was theirs. But do we read this as an endorsement of that spirit?

I think, instead, we might interpret those substantial revisions Bowen made between its initial version for the censor, and the version she published in her own collection later, as editing out the discourses of official feeling that the early version performs so well (a performance legitimated by being un-cut by the censor). As well as ending the piece on what Hepburn rightly interprets as the 'terrifying sentence "we have no feeling to spare"' (48), and cutting her entire discussion of national feeling, Bowen's early version has another notable excision when it describes her neighbourhood: 'Regent's Park, in which I live, backs on Marylebone. [excision] Just inside the outer gates, a few yards from my door, an unexploded bomb makes a boil in the tarmac road' (51). Hepburn suggests that what was excised was a version of the sentence that appears, in the same place, in 'London, 1940': 'Regent's Park where I live is still, at the time of writing, closed: officially, that is to say, we are not here' (422). What is striking about this sentence is the intimations of that 'officially': not only does it name the existence of an 'official' version of life, but it also has two implications – that either that official narrative is erasing its citizens, or that those citizens are not totally regulated by it. Either way, it lends a feeling of subversion.

In reading Bowen's writing from the period, we can position her attention to feeling beyond being a commitment to registering the strange reality of the war. That reality was being actively shaped, rewritten and narrativized by the government through the political uses of feeling, and in her writing, we can see how feelings are being performed as acts of security. We might go back, carefully then, to 'Careless Talk'. Mary represents herself as careful, instructing Joanna to avoid the carelessness revealed by her mentioning her evacuees: '"Yes, and I have evacuees – ". "But we won't talk about those, will we?" said Mary quickly' (753). Mary Dash appears to have perfected the official feeling of cheerful self-censoring that should align her with the national cause. But the original title points us to another affect: 'interesting'. While other characters in the story feign disinterest, or avoid answering, Mary Dash proclaims that '[t]hese days everything's frightfully interesting' (753). Is Mary's interest careless, or carefully construed? Throughout the story she asks uncomfortable questions:

'For instance, can *you* tell me what's become of the Stones?'
'No, I'm afraid I can't. I ... '

'And Edward and I were wondering if you could tell us about the Hickneys. I know they are somewhere in Dorset or Somerset. They're not by any chance anywhere near you? ... Well, never mind. Tell me about yourself.' (750-1)

Later, she asks Ponsonby and Eric about the names and nationalities of people she's seen them with: 'One lives in a perfect whirl of ideas. Ponsonby, who was that man I saw you with at the Meuniere? I was certain I knew his face' (753). People are identified as matters of interest, and, officially, not: 'No, I don't expect you'd know him. He's only been about lately,' said Mary. 'He's an expert; he's very interesting.' 'He could be,' said Eric. 'He was at one time. But he's not supposed to be interesting just now' (751). Twice she pretends Joanna's interest in order to broker conversation between Joanna and the other guests: '"Now you must talk to Joanna,' said Mary Dash. 'She's just brought me three eggs from the country and she's longing to know about everything"' (751); '"You see you've hardly had a word with Joanna, and she's wanting so much to catch up with life"' (754). In her work on 'interesting', Sianne Ngai points out that interest has been perceived as an affect that works to confirm the individuality of the one who declares something as interesting (782). We might notice how often Mary's interest works to draw attention to herself. Perhaps, in Mary's attention to what interests, the story identifies a version of the selfishness of individual feeling intimated in Bowen's 'Britain in Autumn', encoding through Mary's 'frightfully interesting' an excessive feeling that carelessly spends the affective resources that should be saved, undercutting the patriotic cheerfulness she performs. But 'interest', here, might also signal a kind of careful strategy, even as it appears to be careless: Ngai points out that when we determine something to be interesting, that judgement is also a plea for further evaluation. Calling something 'interesting' is a way to keep talking about it and continue giving it attention (814). As Ngai also points out, we say things are interesting when we don't know yet what or how we are feeling. Interest, she writes, often begins with the 'feeling of not knowing exactly *what* we are feeling [...] people often say things are interesting when they aren't sure exactly *how* they feel about them ... yet' (789). Perhaps, in Mary's declarations of interest, we should sense the production of a whirl of chatter whose purpose *is* the material that it produces for her to read, and to scrutinize. Does Mary deserve our suspicion, or are her declarations of Joanna's interest a sign that she may not be as innocent as she seems? Given the work interest does in naming an encounter whose affect is yet to be decided, Mary's final declaration – '"I don't know how I'd feel if I lost three eggs"' (754) – just might be setting off a charge. Feeling emerges, in 'Careless Talk', as a kind of intelligence work in which everyone is involved, and implicated.

Rather than a reality to be represented, then, feelings in Bowen's writing *are* representations, ones that are, in this period, to be performed, fine-tuned and recalibrated in order to signal, sign – and counter-sign – one's orientation to Britain, and to each other. These texts recognize that feelings aren't simply an experience of the war, nor only affected by it. Weaponizable, they are one of its strategic resources, a key technology that supplies a textual strategy to administer, regulate, re-organize and re-orient the public. Not only does 'Careless Talk' represent feeling as representation – a means of performing allegiance by performing official affects – but it also represents feeling as an intelligence work that demands forms of reading attuned to both its politics, and political uses.

Notes

1 'I Hear You Say So' was originally published in *New Writing and Daylight*, September 1945. Unless otherwise noted, stories are cited using the 1999 Vintage edition of *Collected Stories*. For dating see Marcia Farrell's bibliography in *Modern Fiction Studies*, 53 (2) Elizabeth Bowen Special Issue (Summer 2007): 370–400 and the updated version at https://docplayer.net/36841571-Elizabeth-bowen-a-comprehensive-bibliography-compiled-by-marcia-farrell.html [accessed 29 January 2021].
2 Ellmann's 'Shadowing Elizabeth Bowen' offers an invaluable appraisal of Bowen's critical revival.
3 Originally published by Jonathan Cape, there was a second edition in 1947. Nicola Darwood catalogues the contents in her 2016 essay '"The violent destruction of solid things": Elizabeth Bowen's wartime short stories', University of Bedford Open Repository, 1–8, fn 3. https://uobrep.openrepository.com/handle/10547/622413 [accessed 29 January 2021].
4 Ellmann highlights work by Heather Bryant Jordan, Adam Piette, Roy Foster, Gill Plain, and Karen Schneider ('Shadowing', 2003: 156).
5 Hepburn translates from the French 'Panorama du roman', which, translated from English by Pier Ponti, was published in a special edition of *Fontaine* 37–40 (1944): 33–43. It was reprinted in *Aspects de la littérature anglaise 1918–1945* (edited by Kathleen Raine and Max-Pol Fouchet (Paris: Fontaine, 1944): 30–9) and published in German in *Die Neue Zürcher Zeitung: Literatur und Kunst* 168 (4 October 1947): 1–2.
6 For her reports, and the debates these sparked in Ireland, refer to Jack Lane and Brendan Clifford (1999).

7   Published August 10, Issue 20 of *New Statesman* (133–4) and collected a year later in *Look at All Those Roses*.
8   For an image of the announcement see Jo Fox's article, Figure 2. Fox's work on National Archive materials has been a crucial addition to my own on the Kitchen Front Broadcasts via the War, State and Society digitization project. During Covid-19 I've been unable to access archives, and am especially grateful to Fox's archival work.
9   Fox quotes from Paul Addison and Jeremy Crang's *Listening to Britain: Home Intelligence Reports on Britain's Finest Hour, May to September 1940* (2010).
10 Fox refers to Nikolas Rose's *Governing the Soul: The Shaping of the Private Self* (1989).
11 The National Archives: INF 1/250. Without access to these materials I am unable to identify the remaining two.
12 See the Imperial War Museum's collection at https://www.iwm.org.uk/collections/item/object/32270 [accessed 29 January 2021].
13 Fox quotes a Daily Morale Report of 20 July 1940: 'the civilian is beginning to feel, and has been encouraged to feel, that he is in the front line: at the same time, attempts are apparently being made to undermine his status' (946). TNA: INF 1/264.
14 As a member of the editorial board for War, State and Society, Taylor and Francis' digitization project of National Archives materials, I had the opportunity to look at a number of these documents when the project was being launched in 2018 (warstateandsociety.com). An early version of my thinking about Bowen's story appears there in an essay about how these materials can be engaged when teaching literature from the period, particularly in order to retrieve such details from students' tendency to reduce them to either a 'realistic detail' or a 'symbolic motif'.

Works cited

Ahmed, Sara. *The Cultural Politics of Feeling*. Edinburgh: Edinburgh University Press, 2004.

Ashraf, Ana. "'The Ambivalence of Testimony'" in Elizabeth Bowen's *The Heat of the Day* (1948)'. In Sue Kennedy and Jane Thomas (eds.), *British Women's Writing, 1930 to 1960: Between the Waves*. Liverpool: Liverpool University Press, 2020: 109–22.

Bennett, Andrew and Nicholas Royle. *Elizabeth Bowen and the Dissolution of the Novel: Still Lives*. Liverpool: Liverpool University Press, 1995.

Bennett, Andrew and Nicholas Royle. *An Introduction to Literature, Theory and Criticism*. London: Routledge, (5th edition) 2016.

Bowen, Elizabeth. *Collected Impressions*. New York: Knopf, 1950.

Bowen, Elizabeth. *The Mulberry Tree: Writings of Elizabeth Bowen*. Hermione Lee (ed.). London: Virago, 1986.

Bowen, Elizabeth. *Collected Stories*. London: Vintage Random House, 1999 [1980].
Christensen, Lis. *Elizabeth Bowen: The Later Fiction*. University of Copenhagen: Museum Tusculanum Press, 2001.
Corcoran, Neil. *Elizabeth Bowen: The Enforced Return*. Oxford: Clarendon Press, 2004.
Deer, Patrick. *Culture in Camouflage: War, Empire, and Modern British Literature*. Oxford: Oxford University Press, 2016.
Ellmann, Maud. *Elizabeth Bowen: The Shadow Across the Page*. Edinburgh: Edinburgh University Press, 2003.
Ellman, Maud. 'Shadowing Elizabeth Bowen'. *New England Review* 24 (1), 2003: 144–69.
Fox, Joanna. 'Careless Talk: Tensions within British Domestic Propaganda during the Second World War'. *Journal of British Studies* 51 (4), 2012: 936–66.
Gildersleeve, Jessica and Patricia Smith (eds). *Elizabeth Bowen: Theory, Thought and Things*. Edinburgh: Edinburgh University Press, 2019.
Hepburn, Allan (ed). *People, Places, Things: Essays by Elizabeth Bowen*. Edinburgh: Edinburgh University Press, 2008.
Hepburn, Allan. *The Bazaar and Other Stories*. Edinburgh: Edinburgh University Press, 2008.
Hepburn, Allan. *Listening in: Broadcasts, Speeches, and Interviews by Elizabeth Bowen*. Edinburgh: Edinburgh University Press, 2010.
hoogland, renée. *Elizabeth Bowen: A Reputation in Writing*. New York: New York University Press, 1994.
Lane, Jack and Brendan Clifford (eds). *Elizabeth Bowen: Notes on Eire, Espionage Reports to Winston Churchill, 1940–1942*. Millstreet: Aubane Historical Society, 1999.
Lassner, Phyllis. *Elizabeth Bowen: A Study of the Short Fiction*. New York: Twayne Publishers, 1991.
Lee, Hermione. *Elizabeth Bowen*. London: Vintage, 1999.
Magot, Céline. '"Careless Talk": Word Shortage in Elizabeth Bowen's Wartime Writing'. *Miranda* 2, 2010: 1–9.
Ngai, Sianne. 'Merely Interesting'. *Critical Inquiry* 34 (4), 2008: 777–817.
Oxindine, Annette. 'Resisting Dissolution: The Salvific Turn in Elizabeth Bowen's *The Heat of the Day*'. *Renascence* 69 (4), 2017: 200–20.
Porcelli, Stephania. 'Careless Talk Costs Lives: War Propaganda and Wartime Fiction in Elizabeth Bowen's *The Heat of the Day*'. In Stephania Porcelli, Rosy Colombo, Maria Crisafulli, Franca Ruggieri, eds. *Challenges for the 21st Century: Dilemmas, Ambiguities, Directions* (1). Papers from the 24th AIA conference. Rome: Dipartimento di Letterature Comparata, Universita degli Studi Roma Tre, 2003: 107–13.
Schaller, Karen. '"I Know it to be Synthetic but it Affects Me Strongly": "Dead Mabelle" and Bowen's Emotion Pictures'. *Textual Practice* 27 (1), 2013: 163–85.
Sturgeon, Sinéad. 'A Greener Gothic: Environment and Extinction in Elizabeth Bowen's *The Demon Lover* (1945)'. *Éire-Ireland* 55 (3), 2020: 75–94.

6

The Life of Animals: George Orwell's Fiction in the 1940s

Tamás Bényei

The 1940s were Orwell's decade in a very obvious biographical sense. As Richard Rorty remarks, 'We would not now be reading and admiring Orwell's essays, studying his biography, or trying to integrate his vocabulary of moral deliberation into our own unless he had written *Animal Farm* and *1984* [sic]' (169). Rorty describes Orwell as a writer who 'was successful because he wrote exactly the right books at exactly the right time' (170). This assessment is reinforced by John Rodden: 'Within little more than four years in the late 1940s, Orwell rose from a position of relatively modest standing as a London journalist and minor English novelist to a writer of international stature during the last months of his life and a symbolic figure from virtually the moment of his death' (ix–x). The continuing popularity and prominence of these books, which represented a radical change for Orwell after a string of loosely realist novels, led to what Raymond Williams called the critical habit of 'reading Orwell backwards', looking at the earlier texts as preliminaries (qtd. Lea 101). Strictly speaking, the Orwell decade proper probably spans the ten years between 1945, with the publication of *Animal Farm*, and 1955, the consolidation of this period's fiction that Isaac Deutscher famously called 'ideological super-weapons' (qtd. Hammond 17), but, notwithstanding the predictions about the waning of his relevance, Orwell – as David Dwan notes – remains 'part of the political vocabulary of our times' (2). Many readers and commentators feel his work still 'has a lot to tell us about the grammar of key political concepts and the awkwardness of ideals' (9). The exact nature of Orwell's relevance, however, is far from clear, since he has been claimed by Left and Right alike. In 1943, he called himself 'a Socialist by allegiance and a Liberal by temperament' (qtd. Rai 1).[1]

A short piece, 'Revenge Is Sour', published in *Tribune* in November 1945, offers a useful point of entry not only into key themes of Orwell's 1940s fiction but also the specific relevance of Orwell's fiction and non-fiction to that decade. Recalling a visit to a prisoner-of-war camp in Southern Germany, Orwell relates an incident involving their guide, 'a little Viennese Jew', who, 'working himself up into a fury' (3), savagely kicks a German SS officer with horribly deformed feet, a 'real Nazi', who had probably presided over tortures and hangings in concentration camps: 'In short, he represented everything [the guide] had been fighting against during the past five years' (4). The German soldier, thus, becomes the representative of an idea – but only for the 'little Jew'. The narrator, while remaining aloof, studies the 'disgusting specimen', describing him in terms that prefigure Hannah Arendt's idea of the banality of evil. The soldier

> did not look brutal or in any way frightening: merely neurotic and, in a low way, intellectual. [...] He could have been an unfrocked clergyman, an actor ruined by drink, or a spiritualist medium. I have seen very similar people in London common lodging houses, and also in the Reading Room of the British Museum. [...] So the Nazi torturer of one's imagination, the monstrous figure against whom one had struggled for so many years, dwindled to this pitiful wretch, whose obvious need was not for punishment, but for some kind of psychological treatment.[2] (4)

Although the impersonal structures ('one's imagination', 'against whom one has struggled') suggest his involvement, the narrator is careful to detach himself from this mental projection. In fact, the description of the prisoner serves as a corrective downscaling, a 'de-mythicisation' of the monster that – according to Orwell – has taken hold of the Jew's imagination. From this point, the object of Orwell's observant gaze is the Jew rather than the Nazi soldier. Witnessing further humiliations inflicted on the Nazi prisoner, he wonders

> whether the Jew was getting any real kick out of this new-found power that he was exercising. I concluded that he wasn't really enjoying it, and that he was merely – like a man in a brothel, or a boy smoking his first cigar, or a tourist traipsing round a picture gallery – *telling* himself that he was enjoying it, and behaving as he had planned to behave in the days when he was helpless. (4)

Orwell's point is not that the enormity of the Nazi genocide renders any individual act of retribution futile. He is interested in a larger issue, in 'the whole idea of revenge and punishment', which he calls 'a childish day-dream' (4–5). Contrasting the *idea* of revenge, conceived in a condition of utter helplessness, with the reality of the violence fuelled by the idea, he concludes: 'Properly speaking, there is no such thing as revenge. Revenge is an act which you want to commit when you are powerless and because you are powerless: as soon as the sense of impotence is removed, the desire evaporates also' (5). Its reality, no matter how justified, is 'merely pathetic and disgusting.' (5)

Still assuming the role of the detached observer, Orwell goes on to relate how, just a few hours after Stuttgart had been captured, he entered the ravaged city with a Belgian journalist whose attitude towards the Germans was much 'tougher' (6). They come across a dead German soldier, whose 'face was a waxy yellow', and 'on his breast someone had laid a bunch of the lilac which was blossoming everywhere' (6). Orwell notes how the Belgian averts his face; a few minutes later, his companion admits this was the first time he had ever seen a corpse, despite undertaking war propaganda for the BBC's European Service – whipping up powerful emotions through language – for four years. This incident transforms his attitude, restoring his ability to see individual Germans as simply people rather than monsters. '[H]is feelings, he told me, had undergone a change at the sight of "ce pauvre mort" beside the bridge: it had suddenly brought home to him *the meaning of war*' (6) [italics added].

Both incidents are offered by Orwell as parables of something more important than the specific political point made in the piece, to condemn the mass deportation of Germans from East Prussia and other aspects of the vindictive peace settlement. More generally, the article is concerned with the gap between ideas and reality, deploring acts motivated by general ideas, fantasies and rhetoric rather than the particularity of actual experience. The piece of reportage is predicated on contrasting the mental world generated by language (the Belgian journalist) or ideas (the Jewish guide) to the empirical world of objective experience, clearly endorsing the primacy of the latter. For the 'little Jew', mental content overrules physical reality: just as the German prisoner falls short of the image of monstrosity evoked by the idea of a 'Nazi torturer', the reality of revenge – at least according to the narrator, for we never get to hear the guide's thoughts – is less appealing than its idea: 'Somehow the punishment of these monsters ceases to seem attractive when it becomes possible: indeed, once under lock and key, they almost cease to be monsters' (5). It is, however, not only the primacy of mental or physical reality that is at stake: 'Unfortunately, there is often need of some concrete incident before one can discover *the real state of one's feelings*' (5) [emphasis added]. This thesis – illustrated only by the second incident – posits that there is such a thing as the real state of one's feelings and, by implication, a less real one. The story of the Belgian journalist – who succeeds where the guide fails – becomes a parable of one who successfully triumphs over his own feelings – which turn out to have been 'false' – for the sake of a newly born humanism. Humanism is thus presented by Orwell as common sense, supported by the incontrovertible fact of physical suffering. Reality overrides ideology.

One key aspect of the article's relevance is already indicated by the setting. The narrator is an Englishman in Europe, in the thick of historical events – evoking *Homage to Catalonia*, Orwell's 1938 book of reportage about the Spanish war. Orwell is a unique bridge figure in a generational sense whose work and authorial identity encapsulate the 1940s in several ways: having fought in Spain and been an almost *bona fide* member of the dominant group of 1930s writers, he connects the 1930s – identified in V. S. Pritchett's obituary as the 'wintry conscience of his generation' (294) – with the Cold War decades in a way that is comparable only to Graham Greene's position in generational terms (although Greene never aspired to the position of the public spokesman that Orwell claimed for himself in his fiction, essays and journalism). Orwell was a bridge figure also in a geopolitical sense: while his first-hand experience alerts English (British) readers to continental affairs, he is struggling to forge out a viable English role in the new international political alignment of the Cold War. One of the major – and timely – projects in which Orwell was involved during the early 1940s was that of identifying a usable post-imperial kind of Englishness;[3] the aloof, sensible, decently compassionate English observer of the 'madness' of Europeans is part of this self-positioning, and this identity contributed to his high standing among the new writers of the 1950s, Angry Young Men as well as Movement poets (Rodden 10, 19, 47). Englishness remained a concern in his 1940s fiction. Malcolm Bradbury calls *Animal Farm* 'a very English book, smelling both of the British farmyard and a distinctive and traditional sense of liberalism and decency' (xvi), while *Nineteen Eighty-Four* (1948) portrays a Britain shrunk to Airstrip One, a province of one of three global superpowers.

Another topical feature in the aftermath of the Second World War was Orwell's obsession with the workings of power: attempting to come to terms with the politics and psychology of Fascism and totalitarianism in general, he was trying to find the reasons for liberal democracy's inability to offer an adequate response. On the one hand, the post-war years were characterized by – as Joshua L. Cherniss explains in his book on the political philosophy of Isaiah Berlin – considerable enthusiasm for more efficient technocratic administration, regulation and planning: 'even opponents of government regulation acknowledged the need for "adjustment" to the impersonal demands of society' (91). Many observers saw the rise of totalitarianism as the result of chaos arising from individualism, arguing that liberal democracy could be saved only through integration and unity (91), planned by experts and technicians of power.

On the other hand, the immediate past and the events unfolding in the Soviet Union impelled many political philosophers to study the concept of power itself and its abuses. One relevant context for Orwell's many pertinent essays (including those on Burnhamism) and his 1940s fiction is provided by a spate of key texts of political philosophy, like those by Raymond Aron, Isaiah Berlin, Friedrich Hayek, Karl Mannheim or Hannah Arendt's *Origins of Totalitarianism*, published in 1951. In assessing the intellectual tendencies of the period, Berlin identified 'a kind of cautious humanism, respectful both of the truths and methodology of science and of the inner life of the individual', a freedom from dogma and crusading zeal, an 'anxiety to avoid anything exaggerated or outré and too self-revealing', and a determination 'not to be carried away by any wave of violent feeling' (qtd. Cherniss 64). In Berlin's overview, the intellectual climate of the period was represented by figures like Koestler, Silone and Orwell, sharing a 'general distrust of political nostrums and formulas as such, a sense of horror when faced by the inhuman consequences of doctrines and ideas unmodified by understanding or sympathy for the actual predicament of specific individuals or groups in specific situations' (qtd. Cherniss, 64–5). In this atmosphere, Berlin saw 'incorruptible' Orwell as the representative figure with his 'moral severity' and 'rigid integrity' (qtd. Cherniss 65).

Orwell's idea of Englishness, the theme of the contrast between ideas and reality, and his obsession with power are combined in the key preoccupations of works such as *Animal Farm*, *Nineteen Eighty-Four* and many of his key essays. In one of these, 'Politics and the English Language', he states that 'the present political chaos is connected with the decay of language' (139).[4] What connects these two works of fiction is the critique of abuses of language alongside a quest for an honest, truthful language, a concern that is very much in tune with the preoccupations of the 1940s. Christopher Norris condemned what he deprecatingly called 'Orwell's homespun empiricist outlook – his assumption that the truth was just there to be told in a straightforward, common-sense way', claiming that this idea 'now seems not merely naive but culpably self-deluding' ('Language' 242). One of the purposes of the present chapter is to show that, far from being naïve, *Animal Farm* and *Nineteen Eighty-Four* offer a more complex meditation on language, subjectivity and power than the essays.

The 'war of the species': *Animal Farm*

Many of the above concerns come together in *Animal Farm* (written in 1943–4, published in August 1945). The story of the farmyard animals' revolt can be seen in terms of Orwell's quest for an honest and truthful language, or perhaps in terms of his abandonment of any hope for such a language.[5] According to Daniel Lea, the plot of the novel consists of a series of instances of the escalating corruption and perversion of language (112). According to Roger Fowler, who deserves credit for the phrase 'perversion of language' (174), language is also part of the action of the book, and the relationship of language and power symbolized by linguistic actions is a theme examined by this fable (177). Or, as Samir Elbarbary puts it, 'the revolution on the farm is a language-focused enterprise, a product of specifically aggressive linguistic energy, and language, which can effectively control reality, is at the root of the tragic experience rather than merely mirroring it' (35). Given that the opening and closing situations are practically identical, the entire plot can be seen as a pseudo-plot generated by language, evident in Old Major's opening speech, billed in the barnyard as an exposition of his dream that is to become the founding fiction of *Animal Farm*. The animals duly convene to hear the revelation, only for Old Major to say, after a lengthy and highly rhetorical preamble: 'I cannot describe that dream to you' (6). The dream turns out to have been relevant only inasmuch as it puts him in mind of an old song of his mother, of which she knew only the first three words. Instead of the narrative of a dream, as Lynette Hunter says, the animals are offered a carefully composed and perfectly executed speech (180), a sublime piece of political rhetoric, which Fowler calls 'a set-piece parody of, in general terms, political demagoguery, and specifically, the discourse of theoretical Marxism' (175).

In this sense, the pristine, originary moment of the revolution amounts to little more than Old Major's rhetorical *tour de force*. The untold dream remains a literal and linguistic void, into which the possibility of truthful language disappears. Major's speech (re)conceptualizes the non-reflective life of the animals in political terms as a life of slavery and misery, which is not entirely unlike the moment when Molière's M. Jourdain realizes that he has been speaking in prose all his life. The life they have known and endured is redescribed as an unjust and intolerable condition that calls for revolution. The redescription of their world is completed in a series of terminological and conceptual definitions and choices, like the imperative to decide immediately by a vote whether wild animals (like rats) are comrades or enemies (6).

This is the first of many performative speech acts serving to abuse and pervert an ideal, truthful language, a perversion familiar to many in the 1940s from fascism to the ideologues of the Cold War. A typical scene is where, after the expulsion of Snowball, all the animals are gathered in the barn. Standing on the platform 'where Major had previously stood to deliver his speech' (36). Napoleon announces that there will be no more Sunday morning meetings. Though uneasy and resentful, the animals are unable to speak up, except some of the 'articulate' pigs (36), who 'uttered shrill squeals of disapproval'. They are silenced in two, equally vocal ways: by the 'deep, menacing growls' (37) of the dogs surrounding Napoleon and by the sheep who, at moments like this, always break out 'into a tremendous bleating of "Four legs good, two legs bad" which went on for nearly a quarter of an hour and put an end to any chance of discussion' (37). The dogs are not even required to speak – in fact, their function is to enact their original canine identity in the pigs' script, and they are never reported speaking. The bleating of slogans is an instance of the non-communicative abuse of language: it drowns discussion, blanking out any meaning, becoming language without referential value, hardly different from plain bleating as such. There seems to be no middle ground between the inarticulate honesty of the animals and the deceitful articulateness of the pigs. As soon as animal noise becomes articulate human speech, abuse seems inevitable – in fact, the evolutionary leap retroactively corrupts even the noises made by animals. The third, most sophisticated way of silencing the animals makes use of the pretence that they are all equal in terms of language skills and intellect. This is Squealer's job: in every potentially critical moment, he is sent to talk the animals around, which he performs with admirable efficiency and confidence, using a convoluted jargon that is persuasive precisely because it is incomprehensible for the animals. Even in these cases, however, the splitting of language into perverted articulacy and inarticulate noise is present: 'The animals were not certain what the word [tactics] meant, but Squealer spoke so persuasively, and the three dogs who happened to be with him growled so threateningly, that they accepted his explanation without further questions' (38).[6] The soundtrack for Squealer's spiel is the incessant, inarticulate growl of the dogs, a dark, irrational acoustic double which, besides replicating the meaninglessness of Squealer's 'noise', is also the support of absolute sovereignty that is indispensable for the installation and smooth functioning of the Law and of the Symbolic (see Žižek 319).[7]

One result of this strategy is that key political and philosophical terms are hollowed out – for instance, as David Dwan demonstrates, the idea of 'equality', which in 'the vast chasm that exists between, say, naturally clever pigs and incorrigibly stupid sheep appears to decide the case against equality before it is even tried. But the stark differences between species also put banal affirmations of equality under critical pressure and force readers to consider the meaning of ostensibly factual assertions that "All animals are equal". (657). Equality is revealed to be 'an umbrella term for different and sometimes contradictory conceptions of fairness' (679),[8] while in the commandment in question it is used both as a constative and as an imperative. The definition of 'animal' is equally fraught with difficulties – as in the scene when it is explained by Snowball, through a piece of incomprehensible sophistry full of multisyllabic Latinate words, that a bird's wings are not hands (22).

The perversion of language – apart from outright lies used when Snowball is airbrushed out of the history and official memory of *Animal Farm* – works in two basic and contrary ways. On the one hand, propositions are reduced to easily memorisable slogans and clichés that progressively lose their referential valence (even 'Beasts of England' proves to be too much). What begins as 'a complete system of thought' (10), that of Animalism, is reduced first to seven commandments (15), and then to a single maxim: 'Four legs good, two legs bad' (21) – only for both the commandments and the maxim to be further perverted. The other strategy of the abuse of language is to inflate it into a proliferation of meaningless (ideological) jargon or clearly non-referential texts like the lists of record crops; this is indeed the verbal equivalent of the liquid squirt of cuttlefish of which Orwell writes in 'Politics and the English Language' (139). This obfuscation, when language creates its own reference, culminates in the paroxysm of self-generated and non-referential language that is the outcome of the work invented to keep the increasing population of pigs busy. 'Squealer told them that the pigs had to expend enormous labours every day upon mysterious things called "files", "reports", "minutes" and "memoranda". These were large sheets of paper which had to be closely covered with writing, and as soon as they were so covered they were burnt in the furnace' (86–7).

What does *Animal Farm* have to offer in the face of such verbal derangement? According to some readers, it is Orwell's famous or notorious plain style that offers hope by counterbalancing the perversion of language in the story, as indicated by Bradbury (x). Roger Fowler, for instance, claiming that this 'purified language' is 'the foil against which the degradation of language by the pigs is presented' (165), analyses at length the 'simplicity of language' that prevails in the narrative voice, noting its relationship to Orwell's ideas on the politics and 'the morality of public language' (164) as expounded in a series of essays during the 1940s, reflecting on the period's vicissitudes, most famously, perhaps, in 'Politics and the English Language', which distinguishes between the political and the everyday uses of English, claiming that the former is inevitably and incorrigibly corrupt:

> In our time, political speech and writing are largely the defence of the indefensible. Things like the continuance of British rule in India, the Russian purges and deportations, the dropping of the atom bombs on Japan, can indeed be defended, but only by arguments which are too brutal for most people to face, and which do not square with the professed aims of political parties. Thus political language has to consist largely of euphemism, question-begging and sheer cloudy vagueness.[9] (136)

So much has been said about the untenability of Orwell's implied dichotomy, the ultimate impossibility of distinguishing a 'plain', commonsensical, normal language as a kind of neutral background to corrupted or perverted – political, totalitarian, literary, etc. – uses of language, that there is no need to further address it here, apart from noting that Orwell did not fully subscribe to this binarism (see Rorty 174). This becomes clear in *Nineteen Eighty-Four*, but already in *Animal Farm* there are ways in which plain narrative style is contaminated by what is happening to language within the narrated world. To consider just one example, in his otherwise painstaking stylistic analysis of the language of *Animal Farm* Fowler overlooks one feature: a marked preference for impersonal structures. Take the scene in which the pigs appropriate milk for themselves.

> 'What is going to happen to all that milk?' said someone.
> 'Jones used sometimes to mix some of it in our mash,' said one of the hens.
> 'Never mind the milk, comrades!' cried Napoleon, placing himself in front of the buckets. '*That will be attended to*. The harvest is more important. Comrade Snowball will lead the way. I shall follow in a few minutes. Forward, comrades! The hay is waiting.'
> So the animals trooped down to the hayfield to begin the harvest, and when they came back in the evening *it was noticed* that the milk had disappeared. (16) [emphasis added]

The second italicized phrase looks like an echo of Napoleon's apodictic disclaimer; one could even risk that it is a narratorial parody of Napoleon's 'will be attended to'. The hen recalls that Mr Jones used to attend to the milk in a particular way, adding some of it to the food of the animals.[10] Fowler stresses that, unlike in the earlier novels that have a first-person narrator or a single focalizer, in *Animal Farm* 'Orwell creates a sort of *collective* focalization', which, for him, 'represents the ultimate reduction in the status of the narrative voice' (164). The impersonal structure perhaps works as a verbal marker of the idea of collectivism, and its associated verbal ambiguities repeat the ambiguities of collectivism on the level of language: it refers to an act that remains agentless. Thus, the collectivism of impersonality leaves open the question of agency and responsibility. Napoleon obviously uses it in order not to have to call attention to his role in pilfering the shared milk, while the narrator's 'it was noticed' repeats the trick, refraining from identifying those who did the noticing. The same effect is sought in a later scene. ' "That is the true spirit, comrade!" cried Squealer, but it was noticed he cast a very ugly look at Boxer' (55). Even the doubling or echoing is repeated: 'It was given out that the pasture was exhausted and needed re-seeding: but it soon became known that Napoleon intended to sow it with barley' (73). If these instances might be seen as subversions of the pigs' verbal authority, it is also possible to see them, conversely, as sites of contamination, where the manipulative strategies within the story spill out to infect the narrative voice in which they are embedded. In such cases, the narrator clearly manipulates language in ways not unlike the pigs – and, by creating these doublings, he surely calls attention to his own manipulative ruses.

Plain language, thus, can hardly be seen as a real counterforce. If anything might challenge the inevitable corruption of language and the body politic, it is the equally troublesome notion of 'life', one of the key words within the narrative. It is not accidental that Old Major's testimonial speech begins with this promise: 'I think I may say that I understand the nature of life on this earth as well as any animal now living. It is about this that I wish to speak to you' (3).[11] Major next describes the life of farmyard animals in terms that – although evoking Hobbes's characterization of pre-social life – are still non-political and therefore easy to relate to. 'Let's face it, our lives are miserable, laborious, and short. [...] No animal in England knows the meaning of happiness or leisure after he is a year old. No animal in England is free. The life of an animal is misery and slavery: that is the plain truth' (3). The 'plain truth' is, of course, already a political statement, coming as it does after the introduction of the political ideas of 'freedom' and 'slavery'. This ploy is followed by a key rhetorical question which alters the meaning of 'life' by introducing capitalized 'Nature' and the concept of what is natural. 'But is this simply part of the order of Nature? Is it because this land of ours is so poor that it cannot afford a decent life to those who dwell upon it?' (3). Like all rhetorical questions, this one also contains its own answer: the land is fertile enough to support a much larger community that could live in 'a comfort and a dignity that are now almost beyond our imagining' (4). Thus, their present life is indirectly defined as 'unnatural', which brings Major to call the problem by its name: the problem (the serpent in this very English garden of

Eden) is Man: 'all the evils of this life of ours spring from the tyranny of human beings' (5). All this amounts to translating the conditions of life on a farm into political language, identifying the farm as the political system of tyranny, and blaming Man for it, thereby also implying the possibility of other, more just and more 'natural' systems.[12]

The same blurring or subversion can be detected at the level Orwell's treatment of generic conventions. Animal fables are predicated on the absolute difference between Man and Animal, on what Derrida calls the 'pseudo-concept' of the 'animal', used in the singular, 'as though all animals from the earthworm to the chimpanzee constituted a homogeneous set to which "(the hu)man" would be radically opposed' (Mallet x; cf. Derrida 22–3, 31–2). Thus, the translation of class antagonism into the what Derrida calls the 'war of species' (31) that is staged in the narrative entails an asymmetry that is philosophical as much as political: it is a war between a species (Man) and a pseudo-species conglomerate.

Because human beings are involved in the story from the start and especially because the boundary between Human and Animal turns out not to be impregnable after all, Orwell's narrative is subversive on several levels: animals remain animals while allegorizing particular human figures or types – just as, within the farmyard community, some of the animals retain their animal identity (or species identity, like the sheep), while others are full-fledged fable figures with names and individual features. As many readers have noted, Orwell begs the question of the pigs' coup by racializing their superiority: 'with their superior knowledge it was natural that they should assume the leadership' (17). One could argue, of course, that the 'it was natural' locution is one of the subversive textual places, referred to above, that serve to blur agency. A related ambiguity persists concerning language, and, as Christopher Hollis says, the animals in *Animal Farm* do not simply 'speak' (146–7) as they would in a fable: they continue to bleat and whinny and quack and bleat even as they speak (cf. Fowler 177–8), thus, animal noises are not simply metaphors of human speech but also its metonymic extensions. If the point of the animal fable is that animals behave like certain types of human beings or embody certain human features, then the final episodes in which the pigs do behave like generic human beings – rather than certain types of human beings – trigger off a kind of infinity which is already encoded in the starting situation. Rather than two animal species (as in a real fable), the warring parties are humans versus animals, that is, Man versus Animal (pseudo-concept); when the pigs emerge from within the 'animal' group as the 'new humans', this allegorizes the arbitrariness of establishing the human-animal dichotomy in the first place.

When read as a story about actual animals as much as allegorical dummies, the way in which *Animal Farm* defines 'life' becomes doubly interesting. The Major's speech – the Revolution – starts with the redescription of animal life as something that does not follow from nature, more as something imposed on them unnaturally through human oppression and exploitation. This initiates the strategy whereby 'life' in the text is always the life experienced, endured by the underlings: it is always the lives of animals – as distinct from the life of humans and pigs. When the narrator states in a matter-of-fact way that '[t]he seasons came and went, the short animal lives fled by' (85), 'animal life' refers to that of the oppressed animals, even though the word seems to include the life of the pigs as well. Life, then, refers consistently to *zoē* rather than *bios*. On the other hand, the animals themselves (i.e. animals minus the pigs) do include the *zoē* of human beings in their idea of life. This is obvious from Boxer's reaction when, during the Battle of the Cowshed, he thinks he has killed one of the men who attack the farm: '"I have no wish to take life, not even human life," repeated Boxer, and his eyes were full of tears' (28). 'Human life' here is in fact animal life, creaturely life, the life of a creature susceptible to suffering. This, then, is what is meant by the life of the animals – that is, apart from pigs: 'their life, so far as they knew, was as it had always been' (87). They don't really remember historical events;

> [t]here was nothing with which they could compare their present lives: they had nothing to go on except Squealer's lists of figures, which invariably demonstrated that everything was getting better and better. [...] Only Benjamin professed to remember every detail of his long life and to know that things never had been, nor ever could be, much better or much worse – hunger, hardship and disappointment being, so he said, the unalterable law of life. (87)

By 'life', he means creaturely life. Like Koestler's yogi, he remains sceptical about any change because he thinks in terms of unchanging laws of nature and society.[13] His 'animality' (i.e. humanity, creatureliness) is expressed through small gestures of practical caring: he lies down at Boxer's side 'and, without speaking, kept the flies off him with his long tail' (80). Without speaking.

Extinct animals: *Nineteen Eighty-Four*

Antony Easthope, Steven Connor, Alan Kennedy, Richard Rorty and others have demonstrated that, far from a straightforward celebration of individual freedom, *Nineteen Eighty-Four* raises serious doubts about the very possibility of the autonomous subject, performing a demystifying and demythologizing deconstruction of the ideology of common sense, plain language and individual autonomy.[14] In what Easthope called 'probably the greatest and certainly the most famous English novel of the twentieth century' (1999: 155), Orwell's exploration of language and subjectivity takes the unlikely form of a metafictional enquiry, the object of which is the novel genre. Bearing the marks of the conflictual period of its inception, the text privileges both common sense over ideology (purveyed as irrational theories) *and* the autonomous subjective world over the invasive potential of the totalitarian state but does so as part of its preference for the plain language of the novel genre as opposed to other, rhetorical and figurative modes of literary discourse. Orwell's common sense, Cartesian subjectivity and Kantian morality all draw upon the novel as a genre rather than political realities. In 'Literature and Totalitarianism' Orwell appears keenly aware of this connection, as expressed in 'Literature and Totalitarianism':

> We live in an age in which the autonomous individual is ceasing to exist – or perhaps one ought to say, in which the individual is ceasing to have the illusion of being autonomous. Now in all that we say about literature, and (above all) in all that we say about criticism, we instinctively take the autonomous individual for granted. The whole of modern European literature – *I am speaking of the literature of the past four hundred years* – is built on the concept of intellectual honesty, or if you like to put it that way, on Shakespeare's maxim, 'to thine own self be true'. (134)

Although *Nineteen Eighty-Four* is usually considered to be an allegory or a dystopia rather than a novel, Orwell himself referred to it as 'a Utopia in the form of a novel' (qtd. Lea 43). In this text he seems deeply committed to the ideology of the novel as it had been worked out in close alliance with and allegiance to what Easthope calls the ideology of Englishness and liberal humanism. It is possible to read *Nineteen Eighty-Four* as a meta-novel, an apology and a critique of the novel at the same time, a mapping of the ideological unconscious of the novel genre. Thus, instead of simply harnessing the implied ideology of the novel for a defence of liberal humanism, it explores the novel as the embodiment of this ideology, performing a critique of certain humanist assumptions through critiquing the novel itself, thereby putting at risk at each and every moment of its unfolding its own status as a novel.

The world of Oceania is not only anti-narrative, as Steven Connor aptly suggests (207), but thoroughly anti-novelistic. Orwell had no doubt that the novel is the par excellence anti-totalitarian genre: 'in any totalitarian society that survives for more than a couple of generations, it is probable that prose literature, of the kind that has existed during the past four hundred years, must actually come to an end' (134). Connor suggests that the first half of the novel is trying to become a coherent narrative in a non-narrative world, while the second half subjects the first to 'the same kind of rewriting that the Party inflicts on all events that it finds unacceptable' (211–2). We could amend this by claiming that, on the level of the story, Winston Smith's narrative aspires to the status of a novel, while the text itself reads *throughout* as a novel. Even though the novel, as we know it, is clearly unthinkable in Oceania, its spectre haunts Oceania: on the one hand, there exists a kind of text, produced by machines, that is merchandized as 'novel'; on the other hand, the novel is a horizon for texts that strive to become novels. It is as if Winston's story were that part of the text which is in search of the novel as the sense and adequate form of itself, or as if the novel read by us were searching for the reality that it could then represent.

The lack of a coherent narrative identity bothers Winston from the start, impelling him to make repeated attempts to articulate his experience as a narrative that would conform to the criteria of novelistic discourse. Easthope suggests that he is 'expressively writing his novelistic inwardness into existence via the "hurried untidy scrawl" of his diary' (1984: 275), but this is precisely what Winston cannot do. Even though he might be 'a paradigmatic example of the subject of knowledge privileged by realist fiction' (Easthope 1984: 275), his inwardness remains largely inaccessible to him.[15] The recalled childhood scene in which Winston snatches the piece of chocolate from his mother and starving sister (144–5), that is, when the instinct of self-preservation prevails over 'goodness', becomes the starting point of a series, including the 'madeleine scene' of *Nineteen Eighty-Four*, when Julia brings real chocolate to their first date (109), and the scene in room 101, when he betrays Julia (247), conferring upon him 'depth' in a psychological and hermeneutical sense. Winston's betrayal, thus, clinches him as a coherent character, while also discrediting him as a moral agent. As Franco Moretti indicates, the birth of the coherent self-story reveals a radical negativity, an emptiness at the core of the self in an ironic recapitulation of the typical closure of the Bildungsroman: the moment of consent after the individual has successfully interiorized the principles of normality, assenting to them voluntarily (16).

Winston's failure to become a novelistic character is, however, not a moral one: it is due to the fact that Oceania has eliminated the kind of cultural context that novelistic discourse had come to thrive in. As Nancy Armstrong explains in *Desire and Domestic Fiction*, the site proper to the novel genre is where private experience meshes with the public realm, in such a way that the privileged terrain of truths is the personal, private world of everyday life, into which, in modernity the deepest meaning of existence gradually withdrew (39). The ideology of the novel – says Moretti – is 'weak' precisely on account of its hybrid, unclassifiable, malleable nature as a genre, which also allows its efficaciousness as ideology. Its 'weakness' is that of the world of everyday life. It is this everyday life, obliterated in Oceania, that Winston wishes to recover or recapture in his own life as well as among the proles.

Novelistic discourse is identified in *Nineteen Eighty-Four* through being contrasted with texts that could be called anti-novels. Winston begins where the domestic novel began: with the diary. His journal, however, is unable to develop into a coherent text: most of the entries are unintelligible even for Winston, especially the last entry reproduced in the text, his mad account of a visit to a prostitute. From the previous chapter, we know that Winston has no problems writing 'fiction' with fluency; indeed, he even enjoys inventing the spurious story of 'Comrade Ogilvy' (44–5). When it comes to narrativizing his own experience, however, he is at a loss, left with 'the urge to shout filthy words at the top of his voice' (63). On the other hand, we do get the full, 'healthy' narrative in Chapter Six relating, mostly in free indirect discourse, Winston's unsatisfactory and disturbing visit to the prostitute as well as his unsuccessful attempt to render it into narrative form. A 'novelistic' chapter, never exceed Winston's scope of experience and knowledge, it describes his thoughts on sexuality, reminiscences of his wife Katharine, the associations evoked by the encounter, probably very close to the kind of text Winston would write if he could write such a thing.[16]

The true opponent of the Party, thus, is not Winston but the imperturbable narrative voice, in itself a guarantee of 'objective reality': the reality status of the narrated events is never questioned. Thus, the narrative voice is located safely *outside* the collective phantasmagoria of Oceania, what is more, it is able to incorporate even this gigantic madness. O'Brien's threats to Winston to the effect that 'nothing will remain of you' (219) are placed in an ironical context by the mere existence of the narrative voice. Several interpreters have noted the fact that the Appendix, an account of Newspeak, is written in 'normal', Oldspeak English, in the past tense (Saunders 144), using the same reassuring voice of normality.

For the humanist tradition, as Daniel R. Schwarz has noted, narrative voice is the final guarantee of presence (13–14), and, as Alan Singer indicates, it suggests and embodies a sort of timeless, Cartesian cogito (174); equally, it is the place or aspect of novelistic discourse where subjectivity is constituted in the most unassailable – because the least obtrusive – fashion. What speaks here is the 'empty' voice of the ahistorical human(ist) subject, a voice that is never entirely filled by the contingent meanings of the given context, and thereby capable of suggesting the guarantee or illusion of unequivocal meaning.[17]

Deprived of the medium of mediation, normalization and standardization, both the internal memory of the self and collective memory, with its frantic, unceasing rewriting of the past, sink irretrievably into what appears to us novel readers as psychotic fantasy. Winston experiences his internal world as an incoherent series of memories,[18] dreams and present sensations, unable to arrange them into a unified narrative, although his attempts are Proustian in their intensity: 'struggling to think his way back into the dim period of his early childhood. It was extraordinarily difficult. [...] When there were no external records that you could refer to, even the outline of your own life lost its sharpness' (32). Without external armature, his memories remain 'a series of bright-lit tableaux occurring against no background and mostly unintelligible' (9). Like so many heroes of Bildungsroman, Winston is an orphan; unlike them, however, he cannot become a novel, or transform his life into a novelistic plot, partly because he has to dispense with the structures of intersubjectivity (like family and friendship), and partly because he has no adequate mechanisms of signification at his disposal. Moreover, he is denied a novelistic exemplar, because the almost unconscious grammar of everyday life and novelistic discourse have not been allowed to take shape in him. He lacks the intersubjective mechanisms and frameworks of remembering that Maurice Halbwachs considered indispensable to a narrative structure of self-identity and self-understanding. Jan Assmann (49–56) distinguishes two registers or orders of collective memory: communicative memory, which consists in memories of the recent, shared, intersubjective past, and cultural memory – the basic form of which is myth – bound to techniques of recording and retrieval. In Oceania, communicative memory loses its logical, phenomenological and existential primacy to a constructed version of cultural memory – or rather, cultural memory has no time to become history.

The absoluteness of the lack of intersubjective contexts from Oceania is indicated by the fact that the underground movement into which Winston and Julia are initiated by O'Brien – even if it were real – offers the very opposite of a community: all contact between members is forbidden. In terms of intersubjectivity and intimacy, the movement is a ghostly and no less grim replication or travesty of the atomized society of Oceania. O'Brien assures the new recruits that 'you will never have anything to sustain you' (156).

One ambiguous embodiment of the collective nature memory is the rhyme about the churches of London, which, as Lawrence Phillips writes, is 'already an encoded collective memory, or perhaps more specifically, a manifestation of a form of folk history. It is itself a mental map embodying a social network built around the City of London's medieval churches' (142). The rhyme is pieced together by four people, even though the mode of its assemblage also indicates the impossibility of a 'free' novelistic plot, for it is the secret policeman Charrington who supplies both the opening and the closing lines (87–8), while O'Brien turns out to have known the whole thing all along; what is left for Winston and Julia is simply the retrieval of the middle part. The rhyme implies at least three different kinds of remembering. Through its referential content, it recalls the churches of London, emblems of a lost world, *lieux de mémoire*, a link both to the past and to the traditional strategy of *ars memoriae*, a mnemotechnical practice used to develop memory by means of linking concepts to well-known places. It also contains a rudimentary narrative about a debt ('When will you pay me') and a promise ('When I grow rich'), thus indicating the intersubjective nature of narrative identity and counterpointing Winston's inability to conceive such an identity; it is as if the missing internal memories were substituted by the rhyme. The rhyme is also an instance of the retentive kind of memory that Hegel called *Gedächtnis* as opposed to *Erinnerung*, a textual series of lines generated by a verbal automatism that inscribes itself into memory as a meaningless rhyme. Finally, if Winston's story is controlled from the start, the rhyme, with its closed structure and foregone conclusion, can also be seen as a *mise-en-abyme* of O'Brien's proto-novel.

If Winston's mad journal represents one extreme type of the Oceanian anti-novel, the other pole is the multitude of novels manufactured in the Ministry of Truth by novel-writing machines. While Winston's deranged text is all subjectivity, the novels churned out by the Ministry are mad for the opposite reason: they are constructed exclusively out of prefabricated panels, not unlike the rhyme. Implicitly, both types of texts are contrasted with the normal 'novelistic' discourse of the book we are reading, a normality apparent in its very imperceptibility. O'Brien's wry remark – 'No book is produced individually, as you know' (225) – while it may refer to Winston's futile efforts to produce a book (a diary) out of his own resources, also recalls the second type of anti-novel appearing in *Nineteen Eighty-Four*, the texts produced by machines. These so-called novels haunt the entire book, intimating that what is at stake in the ideological function of the novel genre is the insertion of the individual into the symbolic structures of society while letting them believe that they are asserting their individuality. Walter Benjamin associates the novel not only with mass-produced art, but also with the devaluation of immediate experience and the rise of what he calls 'information': news of the world, indeed our own experiences are transformed into processed information, always liable to become propaganda, before they reach us. Oceanian machines are 'writing' the secret double of the novel, constructing the reader, bringing off an unlikely rapprochement between the subject of mass culture and the subject of totalitarian culture.

There is a third anti-novel in *Nineteen Eighty-Four*, which plays an important part in the autopsy of the novel genre, reinforcing the subversive effect of the presence of the mass-produced novels. In the scene that might be read alternately as the apotheosis of novel reading, the novel's *mise-en-abyme*, and its primal scene or primal fantasy, Winston is curled up in his armchair, in what he believes to be a room of his own, reading Goldstein's banned book (which is O'Brien's book and Winston's book as well). Despite the nature of the book, the scene of reading evokes the performative and addressive criteria of the novelistic discourse: Goldstein's book is read by Winston like a novel, for the conditions of reading seem inseparable from what is being read: 'solitude and safety were physical sensations, mixed up somehow with the tiredness of his body, the softness of the chair, the touch of the faint breeze from the window that played upon his cheek' (173). Shortly after starting the book, Winston pauses,

> chiefly in order to appreciate the fact that he was reading, in comfort and safety. He was alone: no telescreen, no ear at the keyhole, no nervous impulse to glance over his shoulder or cover the page with his hand. [...] He settled deeper into the arm-chair and put his feet up on the fender. It was bliss, it was eternity. (163)

The scene encapsulates the essence of the myth – and the ideology – of the novel. According to George Steiner, '[t]he literate middle-class figure, reading a novel which he owns and for which he has a library, in a quiet room in his own house or apartment (silence being a function of size), embodies a complex of economic privileges, stabilities, psychological safeguards, and deliberately nurtured tastes of which Thomas Mann was the last full representative and ironic valedictorian' (104).

In the world of Oceania, Winston's scene of reading is as subversive as the affair with Julia, or perhaps even more so, for Julia's appearance seems to disturb the narcissistic bliss. This narcissism is one of the keys to the ideological function of novels, and it is at this point that *Nineteen Eighty-Four* takes up once again the subversion of the ideology of the novel. Mediating between the individual and the community, the novel offers patterns of subject formation, but not necessarily by representing exemplary instances: it is not through identification with the protagonist that the reader must recognize themselves in the image constructed by the book but through the reading process itself: it is the successful gathering together of the multifariousness of experience into a coherent formation of meaning that functions like a reassuring mirror image. Here, the solitary enclosure of reading appears as the counterpart of the narrative voice.

> The book fascinated him, or more exactly it reassured him. In a sense it told him nothing that was new, but that was part of the attraction. It said what he would have said, if it had been possible for him to set his scattered thoughts in order. [...] The best books, he perceived, are those that told you what you know already. (173)

Such texts hold an image up to us in which we readily see a narcissistic mirror image, providing us with a language that we believe is able to express and articulate our internal disorder in ways that are intelligible for the other. They insert us into the symbolic, transforming us into a subject for the other, while making us believe that what we are 'reading' is a narcissistic self-reflection.[19]

This brings us to a question that at first sight might seem frivolous: could it be that the novel that is being read by us has been manufactured by the Party's machines (or perhaps, like Goldstein's book, produced in a more sophisticated fashion, like a sample 'Oceanian anti-novel' that resembles our 'novel')? Is it possible that, by reading in our room a book in which we are happy to recognize ourselves, we in a sense repeat Winston's error? In *Nineteen Eighty-Four*, novel and non-novel (anti-novel) are locked in a spiralling relationship that could be called dialectical: although Goldstein's book exposes, refutes and contains the entire philosophy of the Party, its negativity turns out to be always already re-contained by the Party. The book called *Nineteen Eighty-Four* in turn exposes, refutes and contains the Party's strategies including the ruse of the Goldstein book, which leaves us in a potentially endless, vertiginous spiral.

What seems to be certain is that, in *Nineteen Eighty-Four*, normality is situated somewhere between the two extreme kinds of anti-novelistic discourse, rather than – as has often been suggested – in the untouched interiority of the mind which is then invaded by external forces. In Orwell's meta-novel, human beings are what Craig L. Carr labels 'socially configured creatures' (100), and what is defined as the merely human, the few cubic centimetres of interiority, is in fact not sufficiently human – as Winston also implies when talking about the defective memory of the proles. Although Winston insists that 'the proles had stayed human' (146), what he means by human is the state of being equipped with an interiorized set of humanist values ('governed by private loyalties [...] individual relationships,' 146), and the proles are dismissed by him as subhuman creatures who have at best preserved the ability to become fully human. This is what undermines the definition of humanity as ordinary humanism. The gesture with which Winston's mother tries to shelter her daughter – together with the similar gesture of the refugee woman in the newsreel (13) – becomes for Winston the irreducible moment of humanity, precisely because these gestures are 'private' (31, 182). Yet, as we have seen, Winston proves to be an abject failure as a human being in comparable moments. Thus, either Winston himself is not fully human or the two women – through their internalized codes – represent something in excess of the human.

The structure of address of *Nineteen Eighty-Four* encourages us to imagine ourselves, even against the logic of the story, like the Winston reading in his armchair and not like him cringing from rats in room 101. The first mirror image is the desired reflection of the autonomous humanist subject communing with another similar subject across vast distances of space and time, a reflection that works like the picture on the wall of the secret room, hiding the camera, hiding the undesired image of room 101 as its own secret and uncanny truth.

At this point let me introduce the glass paperweight, which, though often interpreted as a symbol of the vulnerable interiority of the individual mind, is a multivalent symbol which gathers together not only several themes of *Nineteen Eighty-Four* but also several concerns of the present chapter. For one thing, it serves as the specular origin of the secret room he dreams of renting: 'the idea had first floated into head in the form of a vision, of the glass paperweight mirrored by the surface of the gateleg table' (122). When Winston installs himself in the secret room, the glass paperweight becomes the focus of this personal space, consistently seen by him as a miniature replica of the room itself (130, 134). He often lies gazing into it, finding that:

> The inexhaustibly interesting thing was not the fragment of coral but the interior of the glass itself. There was such a depth of it, and yet it was almost as transparent as air. It was as though the surface of the glass had been the arch of the sky, enclosing a tiny world with its atmosphere complete [...]. The paperweight was the room he was in, and the coral was Julia's life and his own, fixed in a sort of eternity at the heart of the crystal. (130)

The paperweight is, thus, another counterpart of Winston, a narcissistic accessory, literally a looking glass through which Winston sees, opaquely. When he first sees it, the paperweight strikes him simply as a beautiful and gloriously useless object in a world of paltriness and ugliness (85–6), but it soon becomes a memory symbol, a time capsule, 'a little chunk of history that they've forgotten to alter. It's a message from a hundred years ago, if one knew how to read it' (129). Like a drop of amber, it has preserved something that cannot be denied or garbled by language: only a few solid objects like this 'lump of glass' survive the all-out perversion of history and memory (137). Winston's dream of the last glimpse of his mother takes place, as it were, inside the glass globe (142).

What is interesting in Winston's complex and changing images of the paperweight is the elision of its centre. When he calls it 'a chunk of history', Winston is forgetting that in fact the coral in the centre had been 'nature' before becoming 'history' (a man-made object): the animal had to die first before it could be enclosed in the glass globe, transformed into 'art' (or at least artifice). Enthralled by the convoluted transparency of the glass, Winston ignores the 'fragment of coral', which is exposed only when the paperweight is smashed to pieces by the soldiers: 'The fragment of coral, a tiny crinkle of pink like a sugar rosebud from a cake, rolled across the mat. How small, thought Winston, how small it always was!' (190). Even now, Winston compares it to an artificial ornament, and it is too late to note anything besides its tininess.

The coral within the paperweight can be seen in the context of the pervasive animal metaphors of *Nineteen Eighty-Four*.[20] Some of the animal metaphors are unproblematic, as in the episode when Winston observes of his gullible neighbour: 'Parsons swallowed it easily, with the stupidity of an animal' (54). Much more controversial is the treatment of the proles, who are consistently dehumanized through animalization, a strategy that is often deemed to be in line with Orwell's frequently condemned 'obsession with working-class smells and filth' (Rodden 109). In the episode of Winston's slumming, the doorways suggest ratholes (75), with people 'swarming' and 'shooting into them like rabbits' (75). '[T]he sordid swarming life of the streets' (76) is like the village of the Beast-Folk in Wells's *The Island of Doctor Moreau*. At the other extreme, the 'monstrous' prole woman's spontaneous, incessant singing is romantically likened to the song of the thrush (188). Winston's rhetoric of animalization is in harmony with the party line: proles are kept away from politics, not even indoctrinated: 'the Party taught that the proles were natural inferiors who must be kept in subjection, like animals, by the application of a few simple rules [...]. So long as they continued to work and breed, their other activities were without importance. Left to themselves, like cattle turned loose upon the plains of Argentina' (65).[21] Discussing the animal metaphors of the novel, Stewart Cole suggests that 'the shadowy category of the animal in Orwell's work serves to undermine the very humanism that impels it' (341). On the other hand, he concedes that Orwell 'never disavows the human as animal: while falling back upon traditional humanist tropes of ennoblement, he nonetheless asserts our essential animality as an index of our inescapable embodiment' (341). One could even argue that the proles need to be subhuman if the human in its present state means the members of the inner and the outer Party. In fact, their swarming can be seen – in Deleuzian terms – as a potentially subversive social formation. Gilles Deleuze and Félix Guattari describe, 'Schools, bands, herds, populations are not inferior social forms; they are affects and powers, involutions that grip every animal in a becoming just as powerful as that of the human being with the animal' (241). A sense of the animality of the proles is clearly shared by Winston. According to Erika Gottlieb, the rats in room 101 are doppelgängers for Winston, who becomes 'insane, a screaming animal' (247). By allowing himself to be degraded to the level of the 'starving brutes' (246), as Gottlieb says, 'he has become what he had been most afraid of', exposing loyalty and self-sacrifice as sentimental illusions, and man as ultimately a selfish, rapacious beast (71). On the other hand, Winston's transformation can also be seen as a Deleuzian becoming-animal, a line of flight, the moment when he – rather than submitting to the Party – slips out into the realm of the *zoē*.

Seen in this context, the coral within the glass globe shifts its significance once again, recalling an instance when Orwell used coral as a metaphor, in his anti-colonial 1939 essay, 'Marrakech', about the Moroccan city:

> When you walk through a town like this [...], when you see how the people live, and still more how easily they die, it is always difficult to believe that you are walking across human beings. All colonial empires in reality are founded upon that fact. The people have brown faces – besides, there are so many of them! Are they really the same flesh as yourself? Do they even have names? Or are they merely a kind of undifferentiated brown stuff, about as individual as bees or coral insects? (388)

Coral reefs themselves are colonies – if not colonial empires – ecosystems in which it is difficult to tell 'individual' specimens from each other. A coral branch that we often call 'a coral' – like the one within the paperweight – is actually made up of thousands of dead tiny invertebrate animals called coral polyps. The fragment inside the glass globe is not, has never been, a living creature but its exoskeleton. The fact that we have a highly symbolic coral in an empire called 'Oceania' begins to resonate strangely. Creatures of the ocean floor, coral specimens could be seen as similar to the citizens or subjects of Orwell's Oceania: 'fragments' rather than wholes, bits of the 'undifferentiated brown stuff', without individuality in the sense of an enclosed internal world of ideas and emotions. By imagining subjectivity as enclosed in a glass globe as something fragile and beautiful, we are in fact killing it, removing it from its multitudinous life and making it into an exhibit, representing something which does not exist.

As in *Animal Farm*, it is the pseudo-concept 'animal' that is used metaphorically, and the use of the metaphor is further complicated by other instances which veer towards metonymy. Oceanian 'unpersons', a category that comes to include Winston, could be seen as instances of what Agamben calls 'bare life', human life reduced to its biological and physical substratum. This is reinforced by the fact that the animal metaphor is sometimes conflated with that of the monster: in a sentence that also has echoes of the coral motif, Winston 'felt as though he were wandering in the forests of the sea bottom, lost in a monstrous world where he himself was the monster. He was alone' (27). The foreign prisoners are seen by Winston as 'a kind of strange animal' (104), and the room over the junkshop as 'a world, a pocket of the past where extinct animals could walk' (133). In this miniature Jurassic Park, Mr Charrington is mistaken by Winston for an extinct animal like himself.

If in *Animal Farm* the animal metaphor morphs subversively into metonymy, *Nineteen Eighty-Four* presents a scenario that is both similar and inverse: in this extremely urban world, animals are metaphorical (the only exceptions being the thrush, the rats and the bugs in the secret room), but the fact that Winston – like many others – becomes the embodiment of bare life means that animal life is not outside the represented world, but right in its centre – like the fragment of coral.

Notes

1 Orwell's continuing relevance is testified by the multitude of recent monographs, predominantly contextual: Clarke, Colls, Stewart, Gleeson, Goldsmith and Nussbaum, Rodden, Brennan, Ingle, Carr Hitchens, Newsinger, Bounds, Woloch, Lynskey. Textual readings include Connor, Easthope, Saunders, Phillips and Dwan – although Dwan is ultimately interested in Orwell's politics.
2 Orwell's essays are quoted from *The Collected Essays, Journalism and Letters*, Vols. I–IV [see 'Works cited' under Orwell, George for details of these individual essays].
3 To chart these ideas, see Orwell's essays, especially 'The Lion and the Unicorn' published in 1941 and 'The English People' from 1947.
4 This essay was first published in *Horizon* in April 1946.
5 The political debates concerning *Animal Farm* are too well known to warrant further discussion here. For a brief history of the book's reception, see John Rodden

19–26, 384–87. For a scathing indictment of *Animal Farm* from the left, see Sedley, Daniel Lea 15–24, and Paul Kirschner *passim*.

6   The scenario is repeated a few pages later (42–3), when it is announced that Animal Farm would be trading with the neighbouring farms. The same strategy is applied: growling dogs, bleating sheep (a blanket of noise) and the smooth patter of Squealer. Cf. Saunders 14.

7   Napoleon himself does not participate directly in any such silencing, delegating it to several agents. He always speaks briefly and to the point.

8   See also Dwan's slightly revised analysis of *Animal Farm* in his excellent monograph (80 ff).

9   In 'The Prevention of Literature' (1946), Orwell identifies the perversion of language as a necessary consequence of totalitarianism: 'The organised lying practised by totalitarian states is not, as is sometimes claimed, a temporary expedient of the same nature as military deception. It is something integral to totalitarianism, something that would still continue even if concentration camps and secret police forces had ceased to be necessary' (36). See also 'Literature and Totalitarianism'.

10 For a discussion of this scene, see Anthony Stewart 106.

11 This was, of course, before factory farming. In *Animal Liberation*, Peter Singer claims that the animals of Manor Farm are 'happy animals'.

12 Invoking Giorgio Agamben, we could suggest that the revolution begins when Major transforms the farm into a *polity* by redefining *bios* (the biological, natural life of the body) as a kind of *zoē* (the political and ethical life that is characteristic of human beings), thus reversing the exclusion of *bios* which is the condition of proper political – human – life. Thus, *Animal Farm* can be read as a biopolitical allegory of the way modern power politicizes the body and biological life, involving it only to exclude it within the polis as *bare life*.

13 Paul Kirschner considers Benjamin as an authorial figure (765).

14 The conflict between individual autonomy vs totalitarian invasion continues to define much of the critical discourse on *Nineteen Eighty-Four* (cf. Ingle, Sandison, Craig L. Carr 98–100). Alan Sandison sees Orwell as the heir of Protestantism, the fierce defender of the autonomous self, who, however, is also aware that this self is a cultural product rather than a timeless essence.

15 Another possibility is offered by the psychoanalytic reading of Winston as the victim of a regular (Kennedy 84–6) or inverted (Easthope 1984) Oedipus complex.

16 The narrative voice also seems to be in possession of the kind of historical memory the lack of which proves so fatal for Winston. This is obvious from the reference to O'Brien's 'curiously civilized' trick of resettling his spectacles on his nose: 'it was a gesture which, if anyone had still thought in such terms, might have recalled an eighteenth-century nobleman offering his snuffbox' (14).

17 'The new, novelistic point of view is explicitly established by the construction of what would later be called the "subject". It corresponds to the position that

Descartes constructs in the *Meditations* as exterior to the world, as standing steadfastly beyond all possibility of sensory error and also beyond all conceptual doubt' (Cascardi 83).

18 One of his doubles is the old Prole, 'whose memory was nothing but a rubbish heap of details' (82).

19 That Orwell's text is aware of the dystopian elements hidden behind the utopian scene of reading is indicated by the fact that the secret room and room 101 are connected by the motif of the rat.

20 For a discussion of these metaphors from an animal studies perspective, see Cole 342-7 (the coral is not mentioned in his essay).

21 Winston's colleague Syme proclaims unequivocally that 'proles are not human beings' (50).

Works cited

Agamben, Giorgio. *Homo Sacer: Sovereign Power and Bare Life*. Stanford: Stanford University Press, 1998.

Armstrong, Nancy. *Desire and Domestic Fiction*. Oxford: Oxford University Press, 1989.

Assmann, Jan. *Das Kulturelle Gedächtnis: Schrift, Erinnerung, und Politische Identität in frühen Hochkulturen*. Munich: C. H. Beck, 2000.

Benjamin, Walter. 'The Storyteller – Reflections on the Works of Nikolai Leskov'. In Lawrence L. Lipking (ed.), *Modern Literary Criticism 1900-1970*. New York: Atheneum, 1972: 442–55.

Carr, Craig L. *Orwell, Politics, and Power*. London: Continuum, 2010.

Cascardi, Anthony J. *The Subject of Modernity*. Cambridge: Cambridge University Press, 1992.

Cherniss, Joshua L. *A Mind and Its Time: The Development of Isaiah Berlin's Political Thought*. Oxford: Oxford University Press, 2013.

Clarke, Ben. *Orwell in Context: Communities, Myths, Values*. Basingstoke: Palgrave Macmillan, 2007.

Cole, Stewart. '"The True Struggle": Orwell and the Specter of the Animal'. *Literature Interpretation Theory* 28 (4) 2017: 335–53.

Colls, Robert. *George Orwell: English Rebel*. Oxford: Oxford University Press, 2014.

Connor, Steven. *The English Novel in History 1950-1955*. London: Routledge, 1996.

Deleuze, Gilles and Félix Guattari. *A Thousand Plateaus: Capitalism and Schizophrenia*. Brian Massumi (trans). Minneapolis: University of Minnesota Press, 2005.

Derrida, Jacques. *The Animal That Therefore I Am*. David Wills (trans). New York: Fordham University Press, 2008.

Dwan, David. *Liberty, Equality, and Humbug: Orwell's Political Ideals*. Oxford: Oxford University Press, 2018.

Easthope, Antony. *Englishness and National Culture*. London: Routledge, 1999.

Easthope, Antony. 'Fact and Fantasy in *Nineteen Eighty-Four*'. In Christopher Norris (ed.), *Inside the Myth – Orwell: Views from the Left*. London: Lawrence and Wishart, 1984: 263–84.

Elbarbary, Samir. 'Language as Theme in *Animal Farm*'. In Harold Bloom (ed.), *Animal Farm: Modern Critical Interpretations* (New Edition). New York: Infobase, 2009: 35–44.

Gottlieb, Erika. 'Room 101 Revisited: The Reconciliation of Political and Psychological Dimensions in Orwell's *Nineteen Eighty-Four*'. In Peter Buitenhuis and Ira B. Nadel (eds.), *George Orwell: A Reassessment*. London: Macmillan, 1988: 51–76.

Hammond, Andrew. *Cold War Stories: British Dystopian Fiction, 1945–1990*. Basingstoke: Palgrave Macmillan, 2017.

Hollis, Christopher. *A Study of George Orwell: The Man and His Works*. London: Hollis and Carter, 1956.

Hunter, Lynette. *George Orwell: The Search for a Voice*. Buckingham: Open University Press, 1984.

Kennedy, Alan. 'The Inversion of Form: Deconstructing *1984*'. In *Reading Resistance Value: Deconstructive Practice and the Politics of Literary Critical Encounters*. Basingstoke: Macmillan, 1998: 129–48.

Kirschner, Paul. 'The Dual Purpose of *Animal Farm*'. *The Review of English Studies* 55 (222) 2004: 759–86.

Lea, Daniel. *Animal Farm and Nineteen Eighty-Four: A Reader's Guide to Essential Criticism*. Basingstoke: Palgrave Macmillan, 2003.

Mallet, Marie-Louise. 'Introduction'. In Jacques Derrida. *The Animal That Therefore I Am*. David Wills (trans). New York: Fordham University Press, 2008: ix–xiii.

Moretti, Franco. *The Way of the World: The Bildungsroman in European Culture*. London: Verso, 1987.

Newsinger, John. *Hope Lies with the Proles: Orwell and the Left*. London: Pluto Press, 2018.

Norris, Christopher. 'Language, Truth and Ideology: Orwell and the Post-War Left'. In Christopher Norris (ed.), *Inside the Myth – Orwell: Views from the Left*. London: Lawrence and Wishart, 1984: 242–62.

Orwell, George. 'Marrakech'. In Sonia Orwell and Ian Angus (eds.), *The Collected Essays, Journalism and Letters: An Age Like This, 1920–1940*. Vol. I. New York: Harcourt, Brace and World, 1968: 387–93 [1939].

Orwell, George. 'The Lion and the Unicorn'. In Sonia Orwell and Ian Angus (eds.), *The Collected Essays, Journalism and Letters: My Country Right or Left, 1940–1943*. Vol. II. New York: Harcourt, Brace and World, 1968: 56–109 [1941].

Orwell, George. 'Literature and Totalitarianism'. In Sonia Orwell and Ian Angus (eds.), *The Collected Essays, Journalism and Letters: My Country Right or Left, 1940–1943*. Vol. II. New York: Harcourt, Brace and World, 1968: 134–7 [1941].

Orwell, George. 'The English People'. In Sonia Orwell and Ian Angus (eds.), *The Collected Essays, Journalism and Letters: As I Please, 1943–1945*. Vol. III. New York: Harcourt, Brace and World, 1968: 1–38.

Orwell, George. 'Revenge Is Sour'. In Sonia Orwell and Ian Angus (eds.), *The Collected Essays, Journalism and Letters: In Front of Your Nose, 1945–1950*. Vol IV. New York: Harcourt, Brace and World, 1968: 3–6 [1945].

Orwell, George. *Animal Farm*. Introd. Malcolm Bradbury. Harmondsworth: Penguin, 1989 [1945].

Orwell, George. 'The Prevention of Literature'. In Sonia Orwell and Ian Angus (eds.), *The Collected Essays, Journalism and Letters: In Front of Your Nose, 1945–1950*. Vol IV. New York: Harcourt, Brace and World, 1968: 59–72 [1946].

Orwell, George. 'Politics and the English Language'. In Sonia Orwell and Ian Angus (eds.), *The Collected Essays, Journalism and Letters: In Front of Your Nose, 1945–1950*. Vol IV. New York: Harcourt, Brace and World, 1968: 127–40 [1946].

Orwell, George. *Nineteen Eighty-Four*. Harmondsworth: Penguin Books, 1984 [1949].

Orwell, Sonia and Ian Angus (ed.). *The Collected Criticism, Essays, Journalism and Letters of George Orwell I–IV*. New York: Harcourt, Brace and World, 1968.

Phillips, Lawrence. 'Time, Space, and Resistance: Re-Reading George Orwell's *Nineteen Eighty-Four*'. In Nicola Allen and David Simmons (eds.), *Reassessing the Twentieth-Century Canon: From Joseph Conrad to Zadie Smith*. Basingstoke: Palgrave Macmillan, 2014: 134–45.

Pritchett, V. S. 'Obituary of George Orwell'. In Jeffrey Meyers (ed.), *George Orwell: The Critical Heritage*. London: Routledge, 1997: 294–6.

Rodden, John. *The Politics of Literary Reputation: The Making and Claiming of 'St Georg' Orwell*. Oxford: Oxford University Press, 1989.

Rorty, Richard. 'The Last Intellectual in Europe: George Orwell'. In *Contingency, Irony, and Solidarity*. Cambridge: Cambridge University Press, 1993: 169–88.

Sandison, Alan. *George Orwell: After 1984*. Basingstoke: Macmillan, 1989.

Saunders, Loraine. *The Unsung Artistry of George Orwell*. Aldershot: Ashgate, 2008.

Schwarz, Daniel R. *The Humanistic Heritage: Critical Theories of the English Novel from James to Hillis Miller*. Basingstoke: Macmillan, 1986.

Sedley, Stephen. 'An Immodest Proposal'. In Christopher Norris (ed.), *Inside the Myth – Orwell: Views from the Left*. London: Lawrence and Wishart, 1984: 155–62.

Sinfield, Alan. *Literature, Politics and Culture in Postwar Britain*. Berkeley: University of California Press, 1989.

Singer, Alan. 'The Voice of History/The Subject of the Novel'. *Novel* 21 (2–3) 1988: 173–9.

Singer, Peter. *Animal Liberation*. Third Edition. New York: Ecco Press, 2001.

Steiner, George. 'The Pythagorean Genre'. In *Language and Silence*. London: Faber and Faber, 1985.

Stewart, Anthony. *George Orwell, Doubleness, and the Value of Decency*. London: Routledge, 2003.

Woloch, Alex. *Or Orwell: Writing and Democratic Socialism*. Cambridge, MA: Harvard University Press, 2016.

7

Masters and Servants, Class, and the Colonies in Graham Greene's 1940s Fiction

Rebecca Dyer

Graham Greene begins *Ways of Escape* (1980), 'looking back on the circumstances in which [his] books were conceived and written' with a brief anecdote of his convalescing after a surgery at his parents' home in Berkhamsted (9). As he sits down to write, he hears his mother 'discussing a domestic problem with the parlormaid' (13). He reflects then on the vanished world of masters and servants he had known in the early twentieth century: 'How "period" such a title sounds today, and all those other household ranks – kitchenmaid, pantrymaid, nursemaid; I see myself now as a character in a historical novel [...]' (13-14). As this memory and its prominent place in Greene's autobiography indicate, household service was for Greene a necessary condition for his vocation as a writer. So intertwined were servants' working lives with his own that the careful crafting of the first sentence of what was to be his first published novel, *The Man Within* (1929), was interrupted by his mother's instructions to a maid, whom Greene does not describe and who says nothing in his conjured memory. By taking care of essential household tasks, servants indirectly helped Greene to produce or otherwise informed his later work as well. Paul Theroux remarks in his review of the third volume of Greene's biography that a striking and paradoxical feature of Greene's life had been his unusual dependency on outside help for daily matters: 'Greene could not cook, he was incapable of using a typewriter, he did not wield a mop; he was a naturally dependent not to say helpless man. Add to this the astonishing fact that, though a traveler, a seeker of danger, a deeply curious wanderer who was seldom home, he could not drive a car.' Greene also had servants attending to his needs during his stays in Africa – Ali and other servants in Sierra Leone during the Second World War, as I will discuss, and a leper boy in the Congo region while Greene was preparing to write *A Burnt-Out Case* (1960). Some of those servants (perhaps inevitably) found their way into his fiction.

Greene began his writing career on the cusp of a dramatic historical and aesthetic shift. He was one of a number of British authors who wrote master–servant narratives in the 1940s, contributing to a large body of work produced over centuries in a variety of genres and modes. The 1940s narratives are noteworthy in part because actual servants were becoming ever rarer within Britain. In 'Modernity and Revolution', Perry Anderson describes a decline in European artistic innovation during and after the war, a decline which he notes had occurred not coincidentally at the end of the master–servant era: 'Socially, a distinctive upper-class mode of life persisted right down to the end of the 30s, whose hallmark – setting it off completely from the existence of the rich after the Second World War – was the normalcy of servants. This was the last true leisure-class in metropolitan history.' Giles Waterfield explains that during the Second World War, employing a number of servants was seen as unpatriotic by both the government and the public since so many young people were being called up for military service (186). Through travel to the Global South, Greene appears to have created the conditions for his artistic achievement while continuing to experience 'the normalcy of servants' even after the era of live-in servants had come to a close in Britain. Following the war, as the few remaining older servants were joined by migrant workers, Waterfield writes, 'the servant, particularly the manservant, developed into a potent symbol of insubordination and even anarchy in the traditional social order' (186, 190). The figure's potency may be the reason British writers continued to portray servant characters throughout the 1940s, even though only 1 per cent of households in Britain would employ a servant by 1951 (Hobsbawm 278).

Some authors represented masters and servants in the 1940s as part of a long-standing series or set their work during earlier periods when class demarcations were clear and perceived by many to be unalterable. Perhaps because the master–servant relationship was in some ways analogous to the power relations between colonial officials and colonized populations, a few British authors and filmmakers commented either overtly or obliquely on the Empire via these characters. In the 1930s and 1940s, Greene produced works spanning several genres – a travel book, a short story, a novel, and a film – all with African settings or with significant references to the continent. Within these works, he reflects on and sometimes echoes earlier literary treatments of Africa while revealing his general acceptance of the Empire's hierarchies of continents, races, and classes. Yet, as I will argue, he also blends references to Africa and Africans with a form of class travel for his upper-class characters with servants. In a story and a film set in London, 'The Basement Room' (1936), which he adapted with

Carol Reed into *The Fallen Idol* (1948), Greene refers to Africa through a servant character's repeated storytelling. The servant in the film version fabricates a tale of his quashing an African rebellion in a scene that seems to reveal Greene's own ambivalence about the coming postcolonial age. Additionally, despite Greene's characterization of an African servant named Ali in *The Heart of the Matter* (1948), Greene avoids writing about ongoing racial conflicts and makes no mention of the consequences of the Emergency Powers (Defence) Act of 1939, which enabled authorities to detain anticolonial dissidents for the duration of the war. However, as I will argue, even while Greene erases or downplays racial inequality and avoids the subject of organized African resistance to colonial rule, he also represents a master and servant relationship based on companionship and love that at times is capable of transcending race and class divisions.

British writers' servant depictions of the 1940s

Other 1940s publications of the master–servant novel provide a clear contrast to Greene's works with African settings or references. P. G. Wodehouse's novels of the 1940s contained many recurring characters and plot devices and were therefore rooted in the tropes of the past even though their production was influenced by the trying circumstances of the war years. Wodehouse managed even while imprisoned and accused of German collaboration to write four comedic novels featuring master and servant characters.[1] After he made a series of radio broadcasts from Berlin during the war, some libraries in Britain removed his books from their shelves, and a number of newspapers and public figures denounced him. Wodehouse had his defenders, including George Orwell, who argued in 1945 that Wodehouse was oblivious to politics rather than a traitor. Surveying Wodehouse's novels, Orwell noted a continuity – at least since 1925 – in the Jeeves-and-Bertie Wooster creator's manner of conveying a 'peculiar mental atmosphere', 'a harmless old-fashioned snobbishness' and 'a mild facetiousness covering an unthinking acceptance' of the British class system (n.pag). Greene too spoke in an interview of his 'enormous respect' for Wodehouse and described his novels as 'inspired by an infectious *joie de vivre*' (Allain 68).

Other authors of the period represented unruly, even potentially deadly, British servants, who unsettled the established order of society. Ivy Compton-Burnett published four of her twenty novels in the 1940s, including *Manservant and Maidservant* (1947). Despite this novel's setting in a country house in 1892 and many of her characters' adherence to the rigid class arrangements of that earlier era, Compton-Burnett anticipates the class mobility and the British working class's power and class pride during the post-war period through her portrayal of George, an outspoken young servant who had been raised in a workhouse. Compton-Burnett depicts him skewering other servants for their hypocrisy and weakness. He mocks the butler Bullivant's seated position while delivering orders and shows contempt for all the other servants' slavish devotion to the deeply flawed master and his family. When Bullivant reminds his young charge that there is honour in service and that '[t]here is no one, from the first to the last, who does not serve in some way the stratum above himself. Even the Queen is the servant of the State,' George scoffingly replies, 'But not at the sink' (201). Despite Compton-Burnett's gift for writing George's biting retorts, she seems to approve of Bullivant's advice to Master Jasper, one of the children of the house, 'not to foster in George any disposition to terms of equality [...]. It is not a suitable tendency, and would not be to his ultimate benefit' (235).

Albert Memmi has written that the domestic servant is held in contempt by other workers because he is seen as 'a traitor to the common condition of the poor,' who feel they too are diminished by 'the servant's complete debasement, a debasement to which he consents' (179). Compton-Burnett reinforces Memmi's claim through her depiction of a taciturn shopkeeper in *Manservant and Maidservant*, Miss Buchanan, who is unimpressed by titles and property and who questions the elder servants' loyalty to their miserly master and his family. The shopkeeper comes across initially as an ally to George; however, Compton-Burnett depicts him brought low by the novel's end, as he begs for forgiveness at Bullivant's feet after he is caught stealing and plotting his master's murder. In contrast, Miriam, another young servant in the household whose background as an orphan resembles George's, is celebrated for accepting her lowly status and for putting the education she received in a convent to good use by teaching the illiterate shopkeeper to read and write.

Another 1940s character who, like George, refuses his station is Barrett, the malevolent servant in Robin Maugham's second novel, *The Servant* (1948), who entraps his master Tony by arranging the hire of an attractive young maid. By the end, the master has broken his engagement and turned over complete control of his life and property to Barrett. Maugham's novel was later adapted by Harold Pinter and Joseph Losey, whose 1963 film altered the class dynamics and added a number of significant references to the colonies, as I have explored elsewhere.[2]

In what follows, I closely examine portrayals of masters and servants and references to Africa in Graham Greene's 1930s–40s works. Between the world wars, Greene had visited Liberia and Sierra Leone, travelling on foot with

African carriers, a journey he describes in his non-fiction book, *Journey Without Maps* (1936). During his return to England, Greene was writing 'The Basement Room', a story about Baines, a manservant who impresses the master's young son, Philip, with recurring tales of Africa, where Baines claims to have wielded weapons and supervised forty black men. Baines's Africa of 'corruption' and '[s]melling of rot' returns to Philip's mind when he is later deciding whether to reveal Baines's role in his housekeeper wife's death (116). In his unusual rendering of a master and servant in 'The Basement Room', Greene captures the cultural capital that attached to a working-class man making a career and collecting anecdotes in a colony as well as Philip's growing class consciousness as he suffers from Mrs Baines's cruelty. After her death, he runs away from home and discovers in the working-class boroughs of London a world almost as foreign as Baines's Africa.

After serving as an air-raid warden during the London Blitz, Greene sailed in 1941 for West Africa, where, as he wrote thirty years later, he soon 'was ineffectually running a one-man office of the Secret Service' (1971: 26). Stationed in Sierra Leone from 1941 to 1943 as an MI6 agent tasked with decoding the telegrams delivered to the police station in Freetown, Greene later set *The Heart of the Matter* in an unnamed West African colony during the war. He drew on both his knowledge of Conrad and his actual experiences while living solo with 'a couple boys and a cook' in a 'Creole villa' without running water (Sherry 113). Most critics of the novel focus on Greene's representation of Major Scobie, the self-effacing character loosely based on Police Commissioner Brodie, whom Greene worked under in Sierra Leone, and on Greene himself (Sherry 117–18). As Scobie struggles (and fails) not to let down his wife or his mistress and to fulfil his difficult duties without becoming either callous or corrupt, the character enables Greene's questioning of Catholic doctrine about suicide. Given Greene's evident emphases in his novel – or as, Orwell wrote at the time, Greene's depiction of Scobie as 'White all through, with a stiff upper lip [...] gone to what he believed to be certain damnation out of pure gentlemanliness' (1948: 61–3) – it is not surprising that the servant characters have received little scholarly attention. This is a significant critical omission because servants and sex workers are the most prominent African characters in the novel, and, despite Greene's decision not to develop them fully, these characters' interactions with the white characters contribute greatly to the plot and to Greene's meditations on love and suicide. Greene's personal stance in terms of religion – his fervent Catholicism at that time – appears also to have influenced his portrayal of masters and servants and his idea of the 'service' that is required even of someone in the master class. Scobie's devoted servant, Ali, represents in the world of the Greene's novel a complete victim deserving pity, but he also acts at times as his master's protégé and double.

Greene's initial idea of Africa

Greene's deep interest in Africa and his motivation for writing about the continent are clearly laid out in his non-fiction travel narrative, *Journey Without Maps*. Recounting how he prepared for his interwar visit into Liberia, he quotes at length the horrors then in the news about Liberian soldiers brutally attacking native villagers, including small children, and burning newborn babies in huts. After the long, gory quotation, he writes: 'There was something satisfyingly complete about this picture. It really seemed as though you couldn't go deeper than that; the agony was piled on in the British Government *Blue Book* with a real effect of grandeur' (18). About Liberia, founded by American philanthropists and former slave owners at the beginning of the nineteenth century with the intention of its being peopled by black Americans, Greene notes that 'the descendants of the slaves have taken to politics with the enthusiasm of practiced crap players' (19). He admits to a deep attraction to what he described as 'a seediness about the place you couldn't get to the same extent elsewhere' (19). After a list of comparable seedy sites in London, he acknowledges that those cannot satisfy like African seediness: '[T]here are times of impatience, when one is less content to rest at the urban stage, when one is willing to suffer some discomfort for the chance of finding – there are a thousand names for it, King Solomon's Mines, the "heart of darkness" if one is romantically inclined' (19). As this passage indicates, Greene was capable of diagnosing his psychological inclinations very accurately and was hardly unaware of his literary influences. He seems to have been, however, less aware of his ethnocentricity and the blinders (particularly evident in his criticism of the British and of Britain) that his upper-middle-class upbringing and education had placed on him.

About to depart on the steamer from Liverpool, and with his yearning for African seediness at a pitch, Greene makes a morning visit to a pub and observes a small party of middle-aged women and 'an old dirty man of eighty-four' (22). Of the four women, he notes that '[t]hree had the dustbin look; they carried about them the air of tenements, of lean cats and shared washhouses,' and because these three 'must return to the dustbin', their drink with the old man's daughter, home from America for Christmas, 'was perilous, precarious, breath-taking; they were happy and aghast when the old man drew out a pound note and stood a round himself, "Well, why shouldn't he?" the daughter asked them, asked Jackie boy, the bar-tender, the beer advertisements, the smutty air' (22–3). This passage is significant in that it reveals Greene's desire to 'travel' also in terms of class, to be a keen observer, a sensitive instrument (straight from Oxford and his position at the *Times*) noting down, as an anthropologist might do, the 'dustbin' existence of English patrons at the same pub. The vivid anecdote from a Liverpool pub brings to mind a similar scene by T. S. Eliot, whose 'The Love Song of Alfred Prufrock' Greene quotes without attribution in the same chapter. In *The Waste Land* (with its epigraph drawn from *Heart of Darkness*), one woman boasts to a drinking companion about advice to 'make yourself a bit smart' that she had given to a dreary mother of five and wife of a demobbed solider – 'He's been in the army four years, he wants a good time, / And if you don't give it him, there's others will, I said' – revealing a world of petty cruelty in a few deft lines that Eliot interrupts with the bartender's all-caps reminders of closing time (138–39, lines 142, 148–49). Greene's non-fiction pub scene resembles Eliot's, but in Greene's the emphasis is on the pub's atmosphere and the small group's 'air of slightly disreputable revelry' rather than on the particular inflections of working-class British English, even though Greene does note that the old man's daughter 'had caught the American accent' (22). Significantly, Greene thought 'the dustbin look' and 'the smutty air' of Liverpool fitting material for his *Journey Without Maps* to Africa, suggesting in this early travel narrative his manner of representing that other country (in a sense) of the British working- and underclasses while at the same time providing his readers with a taste of the seediness he hoped to find amplified in Africa.

Later in *Journey Without Maps*, Greene sadly contemplates the many books (he lists a few he encountered in the library on the ship bound for Africa) 'written without truth, without compulsion, one dull word following another, books to read while you wait for the bus, while you strap hang, in between the Boss's dictations, while you eat your A.B.C. lunch; a whole industry founded on a want of leisure and a want of happiness' (25). In Greene's concern for commuters and dictation takers, those without the time or inclination to dive into the serious literature he preferred to read himself and to write (even choosing to designate some of his works as 'entertainments' rather than allow them to be taken for his best work), there is a hint of Greene's political vision. These are the working Britons with a bit more status than the party of five in the Liverpool pub whom he had described without sentimentality. Greene as a young man appeared to want to escape the grind of money making, family routine, and controlling bosses, and most of all, to avoid contributing (as a book buyer or writer) to the 'whole industry founded on a want of leisure and want of happiness' (25). His first Africa novel, particularly his characterization of Major Scobie and his servant Ali, reveals another way of considering 'a want of leisure and want of happiness': the master–servant relationship provided an unacknowledged way for the British in the colonies to acquire some leisure time by offloading to Africans the daily necessities of water gathering, food preparation, house cleaning and other menial, time-consuming activities. Even with servants handling those mundane tasks, Greene's official duties as an MI6 agent could be overwhelming: he wrote his mother about being 'rushed off my feet [...]. Stuff accumulates so' and longed for a secretary to relieve 'the donkey work of typing, etc.' (qtd. Sherry 127).

Greene's approach to Africa is also revealed in his attitude towards officialdom and bureaucratic red tape. Laws, especially in African countries, could be gotten around. Before beginning his trek into Liberia with his cousin Barbara on foot from the British side of the border, he notes that white men were forbidden to enter without having paid for an expensive explorer's license that he lacked, and he admits to 'solemnly swear[ing]' on an entry document to abide by the nation's laws (16). Wondering at his willingness to sign, Greene states that his (and humankind's) contradictory psyche is another of his writerly interests: why did he as an avowed Catholic affix his signature solemnly swearing to do something he fully intended not to do? It is as if for him in that time and place, as for many white men before him, the usual rules did not apply. Greene perceptively analysed his motivations to travel to Africa on that first trip, suggesting (as Chinua Achebe and Edward Said would later elucidate about Conrad and other writers) the imprint of earlier European imagery and written representations of the continent and people, prefabricated ideas and stereotypes to which Greene adds his highly personal impressions. Said argues that '[t]he scientist, the scholar, the missionary, the trader, or the soldier was in, or thought about, the Orient because he *could be there*, or could think about it, with very little resistance on the Orient's part,' a claim that could, with only geographic revisions, apply to Greene's repeated presence in and thoughts about Africa (1978: 7).

As John Cullen Gruesser has argued, Greene's 'metaconsciousness about the endeavor of writing about Africa' has to be weighed against his tacit approval of the colonial effort and his avoidance of politics about the region (16). Greene reveals in his travel book that he had no intention of confronting 'the white settler' and the imprint he or she had made on the continent:

> [W]hen I say that to me Africa has always seemed an important image, I suppose that is what I mean, that it has represented more than I could say [...].

[A] crowd of words and images, witches and death, unhappiness and the Gare St Lazare, the huge smoky viaduct over a Paris slum, crowd together and block the way to full consciousness. [...] It is not then *any* part of Africa which acts so strongly on this unconscious mind; certainly no part where the white settler has been most successful in reproducing the conditions of his country, its morals and its popular art. A quality of darkness is needed, of the inexplicable. [...] [W]hen one sees to what unhappiness, to what peril of extinction centuries of cerebration have brought us, one sometimes has a curiosity to discover if one can from what we have come, to recall at which point we went astray. (20–1)

It is striking that Greene claims to have 'always' seen Africa as important and then specifies that he means the unadulterated, truly African 'quality of darkness [...] of the inexplicable' (20), a continent and a culture that cannot claim 'centuries of cerebration' (21). Achebe was to critique this idea that Africa is emblematic of man's ancestral past, a continent trapped at a primitive stage of development. In 'An Image of Africa', he demonstrates how European writers represent even Africa's geographical features as having a beginnings-of-the-earth quality, and he wryly states that Conrad's Congo River 'is not a River Emeritus' and 'enjoys no old-age pension', unlike the vaunted Thames (4). Acknowledging that Conrad did not invent this way of thinking, Achebe explains that 'If Europe, advancing in civilization, could cast a backward glance periodically at Africa trapped in primordial barbarity, it could say with faith and feeling: "There go I but for the grace of God"' (17). For the most part, Greene's thinking conforms to what Achebe expects of Europeans in that Greene travelled to Liberia looking for 'primordial barbarity'. Yet, he appears not to have been comforted by Europe's comparative advances, which he sees as marred by 'unhappiness' and the 'peril of extinction'. Nevertheless, his reflections on 'primitive' Africa are inconsistent and puzzling, as John Airey notes in his analysis of *Journey Without Maps*; 'If the interior of the country is to be considered as seedy, it is obvious that this seediness is very different from the seediness of "civilisation"; the definition of the word evidently needs to be stretched to cover several very different meanings' (n.pag).

Greene appears to have been seeking not just a foil for Europe or an opposition for civilization to measure itself against, but also an opportunity of knowing others at a simple, human level, as indicated by the master–servant pairing of Scobie and Ali in *The Heart of the Matter*, a novel with a clear debt to Conrad's *Heart of Darkness*. Even Greene's use of 'Heart' in the vague title is an echo of Conrad's, but the heart image also refers to Greene's earlier descriptions of the continent as invitingly blank and heart shaped. It is noteworthy that Greene's professed desire to visit the blank spots on the map resembles that of Conrad's

Marlow, who describes Africa on the world map as 'the biggest, the most blank, so to speak – that I had a hankering after' (22). Similarly, Greene decided to take what he would later describe as his 'foolhardy' trip to Liberia because the maps at the time had 'cannibals' marked across a large, mostly blank area (Allain 65).³ Despite all his reading and research prior to his trip, Greene's ideas of the continent remained rather mysterious and vague, and the thought of travelling there occurred to him at incongruous times. In *Journey Without Maps*, after describing his first memory of longing for a woman, his realization at age fourteen of 'the pleasure of cruelty' and 'pain as something desirable,' Greene pinpoints a memory that was for him 'a reminder of darkness' (35): he had observed a young woman who openly wept as she crossed Leicester Square, made a scene in a bar and 'didn't care a damn' (36–37). Bizarrely, given the English setting, Africa then emerged in his mind: 'I thought for some reason even then of Africa, not a particular place, but a shape, a strangeness, a wanting to know. […] [T]he shape, of course, is roughly that of the human heart' (37). As this passage indicates, Greene's thirst for knowledge and sexual experience (implied by the stranger's heartbreak, and the happiness Greene assumed had come before) were loosely connected to a continent offering seediness (as Greene saw it) in the extreme but also requiring a difficult journey that might lead him to the fulfilment of various desires – for love, knowledge and acclaim as a serious writer.

A servant's African tales in Greene's 'The Basement Room' and *The Fallen Idol*

As Greene was travelling home after his first Africa trip, he wrote a story not about the scenes he had just witnessed in Africa, but about strange happenings in a lonely upper-class boy's London household. 'The Basement Room' (1936) was adapted and released as a film in 1948, with Greene famously writing the screenplay over three months while he and Carol Reed were working on the project in adjoining hotel rooms with a shared secretary (Lodge). The original short story provides a clear example of Greene's interest in travelling in terms of class, with the young boy's initial excitement – 'Philip began to live' – and then repulsion and terror as he becomes involved in the complicated lives of his family's live-in servants, Baines and Mrs Baines, with whom he has been left during his parents' two-week holiday (115). The manservant's portrayal is striking in part because he frequently regales the boy, whom he calls 'Phil,' with his experiences as an 'Old Coaster' in Africa, tales which make the servant difficult to place in terms of class (116). At the very least, his portrayal does not conform to the typical hierarchy of masters and servants in England aligning with the colonizer and colonized abroad. Baines boasts to the boy that he once had '"Forty blacks under [him]"' (127), but in the story's present in London, he is living unhappily with his housekeeper wife while trying with stolen hours and half-used pots of makeup (taken from the garbage at Philip's house) to keep another woman on the side.

Greene depicts the masters, on the one hand, as an absence, with Philip's parents away and apparently rarely thought of, and, on the other hand, as a sensitive, nightmare-prone child only slowly becoming aware of adult treachery and his own class positioning. Philip is often called 'Master' by Mrs Baines to highlight his youth and the necessity of his obeying adults, but her references to 'Master Philip' also provides a reminder of his status in the household. Greene depicts Philip as unaware that the Baineses are paid to be there and could be discharged from their jobs for involving the boy so intimately in their marital strife. He is afraid of Mrs Baines, seeing her in her black dress and black cotton gloves as a witch with stale breath, and he is disturbed by her changing moods, as she quickly shifts from commanding, to ingratiating (unsuccessfully offering a bribe of a new Meccano set), to threatening – '"You'll smart; I'll see you smart"' (131). Greene depicts the boy's growing consciousness of his status relative to the servants as he frequently feels protective of Baines. Hearing Mrs Baines shouting at her husband for 'spoiling the boy',

> Philip sadly mounted the stairs to the nursery. He pitied Baines; it occurred to him how happily they could live together in the empty house if Mrs Baines were called away [...]. [H]e sat at the table with his chin on his hands: this is life; and suddenly he felt responsible for Baines, as if he were the master of the house and Baines an ageing servant who deserved to be cared for. (118)

This wish for Mrs Baines to be 'called away' would be soon granted, as if in a fairy tale, and Philip's desire to be rid of her also foreshadows her death. In addition, this passage suggests the boy's growing maturity: he recognizes that feelings of sadness and pity are 'life' and accepts the master's responsibility to repay a 'deserv[ing]' servant for his years of work and devotion.

Mrs Baines's life revolves around cleaning, cooking and keeping the house running smoothly, and thus Philip notes, with some disgust, that her hands are 'dry and white with constant soda, the nails cut to the quick' (120). Through Philip's eyes, Mrs Baines's thorough and frequent cleaning has made the house uninhabitable. He no longer feels comfortable upstairs – normally the master's domain – because Mrs Baines has freedom in his parents' absence to move about there, covering furniture with dust cloths, even muffling the clock. Philip rebels against her rule, stating repeatedly one day that he wants to go for a walk, a minor request that the two servants could easily grant. In Philip's battle of wills with a woman who is in the contradictory position of being both the boy's servant and his minder, Greene depicts the adults' power over the child but also the cruelty of Mrs Baines and the emasculating, even dehumanizing effect she has on her husband:

> 'I want to go for a walk.'
>
> 'Master Philip,' Mrs Baines said. She got up from the table, leaving her meringue unfinished, and came towards him, thin, menacing, dusty in the basement room. 'Master Philip, you just do as you're told.' She took him by the arm and squeezed it; she watched him with a joyless passionate glitter and above her head the feet of typists trudged back to the Victoria offices after the lunch interval.
>
> 'Why shouldn't I go for a walk?'
>
> But he weakened; he was scared and ashamed of being scared. This was life; a strange passion he couldn't understand moving in the basement room [...]. He looked at Baines for help and only intercepted hate; the sad hopeless hate of something behind bars. (119)

As Philip observes Mrs Baines's 'joyless passionate glitter' as she orders him to 'do as you're told', he is also aware of the trudging typists above her head, a reminder of the dismal workaday world threatening to override a child's desire to walk for pleasure. Still, the boy believes the Baineses' cruelty and hatred are also glimpses of 'life'. Telling Mrs Baines he hates her and running for the door, Philip is blocked by the woman 'quivering with excitement' and demanding an apology, but then she becomes 'again as servile as she had been arrogant' and lets Philip pass (120).

Not long after the argument about the walk, Philip sees through a café window 'a different Baines [...]. [A] happy, bold and buccaneering Baines, even though it was, when you looked closer, a desperate Baines' (120–1). He is with a crying girl, who, Philip notes, 'wouldn't wipe her eyes' (121). Greene captures in Philip's chance sighting of Baines at 'a shabby outpost of Pimlico' the boy's keen desire to understand adult lives and secrets (121). As he tries to get a better look at Baines and the young woman, who must be, Philip assumes, Baines's niece, the boy 'was less sheltered than he had ever been; other people's lives for the first time touched and pressed and moulded' (121). Greene then jumps ahead sixty years and provides a glimpse of the emptiness and lovelessness of Philip's life at its close:[4] 'He would never escape that scene. In a week he had forgotten it, but it conditioned his career, the long austerity of his life; when he was dying, rich and alone, it was said he asked: "Who is she?"' (121).

Greene depicts Mrs Baines leaving her post as the joyless enforcer and jailer in the household when she is called away to tend her dying mother. There is notably no concern for the dying old woman or for Mrs Baines's worries. In fact, waking Philip early, Baines 'celebrated at breakfast, restless, cracking jokes, unaccountably merry and nervous' (126). Philip hears more stories of Africa as Baines suggests that all the suffering he had endured there would finally be rewarded: 'It was going to be a long, long day, he kept on coming back to that: for years he had waited for a long day, he had sweated in the damp Coast heat, changed shirts, gone down with fever, lain between the blankets and sweated, all in the hope of this long day' (126). Baines takes Philip around London, treating him to a visit to Green Park, its leaves just beginning to turn for the autumn, the zoo and lunch out. Interspersed with these excursions are Baines's cryptic tales of his manly exploits in Africa, in which he paints himself as the protector of the natives: 'Baines envied no one [...]. "I said don't let me see you touch that black again." Baines had led a man's life; everyone on top of the bus pricked his ears when he told Philip all about it' (127). Philip's exciting day with Baines next brings them home to the basement room and a visit from Emmy. When Baines sends him to check the post, Philip is frightened by the walk alone through the darkened house, where 'the quiet and shadow prepared to show him something he didn't want to see' (128). Running in fear to the baize door, Philip provides a shocked child's perspective on what he finds, another secret to keep from Mrs Baines: 'The girl was already there and Baines was kissing her. She leant breathless against the dresser' (128).

Many of the details of Baines's African stories are reminiscent of Greene's portrayals of British travellers and colonial officials in *Journey Without Maps* and (later) *The Heart of the Matter*. Edward Said has argued that even seemingly inconsequential references to the colonies reveal that the 'texts of Western literature [have] a standing interest in what was considered a lesser world, populated with lesser people of color, portrayed as open to the intervention of so many Robinson Crusoes' (1993: xvi). Baines's African tales' frequent repetition in Greene's story suggests that they are crucial to understanding what makes a manservant in London so alluring to a young boy. These stories and the affair with Emmy are presented as Baines's desperate attempts to reclaim his lost manhood. Without his wife there to check him, he brags to the boy about his strength and bravery on another continent, claiming he had had a revolver there and he would '"have shot to kill"' if the occasion called for it (127). As these stories are repeated throughout the story, there are variations and missing details, leaving some question about their veracity.

'The Basement Room' also contains Greene's interrogation of class as he depicts the boy wandering far from the rules and cold formality of his upper-class home. When Mrs Baines falls to her death in the house after a struggle with her husband, Philip runs away in his pyjamas and slippers to the 'unfashionable end' of the square and beyond, losing himself 'among the fish-and-chips shops, the little stationers selling *Bagatelle*, among the accommodation addresses and the dingy hotels with open doors. [...] [A]s he went deeper he lost the marks of his origin' (134). Here, Greene depicts the boy as a fugitive straying further and further from his loveless home with paid staff, attempting to blend in with common Londoners and trying to convince the adults in a less rigid part of the city that he is a child like any other:

> It was a warm night: any child in those free-living parts might be expected to play truant from bed. He found a kind of camaraderie even among grown-up people; he might have been a neighbour's child as he went quickly by, but they weren't going to tell on him, they'd been young once themselves. He picked up a protective coating of dust from the pavements, of smuts from the trains, which passed along the backs in a spray of fire. Once he was caught in a knot of children running away from something or somebody, laughing as they ran; he was whirled with them round a turning and abandoned, with a sticky fruit-drop in his hand. (134)

Greene represents the boy's idea of the 'free-living' parts of the city, where Philip imagines adults are like Baines in a jovial mood and treat children as equals.[5] In the boy's eyes, the 'dust' and 'smuts' are 'protective' rather than filth to be avoided. These markings from the street make him even more anonymous, even less identifiable as a boy from the other side of the square. Utterly lost, Philip 'began to loiter on purpose to be noticed, but no one noticed him' (135). As he sees his slippers are badly soiled, he feels 'cut off': 'these people were strangers and would always now be strangers; they were marked by Mrs Baines and he shied away from them into a deep class-consciousness' (135). Greene at times provides more than a young boy's perspective, as the reference to Philip's retreat into 'a deep class consciousness' in this passage indicates. After deciding that the only option is to 'surrender, to show you were beaten and accept kindness', Philip asks to be taken to a police station 'where Justice lived' (135). It turns out that

'Justice' – a kindly sergeant with a heavy moustache and six children at home – is reluctant to make too much of a child possibly awakened by nightmares, but Philip insists on having a policeman by his side as he faces the corpse of Mrs Baines.

Returning on foot with a young constable, whose 'nose smelt something', Philip startles Baines (138). As Philip imagines Baines is 'beg[ging] dumbly like a dog: one more secret', the constable reminds Philip of his status within the household that he had almost forgotten under Mrs Baines' reign: 'You're a gentleman. You must come in the proper way through the front door like the master should' (139). Baines approaches Philip 'begging, begging, all the way with his old soft stupid expression: this is Baines, the old Coaster; what about a palm-oil chop, eh?' (140). But Philip is no longer receptive to the servant's charisma or tales: 'The messages flickered out from the last posts at the border, imploring, beseeching, reminding: this is your old friend Baines [...]. But the wires were cut, the messages just faded out into the vacancy of the scrubbed room in which there had never been a place where a man could hide his secrets' (140).

The 'border' in this case appears to be the boundary of class, behind which Philip has retreated, with a policeman there to maintain the division: 'Philip extricated himself from life, from love, from Baines' (139). The 'scrubbed room' signifies Mrs Baines's consistent hard work but also the cramped, embittered existence of a man who claims to have roamed the globe and commanded forty men. Greene moves from young master to servant to narrator in terms of the point of view and from present to future to Philip's enduring memory in the story's devastating ending: '"It was all Emmy's fault," he protested with a quaver which reminded Baines that after all he was only a child; it had been hopeless to expect help there [...]. You couldn't blame him. When he woke in the morning, he'd hardly remember a thing' (140). After Baines's forgiving thought, Greene reminds readers once again of the lasting impact of the kindly manservant on the boy, who saw the constable turn on Baines with 'professional ferocity', asking a variation of the question that Philip would mutter on his deathbed: '"Out with it [...] who is she?"' (141). Readers are left with the image of Philip, sixty years on, slipping into death as he is thinking 'perhaps of the image of Baines: Baines hopeless, Baines letting his head drop, Baines "coming clean"' (141).

When Greene returned to this story in the immediate post-war years, he and director Carol Reed chose a more glamorous setting. They also added evocative props, altered the portrayal of Baines's mistress and infused the servant's African tales with the colonial politics of the late 1940s. The original story's cloistered 'basement room' is transformed into the opulent London residence of a French-speaking ambassador, and the set is teeming with servants and the ambassador's staff. Mrs Baines closely resembles the housekeeper character in the story but is more sinister in that she tracks down the boy's hidden pet snake (one of Greene's additions to the film script) and is shown triumphantly pushing it into the incinerator. She also violently shakes and strikes the boy when she is in a frenzy of jealousy and hatred for Baines and his mistress. Philip – now Philippe – speaks English with an accent and switches to French at times, especially with Baines's 'niece', who is now called Julie. While Baines's girl Emmy in the story is crying and cringing and accepting Baines's gift of used makeup, Julie in the film is an assured co-worker, telling Baines she plans to leave rather than continue meeting in secret and lying. Greene kept Baines's African stories in the film script, but he and Reed depict the boy always initiating the storytelling. Although Baines's claim to have kept his gun seems implausible in the original story, it is a prop that is shown twice in the film (handled first playfully by Philippe and later sadly by Baines as he is preparing to go in for police questioning). Tellingly, the emasculating Mrs Baines is presented as disapproving of the gun, an emblem of her husband's adventurous life before their marriage.

Greene opted while collaborating with Reed to depict Baines's tales of Africa in a less fragmented fashion than in the story; however, in both versions, these tales provide the boy with vision of courage and worldly British manhood as well as an imaginative escape from Mrs Baines's harsh treatment. When in the film Philippe asks Baines about Africa after visiting the lion exhibit at the zoo, the impeccably dressed, urbane servant tells a gunslinger's tale about singlehandedly facing down militant 'blackies': 'They all came up to my hut, hundreds of them, knives, spears, and all I had was that gun. "Clear off!" I said to that king of theirs. "Hop it!"' Claiming to have 'plugged' the king before going in with his fists, Baines gets lost in the tale and says he left the gun behind. Philippe has to remind him that he somehow got it back to London. Instead of supervising forty men as he had in the story, Baines in the 1948 portrayal smirks at the Africans' 'rising' and the 'speechifying' that 'got them properly riled up'. The servant's storytelling thus passes on colonizers' concepts of racial hierarchy while also celebrating threats of violence and suppression of dissent. He warns Philippe that if the Africans had managed to kill him, they would have 'had the taste for blood, like that lion over there'. Notably, there is both a colonizing-justification aspect to Baines's storytelling and (with roles reversed) a connection to Mrs Baines's tyranny and his own stealthy revolt. These references to a 'rising' and subsequent killings relate on the home front to the Baineses' unhappy marriage and Mrs Baines angrily asking her husband: 'You want your freedom?'

Later, when Mrs Baines struggles with Baines and falls to her death, it appears to the boy watching from the fire escape that Baines is at fault, but viewers (unlike readers of the story) know more than the boy and have seen her fall from a window ledge rather than from a push from her husband. Philippe escapes alone into dark, empty streets, running in bare feet until he comes across a kindly policeman. The boy's extended class travel from the story – his wandering into the unfashionable side of the city – is therefore gone, or rather has been reduced to a brief interaction with a prostitute at the police station. In the film version, several avuncular police detectives as well as a doctor are involved in the investigation of Mrs Baines' death, and when asked by a detective what the boy meant when he asked about a killing in Africa, Baines states definitively that he has never been out of the country. Although Philippe tries to protect Baines with lies, the man is cleared by a footprint Mrs Baines had earlier left in the soil from a broken flowerpot. Thus, the bleak ending of the original story, with Philip feeling he has betrayed his friend and then wrecking his own life as a result, has been replaced with Baines almost miraculously freed from his unhappy marriage just as the unscathed young boy (by this point a chattering annoyance to all the adults, as well as to viewers) is returned to his parents.

Greene's own servants and African living arrangements

Greene's personal experiences with African servants undoubtedly influenced his portrayal of Ali and other servant 'boys' in *The Heart of the Matter*, which was published the same year as *The Fallen Idol*'s release. When Greene arrived in Lagos in 1941 to train for his intelligence-gathering position in Freetown, he and his roommate were each assigned 'a boy' and were asked to share an additional 'small boy' (Sherry, 106). In a letter to his mother, Greene describes a detailed daily schedule of juice breaks, cold bath and meals that the servants assisted with (Sherry, 106). Once in Freetown, Green hired a couple boys and a male cook (all Africans) even before he had a place to live, and he claimed to rely on intuition rather than references when selecting his household staff (Sherry 113, 133). Greene then moved into a 'dingy little Creole villa' about two miles from town, and the servants had to bring drinking water from town to be boiled and to carry bath water from a 'native watering hole' in kerosene tins (Sherry 114). Greene borrowed dishes from his cook while waiting for his housewares to arrive and apparently relied on his servants to be his guides, fixers and translators. Greene's writing about his household in the outskirts of Freetown demonstrates his contradictory desires to live at a distance from his class and from other colonial officials while still avoiding some unpleasant realities of 1940s African life. Norman Sherry, Greene's biographer (as well as Conrad's), writes that the rented villa, infested as it was with flies, spiders, ants, and rats and lacking modern conveniences, 'suited Greene's notion of himself, someone who didn't quite fit in, who objected to his own class, bound by conventional values, instinctively. Greene had a longing to be an "undesirable," indeed thought of himself as such' (115).

In *Ways of Escape*, Greene quotes a passage from his journal describing his servant Ali's 'stilted walk with buttocks projecting and the smell of drink', a description that varies markedly from the character with the same name in *The Heart of the Matter* (121). Greene was well aware of the difficulty of his servants' lives outside of work and noted in his journal that one ended up in gaol, the cook went mad and Ali was crying on the job because his brother was dying of gonorrhoea: 'You drink to keep water out of your eyes,' Ali told him (1980: 21). Since the novel is set during the Second World War and draws on Greene's experiences in Sierra Leone from 1942 to 1943, it is quite possible that servants like Ali would be conscripted. The recruitment of colonial troops and African workers for military support roles, such as carrying supplies, relied at that time on a quota system requiring a certain number of conscripts from each village. Training to be a 'personal servant' was an advertised option for African recruits, according to David Killingray, who describes Second World War recruitment brochures depicting African recruits smiling brightly, even when they were wielding pickaxes. Servitude and sewing were also options: 'Soldiers have the opportunity to learn to be a "personal servant" or a "fundi," an artisan' (63).

Race and class in *The Heart of the Matter*

Greene structured his first African novel with a shift in perspective after the first chapter and another at the end after his central character Scobie's death. These shifts might be read as a re-envisioning of Conrad's frame narrative in *Heart of Darkness*, in which an unnamed narrator describes Marlow's 'sunken cheeks' and 'ascetic aspect' before Marlow begins his first-person recounting of his time in the Belgian Congo (16). There are a number of interruptions to Marlow's tale, reminding readers of Conrad's novel of the original storytelling scene with an audience of four on a ship at rest in London in the novel's present, and then the narrative shifts back in time as Marlow continues his tale. Conrad shifts again for a final, brief paragraph to the group gathered on a ship to close the frame after Marlow's storytelling has ended. In Greene's novel, the division between the frame and the heart of the story is marked less dramatically since Greene stays with third-person restricted perspective but shifts from Wilson to Scobie. Opening with Wilson, a newcomer to the colony, enables Greene to introduce readers to the setting and the major cast of characters through Wilson's first conversation with Harris, who has been in West Africa eighteen months. Harris speaks with venom about the Africans, using a racial epithet repeatedly while providing Wilson with some advice that he is clearly not following himself: '"Mustn't call 'em that you know"' (5). Wilson then complains about the '"West Indians [who] [...] rule the coast. Clerks in the stores, city council, magistrates, lawyers – my God"' (5). When Harris points out Scobie, who is passing on the street below, both Wilson and Harris watch 'the squat grey-haired man walking alone up Bond Street', while Harris mockingly describes Scobie's wife as '"the city intellectual"' and claims that Scobie loves the black residents so much '"he sleeps with 'em,"' a bit of gossip that the rest of the novel does not confirm (5–6). After this hate-filled introduction to the colony, Scobie's deeply reflective, empathetic point of view takes over, and the novel primarily stays with him until he intentionally overdoses – with only occasional returns to Harris's or Wilson's perspective, such as during Wilson's visit to a brothel. The ending of the novel, a six-page Part III, closes the frame as three separate conversations unfold, drearily wrapping up the loose ends of Scobie's life.

Notably, the black clerks, city councilmen, magistrates and lawyers and other higher-status Africans and transplanted West Indians who so upset Harris are never mentioned again, except as a brief reference to the ever 'cheerful and respectful' clerks who tolerated the British officials and 'put up with any insult' (6). In terms of more developed African characters, readers are left with Ali, Scobie's household servant. C. L. R. James noted in 1945 that in the few instances when the black man is not entirely excluded from media or artistic representations, 'he is placed in his usual menial position, made the butt of jokes or at the very best is portrayed as a good and loyal servant' (3). Although Greene does not provide fleshed-out African characters beyond the 'good and loyal servant', he does include anecdotes about the locals Scobie encounters while fulfilling his duties as police chief, glimpses of schoolgirls 'trying to wave their wirespring hair', and a half-nude young woman carrying a load whom Wilson watches from afar one day (3). Slightly more developed and less stereotypical are the African prostitute and madam Wilson pays, despite losing his nerve and wishing to get away. In that transaction and in that place, he realizes, the colonial hierarchy of race and class does not apply: 'Here a man's colour had no value: he couldn't bluster as a white man could elsewhere: by entering this narrow plaster passage, he had shed every racial, social and individual trait, he had reduced himself to human nature. […] [H]ere he was simply a man. Even his reluctance, disgust and fear were not personal characteristics' (161). Remarkably, the 'old mammy' who blocks Wilson's exit from the brothel is the African character with the most power and agency in the entire novel. She speaks her language as she gives orders to the girl rather than the rudimentary English the servants use, and she rebuffs his attempts to leave by 'thrust[ing] him backwards with a casual pink palm' (161). Wilson's discomfort in his loss of status is evident: 'A grievance stirred in him, a hatred of those who had brought him here' (161). It is noteworthy that here 'those' remains vague: is his grievance against the government officials who he sent him to such a place, the semi-nude woman on the street who unknowingly fuelled his desire, or the 'old mammy' who insisted he go through with the transaction he had initiated?

Early in the novel, Greene reveals the pecking order among the British characters based on years in the colony, and [he] captures the stinging rejection of class discrimination when Wilson is not wanted at the club, with Fellowes insisting, "'I'm not a snob, but in a place like this you've got to draw the line'" (20). Scobie takes pity on Wilson and invites him to his home, where the young man promptly falls in love with Scobie's literary and socially inept wife, Louise. Scobie appears to recognize their mutual attraction but is relieved rather than jealous. Greene varies the race and class representation beyond white colonial officials and black native workers with his inclusion of Syrian businessmen and smugglers, a Christian named Tallit and a Muslim named Yusef. Greene depicts these men conniving against one another as they try to form alliances with the British, who keep their distance. Harris tells Wilson not to bother wearing a tuxedo and troublesome cummerbund (which notably requires two servants to put on) for a dinner at Tallit's home because he believes Syrians are inferior. Greene depicts Louise as much more status conscious than Scobie. She is so upset that he is being passed over for a promotion to District Commissioner that she arranges to sail for South Africa with another woman from the colony. Feeling responsible for her unhappiness, Scobie makes every effort to raise the money for her passage and ends up borrowing money from Yusef, the more corrupt of the two Syrians.

Greene's portrayal of masters and servants in the colony suggests an arrangement accepted by both the British and Africans. Each colonial officer there appears to have an illiterate, barefoot 'boy' or two to mix their drinks, help them dress, fix their meals and tend to them when they are sick. Readers learn that Ali has been with the Scobies for fifteen years, and in the scenes representing him in some detail, he is invariably serving his master with devotion. After Scobie cuts his hand on a splinter early in the novel, for example, 'The boy made gentle clucking sounds of commiseration: his hands were as gentle as a girl's. [...] Years ago he had taught Ali to bandage: now he could tie one as expertly as a doctor' (31). It is noteworthy in this passage that Ali is compared both to 'a girl' and 'a doctor' with expertise that Scobie had passed on to him, suggesting that Scobie had both encouraged that tender relationship and trusted the potential skilfulness of his servant, enabling the pair's interactions to extend beyond colonial constraints. Greene depicts Ali rewarding Scobie's characteristic reticence and stoicism with even more devoted service and sense of initiative, such as when the master asks for Elastoplast for his wound and Ali insists on applying a full bandage. Ali is also remarkably attentive to Louise. When she sends Wilson into her and Scobie's bedroom to check for rats, he notices 'the dress laid out by Ali for the evening', suggesting Ali's intimate involvement in the couple's home life and his assumption of typically feminine tasks (72).

The master–servant camaraderie is most pronounced during a trip that Scobie takes with Ali and an anonymous driver. When young Pemberton, the District Commissioner of the interior post of Bamba commits suicide, Scobie is called on to travel through the night to make a police report. As Louise and Wilson watch him leaving, Louise comments on Scobie's perpetually inferior status: "'Isn't he the typical second man? The man who always does the work'" (71). Louise's conception of Scobie as 'the typical second man' leaves out Ali, the 'man who always does the work' in the Scobie household and who would be accompanying his master on the difficult journey into the interior. Ali, then, is the second man's second man, the servant of a servant, whose labour remains invisible to anyone (like Louise) with a Eurocentric gaze. Greene suggests elsewhere in the novel that Scobie too feels he is bound to serve and stands ready to act on orders, evident in his misreading of a misspelling in a letter from Helen, his mistress: 'Serius – his eye this time read it as *servus* – a slave: a servant of the servants of God. It was like an unwise command which he had none the less to obey' (183).

While a black policeman drives, Scobie has 'a dream of perfect happiness and freedom' in which master and servant are alone together in a pastoral setting that seems more European than African: 'He was walking through a wide cool meadow with Ali at his heels: there was nobody else anywhere in his dream, and Ali never spoke' (73). The dream reinforces Scobie's idea of Ali as his loyal follower, silently at the heels of his master even in a meadow. When in the dream a snake 'touches his cheek with a cold, friendly, remote tongue', Scobie awakens to find his waiting servant, whose 'tongue' or language remains 'remote' to Scobie:

> Once when he opened his eyes Ali was standing beside him waiting for him to awake. 'Massa like bed,' he stated gently, firmly, pointing to the camp-bed he had made up at the edge of the path with the mosquito-net tied from the branches overhead. 'Two three hours,' Ali said. 'Plenty lorries.' Scobie obeyed and lay down and was immediately back in that peaceful meadow where nothing ever happened. The next time he woke Ali was still there, this time with a cup of tea and a plate of biscuits. 'One hour,' Ali said. (73)

Greene notably reverses the language of service in this passage, with the master 'obey[ing]' his servant's 'firmly' delivered order to trade his seat in the police van for a bed. There is no reference in the text to the way the driver and Ali had passed the night once he had prepared his master's bed, complete with mosquito net, and (soon after) his hot tea. These small acts can be read as emblems of colonial society, in which British routines and necessities have with great difficulty been replicated in the African setting by African subjects to whom they are intrinsically alien.

After Scobie wakes, they are taken by two ferrymen wearing nothing but girdles across the first of three 'dark, styx-like stream[s]' (74). Even if Greene restricts the narrative to Scobie's perspective and leaves much unstated, his depiction of the journey obliges readers to notice the burden borne by the largely silent Africans – the devoted servant, driver and multiple ferrymen working through the night to enable the resolution of a matter affecting only white men. With his head throbbing, Scobie sees 'Ali squatting in the body of the van put[ing] an arm around his shoulder holding a mug of hot tea – somehow he had boiled another kettle in the lurching chassis' (74). Scobie reminisces aloud about a trek he had taken with Ali twelve years prior, and sees Ali 'nodding and beaming' in the driver's mirror at the memory: 'It seemed to [Scobie] that this was all he needed of love or friendship. He could be happy with no more in the world than this – the grinding van, the hot tea against his lips, the heavy damp weight of the forest, even the aching head, the loneliness' (74). Significantly, Scobie's imagines himself being happy with 'no more in the world than' a devoted companion who proffers both creature comforts and thoughtful directives in a few simple words of a shared language. Since this idea of happiness includes loneliness and even a headache, it is in keeping with Scobie's growing asceticism, his idea of how little he needs in the office (just a pair of rusty handcuffs) or at home (no photographs or other personal effects). While Louise accumulates and adds to the couple's library (Scobie's lone book notably a Mende grammar), he gets rid of things and pares down his words to the essentials – writing only 'C died' in his journal after losing his daughter (237).

During his brief time in Bamba, Scobie further removes himself from his loveless marriage as the rigors of the journey and a life-threatening fever increase his dependency on Ali, who meets his needs with kindness and efficiency. The trek into the jungle appears to serve the same function as the 'overarching sky' in E. M. Forster's *A Passage to India* (Bradbury 237). Being unmoored from familiar surroundings and aware of the immense sky, the forest, or even the meadow of Scobie's dream obliges one 'to "invite" everyone to the privileged feast of polite society', as Bruce Robbins suggests about Forster's novel (163). If such an invitation is not proffered, Robbins explains, the 'feast loses its meaning because the uninvited press their faces to the window' (163). Both Scobie's emotional removal from his small family and his immersion in a trans-cultural master–servant relationship reinforce Robbins's argument that servant characters allow a novel to expand beyond the intimates of the protagonist, enabling the author to issue, in Forster's words, 'a universal invitation':

> In order to restore meaning to the world, one must be able [...] to send out wider and wider circles of sympathy, taking in the excluded. Here, [...] in other words, servants intervene in two stages. They signal a withdrawal of meaning from the novel's traditionally exclusive circle of 'personal relations,' but they also push toward the anticipatory constitution of a more inclusive gathering. (Robbins 163)

Scobie's journey with Ali reflects the 'withdrawal of meaning' from the master's marriage as well as his widening 'circles of sympathy,' particularly at the hospital in Bamba, where he comforts a small dying girl (significant in that he had not been physically or emotionally present for the death of his own daughter): 'A memory that he had carefully buried returned [...]. The sweat poured down his face and tasted in his mouth as salt as tears' (112). Scobie also becomes capable of experiencing love again and begins a relationship with the waifish young widow, Helen, whom he meets there. However, despite his empathy and openness during the trek, his relationship with Ali will soon be tainted by his growing doubts about the servant's loyalty.

In all scenes, including the trip to Bamba, Greene depicts the Africans employed by their British and Syrian masters as seldom speaking, and he keeps them largely out of sight. They silently slip around in the dark as they spy for whoever will pay them slightly more (Ali being the one possible exception), and even their fights to the death happen on someone else's order and at a remove from Scobie and the other white residents. Greene depicts one 'boy' making a deal with Wilson to provide intelligence on his employer, his grin 'a gash of white in the smooth grey elephant hide of his face' (156). There are also menacing 'human rats,' whose rumoured existence in the shadows makes the wharf a no-go zone (28). Even Ali, the most developed African character, remains a mystery in that his background, thoughts and life outside of work are completely hidden from readers. His physical concerns are not described directly, and instead become comic anecdotes – *'Ali had to go and have a couple of teeth out the other day. What a fuss he made!'* – included in Scobie's letters to Louise while she is in South Africa, enabling the couple to avoid more serious subjects, such as the state of their marriage (129).

Greene's minimal treatment of Africans led Sarah Milbury-Steen to remark that if not for the war references, the 1948 novel 'would seem timelessly colonial, defined by the office, the club and the colour bar' (47).[6] Greene's lack of development of African characters is in keeping with his failure to acknowledge through his fiction the agency and political power of Africans. He ignores the workers' strikes and collective bargaining of the West African Youth League (WAYL) and other unions that were organizing to bring about better wages and working conditions in the 1930s and 1940s (Denzer 443–46). WAYL's founder, I. T. A. Wallace-Johnson, a writer for the *Negro Worker* and the *African Standard*, helped to get four African city council members elected, including the first West African woman in a British colony. He was arrested in 1939 under the Emergency Act and was imprisoned on Sherbro Island, just off the coast of Sierra Leone. An unsuccessful petition calling for his release was circulated in 1941 among African activists and was submitted to the colonial government around the time Greene was taking up his post (Denzer 445–6). Since Greene was attached to the police station in Freetown, he would likely have known about the enormously popular WAYL's activities. The police even went undercover to infiltrate the league and spy on their meetings (Spitzer and Denzer 569). It is little wonder then that Orwell found fault with Greene's erasure of politics and with his implausible police character, stating in his 1948 review of *The Heart of the Matter* that 'the thing that would actually be in Scobie's mind the whole time – the hostility between black and white, and the struggle against the local nationalist movement – is not mentioned at all' (1–63).

Yet even if African workers' strikes and popular figures like Wallace-Johnson are never mentioned in Greene's novel, he nevertheless conveys the power of African servants who have the insider knowledge to destroy their masters' lives and reputations. It is through a servant boy that the corrupt Syrian character Yusef gets his hands on a signed love letter that Scobie had recklessly written to his mistress Helen. In order to keep Louise who is on her way back from South Africa from reading the letter, Scobie agrees to help Yusef smuggle a shipment of diamonds. Scobie's fall is then brought about through his losing face with his own servant, who witnesses Scobie receiving (via another servant boy) a diamond from Yusef. Scobie is ruffled and sends the diamond back with a threat, explaining that a master has to remain above suspicion to his own servant, who is there at all times, seeing and hearing all, even if he is unable to read or write. Scobie then begins to doubt Ali's loyalty after seeing Ali speaking with another boy, a half-brother who works for Wilson, but Greene leaves readers just as unsure as Scobie about whether the once loyal servant can be trusted. When Scobie asks Ali if he had been offered money to report on him, Ali glowers back at him, his face in the rear-view mirror 'set, obstinate, closed, and rocky like a cave mouth' (213). Is Ali upset because Scobie is wrongly questioning his loyalty or because he has been found out? Greene never answers this question definitively, but Scobie blames himself, recognizing that he began to distrust his servant only after he had become untrustworthy himself. Ultimately, Ali seems very loyal, risking his life to come to his master's aid, even across the deadly wharf at night.

Greene's idea of masters and servants – colonizers and colonized – is revealed in the nature of Ali's death and Scobie's role in it. Greene depicts Scobie having a lapse in judgment when he shares his suspicions about Ali with Yusef, despite knowing well from the blackmail experience that the Syrian cannot be trusted. Yusef sends for Ali through his own 'boy' after insisting that Scobie provide him with a signet ring or another personal item to prove that the order came from him. Greene heightens the Catholic symbolism of Ali's sacrifice by having Scobie decide to send the broken rosary in his pocket. Before learning of Ali's fate, Scobie sits drinking in the gloom of Yusef's living room and reflecting on the years of loyal caretaking he had received from Ali. Yusef lies to relieve Scobie's worries, telling him that 'sometimes boys go back to [the] bush,' but after a long, ominous wait, 'a cry came: pain and fear: it swam up like a drowning animal for air' (229–30). Scobie then rushes straight to Ali's crumpled body as if he knew in advance where he would be killed:

> [T]he body lay coiled and unimportant like a broken watchspring under a pile of empty petrol drums [...]. Scobie had a moment of hope before he turned the shoulder over, for after all two boys had been together on the road. The seal gray neck had been slashed and slashed again. Yes, he thought, I can trust him now. The yellow eyeballs stared up at him like a stranger's flecked with red. [...] He swore aloud, hysterically. 'By God, I'll get the man who did this,' but under that anonymous stare insincerity withered. He thought: I am the man. (230)

In this passage, Scobie speaks both as a policeman fulfilling his official duties and as Ali's avenger – in that he promises to find the culprit. He also recognises he is ultimately responsible for the murder – 'I am the man' – because he had set events in motion and, during the short period when he could have insisted on knowing Yusef's plan, he had relaxed into Yusef's cushions and accepted another drink while Ali was being summoned and brutally dispatched. When Helen (more perceptive than Louise) asks if Scobie was the one who killed Ali, he answers, "'I didn't cut his throat myself [...]. But he died because I existed,'" notably referring to his own existence in the past tense (232). Although Greene does not explicitly present Ali's and Scobie's deaths as a murder-suicide, I believe these acts can be interpreted as such, or, as Gruesser has argued, given Scobie's treatment of a loyal servant, as a colonial official 'giv[ing] the lie to the colonial mission, and the expatriate tradition dictates that he must pay for this with his own life' (30).

Greene hints that Ali's killing (indirectly by his master's hand) is the first painful step towards Scobie's suicide, an indication that Ali was never fully his own man. Ali had been Scobie's only male companion, and they shared many characteristics: both master and servant are gentle and mostly silent; neither draws attention to himself or corrects others' wrong perceptions of his character; each quietly and competently carries out his tasks. No one but Scobie seems to feel the tragedy of Ali's death, an earthshattering occurrence to Scobie that no other character, major or minor, can comprehend: "'What is it, sah?' The corporal whispered, kneeling by the body. "I loved him," Scobie expressing,' expressing a sentiment about his late servant that he could no longer say to his wife (231). Speaking to Ali's 'coiled and unimportant' body, Scobie conveys his deep loss and guilt: "'I've killed you: you've served me all these years and I've killed you at the end of them'" (231).[7] The colonial police captain and his African servant died together (or, rather, one shortly after the other) for Scobie's sense of responsibility to two much less sympathetic women, one of whom is not even bothered by Ali's murder, despite his having served her for fifteen years. Both women quickly move on to other, lesser men, and Scobie's hand in his own death is quickly exposed. Elliott Malamet writes that 'even his suicide, carefully planned so that "no one must even suspect" is uncovered after Wilson inspects the diaries in a prototypical piece of police work' (296). With the novel's bleak ending, in which the numbed responses of the surviving characters are emphasized, Greene seems to be reprising Conrad's ending of *Heart of Darkness*, in which Marlow tells a monstrous lie to comfort Kurtz's Intended and is surprised that an incredibly significant event (to him) hardly makes a ripple: 'The heavens do not fall for such a trifle' (123).

An anticolonial Greene?

Whether real, remembered or imagined, Africa as a subject or setting crucially affects Greene's portrayals of masters and servants in 'Basement Room', *The Fallen Idol* and *The Heart of the Matter*. In addition, perhaps surprisingly, the wide-eyed child Philip and the world-weary police captain Scobie have in common their close relationships with their manservants, who figure in their dying thoughts. Both in the end are masters who have wronged and destroyed their servants, even if unintentionally. Each doubts his servant and then doubts himself before inviting in harsher forces (a policeman and a likely murder conviction for Baines and Yusef and his corrupt network for Ali). These masters, whether they are five or fifty, see the terrible results and end up destroying themselves – Philip over sixty, arid years and Scobie with a carefully planned and disguised overdose of sleeping pills. Greene reveals that both are thinking of their servants as they die, and in both cases, their final words are ambiguous. Philip 'startled his secretary, his only watcher, asking "Who is she? Who is she?" ' (141). Greene's repetitions of elements of that scene had pointed towards Emmy and Philip's inability to place her within his scheme of societal types: he 'thought of mermaids', but that didn't quite fit her 'detachment and mystery of the completely disinherited' (121). But those last words could also be interpreted as Philip rehearsing the constable's question, 'who is she?' addressed with 'ferocity' to Baines after Philip had blamed Emmy for Mrs Baines's death (141). It seems Philip while dying *is* thinking of that interrogation: Greene ends the story with four repetitions of Baines's name as Philip is 'perhaps' reflecting on the moment he witnessed his beloved manservant 'coming clean' (141). Likewise, Scobie calls out to Ali twice in his confusion as the drug begins to take effect and then perceives 'someone [...] seeking to get in, someone appealing for help, someone in need of him' (249). Even Scobie's final words, 'Dear God, I love ...' form an unfinished sentence that Scobie might have completed with 'you' or with Ali, Louise (his wife), Helen (his mistress) or life itself (249).

Although Greene's work seems consistently to emphasize the white traveller and the master, he hints at a more egalitarian political vision in his depictions of wronged servants coming to their masters' minds as they die. Imagining Philip and Scobie paying a heavy price for inadvertent or passive betrayals, Greene represents in the unravelling of their close relationships with servants the dissolution of the Empire – already underway in the 1940s with India's independence in 1947 and Empire Windrush's arrival on British shores in 1948. Perhaps, as Baines's dismissiveness about Africans 'rising' and 'speechifying' in *The Fallen Idol* indicates, Greene was nevertheless reluctant to acknowledge the coming reckoning in the colonies and within Britain as well, once formerly colonized and working-class writers began to publish their perspectives on the erasure or caricature of their people, or the outright racism and classism of earlier British literature. However, by depicting masters destroying themselves when they recognize the human costs of the hierarchal arrangement of society both at home and abroad, Greene anticipates in the 1940s a less rigid world emerging in the post-war period.

Notes

1. Wodehouse wrote *Joy in the Morning* (1946) while he was being held as an enemy adult male in 1940 by the Germans in Belgium. His imprisonment continued in Tort (Poland), where the Germans gave him a typewriter, on which he wrote *Money in the Bank* (US 1942; UK 1946). He wrote *Uncle Dynamite* (1948) in 1944 from a French hospital just after the war, after having been arrested by the French police as a suspected German collaborator. Before leaving France for the United States, where he was to live the remainder of his life, he wrote *The Mating Season* (1949).
2. For a detailed analysis of the differing politics of Maugham's novel and the film adaptation that was Pinter and Losey's fruitful first collaboration, see Dyer, 2015.
3. Valerie Kennedy observes that 'Greene uses the lack of satisfactory maps to suggest that his journey is exploration, not tourism, and also to link the physical journey through West Africa to the exploration of his own psyche' (50).
4. In 'Did the butler do it?' David Lodge notes the difficulty of placing 'The Basement Room' in time given the contemporary setting and references to Philip's death sixty years in the future.

5   Ana Laura Zambrano's analysis of 'The Basement Room' and its adaptation places less emphasis on the class dimensions of Philip's journey. She points out that the boy is drawn to the scenes of family life that he is missing out on himself, such as gathering with loved ones in well-lit interiors and on porch steps (327).

6   Pinpointing a similar tendency in Greene's *The Quiet American* (1955), Matt Steinglass notes that 'almost all of the novel's Vietnamese are "not there" in one way or another [...]. The dynamic Vietnamese – the Vietminh, in particular – are held offstage, spoken of but never seen or heard' (33).

7   See Martin Stollery's analysis of the changes to the plot in *The Heart of the Matter*'s 1953 film adaptation, in which Scobie is attacked by a street gang and dies in Ali's arms. Stollery applies Christine Geraghty's description of 1950s British Commonwealth films to the adaptation. She argues that 'the good white characters must prove their right to take part in Commonwealth affairs by demonstrating their capacity for sacrifice, their unselfish goodness, and their capacity to win, through goodness, the respect that had previously been demanded by the assertion of power' [...] displacing 'the question of political rights into one of humanitarian largesse' (131–32; qtd. Stollery 220). As Stollery notes, Scobie in Greene's novel is a more complicated and corrupt character than Scobie in the film and thus does not entirely conform to this liberal ideal (220).

Works cited

Achebe, Chinua. 'An Image of Africa: Racism in the *Heart of Darkness*'. *Hopes and Impediments*. London: Penguin, 2019 [1975], 1–20.

Airey, John. 'Graham Greene's *Journey Without Maps* and the Fascination of the Abomination'. *De la démocratie au Royaume-Uni: Perspectives Contemporaines* 7, no. 1 (2009). *E-rea: Revue électronique d'études sur le monde anglophone*; https://doi.org/10.4000/erea.849

Allain, Marie-Françoise. *The Other Man: Conversations with Graham Greene*. New York: Simon and Schuster, 1983.

Anderson, Perry. 'Modernity and Revolution'. *New Left Review* 144 (1984): 96–113; https://newleftreview.org/issues/i144/articles/perry-anderson-modernity-and-revolution

Bradbury, Malcolm. *E. M. Forster, A Passage to India: A Casebook*. Macmillan, 1970.

Compton-Burnett, Ivy. *Manservant and Maidservant*. New York: New York Review of Books, 2001 [1947].

Conrad, Joseph. *Heart of Darkness*. London: Penguin, 1995 [1902].

Denzer, LaRay. 'Women in Freetown Politics, 1914–61: A Preliminary Study'. *Sierra Leone, 1787–1987*: Two Centuries of Intellectual Life'. *Africa* 57 (4), 1987: 439–56.

Dyer, Rebecca. 'Class and Anticolonial Politics in Harold Pinter and Joseph Losey's *The Servant*'. *Spaces and Places*, special issue of *Journal of Modern Literature* 38 (4), 2015: 147–67. JSTOR; https://doi.org/10.2979/jmodelite.38.4.147.

Eliot, T. S. *The Waste Land: A Facsimile and Transcript of the Original Drafts*. San Diego, New York, London: Harcourt Brace, 1971 [1922].

The Fallen Idol. Director Carol Reed, screenplay by Graham Greene. 1948. Canal Plus, Image UK, Criterion, 2006.

Geraghty, Christine. *British Cinema in the Fifties: Gender, Genre, and the 'New Look'*. London: Routledge, 2000.

Greene, Graham. 'The Basement Room'. *Twenty-One Stories*. New York: Penguin, 1981 [1936] 115–41.

Greene, Graham. *The Heart of the Matter*. New York: Penguin, 2004 [1948].

Greene, Graham. *Journey Without Maps*. London: Penguin, 1980 [1936].

Greene, Graham. *A Sort of Life*. New York: Simon and Schuster, 1971.

Greene, Graham. *Ways of Escape*. New York: Simon and Schuster, 1980.

Gruesser, John Cullen. *White on Black: Contemporary Literature about Africa*. Urbana-Champaign, Illinois: University of Illinois Press, 1992.

Hobsbawm, E. J. *Industry and Empire: From 1750 to the Present Day*. London: Penguin, 1968.

James, C. L. R. [under the pen name J. R. Johnson]. 'White Workers' Prejudices'. *Labor Action* 9 (17), 23 April 1945: 3; https://www.marxists.org/archive/james-clr/works/1945/04/prejudices.html

Kennedy, Valerie. 'Conradian Quest Versus Dubious Adventure: Graham and Barbara Greene in West Africa'. *Studies in Travel Writing* 19 (1), 2015: 48–65. Taylor and Francis Online; https://doi.org/10.1080/13645145.2014.994927

Killingray, David. *Fighting for Britain: African soldiers in the Second World War*. Rochester, New York: Boydell & Brewer, 2010.

Lodge, David. 'Did the Butler Do it?' *The Guardian*. 4 November 2006; https://www.theguardian.com/books/2006/nov/04/film

Malamet, Elliott. 'Penning the Police/Policing the Pen: The Case of Graham Greene's *The Heart of the Matter*'. *Twentieth Century Literature* 39 (3), 1993: 283–305.

Memmi, Albert. *Dominated Man: Notes toward a Portrait*. New York: Orion, 1968.

Milbury-Steen, Sarah L. *European and African Stereotypes in Twentieth-Century Fiction*. London: Palgrave Macmillan, 1980.

Orwell, George. 'In Defense of P. G. Wodehouse'. *Windmill*, no. 2, July 1945; https://www.orwellfoundation.com/the-orwell-foundation/orwell/essays-and-other-works/in-defence-of-p-g-wodehouse/

Orwell, George. 'The Sanctified Sinner'. Review of *The Heart of the Matter* by Graham Greene. *New Yorker*. 17 July 1948: 61–3; http://home.planet.nl/~boe00905/Orwell-C786.html

Robbins, Bruce. *The Servant's Hand: English Fiction from Below*. 1986. Durham, North Carolina and London: Duke University Press, 1993.

Said, Edward W. *Culture and Imperialism*. New York: Knopf, 1993.

Said, Edward W. *Orientalism*. New York: Vintage, 1978.

Sherry, Norman. *The Life of Graham Greene, Volume II, 1939–1955*. New York: Viking, 1994.

Spitzer, Leo and LaRay Denzer. 'I. T. A. Wallace-Johnson and the West African Youth League'. *The International Journal of African Historical Studies* 6 (3), 1973: 413–52. JSTOR; https://doi.org/10.2307/216610

Steinglass, Matt. 'The Heart of the Matter'. Review of *The Life of Graham Greene, Vol. III, 1955–91*, by Norman Sherry. *The Nation*, 11 July 2005; https://www.thenation.com/article/archive/heart-matter/

Stollery, Martin. 'Scarred by a Cheated Ending/Not Suitable for Audiences in This Colony: The Film Adaptation of Graham Greene's *The Heart of the Matter* in Metropolitan and Colonial Contexts'. *Literature/Film Quarterly* 40 (3), 2012: 216–32. JSTOR; https://www.jstor.org/stable/43798921

Theroux, Paul. 'Damned Old Graham Greene'. Rev. of *The Life of Graham Greene, Volume Three: 1955–1991* by Norman Sherry. *The New York Times Book Review*. 17 October 2004; https://www.nytimes.com/2004/10/17/books/review/damned-old-graham-greene.html?

Waterfield, Giles. 'The Tradition Disintegrates'. In *Below Stairs: 400 Years of Servants' Portraits*, London: National Portrait Gallery, 2004: 183–95.

Zambrano, Ana Laura. 'Greene's Visions of Childhood: "The Basement Room" and *The Fallen Idol*'. *Graham Greene*, special issue of *Literature/Film Quarterly* 2 (4), 1974: 324–31. JSTOR; www.jstor.org/stable/43792838.

8

Purposes of Love: Rethinking Intimacy in the 1940s

Charlotte Charteris

Mary Renault's debut novel, *Purposes of Love* (1939), opens with the death of an infant: the negation – by normative standards at least – of love's legitimizing purpose. Does the loss of this new life invalidate the love that created it? Surely not. And if not, the novel seems to ask, then *why* is re-productivity the standard against which other loves are measured – and so often found wanting? Renault's novel is hardly a 'manifesto' for non-reproductive sexuality, but it does reflect on issues surrounding pre-marital sex, abortion and same-sex desire with a sympathy, openness and humour that looks ahead to the shifting attitudes of the subsequent decade, the 1940s. Now chiefly recalled as a historical novelist, Renault in fact devoted her early career to contemporary fiction, producing six 'medical romances' between 1939 and 1953 that drew on her experiences as a nurse and established her reputation as a writer. With the exception of *The Charioteer* (1953), however, these novels have largely been ignored by critics. Yet they were to prove remarkably prescient, both in yoking intimacy to trauma and rehabilitation, and in questioning the privileged status of marriage, as Jeffrey Weeks notes, as 'the only gateway to status, respectable adult sexuality and parenthood' (15). *Purposes of Love* heralded these preoccupations, its very title evoking the discourse of utility through which female sexuality, in particular, had for so long been regulated, even as it hinted at the plurality that threatened to subvert it. At a time of crisis for the birth rate in Britain, with a second European war threatening a population decimated by the first, the novel radically anticipated current queer debates over society's investment in what Lee Edelman terms 'the absolute value of reproductive futurism' (3).

Set in a large provincial hospital in the late 1930s, *Purposes of Love* is a novel wholly preoccupied with legitimacy, purpose and use-value, its protagonists obsessing over the question of 'whether one has the right to attach any value to oneself whatever apart from one's function in the community' (51–2). Modern medicine's own preference for utilitarian order is enshrined in the hospital's latest architectural addition, 'a new block of the 1930s, an austere functional cube' (3). Yet its halls and wards – each named, in a persistent reminder of past national traumas, for a British military campaign – are peopled by characters who elude classification, resisting medical science's attempts to pathologize them, and instead embracing modes of intimacy and identification that are inherently 'fluid' (141). Their lives and deaths are played out against the ironic echo of the hospital's daily prayer: 'shed Thy blessing on all those who strive to do Thy will and forward Thy purposes of love' (30). In a precursor of wartime life in barracks, the spatial and temporal practices of the hospital complex, while actively seeking to restrict certain forms of contact, unwittingly facilitate others far less likely to 'forward' the ordained purposes of love: 'The ruling ranks, settled virgins whose peace of mind was sufficiently disturbed by the direct manifestations of sex, spared themselves the knowledge of its divagations' (69).

In this 'inverted world' (241) student-nurse Vivian Lingard's ostensibly heterosexual love affair with a young pathologist becomes a source of trauma, a 'continuous nerve-storm' (167) that sees her declining health inextricably linked to the secrecy and subterfuge of maintaining the relationship, of 'all this jumping in and out like a tart' (166). By contrast, Vivian's affair with fellow-nurse Colonna Kimball is characterized by ease and restfulness, with Colonna as willing to take on the role of mother as lover: 'She helped Vivian undress like a mother, folded her things, tucked her in, handed her night-cream and cleansing tissues. Vivian submitted with gratitude' (51). Making love to Vivian 'tacitly, expertly, and with finesse' (44), she is as much an antidote to the conventions that produced the tortured heroine of Radclyffe Hall's *The Well of Loneliness* (1928) as to the competing male sexualities of Renault's own novel:

> Colonna, by all laws of literature, ought to have been plain, heavy, humourlessly passionate and misunderstood, pursuing in recurrent torments of jealousy the reluctant, the inexperienced and the young. She ought to have behaved like someone with a guilty secret. But Colonna, it appeared, accepted her own eccentricities much as she did the colour of her hair, though as a source of more amusement. (44–5)

Some laws, the novel insists, were made to be broken, and Colonna and Vivian are by no means alone in breaking them. Pathologist Mic Freeborn – a man who is, as his surname suggests, himself scarred by the stigma of illegitimacy – is initially attracted to Vivian because of her resemblance to her brother Jan, with whom he is infatuated. As Mic tells Vivian of their own relationship: 'Neither of us [...] has ever been much amused by the standard boy-meets-girl manoeuvres. We are people first, and belong to our sexes rather incidentally' (86). Yet the 'laws' of nature *do* still apply and, suspecting that history may be about to repeat itself, Vivian is forced to the conclusion that, since her love is only of 'use' to Mic insofar as it can 'give him back a little of what he had missed' through his own illicit origins, 'this competitor would have to return to the non-being from which it had come' (186). When she seeks Colonna's help in terminating the pregnancy, her apparent indifference to motherhood leaves Colonna marvelling at Vivian's own largely unexpected resistance to categorization: 'You don't fit into anything' (185).

In fact, by normative standards, Vivian is not 'fit for purpose' either as a nurse – the after-effects of the ergot she takes include dizziness and nausea, and she collapses while on duty – or as a woman. Yet these are not the standards to which Renault holds her, and in the aftermath of Jan's death in a car accident and the shared trauma of loss, it is the rehabilitative purposes of love that are brought into focus. When Vivian declares herself 'beaten' by circumstances, Mic responds: 'So are we all, [...] in one way or another. [...] That's the use of being two' (382). The novel, and the discourse of utility it seeks to rupture, offer a lens through which we might view the earliest workings of what Weeks calls the 'long, convoluted, messy, unfinished but profound revolution that has transformed the possibilities of living our sexual diversity and creating intimate lives' (3). Indeed, in foregrounding non-normative masculinities and femininities and locating trauma and rehabilitation at the heart of intimate life, *Purposes of Love* arguably serves as a starting point for 'an archive of feelings' such as Ann Cvetkovich proposes, a body of 1940s texts that together testify to 'the many forms of love, rage, intimacy, grief, shame, and more that are part of the vibrancy of queer cultures' (7). It is in fact difficult to read Cvetkovich's work on trauma and sexuality *without* noticing the points of contact between 1940s society and our own: 'Sometimes people say we're living in a trauma culture – that it's a time of crisis, and that the crisis is manifest in people's feelings, whether numbness or anxiety, lack of feeling or too much feeling' (15).

For Cvetkovich, however, this recognition of trauma at a national level is itself problematic in its capacity to co-opt, subdue and even erase sub-cultural experiences of trauma. One solution, she suggests, lies in also recognizing that even at times of national crisis – such as that of the Second World War in Britain – the nation itself remains a battleground for those queered by race, gender, sexuality or disability, and making visible 'the forms of violence that are forgotten or covered over by the amnesiac powers of national culture, which is adept at using one trauma story to suppress another' (16). Only by telling these stories does it become possible to expose the queer version of 'national trauma' that so often goes unnoticed because it 'operates in the less dramatic terrain of everyday experience and involves groups of people who make no claim to being representative citizens' (16). In framing traumatic experience as an aspect of everyday life, Cvetkovich's conceptualization of 'queer trauma' (17) at once radically destabilizes conventional approaches to trauma as something necessarily 'catastrophic and extreme' and exposes 'the incommensurability of large-scale events and the ongoing material details of experience' (20). To write of trauma in the 1940s is, for many, not to write of war at all, and what follows takes its cue from Cvetkovich in focusing on intimacy as a source of trauma and rehabilitation for those – children and adolescents, women, the sick and disabled – whose stories resist or disrupt the ways in which war trauma 'can be used to reinforce nationalism when constructed as a wound that must be healed in the name of unity' (16).

This is neither to deny the devastating impact of the war on Britain, however, nor to refute Adam Piette's claim that it 'traumatized British post-war culture' (1995: 1). It is, rather, to acknowledge that – as Sonya Rose suggests (7) – the discourse of 'absolute belonging' that emerged in response to this cultural wounding redefined hegemonic masculinity and femininity in terms of national purpose, placing strenuous demands on intimate life and thus implicitly denying citizenship to those who were unwilling – or unable – to conform to sexual and gender norms. It was an increased pressure on everyday sexual life that *Purposes of Love* would predict, a casual estimation of what Renault's protagonist describes as her own 'survival-value' in the event of war (171) prompting Vivian to muse, 'I wonder if we'd suddenly feel we had to have a baby. They say you do: instinct to perpetuate the race' (172). Similarly, while most of the novels considered below are not set during the war, it remains a persistent and insidious presence, even where the texts themselves appear to occupy only what Cvetkovich terms an 'oblique relation both in content and genre' to wartime culture and its aftermath as 'historical sites of trauma' (20). Those set either wholly or partially within the war's temporal limits – Nancy Mitford's *The Pursuit of Love* (1945) and Henry Green's *Back* (1946) – offer an equally slantwise perspective, only engaging with the war insofar as it intersects with the trauma of sexual and affective life, and the rehabilitative potential of love in all its forms.

Each represents an insight into what Cvetkovich describes as 'the queerness of emotional life' (20), contributing in its own ways to a 1940s archive of feelings that would have to wait until the decade's close – and the serialization of Mass Observation's Little Kinsey by the *Sunday Pictorial* in 1949 – to see any more explicit form of public acknowledgement. Named colloquially in recognition of Alfred Kinsey's ground-breaking study of American sexual life, *Sexual Behavior in the Human Male* (1948), Little Kinsey was the first sex survey of its kind to be undertaken in Britain, and aimed – according to Mass Observation's Tom Harrisson and as recorded by Liz Stanley in her role as editor – at presenting 'the actuality, the real life, the personal stuff of the problem, freed from an excess of methodological and statistical background' (67). The resonances of this aim with those of Cvetkovich's work are striking. As Stanley notes, 'love, passion, desire, pleasure, disgust, distaste, hate, despair; powerful feelings indeed lie behind the statistical headcounts of all sex surveys' (6). Due to Little Kinsey's 'textual reliance on extended quotation, however, they are also there, visible on its pages' (6), the full report arguably constituting a carefully collated archive of feelings in its own right. Read in dialogue with a literature of intimacy that for the most part preceded it into print, moreover, it offers a vindication of those whose fiction questioned or queered the prescribed purposes of love.

This chapter, then, represents a concerted effort to organize some of this 'archival material' into constellations that foreground the everyday stories of queer trauma – and rehabilitation – that have, in many cases, remained hidden from view even to literary criticism by the grand narrative of national trauma in the 1940s. Drawing on contemporary debates in queer theory and gender and sexualities studies as well as historical documents such as Little Kinsey, each of its sections brings together three novels united by their central feeling subject – the repressed adolescent, the rebellious woman, the recovering ex-serviceman – in order to elucidate an alternative teleology of intimate life in mid-century Britain, one that takes account of the personal needs and desires that lie behind public crisis. From the shock of touch and somatic breach experienced by Jocelyn Brooke, Denton Welch and Francis King's motherless schoolboy protagonists, to the ordeals of female embodiment faced by Mary Renault, Nancy Milford and Barbara Comyns's ill-informed heroines, and the recuperative possibilities of medical eros explored by Monica Dickens and Henry Green, this chapter seeks to isolate experiences of trauma and rehabilitation in 1940s fiction that challenge the limits placed upon intimacy by normative society, heralding a 'democratization of intimate life' (Weeks 8) that is still yet to be fully realized.

Repression: Or orphaned masculinities

> The imbrications of trauma and touch are a reminder of how modes of everyday sense experience, and particularly the intimacies of tactile experience in which bodies and things rub up against one another, are connected to trauma as a somatic experience. (Ann Cvetkovich 51)

As a coded shorthand for latent homosexuality, the mid-century usage of 'sensitive' or 'nervous' to describe the ill-at-ease English schoolboy has become so familiar as to warrant little attention from critics, rarely eliciting comment on the literal implications of the terms themselves. When Jocelyn Brooke recalls in his first volume of autobiographical fiction, *The Military Orchid*, that he 'was more-than-usually sensitive' (1948a: 69) as a boy, we are as apt as his contemporary readers were to accept his intended metaphorical meaning without probing deeper. Yet this is arguably to ignore fundamental questions about what it is to engage with the world through heightened 'modes of everyday sense experience, and particularly the intimacies of tactile experience in which bodies and things rub up against one another,' and what it might be to suffer the loss of what Brooke himself termed this 'capacity for feeling' (1950: 138) at a somatic or an emotional level. For the 'sensitive' Brooke, the two – sense and sensibility – are intimately connected, periods of somatic numbness seemingly arising from the need to repress 'unmanly' emotions in times of trauma. As he explains in *A Mine of Serpents* (1949), a dulling of his 'sensibilities' would leave him 'aware of the outside world, but cut off from all sensuous apprehension of it' (190). He might only experience reality from the confines of a 'transparent but impermeable envelope' (190).

Gill Plain has asserted that the 'dominant culture of Englishness, and indeed Britishness, of the 1940s was [...] one of understatement, euphemism and repression' (179). It was, arguably, a trauma culture within which personal grief must be 'covered over' in the name of national unity. For this reason, critics such as Dirk Vanderbeke and Marion Gymnich et al. have seen the period as 'a blank space' (5) in the history of the orphan figure in English fiction. Within the context of an emergent queer literary culture, however, the 1940s in fact produced a series of novels in which orphanhood offered a framework within which to examine the relationship between emotional repression and somatic experience, Brooke's debut novel, *The Scapegoat* (1948), finding parallels in Denton Welch's *In Youth Is Pleasure* (1944) and Francis King's *Never Again* (1947). Narratives of queer adolescence fuelled by repressed grief, despite being set in the 1930s, these novels differ from predecessors such as Christopher Isherwood's *The Memorial* (1932) in focusing primarily on the loss of the mother as a source of heightened sense experience. While neither Brooke nor King were themselves orphans – Welch, like his protagonist Orvil Pym, had lost his mother in childhood – the trope arguably offered a suitably charged context within which to explore their own less-easily explicable adolescent anxieties about losing 'touch' with reality.

For Welch's Orvil Pym, with his mother's death at a distance of three years, the rigid regulatory frame of public school and the 'hard sense of rightness' (20) it has instilled in his older brothers have combined with his father's reserve to firmly establish the limits of emotional expression:

> They had very little to talk about, because the one subject of deep interest to them both was quite banned. Orvil's mother had died three years ago; and he knew that if he even so much as mentioned her, his father's face would freeze and harden, and his voice become abrupt and cruel and contemptuous. She was never to be thought of or considered again – because she had been loved so much. It was disgusting to show that you knew such a woman had ever existed. (10)

Orvil's mother may be of 'deep' mutual interest to father and son, the 'one subject' that might put them in touch with one another, but the subject is only safe so long as it remains deep: buried, hidden from view. She has become an irrevocable barrier between them. Within this context, to 'show' by any external sign of grief that one loved her – continues to love her – is an obscenity, a 'disgusting' and unmanly spectacle. The emphasis on hardness here, as in the reference to Orvil's brothers, draws an implicit connection between emotional and somatic feeling: to 'harden' is at once to become impervious to touch and to being touched – or affected. The masculine code that has kept Orvil's grief in check, in Brooke's *The Scapegoat* it is this very 'cult of hardness' (41) into which his protagonist, Duncan Cameron, is initiated by the death of his mother, an event that coincides with his first term at boarding school. The routine of school life having 'dulled his grief' (7), as he travels to his uncle's farm for the holidays it remains 'to some extent repressed' (7), the transition from his old life tracked across a changing landscape: 'Coming from the softer, more feminine West Country, this eastern land seemed to him bleak, inimical, with a quality of masculine hardness' (6). For Duncan, the necessity of hardening himself to his own emotions triggers a violent physical reaction, after which 'it seemed to him that the conscious, feeling part of himself had been actually wrenched from his body, and now hung suspended in mid-air' (9), proximate but out of reach. It is an experience shared by King's Hugh Craddock, the fire that kills his parents and destroys his home in

India leaving him in a state of suspension in which 'he seemed to exist without feeling and beyond the reach of words' (59).

Within this context, each boy's narrative becomes an active quest for new modes of everyday sense experience, and particularly the intimacies of tactile experience in which bodies and things rub up against one another. It is a quest for something – or somebody – capable of puncturing Brooke's transparent but impenetrable envelope, and with it the barrier to expression. Yet it is also one that is increasingly bound up with each boy's sense of his own emerging sexuality. Their 'rather peculiar' (Welch 49) behaviour is further complicated by repressed grief, which manifests itself in minor illnesses and delinquencies, symptoms of psychological disturbance that go largely unheeded by their guardians. When Orvil's school term is curtailed by illness, Welch's narrator establishes a direct connection between the boy's psychological and physical health: 'Being already very uneasy and anxious about life, he was one of the first to show signs of food-poisoning; but soon two wards [...] were full of other boys [...] showing the same signs' (7). Even Orvil himself is obscurely conscious of the connection, feeling 'delighted and relieved when he knew that he was physically ill at last' (8). Yet his father is oblivious. Orvil is plagued by insomnia, headaches, nausea and vomiting throughout the summer, symptoms exacerbated by his tendency to 'experiment' with unprescribed medicines and unlabelled liquids, for their 'health-giving properties' (30). Nobody notices. Similarly, despite a history of travel-sickness associated with his nerves, when King's protagonist succumbs to seasickness on the voyage to England, he is ignored: 'When he had been ill at home in India, there had always been his mother [...] to fuss over him. Now, no one bothered' (96).

More disturbingly, however, and more significantly in terms of the search for sensuous experience, both Orvil and Duncan take to stealing. While Orvil's activities go unnoticed, in Brooke's *The Scapegoat* Duncan is caught and expelled from public school, his uncle telling neighbours that he is 'home for health-reasons', with ironic, if unwitting, accuracy (64). Indeed, despite the seemingly 'motiveless' (61) nature of the thefts and the arbitrariness of the items stolen, he ignores the signs, maintaining that 'psychology and all that was nonsense, so far as he was concerned' (62). For both boys, the thefts arguably represent an extension of their passion for collecting, a habit of which in Welch's narrative Orvil's brother – more observant than their father – remarks: 'It's a sort of disease – it's a mania' (50). Left to roam about the countryside alone, while Duncan botanizes, trawling his uncle's land for finds, Orvil combs the riverbank and scours junk shops, each of them accumulating objects valued for their sensuous qualities: their colours, their tastes, their smells and, most importantly, their textures. The ways in which they engage with these objects are telling. In *Never Again*, encountering the 'pathetic remnants' of his home is wholly traumatic for Hugh, a disorienting synesthetic experience in which, 'as he touched them, it seemed to him that there clung about them a bitter odour, the smell of burning, which could raise up the dead in all their agony' (67). In Cvetkovich's terms, the encounter is a terrifying 'violation of bodily boundaries' (50) that prompts Hugh to reject the items en masse. For Orvil and Duncan, by contrast, the kinds of sensuous, tactile experience offered by found (or stolen) objects are a gateway to physical intimacy and sexual expression, Orvil's imagination more often turning not on people, but 'from *things* it loved to *things* it hated' (Welch 39) [emphasis added].

With a stolen lipstick, he experiments before the mirror in his hotel room, carefully noting its appearance and smell before making-up: 'Orvil [...] began to cover his lips with a thick layer of colour. Soon they were gloriously cerise and sticky-looking. [...] Still itching to use the paint, [...] he absent-mindedly rouged his nipples until they were like two squashed strawberries' (79). It is, in a sense, a spectacular reprise of his earlier foray into self-flagellation, the 'gashes' and 'crimson marks' (79) he makes with the lipstick imitating those left by a 'short thick strap' of leather found while exploring the hotel: 'He [...] swung his arm across his chest, so that the strap licked round his back, the tip just stinging the tender flesh under his arm. [...] Looking over his shoulder, he delighted in the sore, hot lines on the white skin. They were a brilliant scarlet' (48). Duncan's interactions with his collection in *The Scapegoat* take a similarly sadomasochistic turn when, awaiting punishment by his uncle, he handcuffs himself to his bed. The handcuffs – a pair of 'heavy steel rings' that Duncan has treasured since finding them in the box-room (1948b: 52), and often 'fingered' (70) in contemplation – cannot be unlocked by the wearer, and it is left to his mortified uncle, on finding him, to 'release the trapped hands' (92). As Cvetkovich suggests, in these intimate encounters with objects, touch, as a not unpleasable 'breach of bodily boundaries, [...] creates a continuum between the physical and psychic, between the sexual and emotional' (51). Indeed, as experiments in how bodies and things rub up against one another, they arguably rehearse encounters with other bodies, bodies 'othered' by age and class, their strange textures, accents and odours offering forms of somatic experience capable of penetrating to the emotions.

All three boys forge intense, if fleeting, intimacies with older working-class men. Described in Brooke's *The Scapegoat* in terms of 'rough and weather-worn' skin, 'unfamiliar speech,' and 'animal, foxy scent' (5), these men provoke conflicting reactions, each protagonist – like Duncan – finding 'primary disgust modulated [...] into a peculiar and inadmissible pleasure' (31). Nowhere is the 'sensual excitement' (115) aroused by such masculinities more in evidence than in Orvil's case, Welch's novel climaxing in a spectacular return of the repressed – elicited by a single touch. Orvil is tantalized by his first glimpse of a young school-master with two boys on the river, a 'burning pang of longing' produced in him by their pseudo-militaristic yet sensual appearance in 'khaki shorts, [...] their chests and arms [...] brown as burnt sugar' (34, 31). Finding their makeshift camp, he watches 'hungrily' as the boys go about their tasks, eagerly doing the man's 'bidding' (34) while also engaging him in 'brawling and rough sport' (35), a scene that appeals to Orvil's own sadomasochistic tendencies. The man then reads to the boys on the grass, the sight of them 'rubbing up against his legs' and the physical contacts with which he responds – an ear 'tweaked' here, a toe 'jutted [...] into one of their rumps' (35) there – proving too much for Orvil: in his 'frustration and excitement' (36) he is caught masturbating in an abandoned garden on the way back to his hotel. Only once the boys have left does he encounter the school-master face to face, the man offering him shelter during a storm, and with it an opportunity not only to indulge his senses among the man's possessions but to engage in bodily contact with their owner by proxy. Lent an old dressing-gown while his clothes dry, and informed that it belonged to a friend lost in the last war, Orvil muses: 'A dead man's body used to lie between these folds – they've felt him a little hot, a little sticky, a little cold with gooseflesh and the small hairs sticking straight up all over his arms' (62).

'A tremor, like a weak orgasm' (65), runs through Orvil's naked body as he hugs the dressing-gown to himself, and his pleasure is only intensified by the suggestion that he clean the school-master's shoes:

> As he thrust his hand into one of them, he thought, 'It's [...] like a dark cave. [...] You can only feel along the walls blindly.' He placed his fingers in the little hollows – like a string of graded pearls – made by the toes. He traced the curve where the ball of the foot fitted. Pressing his knuckles up, he touched the overarching leather, which seemed cracked and yet humid. (69)

Orvil's 'thrust' is an act of penetration, a breach of boundaries that creates a continuum between the physical and the psychic, the tactile play of his fingers over the physical impressions left by the man's foot forging figurative impressions in the boy's mind. He touches and is touched, even if he is unable to express this, in a way that prefigures the pair's final encounter. Walking the tow-path on the last day of the holidays, Orvil thinks of his mother, his emotional connection to her reinforced by his physical engagement with the 'agate chicken' given to him by her: 'Abstractedly he rubbed it up and down on his trousers, and polished it till its little round eye sparkled [...] wickedly; then he breathed on it and covered it with a diamond dew. He popped it into his mouth and sucked it as if it had been a large sweet' (115). The 'unbearable flow' of his thoughts (115) prompts a physical desire 'to be near someone of good sense and strength' (116), and he is drawn to the school-master's hut, where his by-now habitual voyeurism finally leads to trouble: 'The man suddenly threw himself forward and tackled Orvil. He only managed to imprison one foot, but at his touch Orvil seemed to go mad' (118). With a touch, the school-master penetrates the transparent envelope of Brooke's analogy, opening up the continuum between the physical and the psychic, the sexual and the emotional. It is a consummation, a 'frenzy' (118) of physical violence overflowing in a surfeit of bodily fluids – blood, saliva and tears – before giving way to a verbal outpouring of repressed grief that leaves Orvil utterly spent, sure 'he could never speak again' (122).

What is striking about the memories to which Orvil gives vent is the way in which they resurrect his mother, their verbal expression at last freeing her image from the trappings of the grave that – in the daily effort to keep her figuratively buried – have dominated his silent recollections of her. Until this moment, the reader has seen her only as a corpse, a terrifying spectre 'struggling out of the earth' (18) in an attempt to reach him. With the shock of that longed-for physical contact, however, she comes to life. The school-master's touch draws from the formerly reticent Orvil a flood of tactile memory that evokes the intense physicality of his relationship with his mother and redefines orphanhood as a peculiar form of sensory deprivation: 'Sometimes we used to quarrel and then she'd hit me and I'd hit her back' (120). Firmly yoking sense to sensibility, Orvil's most intimate memories of his mother fuse in tragi-comic detail his pleasure in sensuous objects with his sadomasochistic streak, rejecting the hardened masculinity of his surviving relatives for the queerness of feeling itself: 'Once she tried to beat me with her ivory hair-brush and she got so excited that she used the wrong side and printed me all over with bristle-marks' (120).

Rebellion: Or governing bodies

To construct some bodily feature or process, to describe it in a certain way or to lay social emphasis on some aspect of the body is [...] to exercise control or constraint. [...] Similarly, to regulate or to exercise control over the body or bodies is to see these bodies in a particular way and to privilege certain understandings or constructions as against others. (Sue Scott and David Morgan viii)

For women, the 'social emphasis' on certain bodily processes reached an apotheosis in the 1940s. Even as it became increasingly difficult for the state to police modes of female embodiment and sexual behaviour in real terms, as Maroula Joannou explains, women remained subject to intensified 'propaganda, discourses and pressures during the war, many of which depended on the uses and meanings of their bodies' (68). For many, for perhaps the first time in their lives, womanhood itself became a conscious source of trauma under these pressures. For others, however, this was not a new problem, the biologically and socially prescribed 'uses and meanings of their bodies' having long proved incompatible with their own needs and desires. Yet, in bringing the formerly private issues surrounding fertility, reproduction and motherhood into the public sphere, discourses that stressed what Wendy Kline terms women's 'reproductive duty to the nation' (63) also opened up a space for debate and dissent. Within this context, so-called women's problems arguably became the nation's problems, an implicit conflation that saw the everyday traumas of female embodiment – menstruation, intercourse, morning sickness, childbirth and illegal abortion – discussed more freely by female novelists who sought to take back discursive control of their bodies. Writing about the most intimate of experiences with honesty, sympathy and humour, these authors challenged both literary and bodily norms, and exposed the ways in which, as Cvetkovich observes, 'the normalization of sex and gender identities can be seen as a form of insidious trauma, which is effective precisely because it often leaves no sign of a problem' (46).

A queer comedy of manners that seeks to puncture the assuredness with which female same-sex desire is pathologized by a – largely male – medical profession, Mary Renault's *The Friendly Young Ladies* (1944) is a novel in which, as Julie Abraham asserts, the 'expected relationships among gender, biological sex, and sexual behaviour are all undermined' (83). Yet it is also one that refuses to conform to a 'lesbian' tradition that Abraham sees as characterized by 'an excess of sex, sin, and torment' (1). Just as *Purposes of Love* finds nurse Colonna Kimball quite 'shameless and deliberate' (45) in both appearance and conduct, so Renault's *The Friendly Young Ladies* offers, in Leonora 'Leo' Lane, a heroine confident in her body whether clothed or unclothed. The distinction is important, for despite appearing more often in the habit of a 'slim shabby boy' than in that of 'a female manifestation' (169; 146) more acceptable to normative society, Leo cannot simply be read as a figure attempting to cover over her biological sex. She is by no means ashamed of her body. Whatever else naïve little sister Elsie might miss – she lives with Leo and her lover Helen Vaughan aboard their houseboat for several months without guessing the nature of their relationship – this is plain to her on observing Leo naked in the galley: 'Her body was straight, firm and confident; it moved as though clothes were an accident about which it had no particular feeling, for or against' (82). Leo is in her element, her movements so easy that a fully clothed Elsie senses 'a kind of arrogance in that slender, fluent shape with its small, high breasts, straight shoulders and narrow hips which made her feel as if it were she who had been stripped' (83), and found wanting. The fluency Elsie identifies here is symbolic of Leo's whole attitude to gender and sexuality, as scripts that can be learned, performed and subverted. They are, as Judith Butler (1999) might argue, repeated stylizations of the body over which Leo exercises control.

It is only when Leo is forced to relinquish control of her body, when her biological sex asserts itself in bodily processes that reduce her to the sum of her anatomical parts – and, with that, to her prescribed social function – that she becomes vulnerable. When Helen finds her unwell one evening, it becomes evident that this is not simply the result of having fallen in the river during a bet with a friend, as Helen asks:

> 'But why on earth? Why didn't you tell him you had an off day, like anyone else would?'
> 'Maybe they would, in one of your filthy hospitals.'
> 'Oh, nonsense. It isn't 1890.'
> Leo's mouth shut in a straight obstinate line. After a while she said, awkwardly, 'It makes you feel a fool.'
> 'I just don't get it. Joe of all people, too. I don't know what you've noticed [...] to make you think his mother didn't instruct him in the facts of life.'
> 'There are times,' said Leo, 'when the facts of life strike me as so damned silly I stop believing in them. [...] A smoke's all I want, and I'll be fine.' (131)

A trained nurse, Helen's recourse to 'facts' in broaching the subject of Leo's monthly period may be professional instinct, but it is also a challenge both to Leo's rather conventional squeamishness on the topic, and the reader's own. For all its subtlety, the passage is a transgressive move by Renault, since as Sophie Laws argues it is hard to 'isolate "meanings" of menstruation in our culture apart from the idea that it is *something which must be hidden*' (42) [emphasis in original]. Indeed, the reference to 'filthy hospitals' is resonant with the 'pollution beliefs' that still surround menstrual blood today and prompted several pseudo-scientific attempts to isolate its 'poisonous element' during the 1940s: 'Pollution beliefs [...] define, according to the dominant ideology, what is "matter out of place" and this in turn makes it clear who has control of such social definitions' (Laws 36). As Laws illustrates (36), the studies of the 1940s were exclusively male-authored, attempting to stablish a modern, 'rational-scientific' basis for fears that were firmly rooted in superstition. In Renault's narrative, Leo's dismissal of the 'facts of life' as 'damned silly' is, then, a rejection of a particular brand of masculine interpretive logic, a pathologizing instinct represented in the novel by doctor and amateur-psychoanalyst Peter Bracknell, who flirts with Elsie, Leo and Helen while treating them all as 'female cases' (2014b: 199) simply needing 'to be cured' (313).

When neither Leo nor Helen proves willing to submit to the 'logical procedure' (204) of his seduction, he refuses to accept Helen's account of their pleasure in each other: 'I keep telling you, we live together because we enjoy it. Anyone would think, to hear you talk, that we were a married couple' (249). What Peter fails to understand is that, for both women, the relationship is a rejection rather than an emulation of marriage. Helen speaks from experience, having refused to marry a former male lover, only to fall victim to a perverse masculine logic: 'Finally he tried to make me have a baby so that I'd have to. He said it was for my good. I [...] just packed and went' (250). Free from such coercion, her relationship with Leo represents bodily autonomy, a chance for each of them to dictate the uses and meanings of their bodies for themselves. Yet, this route to bodily autonomy was not open to every woman, the degree to which it depended upon financial autonomy – or, at least, financial stability – finding expression in very different ways in Nancy Mitford's *The Pursuit of Love* (1945) and Barbara Comyns's *Our Spoons Came from Woolworths* (1950). Focusing on young married women at opposite ends of the social scale, these novels examine the connection between the everyday traumas of womanhood and the inadequacy of sex education for girls, exposing the ways in which the 'facts of life' are themselves socially constructed and controlled. Indeed in Mitford's novel, while Linda Radlett spends her childhood in the eponymous pursuit of love, she gains little by her enquiries, retaining into adulthood what one friend terms with chilling accuracy 'an intensely romantic character, which is fatal for a woman' (76). Firmly against 'the education of females' (20) on principle, her father refuses to send her to school, thereby denying her access both to accurate information about sex and to the skills necessary for achieving financial independence. Linda, for all her ingenuity, leaves her father's home for her husband's with 'some curious ideas' (14) about sex and childbirth acquired from a combination of novels, psychology textbooks and manuals of animal husbandry.

Given this frame of reference, it is hardly surprising that Linda announces her first pregnancy with the words, 'I am in pig, what d'you think of that? [...] I feel awfully ill, I must say' (84). Linda's humour, like her author's, is a defence mechanism. Yet it also reveals her own half-conscious sense of the social emphasis on her body as good breeding stock. The admission of illness is uncharacteristic, however, given her commitment to maintaining – even as her marriage fails – what her cousin terms 'a perfect shop-front' (78). It is a mark of its severity that she alludes to her morning sickness at all, but it proves only a prelude to the physical trauma she undergoes in childbirth, her cousin's description of her again grimly prophetic: 'She was ill for a long time before, and very ill indeed at her confinement. [...] She [...] looked like a corpse' (85). Linda is warned by doctors that any subsequent pregnancy could kill her. The experience casts a shadow over Linda's emotional life, leaving her 'unhappy in her marriage, uninterested in her child, and inwardly oppressed with a sense of futility' (87), all symptoms suggestive of post-natal depression. It is only as she begins – after an ill-fated second marriage that leaves her stranded in Paris – to take conscious control of her body, that she recovers, a final passionate affair affirming Cvetkovich's identification of the body as 'the site where trauma can be both manifested and cured' (55). In the debonair Fabrice de Sauveterre Linda at last finds 'the authentic face of love' (Mitford 139), a heady mix of 'strong and impelling emotion' and 'what she had never so far felt for any man, an overwhelming physical attraction' (137). For the first time, she experiences sexual satisfaction, concluding that neither of her former husbands 'had an inkling of what we used to call the facts of life' (147). Yet, her new-found pleasure in her body is also a product of her own rejection of the 'facts of life' as she has always understood them, of the bodily norms and expectations constructed as 'facts' by normative society. This freedom from restraint is expressed in bodily terms, initially 'disconcerting' the experienced Fabrice, who asks: 'Do you always laugh when you make love?' Informed that 'most women' do not, Linda responds simply, but sincerely: 'How extraordinary – don't they enjoy it?' (147).

Linda dies in childbirth, carrying a son to full-term with a kind of bodily determination that confounds the predictions of her friends: 'Linda may miscarry, [...] and I'm sure it's to be hoped she will' (191). This will-to-birth turns the naïve misapprehensions of Comyns's Sophia Fairclough on their head: 'I had a kind of idea if you controlled your mind and said "I won't have any babies" very hard, they most likely wouldn't come. I thought that was what was meant by birth-control, but […] that idea was quite wrong' (2013: 26). She is not alone in her ignorance. Little Kinsey had noted in 1949 that women were 'worse informed than men' on the subject, reporting that many 'either do not know what birth control is or else confuse it with something else', a pattern that arguably rendered Mass Observation's female panel-members 'more willing than men to accept the comparatively new principle of sex education' (Stanley, 96, 192). Comyns had dealt with the inadequacies of education for girls on a formal level in *Sisters by a River* (1947), maintaining the spelling mistakes, grammatical errors and infantile colloquialisms of her female narrator throughout, despite ensuing difficulties in finding a publisher. In *Our Spoons Came from Woolworths* she concentrated on the implications of such ignorance for the experience of female embodiment, foregrounding 'upsets' of the kind Little Kinsey attributed to the 'belated or haphazard discovery' (Stanley 83) of the facts of sex and childbirth.

For Sophia, the trauma of giving birth for the first time in a large 'prison-like' public hospital is profoundly increased by the 'impatient' yet uncommunicative nurses, alien equipment and inexplicable questions, which leave her feeling 'dreadfully shamed and exposed' (Comyns 2013: 48, 50, 52) both physically and emotionally:

> When they had finished asking questions one of the nurses shaved me. This was a bit difficult, because the pains kept coming and it was difficult to keep still. When she had finished, she put very strong disinfectant on me. This smarted a lot, but it was almost a relief to have a different sort of pain. Then they gave me an enema, the first I had ever had, and it shamed me a lot, but the next thing they did was even worse – a large dose of castor oil which made me dreadfully sick for hours. (49–50)

There is a child-like simplicity about Sophia's first-person account that renders it at once more immediate and more horrifying. She is hustled from one 'torture chamber' (50) to another, eventually finding herself on a labour ward, where she is 'sick all over the bed' (51). Denied agency over her body and yet held wholly responsible for its failures, she is labelled 'dirty' and 'disgusting' (49, 51) by the nurses, who – despite having administered it – seem as appalled as Sophia herself when 'without any warning the wicked castor oil acted and I was completely disgraced' (51). For all the abject horror of this experience, Sophia adores her son, only poverty – and the refusal of her painter husband to find regular employment – forcing her out to work as an artist's model within weeks of his birth. Sophia's body becomes the couple's only source of income, and when this is jeopardized by another pregnancy, she is forced into an illegal abortion by her husband. Her reticence on this subject is, like her earlier candour, an act of discursive control: 'I don't feel much like writing about the actual operation. It was horrible and did not work at all as it should. I couldn't go to hospital, [...] but eventually I became better. But my mind didn't recover at all' (99). Just as with Linda, Sophia's emotional recovery becomes possible only through active defiance of coercive bodily norms and expectations, an adulterous affair introducing her belatedly to a guiltless sexual pleasure. 'I just felt awfully happy I had had this experience,' she explains, 'which if I had remained a "good wife" I would have missed' (105), her use of quotation marks symptomatic of the divergence of her values from those of normative society. It is an experience that redefines the purpose of physical intimacy, challenging the prescribed 'uses and meanings' of her body, and lending it a new social emphasis: 'I had had one and a half children, but had been a kind of virgin all the time. I wondered if there were other women like this, but I knew so few women intimately it was difficult to tell' (105–6).

Reconnection: Or nursing strangers

> The bedside [...] serves both as a real-world place and as a metaphor: the actual site of privileged medical exchanges and a theoretical space where patients encounter the representatives of medical logos. In its metaphoric sense, the bedside functions as an edge, a boundary or borderland where two adjacent worlds touch and sometimes collide. (David Morris 27–8)

The penultimate chapter of Monica Dickens's *Flowers on the Grass* (1949) finds protagonist Daniel Brett in a hospital bed, his bedside serving as a point of convergence for those whose worlds he has touched or collided with throughout the novel, the otherwise disparate scraps of 'a patchwork life' (212). Daniel's bedside becomes a synecdoche for his post-war life, the chapter a synecdoche for the novel, illustrating the inherent queerness of intimacy in a traumatized world where – for many – everyday life has begun to resemble that of the hospital itself: 'Odd how your life was made up of little bits of other people. You were close for a time, but it was touch and then away, like flies on a ceiling. In hospital you got to know people so intimately, and then never saw them again' (290). Indeed, in following its 'fugitive' protagonist (10) to this point of physical crisis, *Flowers on the Grass* arguably traces the post-war origins of a process through which, as David Morris explains, 'patienthood has expanded far beyond the image of a single person who occupies the sickbed' (28). In his landmark study of the role of eros in illness, Morris draws on medical sociology (Smith and Christakis 2008) to describe how the conventional dyad of patient and doctor, once 'almost like a traditional romantic couple' (27), has been queered by the emergence of 'supra-dyadic' networks: 'Supra-dyadic effects extend in networks beyond a single patient to include not only spouses or parents but also children, relatives, neighbors, paramedical help, and others, from the playmates of children and the neighbors of neighbors to far-flung friends of friends of friends' (28–9). Morris sees this as a relatively recent phenomenon, an outcome of the largely unseen conflict between medical logos – the operations of science and reason within the context of health and illness – and medical eros – the operations of desire within that same context. For him, the 'supra-dyadic bedside' (29) is perhaps best captured by Susan Sontag's 'The Way We Live Now' (1986), in which readers encounter a nameless HIV/AIDS patient exclusively through the conversations of his acquaintances. Yet, Dickens had arguably achieved this effect with *Flowers on the Grass* nearly forty years earlier, the innovative form of her novel – in which her troubled protagonist, a widower and ex–prisoner of war, appears only as a transient figure in other people's lives – highlighting the need for a supra-dyadic approach that took into account the role of desire in dealing with the traumas of post-war life.

Each chapter of *Flowers on the Grass* offers an account of Daniel – Danny, Dan, Mr Brett – from a single viewpoint, his role – husband, colleague, lodger, school-master, patient – differing according to the identity of the viewer, for whom the chapter is named. We are denied insight into his thoughts and feelings other than as they emerge from dialogue and have to instead rely on the speculations of his interlocutors, only our privileged access to wife Jane – the opening chapter focuses on her thoughts in the moments before her death and that of their unborn child in a household accident – giving us any advantage over the other strangers whose lives he touches. Only 'The Nurses' deviates from this pattern, the penultimate chapter combining the perspectives of several healthcare professionals, whose ministrations at Daniel's 'real-world' bedside are symbolic of those of the novel's other characters at its 'metaphoric' equivalent. Each of those who will eventually find themselves at his hospital bedside nurses him to some degree, the process fulfilling as deep-rooted a desire in each of them as in their patient, the 'loving need' that nurse Jacky Sanders sees as her vocation: 'Now she knew that she would never give up nursing for [...] anybody. This loving need that drove her could never be satisfied anywhere else' (289). Jacky's insight makes cogent the link between eros and illness in a way that illuminates the operation of desire in Daniel's previous encounters. Even for Jane, any sexual attraction to Daniel seems alleys to have been contingent upon her desire to care for him, her 'loving spirit' responding to some unspoken need in him: 'She had wanted to look after Daniel for the last twenty years, ever since she was nine, when she had seen him at his mother's funeral' (11).

She is only the first in whom he inspires this sense of purpose. The trauma of losing her cruelly shatters the fragile domesticity she has 'discreetly' (10) built up around him, reawakening the 'restless spirit' (19) with which he returned from Germany, and with it, that aura of 'detachment' (24) and careless 'neglect' (15) to which Jane was herself first attracted. For lonely college librarian Ossie Meekes, Daniel has always had 'that tantalising detachment of self-sufficiency that made you want to make him [...] need you, if only for the occasional laugh' (29). The desire to be of use in the aftermath of Jane's death sees him 'proposing' (33) to Daniel, offering to 'run the house' (33) in her stead, a queer model of domesticity that – while it suits both men for a time – courts controversy among family and friends: 'It's all wrong, you know, these two men living here together in this way with no one to look after them' (43). Yet, Ossie *does* look after Daniel, a task that becomes both more challenging and more intimate as Daniel takes to self-medicating on spirits. Called upon to undress a belligerent Daniel and put him to bed, he finds 'he quite enjoyed doing all this, and could understand why women liked to be nurses' (40). This pleasure in 'being needed' (48) by Daniel is shared by Mumma Weissman, the Jewish matriarch whose grown-up family Daniel lodges with several months later, brought 'physically so low that he had to let himself be looked after,' willing or not: 'The others were so independent now. They did not need her as she felt that Daniel did' (86).

The supra-dyadic bond that develops between them during Daniel's illness – Daniel 'obstructive and remote' (42) as ever, Mumma patient and intuitive – illustrates the ways in which for Morris eros 'makes its presence known obliquely through passionate refusals, grief, or anger. It produces gaps as palpable as the vacant space in a once-shared marriage bed' (25). Even as Daniel's health improves, Mumma is able to trace in his silences, omissions and protests the gap left by Jane, identifying in his physical maladies a manifestation of the psychological trauma of loss: 'He has kept some trouble inside himself and it has made him ill' (93). Indeed, while Mumma never learns from Daniel precisely what that 'trouble' is, she comes closer to understanding him – and his state of mind – than anyone before Valerie March. In Valerie, however, he meets his match: a widow with a young son, she takes him in as a paying guest, an 'effortless intimacy' (162) growing up between them largely as a result of her refusal to indulge him. While she nurses him with efficiency and care, first through a gunshot wound – inflicted by an ex-student – and later a bout of flu, she is not afraid to challenge him: 'You must be terribly unhealthy, Dan, to have gone so septic' (140). When both Daniel and Valerie's other lodger fall ill in quick succession, the comparison does not favour Daniel. Alec Piggott makes 'a heartbreakingly good patient' (157) while Daniel proves to be 'the worst patient Valerie had ever nursed,' even with son Pip helpfully 'ordering him about like a male nurse' (165).

She is clear-sighted enough to analyse her own motivations, however, briefly escaping 'the concentrated atmosphere of sickness and inaction' at home (168) to consider – quite calmly – a tepid proposal issued from beneath Daniel's bedclothes. She watches a 'shy, ill-matched' young couple (170) in a Lyons Corner House:

> They needed each other more for comfort than passion. They had found, as they grew forlornly up, that human beings are not strong enough to carry their lives alone, and that neither families nor friends nor even doting mothers can give the secret, saving support that comes only from the mysterious relationship of marriage. [...] In the cinema they would cling, not so much from a sex urge as from their fundamental need to cling. (171–2)

She is herself deeply conflicted: having, like Daniel, previously married for love, she remains – despite, or even because of, the trauma of loss – somewhat idealistic, acutely aware that 'with her single experience she could not imagine what a marriage without love would be like' (167). Yet, she has also criticized Daniel for his detachment in the past, suggesting that he 'had no right to make a show of being so fugitive in a world where people had to share each other's lives or die of loneliness' (153). The couple in Lyons invoke an epiphany as keen as 'those revelations you get under gas at the dentist' (170), the medical simile highlighting the overlap between the experience of illness, and that of what Morris terms the 'inner life' of desire (6). In a world in which loneliness is a terminal illness, the desire for comfort – to care and to be cared for – outstrips the desire for passion, subordinating the sex urge to other forms of intimacy. In Dickens's narrative neither she nor Daniel are 'strong enough to carry their lives alone,' Valerie realizes, and under such circumstances they have every right 'to choose each other and cling' (170). It is arguably this 'fundamental need to cling' that sees paralysed young housepainter Sonny Burgess and his fiancée married on the hospital's fracture ward in the novel's penultimate chapter. The wedding is a triumph of medical eros, though the cleaning regime ordered by Sister Ferguson is an insidious reminder of medical logos at work, the probationary nurses tasked with its completion complaining: 'Anyone would think it was going to be a surgical operation instead of the happiest day in Sonny's life' (282). The subsequent improvement in Sonny's response to treatment suggests it could hardly have been more medically effective if it was. More than this, the event extends and enriches the supra-dyadic network to which both Sonny and Daniel belong, allowing Daniel himself to acquire what he calls 'the habit of being any use to anyone' (291). The novel's final chapter, an epilogue from Nellie Burgess's point-of-view, finds the young couple – wheelchair and all – beginning their married life together in Daniel and Jane's cottage.

'Eros and illness both usually send us under the bedcovers,' suggests Morris (27), and both Henry Green's *Back* (1946) and Mary Renault's *North Face* (1949) exploit this overlap, climaxing in scenes that – like Sonny and Nellie's wedding – queer the distinction between consummation and rehabilitation. In focusing on ex-servicemen psychologically damaged, like Daniel Brett, not merely by their war service but by the devastating loss of what peace had seemed to promise, both novels also offer perspectives on the intimate connections forged between strangers in civilian life, and their supra-dyadic effects. In Green's narrative a harassed Nancy Whitmore complains after reviving Charley Summers from a dead faint on her hall floor, 'I don't know where we're coming to with the war effort, but I can't find time to nurse strangers' (49). Yet this is precisely what she proceeds to do, eventually taking on the care not only of Charley, but also of her estranged father and his ailing wife. Charley falls under the category of 'strange men' (47) in several senses: not only is he entirely unacquainted with Nancy herself, his behaviour is 'more than a bit queer' (112), both here and throughout the novel. An amputee and ex-prisoner of war, he is repatriated only to find that his lover Rose Phillips has died in his absence but is unable to grieve openly for fear of alerting her husband to their adulterous affair. When he is given Nancy's address by Rose's father, he becomes convinced that she is Rose, refusing for some time to accept that she is in fact her half-sister.

The psychological burden of his 'secret' (78) knowledge leaves Charley 'empty, and ill' (45), and wondering – on a second visit to Nancy's – if 'he would be sick all over the carpet' (67). As his physical health deteriorates and his reticence increases, almost everybody he comes into contact with has an opinion on what the 'trouble' (108) is, more than one concluding 'that these repatriated men came back very queer from those camps' (120). In fact, the general consensus is that

Charley's is a sexual problem, his boss advising him: 'It's sex is the whole trouble. There you are. Sex. [...] To put it in a nutshell, after the bad time you've had, you want to marry and settle down' (186–7). Nancy alone appears alert to the more complex operation of eros within the context of injury and illness, registering the ways in which it suffuses Charley's experiences of both physical and psychological trauma, marking them, in Morris's words, 'with damage, deficit, forfeit, and loss: loss of health, loss of function, loss of future' (25). Whatever it is, to Nancy's mind as to Morris's, eros 'is *not* identical with sexual activity' (5) [emphasis original]. It inhabits, and is simultaneously inhabited by, limitless emotional content. Nancy – a young widow like Valerie March – is perceptive enough to realize that it is not passion but comfort that Charley desires, clinging to the image of Rose not from the sex urge, but from the fundamental need to cling. Indeed, with its combined implications of both proximity and urgency, the verb 'to cling' perfectly captures Charley's attachment to Nancy in Green's novel, first as an embodiment of Rose and later as a reassuringly 'solid' body (140) in her own right. Finally reconciling himself to her true identity, as Charley spends more time with Nancy, he is startled to find he is 'beginning to feel easy and comfortable' (137). When she is with him, his nerves are 'quietened by having her there' (190), without the need for words. Nancy responds to this unspoken need, deciding that 'what she liked about Charley was how he did not ask for anything, however small, although his need was desperate, a child could tell it' (199). While she wonders, 'if he didn't, or just couldn't, tell [...] something of all that went on behind those marvellous brown eyes,' she is certain that she is 'needed as she could never be by almost anyone, that more than anyone in the world [...] it was Charley Summers who must have her' (199). Granted the access that is so categorically denied us by Dickens's narrative, however, we *are* privy to what goes on behind those marvellous brown eyes and can trace Nancy's evolution for Charley into 'an embodiment of everything comforting, and true, and good' (202).

Yet he remains unable to express either these sentiments or the grief and suffering that have led up to them. It is Nancy who proposes marriage, and is accepted, in a radical reversal of normative gender roles that also sees her taking the sexual lead by making the proviso 'that they should have a trial trip' (207). Charley shyly enters her room that same night:

> Then he knelt by the bed, having under his eyes the great, the overwhelming sight of the woman he loved, for the first time without her clothes. [...] She had shut her eyes to let him have his fill, but it was too much, for he [...] buried his

face in her side just below the ribs, and bawled like a child. [...] His tears wetted her. The salt water ran down between her legs. And she knew what she had taken on.' (207)

Green exploits the implicit overlap between marriage-bed and sickbed, the 'overwhelming sight' of Nancy's naked body bringing Charley not to sexual, but emotional climax. Nancy herself is 'wetted' by his tears, in an authorial sleight-of-hand that sees not semen, but 'salt water' running 'down between her legs.' Here, medical eros again comes into its own, the episode illustrating the role of intimacy in rehabilitation. It is nonetheless a daring scene since, regardless of its outcome, in its intent the 'trial trip' troubles the moral imperative against pre-marital sex in a way that would not be discussed openly until Little Kinsey appeared. Surprisingly, as Stanley's edition reveals, while the report found that more people were 'more strongly opposed to extra-marital relations' than to any other practice (133), it also identified what many saw as the mitigating emotional content of certain kinds of pre-marital sex, highlighting cases where 'feeling' was 'as important a sanction to intercourse as marriage' itself: 'Sex relations between two people who are in love, engaged, or somehow unable to marry, are far more often condoned than sex relations based largely on physical attraction alone' (135, 134–5). One interviewee went so far as to assert that it was necessary 'to try people out' (138) before marriage in order to avoid disappointment. This is, in essence, in Green's novel precisely Nancy's motivation, and – in a world in which comfort is more valuable than passion – she is satisfied: 'It was no more or less, really, than she had expected' (207).

Stanley records that the report's compilers were at pains to stress the potential 'cleavage between attitude and habit' (133), and indeed, the climactic scene of Renault's *North Face* accords with *Back* in implying that the 'trial trip' was more common in practice than attitudes suggest. Set in a post-war Yorkshire boarding-house, the novel focuses on the solitary Neil Langton, an amateur climber who – mourning the loss of his wife to a GI and the death of his infant daughter in a house-fire – has 'existed for some months untroubled by any human contacts' (2014c: 28) while awaiting his decree absolute. Neil's arrival, falling in 'one of the all-female spells' (5) at the guest-house, is something of an event, and – appearing in the lounge unkempt, 'shockingly thin' (14) and late for tea – he 'finds himself confronted with two strange women' (17), with whom contact is unavoidable. These peripheral characters have been described by Sarah Dunant as 'more entertaining' than the 'rather laboured love story' (ix) about which Renault's novel ultimately turns. Yet it is precisely this imbalance that lends *North*

Face to analysis in terms of the supra-dyadic bedside: everyone, it seems, has an opinion on Neil's 'case-history' (111). While landlady Mrs Kearsy is prompted to 'palliative platitudes' (15) by Neil's appearance, for closeted academic Miss Searle, his arrival in the lounge brings with it an 'aura of male negativism like a cramp in the back of her neck' (17). With the 'clinical' instincts of the professional nurse, however, Miss Fisher attempts to diagnose 'what he was convalescing from' (17). At odds both with their surroundings and with each other, Miss Searle and Miss Fisher function as a kind of modern chorus, each responding to the 'goings-on' (108) at the boarding-house after her wont: while Miss Fisher regards 'prudery as a social crime' (9) from which nursing has freed her, to an appalled Miss Searle the 'whole world seemed to have become obscene' (112). In spite of their years, in assessing Neil's motives and those of the other guests, neither seems emotionally mature enough to see beyond the sex urge.

Such 'goings-on' escalate with the arrival of Ellen Shorland. An orphan on the cusp of womanhood, in mourning for a fiancé lost to the war, she is – like Neil – a victim of a trauma culture in which 'the personal' has become so 'completely insignificant' as to leave one 'feeling that one hasn't the right to feel' (130–1). It is ironically symptomatic of that culture's capacity to homogenize suffering that Neil himself labels it 'the sickness of the age' (131). Neil and Ellen meet as strangers but are drawn together by an 'instinctive need' that exceeds the limits of sexual desire, the relationship itself becoming an experiment in whether – damaged as they both are – they remain 'as fit as any for love' (199). In a novel characterized by anti-climax, the couple's 'trial trip' is no exception, the physical merely punctuating the emotional in a bedroom scene that again blurs the distinction between consummation and rehabilitation. While the bedclothes are 'tangled' into 'a churned-up heap' beneath them (289) in the throes of feeling, the sexual act itself occurs only as an afterthought, Ellen choosing to 'part with her virginity as a casual epilogue, after an exhausting emotional crisis, in the abrupt and flickering desire of weariness' (293) rather than passion. Sex is a salve, a balm applied – like the flavine cream applied to Neil's injured hand earlier that night – to a 'gritty, ragged-edged, ploughed-up wound' (272). Like Mic and Vivian of Renault's *Purposes of Love*, Neil and Ellen accept that 'physical love had become almost irrelevant, but might make them feel better' (196).

A decade after the publication of her debut, Renault continued to question the purposes of love, her voice just one of many that saw its rehabilitative potential in a world in which everyday life had come to resemble the traffic of a busy trauma ward. While the 1940s had given rise to a narrative of 'national trauma' that figured the war as a wound that must be healed in the name of unity, these writers sought to expose the fault-lines so hastily covered over by this narrative, telling the stories of those for whom the nation itself remained a battleground and a daily source of trauma. Marked out by their resistance to the demands placed upon intimate life by normative society, the novels they produced represent – when read as a body – an archive of feelings that arguably paved the way for the frankness and diversity of response by which interviewers, according to Stanley, confessed themselves 'constantly surprised' (71) while questioning members of the British public for Mass Observation's sex survey. The report's serialization in the *Sunday Pictorial* in 1949 offered documentary evidence for what it termed the 'atmosphere of emotionality' (77) surrounding everyday sexual life, testifying to the lived reality of a range of feelings – from numbness, grief, shame and disgust to desire, solace, liberation and pleasure – that had been anticipated by a fiction of queer trauma and rehabilitation amassed over the preceding decade. In this, the world we had won, it was becoming clear – for perhaps the first time in British history – that, as Cvetkovich would later assert, it was 'no longer useful to presume that sexuality, intimacy, affect, and other categories of experience typically assigned to the private sphere do not also pervade public life' (32).

Works cited

Abraham, Julie. *Are Girls Necessary? Lesbian Writing and Modern Histories*. London and New York: Routledge, 1996.
Brooke, Jocelyn. *The Military Orchid*. London: The Bodley Head, 1948a.
Brooke, Jocelyn. *The Scapegoat*. London: The Bodley Head, 1948b.
Brooke, Jocelyn. *A Mine of Serpents*. London: The Bodley Head, 1949.
Brooke, Jocelyn. *The Goose Cathedral*. London: The Bodley Head, 1950.
Butler, Judith. *Gender Trouble: Feminism and the Subversion of Identity*. London and New York: Routledge, 1999.
Comyns, Barbara. *Sisters by a River*. London: Eyre & Spottiswoode, 1947.
Comyns, Barbara. *Our Spoons Came from Woolworths*. London: Virago, 2013 [1950].
Cvetkovich, Ann. *An Archive of Feelings: Trauma, Sexuality, and Lesbian Public Cultures*. Durham, NC: Duke University Press, 2003.
Dickens, Monica. *Flowers on the Grass*. London: Michael Joseph, 1949.
Dunant, Sarah. 'Introduction'. In M. Renault, *The Friendly Young Ladies*. London: Virago, 2014: v–xii.
Edelman, Lee. *No Future: Queer Theory and the Death Drive*. Durham, NC: Duke University Press, 2004.
Green, Henry. *Back*. London: Harvill Press, 1998 [1946].

Hall, Radclyffe. *The Well of Loneliness*. London: Jonathan Cape, 1928.

Isherwood, Christopher. *The Memorial: Portrait of a Family*. London: Hogarth Press, 1932.

Joannou, Maroula. *Women's Writing, Englishness and National and Cultural Identity: The Mobile Woman and the Migrant Voice, 1938–62*. Basingstoke: Palgrave Macmillan, 2012.

King, Francis. *Never Again*. Richmond, VA: Valancourt, 2013 [1947].

Kline, Wendy. *Building a Better Race: Gender, Sexuality, and Eugenics from the Turn of the Century to the Baby Boom*. Berkeley: University of California Press, 2001.

Laws, Sophie. *Issues of Blood: The Politics of Menstruation*. Basingstoke: Macmillan, 1990.

Mitford, Nancy. *The Pursuit of Love*. Harmondsworth: Penguin, 2010 [1945].

Morris, David B. *Eros and Illness*. Cambridge, MA: Harvard University Press, 2017.

Piette, Adam. *Imagination at War: British Fiction and Poetry, 1939–1945*. London: Papermac, 1995.

Plain, Gill *Literature of the 1940s: War, Postwar and 'Peace'*. Edinburgh: Edinburgh University Press, 2013.

Renault, Mary. *Purposes of Love*. London: Virago, 2014a [1939].

Renault, Mary. *The Friendly Young Ladies*. London: Virago, 2014b [1944].

Renault, Mary. *North Face*. London: Virago, 2014c [1949].

Rose, Sonya O. *Which People's War? National Identity and Citizenship in Wartime Britain, 1939–1945*. Oxford: Oxford University Press, 2004.

Scott, Sue. and David Morgan. 'Introduction'. In Sue Scott and David Morgan (eds.), *Body Matters: Essays on the Sociology of the Body*. London: Falmer, 1993: viii–xi.

Smith, Kirsten P. and Nicholas A. Christakis. 'Social Networks and Health'. *Annual Review of Sociology* 34, 2008: 405–29.

Sontag, Susan. 'The Way We Live Now'. *The New Yorker*, 24 November 1986: 42–51.

Stanley, Liz. *Sex Surveyed, 1949–1994: From Mass-Observation's 'Little Kinsey' to the National Survey and the Hite Reports*. London and New York: Routledge, 2014.

Vanderbeke, Dirk and Marion Gymnich et al. *The Orphan in Fiction and Comics since the 19th Century*. Newcastle-upon-Tyne: Cambridge Scholars, 2018.

Weeks, Jeffrey. *The World We Have Won: The Remaking of Erotic and Intimate Life*. London and New York: Routledge, 2007.

Welch, Denton. *In Youth Is Pleasure*. London: Enitharmon Press, 2005 [1944].

9

No Concession to 'English' Taste? Refugees from National Socialism Writing in Britain

Andrea Hammel

The contribution that refugees from Central Europe made to British culture and society has been recognized in many areas, such as music and art, with the celebration of individuals such as the conductor Sir Georg Solti and the painter Frank Auerbach. However, there are a few first-generation refugees who are currently not anywhere near as well known for their contribution to English literature. This chapter will outline some of the circumstances that led to this discrepancy and try to rehabilitate some forgotten writers and their works.

In the English-speaking world (as well as in Germany and Austria) writing by refugees from National Socialism is called Exile Literature. However, if we look at English-language literary histories or critical works, those writers who had to flee Continental Europe due to National Socialist persecution do not feature in the discussion. For example, Andrew Gurr's *Writers in Exile* charts exile as the central theme of modern literature: using the examples of Katherine Mansfield, V. S. Naipaul and James Joyce. Gurr claims that 'exile creates the kind of isolation which is the nearest thing to freedom that a twentieth century writer is likely to attain' and that 'the normal role for the modern creative writer is to be an exile', but he does not discuss any writers that fled to the UK in the 1930s and 1940s (17, 13). Similarly, Michael Seidel argues in his study *Exile and the Literary Imagination*, which focuses on a critical reading of a small number of canonized writers, such as Conrad, Joyce, Sterne, James and Nabokov, that 'imaginative powers begin at the boundaries of accumulated experiences' (2) and that exile is not only the 'symptomatic metaphor for the narrative imagination, but also its material resource' (8); but he completely ignores exiles from National Socialism and their work. These studies give priority to well-known literary figures and a high-modernist canon. The focus is also very male-centric. But even feminist challenges to this viewpoint concentrate on the traditional English canon: Jane

Marcus draws on her research on Virginia Woolf to argue that a woman 'is always in exile by speaking *his* tongue, so further conditions of exile simply multiply the number of her "veils"' (270).

I have discussed elsewhere that there is nothing straightforward about the intersection of oppressions or the 'opportunities' that women writers fleeing National Socialism experienced (Hammel 2008). Following some historical details of the extent of the migration of German-speaking exiles during the period, I will discuss the exile experiences of perhaps the most well-known exile writer, Stefan Zweig, before going on to examine the difficult choice faced by other exile writers, such as Robert Neumann and Hilde Spiel, as to whether or not they should try to write in English. The second half of the chapter will include the discussion of a number of women writers, their work and their position as women refugees in the UK. According to Marcus, feminist readings of exile literature need to understand the multiple displacements in women authors' lives and their texts and acknowledge that 'displacement and distance are obviously different for women which are already displaced by gender within their home culture' (273). Through case studies of Hermynia Zur Mühlen and Anna Gmeyner, I hope to show how exile writers created a space of possibility that was separate to both their home and host cultures but nonetheless central to both the political zeitgeist and the cultural imaginary of the period.

Refugees from National Socialism in the UK

As Grenville indicates in *Jewish Refugees from Germany and Austria in Britain, 1933–1970* (2010), at the outbreak of the Second World War in September 1939, over 60,000 German-speaking refugees, not including children, are said to have been resident in the UK (xi). After the outbreak of hostilities very few civilians could arrive in or leave the UK, so this number of refugees from National Socialism in the UK remained steady, at least during the first half of the 1940s. This makes the UK the country that took in the largest number of refugees in proportion to its population. Many of the refugees arriving before 1938 were political opponents of the National Socialist regime, and this included writers, journalists and those interested or active in the creative arts. Some of these early refugees were Jewish, and thus doubly in danger of persecution. After the annexation of Austria in March 1938 the number of refugees trying to flee to the UK rose sharply, and the number included many more writers and artists. Finally, the Pogrom perpetrated against the Jewish population of the German

Reich and the annexed Austria in November 1938 acted as a catalyst for an even larger number of Jewish citizens to try and find refuge outside Germany.

The relatively large number of refugees in the UK and the post-war success of some individual former refugees led to the myth of exemplary British hospitality. But over the last two decades this has been challenged frequently (see, for example, London 2000): in fact, British immigration and refugee policy was repeatedly made more restrictive in response to the increasing numbers of Continental refugees anticipated. Latent British anti-Semitism, xenophobia and the fear that admittance would have a negative impact on the British labour market and on the difficult economic situation at the end of the 1930s influenced the British government to tighten admission criteria. Successive governments were not willing to invest in much organizational and financial support for those fleeing persecution. Even the now-so-celebrated Kindertransport child refugees were able to come to the UK only due to the efforts of large numbers of British citizens who gave their money and their time to assist the children. The government even demanded a guarantee of £50 for each child to ensure they would not become a financial burden to the state (see Hammel 2020).

Stefan Zweig: Between privilege and despair

The most well-known writer to flee to the UK was Stefan Zweig, who arrived in London in October 1933. Born in Vienna into a wealthy Jewish family in 1881, he had aspired early on to be part of a European cultural elite working towards greater European cultural unity. This aim was shattered for the first time by the outbreak of the First World War and then by the rise to power of fascism.

Zweig was a very productive author of poetry and prose and widely translated: by the 1930s his books had been translated into thirty languages. He also gathered many European literary figures in his home outside Salzburg in Austria for intellectual exchanges, such as the writers Thomas Mann, H. G. Wells and James Joyce. Like many others, he was initially disinclined to leave Austria despite the fact that his books were on the National Socialist list of prohibited texts, and copies were destroyed in the book burnings in May 1933. His journey to the UK in autumn 1933 was voluntary, and it has often been remarked upon that England was an unusual destination for someone who seemed more at home in Central and Southern Europe and rarely expressed public political opinions (see Dove 2000: 33). However, he had the means to travel, and difficulties in his first marriage might have contributed to the decision.

Zweig is said to have preferred a quiet life; he rented a flat in central London and spent much time in the Reading Room of the British Library researching his next books. After a few months in Britain, he travelled back to Austria in January 1934 but was extremely perturbed by the political developments towards Austro-Fascism and quickly returned to London. As Dove notes, by February 1934 he felt that his exile had begun in earnest. Zweig continued to work on biographical studies of great Europeans and quickly added *Erasmus of Rotterdam* (1934) to *Joseph Fouché* (1929) and *Marie Antoinette* (1932). The publication of his next book *Maria Stuart* (1935) – a biography of Mary, Queen of Scots, titled *The Queen of Scots* in the English translation – cemented Zweig's reputation in the UK, but this did not mean that he sought to be part of the British literary scene. Zweig is sometimes described as melancholic and was possibly suffering from depression. Despite his success and financial security, the political changes on the Continent hit him hard, and he became more reclusive. After the annexation of Austria, he applied for British citizenship, a process that was complicated and slow despite his privileged position, reputation and wealth.

Zweig remained prolific in exile, publishing a book a year until the outbreak of the Second World War: *The Queen of Scots* (1935) was followed by *The Right to Heresy* (1936), *The Buried Candelabrum* (1937), *Magellan* (1938) and *Beware of Pity* (1939). With the exception of the last book, all were published in German by Reichner first, and then, as Dove details, in English by Cassell: 'confirming Zweig's emergence as a bestselling author in Britain, in parallel to his disappearance to his German-speaking readership' (2000: 143). But Zweig was not only successful in the UK, he was one of the most successful writers worldwide in the 1930s. In 1936 he went on an extensive speaking tour on the invitation of the Brazilian government. He was received by the Brazilian president and celebrated all over the country. Zweig seems to have been blind to the authoritarian aspect of the Brazilian regime and, as cited by Dove, Zweig called Brazil 'a land of the future' (2000: 211). Back in the UK, he became more and more depressed, partially due to the irretrievable breakdown of his first marriage, but also due to the fact that he was living in exile. As quoted by Dove, he wrote in a letter to the writer Romain Rolland: 'Emigration undermines and slowly kills you' (2000: 145).

It is not surprising that the annexation of Austria by National Socialist Germany on 12 March 1938 pushed Zweig deeper and deeper into depression. A large number of friends from Austria, many writers and cultural figures, approached him for urgent help to escape. He was appalled that the general public in the UK was indifferent to the plight of many in his home country. In the midst of these difficulties, he started to plan his memoir *The World of Yesterday*, which portrays the end of the Austria and Austria-Hungarian Empire in which Zweig himself grew up. This complicated longing for the multi-culturalism of the Austro-Hungarian Empire is a feature in a number of other exile writers' works, such as Hilde Spiel's *The Fruits of Prosperity* and Hermynia Zur Mühlen's *We Poor Shadows*, which are discussed below.

Zweig was also surprised by the calm with which the British public received the news of the outbreak of the Second World War. By this time, he had left London, married a German woman, writer Friderike Maria Burger, and eventually he purchased a house in Bath. This is generally seen as a commitment to Europe, and a sign that he by then had given up plans to emigrate to the United States (like other famous German-language writers such as Mann or Feuchtwanger) or even South America. However, as Dove records, his letters show how disturbed he was by the German advances on the Western front (2000: 188). His status as a bestselling author allowed him to still travel in a limited way, and he visited Paris in spring 1940 for a number of speaking engagements. But international relations were clearly becoming more difficult. When he received another invitation to visit Brazil again, he dithered, though he did accept it in the end. He was aware of the dangers of crossing the Atlantic, and of the possibility that he might not be able to return to Europe. But the pull of escaping the demoralizing situation in Europe and being able to perform as the celebrated author as well as the push of fearing for his life as a Jewish exile in the UK in the case of an invasion proved too much. Zweig and his wife set sail first to New York and from there to South America. Dove outlines plausibly that Zweig always intended to return to England, leaving behind his house, his papers, his library and the manuscript for the study of the next great European, his *Balzac* manuscript (2000: 209). But the German U-Boat attacks in the Atlantic made a return journey inadvisable. First Zweig extended his tour of South America with a speaking tour of Northern Brazil. Despite travelling back and forth once to New York, the further journey to Europe could not be undertaken, and the couple returned to Brazil and took a house on the outskirts of Petropolis. Being able to stay in one place initially cheered him up, but after a few weeks Zweig fell deep into depression. He was in despair about the war, growing old and not being productive. In a letter quoted by Dove, Zweig wrote that always speaking in a foreign language was tiring and that he was constantly 'afraid of forgetting my own language' (2000: 213). He managed to finish his celebrated memoir *The World of Yesterday*, first published in English in 1943, with the narrative ending abruptly in 1939. Not long after,

Stefan and Lotte Zweig ended their own lives on 22 February 1942 to the shock of the literary world.

Changing language

Like Zweig, most writers-in-exile feared losing their language: they felt that they might be losing the tools of their trade if they were no longer surrounded by the German or Austrian culture and the German language. Some feared the loss of mother tongue might threaten a diminishment in their whole professional as well as personal identity, which was so bound up with the German language and culture. 'You have to write in the language of your surroundings, anything else will be a dead creation,' argued the exile writer Ernst Bloch in an article first published in July 1939 (83).[1] Many felt it was imperative to preserve their mother tongue as a source for creative writing, as opposed to starting to use another language for their creative work. Many exile writers also believed that they had a duty to preserve an alternative version of the German and Austrian culture to that promulgated by National Socialism. Therefore, as F. J. Wehage sets out, a significant number of exiled writers and artists claimed to represent 'the Other Germany' (421ff). They did so by upholding the German language as well as German literary and artistic traditions, and by trying to build on an earlier cultural history that was now being rejected by National Socialist cultural policy.

Many well-known writers insisted that they could not be creative in a language that was not German. The German playwright and novelist Lion Feuchtwanger, who lived outside Germany from 1933 onwards, upheld this view: 'One cannot write, one cannot create in a foreign language' (qtd. Krohn et al., ix). Feuchtwanger was an established writer and on a tour of speaking engagements in the United States at the time of the National Socialists' takeover in 1933. His novel *Jud Süss* (1925) had been very successful and was translated into seventeen languages by 1931. As was the case with Zweig's work, this meant that publishers were willing to continue to arrange for his work to be translated after 1933 and his popularity with an English-speaking audience afforded him a degree of financial security. He could thus continue to write in German and did not need to change his view that creative writing should take place only in one's first language.

Other less well-known writers were in a different position: if they chose to continue to write in German, they would only be published by exile publishing houses or maybe in Switzerland; otherwise, they had to try to get their works translated. Like Feuchtwanger and Zweig, the Austrian-born Robert Neumann was also on a professional engagement abroad in the early 1930s. Neumann had come to London in 1933, not as a refugee but to start research for a biography of the arms dealer Sir Basil Zaharoff commissioned by a London literary agent. Neumann returned to Austria at the end of that year to see his wife and son, but in February 1934 – similarly to Zweig – he permanently settled in London. Interestingly, over the next two years Neumann visited the Austrian countryside and Vienna several times until in 1936, when he was mistaken at the border for a German communist and arrested. This experience stopped him from returning to Austria for visits, something that was to become impossible for a writer with a Jewish background after the annexation of Austria in 1938 anyway. Neumann's reputation in the German-speaking world was based on his parodies; his volume *Mit fremden Federn* (1927) had brought him overnight fame. Parody is, of course, a culturally specific genre and does not lend itself to easy translation. The aforementioned Zaharoff project was a complicated endeavour which became a success only after years of stops and starts, especially because the publishers feared litigation from the armaments industry. However, by 1939, 35,000 copies had been sold, which, as Dove explains, did much to alleviate Neumann's financial difficulties (1994: 162).

When Neumann settled in the Britain he apparently spoke little English, but five of his earlier novels had already been translated from German into English and published by the small British publisher Peter Davies. He offered his already published German-language oeuvre to British publishers with limited success. Eventually Neumann's novel *Die Macht* (1932) was translated by Dorothy Richardson, who usually translated from French into English, as *Mammon* (1933). Richardson was also asked by the publisher to condense the novel and shortened it by a third. The end result upset Neumann to such an extent that he demanded that the edition should be scrapped.

Having had to leave the Austrian and German market behind, it quickly became obvious to Neumann that his works had to be written primarily for translation. As Dove points out: 'The pattern of publication of his work up to 1939 exemplifies the rapid contraction of German-language publishing outside the Third Reich and the German author's growing dependence on the English-speaking market' (64). Neumann's novel *Struensee* (English language title: *The Queen's Doctor*) is a good example of this phenomenon: he wrote it quickly in 1934 and finally it was published in German first by the exile publishing house Querido in Amsterdam in 1935, but it was expected to reach a wider audience in the English translation by Edwin and Willa Muir which was published by

Gollancz in 1936. It is a historical novel, which was a popular genre among exile writers for a number of reasons, including the fact that it gave the writer the opportunity to criticize National Socialism and related fascist or dictatorial tendencies without writing about it directly. In *The Queen's Doctor*, Neumann, for example, parodies the situation of a benign ruler, here a Danish king, who is not aware of certain actions of his civil servants. This can easily be read as a parallel to the relatively common view in Germany in the 1930s that Hitler did not know what the barbaric SS was doing. Additionally, historical novels were clearly popular with the European readership, including the British audience. Apparently, as Dove relates, Neumann chose the subject matter on the advice of Zweig who – as described above – had just had a significant success with his historical novel, *Marie Antoinette* (2000: 67). As Neumann had not been happy with the English versions of his other novels, such as *Mammon*, it seems that he wanted to make sure that the translation for *Struensee* was of a high calibre. He thus asked to receive parts of the translation for checking while it was being undertaken by the Muirs, who were prominent translators from German into English, perhaps best known in this respect for their work on Kafka. Victor Gollancz certainly liked the finished product and congratulated Muir on his translation (see Muir 1968).

Although Neumann was not as well known as Zweig when he fled to the UK, he was a recognized author with a loyal readership. The Austrian-born exile writer Hilde Spiel, however, was much younger (born 1911) than Neumann (born 1887) and had only published one novel before she decided to leave Austria and move to the UK in 1936. Spiel and Neumann knew each other well. They had both frequented the Café Herrenhof in Vienna, which had been popular with established writers as well as those at the beginning of their literary careers. Spiel showed Neumann the manuscript of a novella while still in Vienna. Although this novella was never published, Neumann encouraged her to write the novel *Kati auf der Brücke*, which subsequently came out with Paul Zsolnay Verlag in 1933 on the recommendation of Neumann. Like Neumann, Spiel did not undertake the hasty, desperate flight to come to the UK that some other refugees had to make. Hers was a much more ordered move. She arrived after finishing her doctorate in Vienna, having followed her fiancé, the German journalist Peter de Mendelssohn. Although Spiel was from a Jewish background, her parents had both converted to Catholicism, and she had lived the life of an intellectually curious young woman who enjoyed the company of different groups of people regardless of political allegiances, including a number of male admirers, in the early to mid-1930s. Spiel sometimes portrayed her decision to go into exile as more voluntary than it was: after the annexation in 1938 she certainly would have had to fear for her life because of her Jewish background.

Spiel continued her literary as well as her journalistic career in the UK. Before March 1938 she made her living by selling her writing in German to Austrian newspapers and magazines, while de Mendelssohn, whom she had married in 1936, initially worked as a foreign correspondent for German-language newspapers in London. However, the couple and especially de Mendelssohn realized that this income stream would not last. As Dove explains, De Mendelssohn seems to have been one of the strongest advocates of a language switch to English amongst the German and Austrian writers in the UK (2000: 222). As Spiel later recounted, besides her work for Austrian newspapers, she earned her first money in the UK by placing short stories written in German, then translated by de Mendelssohn – in British newspapers: 'A little cheque arrived for my short stories, which had been translated into English by Peter and which were published by the *Daily Express*' (1994: 152). Her first novel published in the UK was *Flute and Drums*, written in German, translated by her husband with the help of a friend Eric Dancy and published by Hutchinson in London in 1939.

Shortly thereafter, de Mendelssohn and Spiel decided to change from German to English as their first language for creative and journalistic writing. They wanted to become English writers. In her autobiography, Spiel describes this process and names her husband as the driving force for 'our entrance into the English language, into the written English word, eventually into the community of writers in this country. Peter has made further advances than me' (1994: 154). As Dove records, De Mendelssohn had had a very cosmopolitan upbringing: he lived in an international artists' community and had attended the international Free School in Dresden where he had been taught English by Willa Muir, who later translated Neumann's novels together with her husband (1994: 100).

De Mendelssohn's and Spiel's decision in favour of a language switch was clearly based on many reasons, pragmatic ones such as finances and career advancement, but also ideological and social ones: Spiel and de Mendelssohn wanted to be part of a country that was democratic and took a stance against National Socialism, and also to be part of a community of writers that shared their attitude to social commitment and aesthetic debate. It was not an easy process and, as she later recorded, Spiel complained to Neumann about the difficulty of writing in English. Neumann pointed out, on the basis of their shared Jewish heritage: 'They burnt our ancestors at the stake. I think you might manage to learn to write in another language' (1994: 155). Both Spiel and de Mendelssohn were successful in their language switch and both seem to have been accepted within British literary and journalistic circles during the war, including those surrounding the *New Statesman*. Spiel also cites the opportunity to experience a British childhood by proxy, after the birth of her daughter Christine in 1939 and her son Felix in 1944, as an advantage in the acculturation process.

Spiel set out to write her next novel after *Flute and Drums* in English. She mentions work on *The Fruits of Prosperity* for the first time on 7 January 1941 in her diary, which novel is set between 1873 and 1881 in Austria and examines the multiculturalism, including the experience of Jewish subjects, of the Habsburg Empire (see Hammel 1998). Spiel herself stated that she tried to examine the roots for Austrian anti-Semitism of the twentieth century and that the novel represents 'the search for the roots of my own epoch in which the Jewish problem is moving towards a catastrophic solution' (qtd. Strickhausen 1996: 146). However, the novel, though written in English, was never published in the UK. Spiel was of the opinion that British publishers did not think that the Austrian topic would be of interest to the British readership (see Strickhausen 1996: 146–7). Consequently, Spiel herself translated extracts from the manuscript into German and they appeared in the exile publication *Die Zeitung* in London between 1941 and 1946. Forty years later, *The Fruits of Prosperity* was finally published in German as *Die Früchte des Wohlstands* in 1981.

The end of the Second World War constituted a shift for Spiel regarding her identity as a writer and citizen. From being an exile who had successfully integrated both linguistically and culturally in Britain, she became someone who might be in the UK only temporarily and might be able to return to her birth country. In her autobiography Spiel writes about this process as a very painful development and recalls a conversation with Kingsley Martin, the editor of the *New Statesman*: 'Kingsley Martin declared: "Now the war is finished" and addressing us, he said: "I suppose you will return to your country?" Thus we knew but did not want to admit it: nine years of acculturation into an English world had been futile' (1994: 206).

As I have discussed elsewhere (see Hammel 2017), this statement is based on a narrow definition of belonging and identity, which is not untypical for her generation and for an exiled writer. Her disappointment at not being recognized fully as an English-language author is understandable but did not only hail only from her position as an exile writer. Spiel was frustrated that she had not been able to write and publish more during the war. But there were many reasons for this, most of which had little to do with being an exile from Austria. Spiel had had two children (and a miscarriage) between 1939 and 1944. She experienced domestic life as a woman with a young family as restricting, calling her suburban domicile in Wimbledon 'a green grave' (1992: 105). As Strickhausen notes, she also felt an acute tension between her career as a journalist and her career as a writer, believing the journalism was a way to earn a living, but that it detracted her from her true calling as a writer of fiction.

Neumann was disappointed by the low sales of the British and American editions of his novel *A Woman Screamed* (1938). Neumann's next project, again written in German, but first published in English, was a book with an exile theme: *By the Rivers of Babylon* (1939) had ten individual stories of Jewish exile at the centre. As Dove reports, this book finally established Neumann's reputation in Britain: it received praise from H. G. Wells and was positively reviewed by *The Sunday Times*, the *New Statesman* and the *Times Literary Supplement*, and in November 1939 it became the *Evening Standard's* Book of the Month (1994: 169).

However, a few months later, in May 1940, like so many fellow refugees from German and Austria, Neumann was interned as an enemy alien. Like many others, he felt traumatized by the experience and, although he was released relatively quickly, the experience had a negative impact on his mental and physical health. Another consequence was that after his internment he found it more difficult to find employment. Neumann had not been able to live on the proceeds of his creative writing, and he had worked for the film industry and the BBC, especially its German-language service. Because of these difficulties, he decided to switch to English as the language of creative production and completed the novel *Scenes in Passing* (1942) after being released from internment. There were clearly financial pressures that pushed Neumann in the direction of a language switch, but there were also ideological and psychological reasons. After having experienced internment and thus being lumped in with other German speakers he felt he had nothing in common with, he wanted to identify with Britain. Observing the developments of the Second World War, Neumann also felt he did not want to write in the German language anymore, the language of National Socialism and the enemy. Neumann wrote about 'a second virginity' in relation to his language switch (1968: 186). Some, including on occasion Neumann himself, were critical of his accomplishments in the English language. Neumann called the English of *Scenes in Passing* a language 'that those who are not English consider English' (1963: 157). His next novel *The Inquest* (1944) became his most successful English-language novel. It was translated into several languages. It is set at an Austrian exile theatre in London and structured as a narrative where the main character has to investigate a story of emigration and exile.

Some Exile Studies scholars such as Richard Dove and Ian Wallace are critical of the achievements of writers who switched languages. Both argue repeatedly in their assessment of Neumann's work that the high linguistic quality of *Scenes in Passing* and subsequent novels might have been due to first-language proof-readers and editors (see Dove 1994; Wallace 171–2), but this seems to say more about the cultural politics of the critic than the style of the novels. Additionally, Dove argues that despite their many accomplishments, exile writers, including De Mendelssohn and Neumann, made no concession to 'English taste' – even when writing in English – and they were only able to offer 'an exile's view of England' (1994: 113). There is an outdated value judgement in these assessments. From the viewpoint of twenty-first-century criticism, we would not seek to criticize a Black British writer for offering a Black British view; rather, we would try to celebrate a diversity of views.

Neumann wrote seven novels in English and worked for the film industry and in 1943 he was appointed editor of the Hutchinson International Authors series, which was very successful. In 1946 he wrote and published *Children of Vienna* which was popular internationally and was translated into twenty-five languages, amongst them a translation into German which was undertaken by Franziska Becker who later became Neumann's wife. There are parallels between this publication and articles by Spiel in the *New Statesman*, which aimed to explain the situation – and the difficulties – of continental German and especially Austrian culture to a British and ultimately an international readership.

Both Neumann and Spiel themselves, and many of their critics, focus on their work and life as being located in between the German and English languages and in between the two countries. Spiel speaks explicitly of leading a 'Zwischenexistenz' (1994: 153), an in-between existence. Often, however, their 'inbetweenness' is assessed in a negative way as a failure to belong. However, cultural theorists of the late twentieth and early twenty-first centuries would argue that there is no static culture that you can belong to, that culture is an activity and a practice that you undertake, and that all culture is representation (see Bhabha 1994). If someone writes a novel in English, it is English literature.

Women exile writers

Women exile writers, artists and musicians had even more difficulties on the road to success than their male counterparts. Even those with careers of their own before having to flee from the Continent, such as the composer Julia

Kerr, found it hard to re-establish themselves. Alfred and Julia Kerr fled with their children Martin and Judith in 1933, first to Switzerland, then to Paris and eventually to London. The renowned theatre critic Alfred Kerr found it impossible to adapt to life in London and make a living. Thus, his wife had to work as a secretary to support the whole family. Dove writes: 'Exile had probably treated her more cruelly than her husband. It was she who had to support their family throughout their early years in England, working long hours in poorly-paid secretarial jobs and thereby sacrificing any chance of achieving her artistic and musical ambitions' (2000: 226). They were, of course, the parents of Judith Kerr, the famous English children's author – she wrote *The Tiger Who Came to Tea* (1968) – who recounts a fictionalized version of her family's exile in the novels *When Hitler Stole Pink Rabbit* (1971) and its sequels. Nonetheless, despite the challenges they faced, a number of remarkable women authors did manage to write while in exile in Britain. In the remainder of this chapter, I discuss the careers of two of these authors, Hermynia Zur Mühlen and Anna Gmeyner, as case studies of women writers in exile from National Socialism.

Hermynia Zur Mühlen

Zur Mühlen was a well-known translator and the author of novels and short stories in the 1920s in Germany. Her biography and career are often separated into two phases: her early work as proletarian-revolutionary writer and her second phase which is variously defined through her exile, her turning away from communist politics or through her production of popular fiction (see Matt 1986). Born as Countess Crennville in 1883 into the Austrian aristocracy, Zur Mühlen experienced an interesting, but at the same time restless, early life. This included travel across continents with her father who was a Habsburg diplomat, training as a primary school teacher, work experience at a book binders and marriage to a baron, Victor von Zur Mühlen, before she seriously started her career as a writer. After her divorce from the Baltic aristocrat, and a lengthy time spent in Davos recovering from respiratory problems, she moved to Frankfurt am Main in 1919 together with her partner Stefan Isidor Klein, a Hungarian translator of Jewish descent born in Vienna whom she had met in Switzerland. First, she earned her living mainly as a translator, her privileged international education enabling her to take on translation from English, French and Russian into German, especially socially critical work. A member of the German communist party (KPD) from 1919 onwards, and sometimes known as the 'Red Countess', she also wrote articles for left-wing and communist newspapers. Her first book publication was a collection of fairy tales entitled *What Friends Told*, which appeared in 1921 in the series 'Fairy Tales for the Poor' with the Malik Verlag. This publication can be seen as her breakthrough as a writer. It was followed by two novels *Der Tempel* (1922) and *Licht* (1922) and a collection of novellas entitled *Der Rote Heiland* (1924), as well as detective fiction which she published under the pseudonym Lawrence H. Desberry such as *Der blaue Strahl* (1922) and *An den Ufern des Hudson* (1925) and the political thriller *Die weiße Pest* (1926), published under yet another pseudonym, Traugott Lehmann.

Her literary strategy was to use popular genres such as the detective novel, the romantic novel and the fairy-tale genre to convey radical content. She became a widely read author in the German-speaking world who brought her reputation with her to the English-speaking world as demonstrated by the fact that the BBC aired a tribute to Zur Mühlen in 1943, on the occasion of her sixtieth birthday. However, the processes of dislocation she experienced through exile and the end of the 1930s culture she came from have caused her to largely disappearance from reception history.

Zur Mühlen left Germany after the National Socialist takeover, losing her literary network and her library. With her partner Stefan Klein she relocated to Vienna in 1933 and continued to publish anti-Nazi literature such as the novel *Unsere Tööcher die Nazinen*. Her principled anti-fascist stance led her to lose publishing opportunities and access to most of her remaining wealth. When National Socialist Germany annexed Austria she knew she had to flee and left Vienna overnight and driving across the Czech border, pretending to be on a day trip. She arrived in Bratislava in March 1938 with her partner and her two dogs but without any possessions. After the German occupation of Bohemia in March 1939, the couple had to escape again: via Hungary, Yugoslavia, Italy, Switzerland and France. They reached London on 19 June 1939. By that time Zur Mühlen was not a well woman in Britain and had no financial resources left. There is evidence that she might have hoped to escape to the United States, and she was certainly in regular contact with Hubertus Prinz zu Löwenstein, the President of the American Guild for German Cultural Freedom. Her biographer Manfred Altner claims that she sent twenty-nine novellas, short stories and radio plays to the US publishers and magazines but to no avail. It is thus not surprising that, following the examples of Zweig and Neumann, she chose the genre of the historical novel, or more precisely the family saga, as one that was likely to sell. However, as discussed above, subverting traditionally conservative genres was a long-standing strategy in her literary output, and Zur Mühlen sought to do the same to the genre of the historical novel. While Zweig wrote about major figures in European history, and Neumann made a court physician the central character of his historical novel, Zur Mühlen takes this one step further and creates a family saga where the Congress of Vienna is seen through comments made in the women characters' boudoir integrated with a heterogeneous range of topics of conversation, including a discussion of breastfeeding.

We Poor Shadows (1943) and Came the Stranger (1946) were originally intended as parts one and three of a trilogy comprising what Zur Mühlen described as a Forsyte-like family saga (although she either abandoned or never wrote the intended middle volume). As I explore elsewhere, it is slightly unclear at which stage of her exile she wrote them (2008: 177). However, both novels were written in German first and then translated by the author herself and published by Frederick Muller in London. Both parts of the family saga were positively reviewed in the *Times Literary Supplement*. The German versions would appear in Austria only in 1994 and 1996.

One way of recovering the significance of these English novels by Zur Mühlen is to think about them in the context of Georg Lukács's *The Historical Novel* (1969). Originally writing in the 1930s, Lukács recognized the centrality of the historical novel for exile literature: 'This democratic protest movement has created a new type of historical novel which, chiefly in the literature of the German-antifascist emigration, has become a central problem of letters in our day' (307). Lukács praised the exile writers for overcoming what he sees as the previous problem of historical narratives, namely the lack of connection between history and present. He saw the historical novel as a tool against the misuse of history by the National Socialists and proclaimed the works to be 'a humanist declaration of war against fascist barbarism' (325). However, it is not only this positive assessment of the genre of the historical novel that makes Lukács an important contributor to this debate. His outline of the development of historical narratives is also significant for the analysis of Zur Mühlen's novelistic practice. Lukács described the French Revolution, the revolutionary wars and the rise and fall of Napoleon as the beginning of history as mass experience. Whereas earlier wars had been waged by professional armies, the French had to create a mass army against the coalition of absolute monarchies. Thus, according to Lukács, the purpose of the war had to be made clear to the masses by means of propaganda, which had the effect of increasing individual awareness of the influence of history:

> Now if experiences such as these are linked with the knowledge that similar upheavals are taking place all over the world, this must enormously strengthen the feeling first that there is such a thing as history, second that it is an

uninterrupted process of changes and finally that it has a direct effect upon the life of every individual. (20)

Significantly, Zur Mühlen set *We Poor Shadows* during the period succeeding the Napoleonic wars and, in the characters Victoire and Joseph, shows individuals who are aware that their lives are being directly shaped by history.

Following the *Anschluss* most of the Austrian exile groups had an especially strong interest in this preservation of national culture but they were aware that the distinction between Austria and Germany was now unclear to the Allies. The world at large had to be convinced that Austria was an independent nation, and that it should be a separate state after the war. To this end the Free Austrian Movement in Great Britain (FAM) was founded on 3 December 1941. The Moscow Declaration passed on 30 October 1943 was the political manifestation of the success of this policy. The concluding parts of the declaration confirm the Allies' desire to annul the *Anschluss*, which is quoted by Robert H. Keyserlingk:

> The Governments of Great Britain, the United States and the Union of the Socialist Soviet Republics, having taken counsel together, hereby declare that they regard the *Anschluss* imposed upon Austria by Germany as null and void and that, being determined that Austria shall never again be allowed to become a strategic base for German aggression in Central and South Eastern Europe, they desire to see re-established a free and independent Austria which, in association with neighbouring states, shall be assured of that economic security which is the only basis for political freedom and lasting peace. (140)

The question of the intended audience for Zur Mühlen's family saga is a fascinating one. Obviously, she had planned the publication of the first part at least – and it might be reasonable to assume of the other one or ones as well – in German. Was the decision to publish an English language edition a purely practical and financial one or did it constitute her contribution to the promotion of Austrian culture in Britain? Was the latter intention compatible with the decision to promote the books as by 'Countess' Hermynia Zur Mühlen, a title she had long since discarded? The resurrection of the aristocratic title suggests that Zur Mühlen saw the necessity for some reconciliation with her past in order to create a vision for the future.

We Poor Shadows focuses on one aristocratic family, the Herdegens, direct ancestors of Clarisse Herdegen, the main character of *Came the Stranger*. The narrative follows the family history through five generations from 1814 to the aftermath of 1848. The oldest member of the family is the matriarch Grandmama Inez, a Spanish Catholic. She is shown as an influential woman who married into the Austrian dynasty. By the end of the novel the late Inez's great-great-grandson baby Joseph is born during the gunfire of 1848. The narrative is rooted in the tension between continuity and change. The family's geographical location marks the position of continuity: this is represented by the country estate, Wohan, in Bohemia, and, to a lesser extent, the Palais in Vienna. The generational structure of the novel is supported by an omniscient narrator who moves from character to character, and therefore moves along with the generations and gives the narrative continuity, although there is a stronger emphasis on the middle generation. This typical family saga cycle of birth, youth, frustrated dreams, settling into middle age, old age and death structure can be read as representing a resigned mood but Zur Mühlen manages to weave several critical undercurrents into the historical narrative: first, misunderstandings between the different European nations; second, the break-up of class divisions; and third, the position of women.

The theme of European multiculturalism is related less to the different nations of the Habsburg Empire, which is the focal point of Spiel's *Fruits of Prosperity*, but rather to European politics following the Congress of Vienna (1814–15). The Congress is viewed with historical hindsight as a potential source for a new European political landscape, which did not materialize. Criticism of the wasteful extravagance of the countries' leaders while the population was going hungry is expressed through the eyes of the common people. Scenes of discussions in the streets intermittently appear in the development of the novel, almost like a commentary, or like the chorus in a classical drama. This has the effect of questioning the centrality of the aristocracy at the heart of the novel and political developments, while at the same time describing the status quo.

The country estate Wohan, far away from the platform of high politics in Vienna, allows for more transgressive developments across class and national boundaries. Here the non-aristocratic characters actually interrelate with the Herdegen. First and foremost, there is Bozena, a farmer's daughter who is seduced by Stanislas, Inez's oldest grandson. Grandmaman Inez forces the couple to get married, against the wishes of the eighteen-year-old and his mother Ludmilla. What on the one hand is a dogmatic and cruel move is shown in a more differentiated way in the narrative. Bozena is not depicted as a simple peasant girl who is grateful that the young count will marry her. She has her own sexual desire and is shown to fancy the second gardener. By forcing Stanislas to marry a woman situated below him in the class structure, rather than just paying her off as suggested by the arrogant Ludmilla, Inez acknowledges the equality of all human beings, a view which is based on her Christian faith. Bozena's parents provide another case for the depiction of the interrelationships across class boundaries. Zur Mühlen creates a rupture in the class-constrained narrative by deploying her usual irony: when Stanislas comes to asks Bozena's parents for permission to marry her, Bozena's mother falls into a lament about the situation and tells him what great chances Bozena would have had with the second gardener. The embarrassed Stanislas stammers about being a good match. Thus Zur Mühlen's narrative provides space for small transgressions in an otherwise restrictive society. By not engaging in the romantic notion that everyone lives happily ever after in such a marriage across class boundaries, Zur Mühlen avoids the pitfalls of romantic escapism, which would re-enforce, rather than weaken, the nineteenth-century class structure.

Italian scholar Claudio Magris sees writers creating models of the monarchy and the state as a guarantor for continuity. Quoting Stefan Zweig and Joseph Roth, Magris points out that these authors did acknowledge the mediocrity and ineffectualness of the monarchy and imperial administration, but that the Habsburg Empire nevertheless became their ideal fatherland in their memories and their literature (see Magris 2001: 8). Continuity on the public political level is discussed in a different way in *We Poor Shadows* than in equivalent books by male authors such as Zweig. Having children and looking after the land in Bohemia signify continuity for Hermynia Zur Mühlen rather than generations of men devoted to diplomatic service.

Zur Mühlen's narration of history stays very much behind the scenes, inside the bosom of the family. In the beginning of the novel during the Congress of Vienna, a ball is held in the Palais Herdegen, but the reader is only introduced to the events in the boudoir where Marie Christine gets ready for the evening or to the conversations in one of the side rooms. Significantly the narrative development of the family saga with its births and deaths is interspersed with short chapters based on historical figures and events. These stylistically different chapters which focus on Metternich or Napoleon create a rupture in the main narrative and can be read as Zur Mühlen's questioning the narratability of history in a traditional manner. The stream-of-consciousness passages do not mark the pomposity of an official historical meta-narrative, but the fragmented nature of human historical consciousness. Showing historical events as impinging intermittently on the consciousness of the characters opens up the novel to a far more modern reading than a traditional description of historical events would have done. Writing as a refugee gave Zur Mühlen a heightened insight into the differentiated historical consciousness and led her to question official versions. Although most of the characters' attempts at political reform fail, it shows the possibilities of 'what could have been'. For Zur Mühlen a reconnection of the development of Austria with these revolutionary and reformist moments was the desired outcome of her historical novels are her contribution to the process of a post-war cultural and political re-establishment of the country within a democratic Europe.

Came the Stranger connects the historical narrative of *We Poor Shadows* to the present. The female main character Clarisse Herdegen runs a rose farm from the ancestral Wohan estate. The novel is tightly structured into three parts and culminates in Czechoslovakia over the winter of 1938–9. *Came the Stranger* thus connects the earlier historical developments of the Austro-Hungarian Empire with contemporary developments and the refugee crisis of the later 1930s. The stranger of the title is a National Socialist German who sows divisions in a Czech community. However, although some characters argue that everyone had got on before he appeared, Zur Mühlen does not create a naive before-and-after scenario by creating complex tensions between Sudeten Germans, Czech supporters of Thomas Masaryk, Jews, Slovak separatists and characters of Hungarian descent.

Anti-Semitism and the racial ideology of National Socialism are foregrounded in this novel: Zur Mühlen provides insights into the economic, historical and psychological background of discrimination and persecution for the 1940s reader. The novel provides an interesting angle on refugee issues. Many exile writers understandably portrayed the exile experience from the viewpoint of those that had to flee their home country. Here we are given a glimpse into the receiving society: Clarisse Herdegen helps dejected and forlorn refugees who come to Bratislava. She uses her resources to assist them and feels proud to be able to provide a safe haven, albeit temporarily.

Again Zur Mühlen uses irony, such as when the Herdegen relative Tante Annerl, a refugee from Austria, describes how she got an old man out of a sticky situation with a National Socialist on the streets of Vienna by claiming that she was keen to give Hitler 'a welcoming party' and the National Socialist naively interpreted her words in a positive way. Some of Tante Annerl's relatives eventually flee to Britain.

Interestingly, having to move away from one's homeland is described as a common experience for many of the Herdegen women ancestors, who upon marriage had to leave their home country and in some cases mother tongue behind. This is a reminder of the specificity of women's experiences as a metaphorical exile from a patriarchal society as discussed in the introduction to this chapter. *Came the Stranger* and the novel discussed below, Anna Gmeyner's *Café du Dôme* (1941), are clearly exile novels, i.e. works that discuss the actual experience of flights and settlement under forced conditions, but they also connect to a feminist discussion of metaphorical displacement due to patriarchal oppression.

Anna Gmeyner

Gmeyner was born in 1902 in Vienna into a middle-class Jewish family. She attended the same progressive girls' grammar school as Hilde Spiel would nine years later and had ambitions to become a writer from a very young age. Gmeyner's initial breakthrough came as a dramatist within the left-wing cultural circles of the Weimar Republic. Having followed her first husband, a biologist, to Scotland, she witnessed the Scottish mining community during the General Strike of 1926. In the manner of a participant observer, she decided to live among the miners and their families in Fifeshire. Gmeyner used this material for her first play *Heer ohne Helden*, which was first performed on 27 October 1929 in Dresden. On 26 January 1930 the 'Theater der Arbeiter', a troupe founded by a workers' cultural organization associated with the German communist party KPD, performed the play at the Wallner-Theater in Berlin. Unsurprisingly, theatre critics were divided along political lines about the play: the right-wing *Lokalanzeiger* called the performance 'Bolshevist Hate Speech' whereas the communist *Rote Fahne* (a publication that Zur Mühlen wrote for frequently) commented that the play portrays the divisive revolutionary class struggle successfully (see Stürzer 1993: 31).

For her next play, *Zehn am Fließband*, Anna Gmeyner studied the world of her characters again by working on an assembly line at a Siemens factory in Berlin. The play dealt with the workers' fears of increasing mechanization and unemployment. No conventional theatre was interested in performing the play, but the official Agitprop-Troupe of the International Workers' Aid 'Kolonne Links' included it in their repertoire. Gmeyner's third play, *Automatenbüfett*, was performed for the first time on 25 October 1932 by the Thalia Theater in Hamburg. The play then moved to Berlin where it was performed at the Theater am Schiffbauerdamm, where Bertold Brecht's *Threepenny Opera* was first performed in 1928, between 25 December 1932 and 11 February 1933 which means that it was still performed after the National Socialist rise to power in January 1933. However, the performance changed after 20 January 1933 as a number of the cast had to be replaced because the fear of arrest motivated many of the actors to leave Germany.

Gmeyner herself went to Paris in 1933, where she worked with the film director Georg Wilhelm Pabst until her emigration to Britain in 1935. In Paris, Gmeyner met and married her second husband, the Russian philosopher Jascha Morduch. He was a British citizen and had family in Britain, and in 1935 they resettled in London. Failure to find further employment in the film industry had contributed to the impetus to for this decision. Her involvement in left-wing cultural politics continued in Britain. In 1938 she read from her first exile novel *Manja* (1938) at the launch of the Free German League of Culture in London, a communist affiliated cultural association, as alluded to by Heike Klapdor-Kops (11). *Manja* was first published in German in Amsterdam before an English translation was published in the United Kingdom (as *The Wall*) and in the United States (as *Five Destinies*). The novel was subsequently republished in the UK by Persephone Books in 2003 under its original title of *Manja*. The plot concerns five families and their children providing a cross-section of German society and covers the period from the children's births in 1920 through to 1934. Anne Stürzer claims that Gmeyner's exile work is disappointing and less radically political and that her post-war move towards mysticism and esotericism is already detectable in her first two novels published in Britain, *Manja* and *Café du Dôme* (204–5). This view can easily be contradicted by examining the case of *Café du Dôme*.

In Britain Gmeyner worked under the *nom de plume* Anna Reiner that she had used for all her work since 1933 to protect her relatives left behind in Austria. She contributed to a film for the Boulting brothers, *Pastor Hall* (1940), which was an adaptation of a play by Ernst Toller, based on the story of Martin Niemöller, and is credited as one of the screenwriters together with Leslie Arliss and Hayworth Bromley. Gmeyner was probably working on *Café du Dôme* while writing the screenplay.

Café du Dôme was originally written in German, but only ever published in an English translation undertaken by Trevor and Phyllis Blewitt for Hamish Hamilton. J. M. Ritchie suggests that the achievement of managing to sell a novel which needed to be translated to a British publisher is proof of Gmeyner's early success as a writer in Britain; an achievement which was later consolidated by the post-war novels she wrote in English, under her married name Anna Morduch, such as *A Jar Laden With Water* (1961) and *The Sovereign Adventure* (1970), as detailed by Ritchie (216). From the edition of *Café du Dôme* consulted for this chapter it can also be deduced that – after its original publication in June 1941 – it was reprinted three times in as many months, supporting the claim that it was well received by a wartime British readership. As with *Manja*, *Café du Dôme* was also published in an American edition, which appeared in 1942 entitled *The Coward Heart*.

Café du Dôme is set in Paris between 14 July 1936 and 14 July 1937, which can be deduced from the first and last chapters and references to the Spanish Civil

War. The narrative focuses on one main female character, Nadia Schuhmacher. The novel opens with Nadia, a Russian-born, German-speaking refugee living in Paris, attempting to facilitate her husband's release from Dachau concentration camp. Peter Schuhmacher is an active communist, and the novel focuses more on political exiles than on those who had to leave Germany because of their Jewish background, which is also consistent with the time span of the narration. Jewishness or racial persecution is mentioned only as a by-line and does not get such central attention as in Gmeyner's earlier novel. The multi-perspective structure is also not as formally developed as in *Manja*; there are, however, a number and sub-plots, which diverge and converge in a complex manner. The place where the different strands of the plot and the different characters come together is the Café du Dôme, which gives the novel its title. Historically, this café in the centre of Paris was known to be a meeting place for German intellectuals even before the First World War and remained so after 1933, when numerous refugees arrived from Germany. Elsewhere, I have described this type of exile novel as kaleidoscopic in the sense that Gmeyner describes Nadia's husband as 'enjoying the kaleidoscopic life at the *Dôme*, with its sudden and fleeting glimpses into the lives and destinies of all kinds of people' (Reiner 1941: 144; see Hammel 2008). This is a literary construction which allows characters from different classes and in different situation to be portrayed simultaneously. It is also a reflection of the unstable refugee experience: fluid, fleeing from one place of refuge to the next.

Café du Dôme can also be read as a criticism of other political exile novels. Gmeyner's text is self-reflexive towards the position of a writer and the exile narrative as such. Her narrative technique in *Café du Dôme* consciously builds on the multiperspectival view of the inhabitants of a block of flats from her film work (see Stürzer 1993: 202):

> It was all like a modern theatrical set: you saw a cross-section of houses in which people lived and died side by side, only the audience being privileged to see all the scenes at once, and the lights going on in one of the cells and going out in another. But here in the Dôme the production was rather different: everything happened all over the place and simultaneously. (311–12)

This attempt to convey simultaneity indicates Gmeyner's commitment to representing the complexity of modernity and refutes the view, which has exerted a disproportionate influence over the reception history of exile literature until recently, that most novels with an overt political message are stylistically conservative.

Gmeyner's targets include the conventional gender politics of the political left. As in *Manja*, she uses motherhood as a means of transgressing boundaries.

The conventional attitude of political activists is exemplified by Peter, who has the attitude that 'children make men reactionary and women fat' (277) thus linking the reactionary nature of his conventional left-wing political activism to sexism, reducing women to beautiful accessories of revolutionary men. Nadia's rejection of Peter, the discussion between Nadia and her friend Irene that having and bringing up a child without a father is a preferred option – 'it belongs to us alone, it's our business, not theirs' (309) – and the rejection of the happy end of the romantic novel, where Nadia would get together with Martin Schmidt, are strong indicators that the novel aims to show the possibility of alternatives to existing societal structures.

Gmeyner's alternative scenarios also include the possibility of physical attraction between women. She subverts the conventional feminine setting of a beauty salon into a space for mental and physical intimacy between Nadia and Irene. While assessing their different lives and giving each other advice about their relationships with men, the possibility of physical attraction between women is also present: 'It gave Nadia pleasure to gaze upon the beauty of Irene's tall faultless body as she strode indolently to the door' (185). Although Irene explicitly states that she has no lesbian tendencies, albeit with regret, the possibility of an alternative to heterosexual relationships is clearly open in the narrative. This exploration of different sexualities, together with the representation of other strong bonds between women, indicates Gmeyner's interest in finding alternatives to the male-dominated society and political and cultural structures of her time.

Jane Marcus states that it is the task of the critic to understand 'the ethics of the woman writer's elsewhereness. For elsewhere is not nowhere. It is a political place where the displaced are always seen and see themselves in relation to the "placed"' (270). A writer such as Gmeyner can be positioned in a variety of 'elsewherenesses', as a Jew, as a disillusioned socialist, as an exile and as a woman, while still inhabiting a specific political place. This is reflected in *Café du Dôme*, where alternative scenarios regarding political ideology and gender relations are part of the narrative's alternative elsewhereness.

Conclusion

Thinking about the novels – especially those originally, or only, published in English – of Gmeyner, Zur Mühlen, and the other exile writers discussed in this chapter, as embodying elsewhereness helps explain why they do not fit easily into the reception histories of national literatures. Politically these writers were at the heart of the zeitgeist of the second half of the 1930s and the first half of the 1940s, but culturally they were only ever at the margins of British life. Following the Second World War, their concerns seemed dated and foreign to an insular post-war British culture. For decades there has been no real place for these works in English literature. However, paradoxically perhaps, the current British identity crisis with respect to Europe provides a juncture in which it is worth looking back again at a time when exiles from the continent came to Britain in flight from totalitarian oppression and London became the capital of free Europe. Although the works examined in this chapter have generally been neglected or marginalized, their publication and readership at the time testify to the existence of a wartime cultural imaginary – a heterotopian conception of the possibilities of elsewhereness – that was international. It is hoped that this chapter, by reintroducing these texts to the record of British fiction, will prompt both further research into this aspect of 1940s culture and comparative analysis with other marginalized and transgressive works that have an uneasy relationship with canonical English literature.

Note

1 Translations from German to English are by the author of this chapter unless otherwise acknowledged.

Works cited

Anderson, Harriet. *Utopian Feminism. Women's Movements in fin-de-siecle Vienna*. New Haven and London: Yale University Press, 1992.

Bhabha, H. K. *The Location of Culture*. London: Routledge, 1994.

Bloch, Ernst. *Vom Hasard zur Katastrophe: Politische Aufsätze 1934–1939*. Frankfurt: Suhrkamp, 1972.

Dove, Richard. "'Ein Experte des Überlebens": Robert Neumann in British Exile 1933–45'. In Ian Wallace (ed.), *Aliens – Uneingebürgerte: German and Austrian Writers in Exile*. Amsterdam: Rodopi, 1994: 159–94.

Dove, Richard. *Journey of No Return: Five German-speaking Literary Exiles in Britain, 1933–45*. London: Libris, 2000.

Gmeyner, Anna. *Manja*. Mannheim: Persona, 1987.

Grenville, Anthony. *Jewish Refugees from Germany and Austria in Britain, 1933–1970*. London: Vallentine Mitchell, 2010.

Gurr, Andrew. *Writers in Exile*. Brighton: Harvester Press, 1981.
Hammel, Andrea. 'Hilde Spiel and the Possibility of a Multicultural Society: *Die Früchte des Wohlstands* and *Mirko und Franka*'. In Allyson Fiddler (ed.), *'Other' Austrians: Post-1945 Austrian Women's Writing*. Berne: Peter Lang, 1998: 129–39.
Hammel, Andrea. *Everyday Life as Alternative Space in Exile Writing: The Novels of Anna Gmeyner, Selma Kahn, Hilde Spiel, Martina Wied and Hermynia Zur Mühlen*. Oxford: Peter Lang, 2008.
Hammel, Andrea. 'Translating Cultures and Languages: Exile Writers between German and English'. In Joan Boase-Beier et al. (eds.), *Translating Holocaust Lives*. London: Bloomsbury Academic, 2017: 127–44.
Hammel, Andrea. '"I Remember their Labels Round their Necks": Britain and the Kindertransport'. In Tom Lawson and Andy Pearce (eds.), *The Palgrave Handbook of Britain and the Holocaust*. Cham: Palgrave Macmillan, 2020: 93–111.
Keyserlingk, Robert H. *Austria in World War II: An Anglo-American Dilemma*. Kingston and Montreal: McGill-Queen's University Press, 1988.
Klapdor-Kops, Heike. 'Vorwort'. In Anna Gmeyner (ed.), *Manja*. Mannheim: persona, 1987: 5–12.
Krohn, D. et al. (eds). *Übersetzung als transkultureller Prozess: Exilforschung: Ein internationals Jahrbuch*, 25. Munich: edition text+kritik, 2007.
London, Louise. *Whitehall and the Jews 1933 to 1948*. Cambridge: Cambridge University Press, 2000.
Lukács, Georg. *The Historical Novel*. Hannah and Stanley Mitchell (trans). Harmondsworth: Penguin, 1969.
Magris, Claudio. *Danube: A Sentimental Journey from the Source to the Black Sea*. Patrick Creagh (trans). London: Harvill Panther, 2001.
Marcus, Jane. 'Alibis and Legends: The Ethics of Elsewhereness, Gender and Estrangement'. In Mary Lynn Broe and Angela Ingram (ed.), *Women's Writing in Exile*. Chapel Hill and London: University of North Carolina Press, 1989: 269–94.
Matt, Susanne. 'Hermynia Zur Mühlen (1883–1951). Von der proletarisch-revolutionären Schriftstellerin zur Unterhaltungsliterautorin', unpublished MA Thesis, University of Vienna, 1986.
Muir, Edwin. *An Autobiography*. London: Methuen, 1968.
Neumann, Robert. *Ein leichtes Leben*. Munich: Desches, 1963.
Neumann, Robert. *Vielleicht das Heitere*. Munich: Desches, 1968.
Reiner, Anna. *Manja*. Amsterdam: Querido, 1938.
Reiner, Anna. *Café du Dôme*. Trevor and Phyllis Blewitt (trans). London: Hamish Hamilton, 1941.
Ritchie, J. M. 'Anna Gmeyner and the Scottish Connection'. In Alan Deighton (ed.), *Order from Confusion. Essays presented to Edward McInnes on the Occasion of his Sixtieth Birthday*. Hull: University of Hull, 1995: 205–22.
Seidel, Michael. *Exile and the Literary Imagination*. New Haven and London: Yale University Press, 1986.

Spiel, Hilde. *Welche Welt ist meine Welt: Erinnerungen 1946–1989*. Hamburg: Rowohlt, 1992.

Spiel, Hilde. *Die hellen and die finisteren Zeiten: Erinnerungen 1911–1946*. Hamburg: Rowohlt, 1994.

Strickhausen, Waltrud. *Die Erzählerin Hilde Spiel oder 'Der weite Wurf in die Finsternis'.* New York: Peter Lang, 1996.

Stürzer, Anne. *Dramatikerinnen und Zeitstücke: ein vergessenes Kapitel der Theatergeschichte von der Weimarer Republik bis zur Nachkriegszeit*. Stuttgart and Weimar: J. B. Metzler, 1993.

Wehage, F. J. 'Das "Andere" Deutschland 1933–1945'. *Neophilologus*, 1985: 421–36.

10

Un-British: The Transatlantic Crime Film Connection

Glyn White

This chapter investigates the relationship between popular fiction of the crime genre and British cinema in the 1940s, particularly adaptations made in the second half of the decade of works by Graham Greene, James Hadley Chase and Gerald Kersh, by tracking transatlantic currents in film and literature and mapping their varied critical receptions within the context of 1940s criticism. While the focus of this chapter is on British writing and British cinema neither can be fully understood without reference to the wider international political and economic factors at play.

During the 1940s, the cultural gravity of the United States in Britain grew significantly for a number of reasons. First and foremost, Britain was dependent on essential support in credit and shipping once the rest of Europe had become either neutral or had been conquered in 1940. Second, there was an increased exposure to actual Americans after the United States joined the war effort in 1941 and, third, permeation by American media increased. Popular print culture made its way to British shores much more directly than through the international machinations of publishers in the form of publications sent and issued to American servicemen. The American Forces Network was set up for US bases in 1943 importing US domestic music and comedy shows (minus adverts). The chief difference to British Forces Network was that the American Forces Network played considerably more American music than the staid BBC and Andrew Crisell's *An Introductory History of British Broadcasting* indicates that:

> By 1944 American variety shows were being syndicated to the BBC, and British listeners became captivated by such stars as Bob Hope, Bing Crosby, Glenn Miller, Jack Benny, the Andrews Sisters and Frank Sinatra. It is perhaps at this point that British popular culture began to be dominated by that of America. (65)

Increasing awareness of US comedy and musical performers through radio was, however, only adding to the influence of Hollywood films on British popular culture during the medium's peak decade of attendance. In *Transatlantic Crossings: British Feature Films in the USA* Susan Street notes that 'The study of "transatlantic crossings" is a complex area that needs to be understood with reference to economic and cultural factors. [And that:] With a home market that was dominated by Hollywood [...] British film producers could not isolate themselves from the imperatives of international competition' (2002: 218). The topic Street pursues expands the study of British cinema by looking at the fortunes of British-made films in the United States but the reverse of its premise – studying American films in Britain – would be a dauntingly large task given that what the cinema actually means in Britain is predominantly American films, both now, in the 1940s and earlier.

The dominance of Hollywood products over those of the British film industry followed on from the Great War and led, in 1927, to the creation of a government-imposed quota system that obliged film distributors and exhibitors to handle a percentage of British films. By the mid-1930s one unintentional consequence of this system was the so-called *quota-quickie* – cheaply made British films fulfilling the requirements to allow exhibitors to screen the American films audiences wanted to see. Investing heavily in a British film was a risky proposition; audiences were fickle and, if the film failed in Britain, there was little chance of overseas sales. The imbalance is summed up by C. A. Lejeune, writing in 1940, cited by Anthony Slide: 'We know that if we make bad pictures in this country the Americans don't want them – even our own countrymen are not very keen on bad English pictures. Perhaps even less do the Americans want *good* British pictures. Since when has a powerful industry encouraged foreign competition[?]' (227).

While *The Private Life of Henry VIII* (1933) starring Charles Laughton had been an unprecedented success for a British film in America, most follow-ups did little business. Instead, it was Hollywood studios that mined British historical and colonial subjects in films such as *The Private Lives of Elizabeth and Essex* (1938), *The Adventures of Robin Hood* (1939) and *The Sea Hawk* (1940) or *The Lives of a Bengal Lancer* (1935), *Storm over Bengal* (1938) and *Gunga Din* (1939). Some Hollywood studios entered into co-productions such as the Gaumont-British/MGM *The Lady Vanishes* (1938) from Ethel Lina White's 1936 novel *The Wheel Spins*, or made their own productions on British soil such as *Goodbye Mr Chips* (1939) from James Hilton's 1934 novel.

After 1939, however, things changed. In Great Britain, according to Tom Ryall: 'Fewer films were produced [in the 1940s] than in the 30s – around 500 compared to more than 1,200 – but critics noted the emergence of what they termed a new "quality" or "prestige" cinema' (30). The motivations changed during wartime, too. Rather than simply seek profit in the American market, the British government encouraged film producers to draw on and develop American sympathy for the country's plight when it stood isolated, bringing films with clear propagandistic value like *49th Parallel* (aka *The Invaders*) (1941) and *In Which We Serve* (1942). Other ways the coalition government pursued this aim are detailed in Nicholas John Cull's *Selling War: The British Propaganda Campaign against America 'Neutrality' in World War II* (1995), include rolling out the red carpet for American journalists in Britain (see Chapter 2) and supplying information to American newspapers that was more graphic than that which British newspapers were allowed to report (see, for instance, Cull's picture section between pages 134 and 135 showing victims of the Coventry bombings). American interest in what was happening in Britain, stimulated by newspaper and radio reports, affected publishing, too, and Cull notes that:

> In the early summer of 1941, three books dominated American [bestseller] lists, and all three were British. The first was an anthology of Churchill's speeches, and the other two were novels: *Random Harvest* by James Hilton (author of *Lost Horizon* and *Goodbye Mr. Chips*), and *This Above All*, by Eric Knight, an expatriate Yorkshire writer best known as the author of *Lassie Comes Home*. (178)

Additionally, coming from a source in close communication with the Ministry of Information were Scottish-born but US-resident Helen MacInnes's espionage novels, *Above Suspicion* (1941) and *Assignment in Brittany* (1942), which were successful and were both seized upon by Hollywood and filmed in 1943. Hollywood's interest in Britain during wartime is epitomized by *Mrs Miniver* (1942), its huge box-office success and the fact that it won six Academy Awards (see Chapter 3).

The war-straitened British film industry focused on fewer and better productions for its home market and what gained critical favour in Britain ('*good British pictures*') turned out to be very specific. As Andrew Higson notes, 'British cinema as a whole has habitually been thought through (that is, constructed) in terms which derive from the documentary idea' (73). In the early 1940s critics revered a combination of studio realism and documentary techniques focusing on obligation to community and the war effort or what John Shearman called in

1946 the 'wartime wedding' of documentary and fiction (cited Chapman 2000: 204). The 'pantheon' of films in this mode is listed by James Chapman as *In Which We Serve* (1942), *The Foreman Went to France* (1942), *Nine Men* (1943), *Fires Were Started* (1943), *Millions Like Us* (1943), *San Demetrio, London* (1943), *The Way Ahead* (1944) and *The Way to the Stars* (1945) (2000: 194). Chapman points out that this canon was developed through the denigration of films made earlier during the war and avoided films which were controversial at the time, such as *The Life and Death of Colonel Blimp* (1943) (2000: 196–7). In a detailed study of the corpus of British film criticism across the years 1942–9 written for *Screen* in 1979 and appearing in its definitive form in 1996, John Ellis draws out the language 1940s critics shared in attempting to promote their views. These include ideas of realism, restraint, understatement, unobtrusive style and good taste, which overlap with other existing discourses, particularly the BBC's remit to inform, educate and entertain, and Leavisite literary criticism ('organic unities') (1996: 76). Conversely, films which showed stylistic excess, emotional content and acknowledged the existence of different standards with regard to sex and class were not well received. According to Jeffrey Richards:

> The 1940s saw a [...] polarisation of styles and values. On the one hand there were the critically respected films about 'the people's war', black and white, semi-documentary features with realistic contemporary settings, ordinary people both in the services and on the home front, and the foregrounding of emotional restraint, service and sacrifice. On the other hand there were the critically excoriated Gainsborough melodramas, with their spectacular costumes, conspicuous consumption and extravagant goings-on. (139–40)

Gainsborough Studios' period melodramas such as *The Man in Grey* (1943), *Fanny by Gaslight* (1944) and *The Wicked Lady* (1945) were highly popular with British audiences and featured various permutations of stars, including Stewart Granger, James Mason, Margaret Lockwood and Phyllis Calvert. Nevertheless, 'Gainsborough horrors' was the term used for them by contemporary critic Richard Winnington (quoted in Ellis, 71) and Julian Maclaren-Ross suggested, in a discussion of British cinema first published in *Penguin New Writing* in 1947: 'One may, I suppose, comfortably ignore vulgar nonsense like *The Wicked Lady*, *Caravan* [1946] or *The Madonna of the Seven Moons* [1944]' (263). Their critical marginalization has a number of causes. As Sue Harper argued in 1994, with their prominent and active female characters and high emotional key these Gainsborough melodramas appealed to a female audience, one that was habitually disregarded in literary criticism of the time. Furthermore, as Richards says (drawing on Peter Brooks), melodrama 'functions as ritual and catharsis' and 'one of the great appeals of melodrama is thus the possibility of saying the unsayable, resisting control and accommodations, and rejecting the class system or sexual repression' (142). These are not the reasons given by 1940s critics for sidelining them, or the crime-novel adaptations we shall focus on below, but rather for a lack of conformity to the idea of 'quality' in film-making.

Films drawing on canonical literature such as *Henry V* (1945), *Great Expectations* (1946), *Oliver Twist* (1948) and *Hamlet* (1948) did so much to boost the prestige of British film during the 1940s they were immune to criticism on the grounds of quality but adaptations of contemporary writing were not. These attitudes in film criticism held sway for a long period afterwards, effectively excluding what Julian Petley named 'the lost continent' of genre and non-realist film-making (1986b). This is the area inhabited by the texts and adaptations I want to focus on in the following sections.

Genre versus literature: The imaginary America

A mean undercurrent of popular literature delivered the transgressions of the American underworld to British readers. Inspired by W.R. Burnett's *Little Caesar* (1929), this subgenre of crime writing was solidly established in Britain by Edgar Wallace, the journalist and prolific popular novelist, whose gangster novel *On the Spot* (1931) was a significant success, with the British stage production launching Charles Laughton's career. The American underworld strengthened its grip on the British imagination with the archetypal early sound gangster films *Little Caesar* (1931), *The Public Enemy* (1931) and *Scarface: Shame of a Nation* (1932). The post-Prohibition crime wave in the United States that peaked in 1933–4 was heavily reported in the British press. This interest was quickly perceived as a threat to moral order and British censorship prevented domestic attempts to exploit audience interest meaning neither *On the Spot* nor Wallace's follow-up *When the Gangs Came to London* (1932) were filmed. Instead, the American crook became a stock comic character as seen, for example, in *Where There's a Will* (1936) and *Hey! Hey! USA!* (1938). British demand for more of the American underworld was instead catered to by cheap fiction tapping into the American pulp style by prolific British writers like James Hadley Chase and Peter Cheyney (creator of Lemmy Caution). Steve Holland notes that *No Orchids for Miss Blandish* (1939), Chase's debut novel, 'sold over a million copies in five years' (28) despite paper rationing, and, according to Joseph MacAleer in *Popular Reading and Publishing in Britain 1914-1950*, became probably 'the most notorious and widely-read bestseller of the Second World War – among the working classes' (cited Holland 29). George Orwell is more specific in dating its success, suggesting that it 'seems to have enjoyed its greatest popularity in 1940, during the Battle of Britain and the blitz' (n.pag).

No Orchids for Miss Blandish tells the story of cheap crooks who plan to steal a necklace but end up kidnapping its wearer after killing her escort and then coincidentally fall foul of more fearsome criminals, the Grisson gang, led by Ma Grisson, a character based on the FBI's self-serving presentation of the Barker/Karpis gang supposedly being led by Ma Barker. The Grissons take the ransom but keep the victim who is desired by the psychopathic Slim Grisson. After three months Miss Blandish's father hires private eye Dave Fenner to investigate and he locates her through the violent interrogation of a gang member, bringing about a raid on the gang's nightclub hideout and beginning a manhunt for Slim and his captive. In the shocking denouement the rescued, but traumatized and possibly pregnant, Miss Blandish commits suicide rather than try to return to normal life. Fenner recognizes the trauma the victim is likely to feel, but it does no good.

Orwell introduces the novel, midway through his 1944 essay 'Raffles and Miss Blandish', with 'Now for a header into the cesspool' (n.pag). Depending on which of the several versions of this multi-focalized gangster novel you have read it may seem as if Orwell is rather easily shocked and reads things into the narrative, but he summarizes the 1939 original, much the toughest version. Therein Eddie is given the excessive beating Orwell describes and Rocco, the rival gangster with a grudge against the Grissons, dies orgasmically. The 1942 edit is a little more circumspect. An American 1948 edition (aka *The Villain and the Virgin*) tones things down significantly. Finally a 1961 revision by the author is again substantially different. The original version (and the first edited version) ends with a rich woman in a car being only mildly disconcerted to hear of Miss Blandish's demise.

The reason for the different versions was largely to avoid censorship. Representation of violence was less frequently prosecuted than that of sex, but *No Orchids* brings them together. Slim Grisson is excited by the opportunity to kill the kidnappers slowly and afterwards he 'was relaxed and eased like a man sexually satiated' (33). When Rocco, who has rescued Miss Blandish for his own purposes, realizes Slim has found them and is behind him with a knife we learn:

> The seed in his loins suddenly began to spring. He couldn't do anything about that either. It just came from him, unexpectedly and as a relief. He felt for

the last time that urgent ecstasy that had been so necessary to him in his short life. He felt his muscles relaxing to it, and then the steel blade wiped out everything. (115)

Afterwards Slim tries to persuade Miss Blandish to disguise herself in Rocco's clothes and becomes aroused. A description of the coupling is substituted by the following paragraph: 'A large bluebottle settled on the bloodstain on Rocco's coat. It stretched its legs and buzzed excitedly. It remained there some time, enjoying itself' (123). The fatal ending for Miss Blandish is frequently prefigured; gang member Eddie says, '"One look at her an' a corpse would have wicked thoughts!"' (21). When she is drugged by Ma for his use, Slim observes that amusing himself with her is 'like playing with a corpse' (80); a witness to her nightly walk says '"She looks like a walking corpse"' (93).

No Orchids' most literary precursor is William Faulkner's *Sanctuary* (1932) which according to Julian Maclaren-Ross, writing in the *TLS* in 1953, 'has since inspired a school of sensationalism which its begetter may, with reason, hold in abhorrence, certainly the sheer savage tension of the original has not been surpassed by any of its imitators' (331). Yet while *Sanctuary* is embedded in the deep South of the United States, *No Orchids* inhabits a much less specific version of that country, a composite generic America culled from pulp fiction and gangster films rather than actual experience.

The novel represents a violent, unpredictable and sadistic milieu which Orwell equates with bully-worship and fascism: 'a daydream for a totalitarian age' (n.pag). For Ernest Mandel in *Delightful Murder* (1984): 'The fact that such novels enjoyed tremendous success clearly confirms their status as reflections of a sick society: they were phenomena of social decomposition' (94). As Colin Watson suggests in relation to *No Orchids* in *Snobbery with Violence* (1971): 'It is a calculated, if clumsy, attempt to titillate by projecting its English author's idea of how American gangsters go about being beastly to one another and to their women' (242). This imaginary version of America appals Orwell most of all, since he notes disapprovingly that 'Evidently there are great numbers of English people who are partly americanized [*sic*] in language and, one ought to add, in moral outlook' (n.pag). Orwell finds the book's morality problematically ambiguous:

> Today no one would think of looking for heroes and villains in a serious novel, but in lowbrow fiction one still expects to find a sharp distinction between right and wrong and between legality and illegality. The common people, on the whole, are still living in a world of absolute good and evil from which the intellectuals have long since escaped. (n.pag)

He is somewhat missing the point, made by Holland, that the book does demonstrate that 'crime does not pay' (82), though it also shows terrible things happen to the innocent, and the upper class.

As Orwell records, while the excesses of *No Orchids* went unchallenged, Chase was fined for obscenity in 1942 after the publication of *Miss Callaghan Comes to Grief* (1941) (see Holland 111 for details). The title character is a dead prostitute in the St Louis morgue seen by drunken journalists escaping a heatwave in the prologue. Her fate leads one of them to recount the rise and fall of a gangster called Raven (the name of Greene's anti-hero of 1936 entertainment *A Gun for Sale*). Instead of bootlegging being Raven's route to the top, as in archetypal gangster films of the early 1930s, he takes over by brutally and murderously seizing control of the vice industry. Possible witness Mrs Sadie Perminger is picked out by Raven and undergoes a process of 'white' slavery. Later, in a grim scene, she distracts him from his train set and: 'Grinning at her, Raven pushed her flat and then, amid the railway, flattened by their bodies, he had her' (122). Journalists and the FBI finally stop Raven's rise but before he is formally executed by electrocution he gives a short speech about the necessity of the role of vice in the sexual economy which he is vilified for supplying: '"If you guys didn't want women, my racket wouldn't have lasted long. Don't forget that. All you smug-lookin' heels who've come to see me burn are as much to blame as I am"' (173). Sadie, looking 'a little mad' (174), spits in the face of his corpse. The novel is relentlessly nasty, casually racist (143) and queasily ambivalent about its prurient interest in the experience of victimized female characters. What is today called 'rape culture' is manifested surprisingly openly in 1940s popular literature. The text is capable of highlighting the everyday sexist abuse to which Perminger's employer Caston subjects his secretary (67–71) but hypocrisy is evident; when the underlying rage of the exploited women results in violent revenge on two gangsters, it is treated as a horror scene (133–5).

Occasional lurches into gothic horror in Chase's stories relate his work back to the 'shocker' style of film thriller of the 1930s. James Chapman suggests, 'it was the thriller's origins in a stream of lowbrow popular culture which has caused its neglect by film critics' (1998: 80). Films like *The Ghoul* (1933), *The Terror* (1938) and *The Dark Eyes of London* (1939) 'presented a violent disruption of the normal patterns of life through malevolent and sometimes supernatural forces which cannot be contained within the restrictive boundaries of the orthodox realist aesthetic' (90). Chase's novels regularly reject the standard realist aesthetic of the crime genre they ostensibly belong to. Several gangsters are killed in *Figure It Out for Yourself* (1950) by packs of rats lurking in the mine used to store crates of reefers (a late 1940s US moral panic) and murderous mental patients are set loose in *Lay Her among the Lillies* (1950) and the sequel to *No Orchids, The Flesh of the Orchid* (1948). *Make the Corpse Walk*, published in 1946 under the pseudonym Raymond Marshall, has an element of the supernatural both in the title and with the introduction of Voodooism (probably stimulated by the 1943 Jacques Tourneur film *I Walked with a Zombie*). Stepping away from American settings, it is based in London, with the plot revolving around the crazed obsession of millionaire Kester Wiedmann about having his twin brother resurrected and the gangsters he pays to arrange it. Wiedmann's vicious chauffeur, Joe Crawford, incorporates an element of Pinkie from Greene's *Brighton Rock* (1938) in that he is good at facing people down, but physically incapable of being the thug he would like to be. To thwart Kester's plans Crawford kidnaps the corpse and delivers the trunk to heroine Susan Header, directing her through a criminal contact to hide the body in a wax-modeller's cellar. American gangster Butch kills two men, and gets the better of Detective Adams before the flying squad turns up – 'these damn British cops were dynamite' (151) – but it is Susan who captures him. Wiedmann rewards her with £5,000, before he is certified mad, and she considers using these funds to open a detective agency (157). This conclusion suggests that despite a handful of murders and a suicide the novel is meant to be read as a playful romp. It was clearly unsuccessful given that Chase did not pursue this style.

Another indication that Chase wanted to escape the morbidly violent imaginary version of America is *More Deadly than the Male* published under another pseudonym, Ambrose Grant, with Eyre and Spottiswoode in 1946. In a British setting the protagonist is George Fraser, an educational book salesman and fantasist who claims – in weak moments – to have been a gangster in America. His prize possession is a Luger taken from his uncaring father, which is significantly stiff-triggered and unloaded. When Sydney Brant, a scar-faced petty criminal, tries to lay low in the book racket his con-man skills are much more effective than Fraser's approach. Learning of Fraser's fantasies, Brant manipulates him into a revenge scheme through his attraction to Brant's 'sister' Cora. Fraser is meant to be the fall guy for the resulting murder, but the rival gang conceals the body, regroups under the murdered man's mother and kills Brant. Now feeling responsible for Cora, George tries to assert himself by a series of fuel station robberies across London but Cora still leaves him to work as a prostitute for gangster Little Ernie. George shoots Ernie and tells the rival gang where to find Cora, before revealing all to the police. The 1940s is, of course, the decade of the femme fatale, but it might equally be the decade of the manipulated male protagonist.

Chase's female characters are no longer victims like Miss Blandish but the tormentors of men, dangerous in their own right (like Ma Grisson). The majority of Chase's novels of the 1940s have female villains, culprits and gang leaders. Often his novels are awkwardly plotted, not entirely convincing in their American settings (while Orwell was impressed, tellingly Chase was not a success in the United States), and yet in their violence and sexuality they are remarkably raw and troubling. And they sold well. Concluding his essay 'Raffles and Miss Blandish' Orwell admits: 'one is driven to feel that snobbishness, like hypocrisy, is a check upon behaviours whose value from a social point of view has been underrated' (n.pag). This indicates, in capsule form, the forces at play in British cultural criticism in the turbulent 1940s; intellectual disapproval of popular taste where it conflicts with standards of class and sexuality and particularly when it leans towards American culture. An association between criminality and Americanization develops among British intellectuals, and the crimes revealed in the so-called cleft chin murder case are suggested as confirmation by Orwell in 'The Decline of English Murder' first published in *Tribune*, 15 February, 1946: 'Perhaps it is significant that the most talked-of English murder of recent years should have been committed by an American and an English girl who had become partly Americanized' (n.pag).

Filming Greeneland

While Greene's novels of the 1940s are dealt with elsewhere in this collection (see Chapters 2 and 7) his transition from a writer of note to pre-eminence in the field of literature during this decade cannot have been hurt by no less than nine feature films based on his works being made and released in the decade. This was a considerable change of pace from the 1930s, during which, aside from film reviewing, Greene was involved in three films. His novel *Stamboul Train* (1931) was filmed by Twentieth Century Fox as *Orient Express* (1933), and he was responsible for the screenplays of John Galsworthy adaptation *Twenty-one Days* (1937) and the crime film *The Green Cockatoo* (1937). That the last of these reached the screen only in 1940 is indicative of trouble ahead for the crime genre (see Pulver 2010: 87).

The first Greene-based film made in the 1940s was Ealing Studios' adaptation of the short story 'The Lieutenant Died Last' published in *Collier's* in the United States in late June 1940. Greene had briefly been at the Ministry of Information before being posted to Sierra Leone and, though the story paints far from an idyllic portrait of Britain, this publication may have been an incidental part of his MoI role. Penelope Houston's detailed research on the resulting film, *Went the Day Well?*, suggests that Greene may have discussed an adaptation with the director, Cavalcanti, a personal friend, but made no contribution to the script of the film which was released in October 1942 (often thought to have been released in 1943). Even with this release date the topicality of the film – invasion by German paratroops – was rapidly receding. However, this was not the case when it was scripted and shot. *Went the Day Well?* tells the story of Bramley End's brief capture by the enemy from the (reassuring) point of view of the future. In the flashback that forms the narrative the village is betrayed by the squire, Wilsford (Leslie Banks), who uses his status to give plausibility to the Germans wearing British uniforms. Once the occupation is revealed, and the Home Guard have been ruthlessly disposed of, the villagers are forced to fight back individually. The stock characters of cosy rural life become casualties in startling changes of tone, literally when they are killed, but equally when we learn what they are capable of. William Whitebait described it as 'a mixture of friendly human nature and waking nightmare' (cited in Houston 54). After several unsuccessful attempts to communicate with the authorities, the efforts of an evacuee and the local poacher (the protagonist of Greene's short tale) succeed, but there are more casualties in the villagers' defence of the manor house. Some contemporary criticism found it violent and objectionable, while C. A. Lejeune felt it lacked 'talent and taste' and the *Kinematograph Weekly* described it as 'Fair average thick-ear fiction for the unsophisticated masses' (Houston 53, 54). Objections seem primarily based on judgements of plausibility and realism. As Houston concludes, this film is not 'the grim, strenuously "realistic" study of a village under occupation which might have won more immediate approval from the critics. [… Instead it] had a kind of freedom to make it up as it went along, rather as Bramley End has to take its fate into its own hands' (59). This is where the film earns its longevity. The fighting is led by a son of the village on leave from the Navy and non-local land girls. While the lady of the manor plays a key role in the defence, Wilsford is still trusted by the majority until the very end. In line with Greene's tale of a poacher who barely understands the nature of modern war, the battle is almost instinctual. It is, as Houston says, 'the only British feature film made during the war to deal seriously […] with the prospect of invasion, to show British civilians coming to grips on home ground with the German army' (9). That they do so largely without leadership, in the light of the French experience of Vichy government, is rather extraordinary.

This Gun for Hire (1942) is the Hollywood adaptation of Greene's 1936 novel *A Gun for Sale*. Where the novel was concerned with the build-up to a second war and unleashed its criminal underclass anti-hero, Raven, on those who sought to cause it, situations had clearly changed radically by the time the film was made. Relocation of the story from Britain to the United States also had to be accommodated. Instead of attempting to spark a war to revitalize his business interests, the capitalist villain wants to sell poison gas formulae to the Japanese. Adapted by W. R. Burnett and Albert Maltz (one of the Hollywood 10) Paramount's adaptation benefits from the first pairing of Veronica Lake and Alan Ladd. Given a deformed wrist rather than the badly fixed hare lip that Greene used to mark him out, Ladd's trench-coated Raven was hugely influential in French Cinema when it was finally seen along with other early 1940s Hollywood films after liberation. It is among the ten films listed by Raymond Borde and Étienne Chaumenton in *Panorama du film noir Américain 1941-53*, their 1955 essay identifying of the arrival of film noir in 1946.

Greene's work was in demand from Hollywood studios because it fitted with the tone of filmmaking which French critics would later identify as 'noir'. Greene was thrilled to hear Fritz Lang would direct *The Ministry of Fear* (1944), with Ray Milland starring, but was disappointed with the results. The adaptation had been written by Seton I. Miller, who had graduated to becoming producer, too, and Lang was unable to affect the script as he expected. In order to allow the ending as written, the protagonist's guilt was changed from being responsible for his wife's death to merely enabling her suicide. The passage in the book where the protagonist loses his memory due to the after-effects of an explosion was also minimized. Nevertheless, the disorientated, guilty, out-of-his-depth, hunted and deceived protagonist looks ahead to the protagonists of later noir films.

Other Hollywood adaptations had less impact. *The Confidential Agent* (1945), starring Charles Boyer and Lauren Baccall, is among the most faithful Hollywood adaptations of Greene, staying close to the 1939 novel, but lacks spark and, sold on romance rather than intrigue, it was a box-office disappointment that nearly derailed Baccall's career in her second film. The adaptation of *The Power and the Glory* (1939) as *The Fugitive* (1947) was directed by John Ford for his own company, and filming in Mexico with a Mexican crew free of studio oversight, he chose to make something expressionist and noir in atmosphere that was faithful to Catholicism rather than to Greene's story (which would likely have mired the project in controversy).

The success of British costume dramas in the mid-1940s led to Greene's historical first novel *The Man Within* (1929) being adapted in 1947 in a film also known as *The Smugglers*. But the concerns of the narrative do not sit well with the period setting, or perhaps with the historical moment at which it was made. Greene's interest in morality would be best served by a contemporary setting as in *The Fallen Idol* (1948) from Greene's 1935 short story 'The Basement Room' (see Chapter 7), but the successful and close collaboration between Greene and the director, Carol Reed, led to them working together again in *The Third Man* (1949). This film, and the adaptation of *Brighton Rock* made in 1947, will be set in the generic context in the next section.

'The spiv cycle'

The 'spiv' was an urban black-market racketeer, profiteering from wartime shortages and rationing. According to Andrew Spicer: 'The spiv was a dark version of the Rogue, the symbol of the licentiousness and criminality released in wartime, an image of that "other war", conducted by amoral opportunists and shirkers, that threatened the values of order and community' (27). The real-world character drew on the gaudy style of the Hollywood gangster, and British films began to reflect his existence beginning with *Waterloo Road* (1945), with Stewart Granger, slightly larger than life star of Gainsborough melodramas, playing this role opposite 1940s everyman, John Mills.

In the post-war period the obstacles to British crime narratives emulating American ones had diminished for a number of reasons. First, after the violence of the war, restrictions on screen violence seemed petty and British films followed American examples in becoming darker, both visually and morally. In other words, certain genres of British cinema were already influenced by what would eventually come to be called film noir. Second, wartime and post-war rationing created a situation where laws of supply and demand produced a moral twilight suitable for the rise of racketeers, broadly comparable to that of prohibition era. As Robert Murphy explains in an essay that introduces the term 'the spiv cycle' (1986b: 302), this meant that gangster activities such as 'Prostitution and drug trafficking could be toned down in favour of unprohibited subjects like smuggling and warehouse theft' (300).

Early film versions of the spiv character as criminal antagonist include *Appointment with Crime* (1946) with William Hartnell and *Dancing with Crime* (1946) with Bill Owen. *They Made me a Fugitive* (1947), expanded by Noel Langley from *A Convict Has Escaped* (1941) by Jackson Budd, tells the tale of a jaded RAF veteran Clem Morgan (Trevor Howard) who is drawn into the criminal enterprises of Narcy (Griffith Jones) run from the Valhalla funeral parlour. Class antagonism is part of their uneasy relationship. Eventually Morgan learns Narcy deals in cocaine ('sherbet' in the film) and they fall out, with Morgan being framed, jailed and having to escape to clear himself, ultimately killing Narcy but incriminated by his dying breath. Directed by Cavalcanti, the film uses expressionistic cinematography and, in the words of Robert Murphy, 'the conventions and concerns of film noir are shown as effective in a British as much as in an American setting' (2013: 94). Film noir's influence on British films was by no means confined to this cycle, but the tonal fit is very good. As we have already seen, American adaptations of British crime and spy narratives by writers such as Greene and MacInnes were, however compromised, feeding into the early 1940s development of noir.

Brighton Rock (1947), directed by John Boulting, stars Richard Attenborough as Pinkie, the young leader of a racetrack protection racket and William Hartnell as his lieutenant, Dallow. It comes from Greene's 1938 novel via his 1943 play with the screenplay by Greene and Terence Rattigan. The film makes explicit in its preface that it is set in pre-war Brighton, not the present – presumably a condition of location filming – but as a manoeuvre to avoid contemporary controversy this device was unsuccessful. Greene found himself defending the film from *Daily Mirror* critic Reg Whitley, who described it as 'False, cheap, nasty sensationalism' and went on to appeal to the censor to think of what it would do to the country's reputation overseas:

> British films are getting a break on foreign screens. *Brighton Rock* probably is set for a big showing in the 2000-odd theatres owned by Warner Bros in America. So it is important that overseas should not get the impression made by our recent films, that we are a nation of toughs who rival in brutality the Chicago gangs in their heyday. (Cited in Falk 2000: 41–2)

The film does have moments of shocking violence, such as when Pinkie and Dallow visit the bookie Brewer, or when Pinkie is double-crossed at the racetrack, but the gang is decidedly small scale. Pinkie is totally overawed by the big shot gangster, Colleoni (Charles Goldner), who stays at the Metropole hotel while he is refused a room there on his honeymoon night. The level of violence is also very British. A gun is introduced in the closing stages but for use in a suicide pact between Pinkie and his new wife (witness) Carol Marsh and isn't fired. Yet this realism is part of the problem for critics; it is tawdry and squalid, an aspect of British society they did not wish to consider. Responding to another film in the cycle, *It Always Rains on Sunday* (1947), from Arthur La Bern's first novel, C. A. Lejeune suggested in the *Observer* of 30 November 1947 that 'those artists who work with the deliberate exclusion of beauty are misinterpreting the temper of the people. The adulation of the spiv and all that goes with him is simply a pretence of the unfit and mannered minority, and the sooner his cult is expelled from the cinema, the better for us all' (cited in Ellis: 80). Lejeune's claim to be able to interpret the temper of the people is clearly questionable, and not all critics agreed (see Murphy 1986b: 298). Films about what was happening in the underbelly of British society continued to be made, such as *Good Time Girl* (1948) also from a La Bern novel, with Jean Kent, Herbert Lom and Griffith Jones, not because film producers were determined to throw their money away, but because audiences attended. Yet the critics were not alone in their opinions of crime films: powerful voices in government were speaking in similar terms. This is President of the Board of Trade Harold Wilson speaking in the House of Commons in June 1948:

> We are getting tired of the gangster, sadistic and psychological films of which we seem to have so many, of diseased minds, schizophrenia, amnesia and diseases which occupy so much of our screen time. I should like to see more films which genuinely show our way of life [...]. (Cited in Charles Barr: 14)

Such voices counted when the British film industry was in its most turbulent period. Film-making was not included in state provision for the arts and remained commercially driven. Pre-war quotas had been slackened on the basis of mutual interest during wartime, but the 1947 balance of trade crisis resulted in a 75 per cent duty being imposed on film revenue being taken out of the country and Hollywood boycotted Britain in response. The flood of American films that came when the duty ended in 1948 caused problems for the Rank organization which lost heavily by showing mainly British films produced in the interim. As Murphy puts it, 'British films had proved increasingly popular in the war years, but they still constituted a small percentage of the total supply, and British audiences were not so patriotic as to stomach only a diet of British films' (1986a: 61). As President of the Board of Trade, Wilson reimposed a quota of 45 per cent British pictures in 1948 which settled back to 30 per cent in 1950 and stayed there until the quota system was finally abolished in 1983.

Here, then, was another reason for critical hostility to crime films which were not seen to reflect 'our way of life' positively against other ways. Ellis shows there was already a view among critics about America's pernicious influence through cinema by citing Jympson Harmon from *Sight and Sound* in 1946, an anonymous *Evening Standard* reviewer from 1948 and Jan Read from the *Penguin Film Review* in 1948:

> The main problem has been an 'imposition on the British character of foreign manners talk and thought by films from overseas,' which in practice means America. The seemingly endless flow of 'puerile pulp, synthetic sex and Technicolor goo,' can be attributed to 'the fact that the average mental age of the American audience is round [sic] 15 years.' (1996: 87)

As we have seen in our earlier discussion of Hadley Chase and Orwell's response to the cleft chin case, there is a particular critical association between criminality and Americanization, too.

These currents in criticism would inevitably unite in hostility to the next significant British-made crime film, *No Orchids for Miss Blandish* (1948), starring Linden Travers as Miss Blandish, and Jack La Rue as Slim Grisson. Hadley Chase's novel was adapted by the director, St. John Legh Clowes, with Robert Nesbitt, from the 1942 stage play which had starred Robert Newton and Linden Travers. The two-stage adaptation has an interesting effect on the relationship between the title character and the lead gangster. Robert Aldrich's 1971 adaptation is much truer to the text, though seemingly adapted from an expurgated version. The first cinema adaptation, needing to adapt to the demands of the Production Code, changes the relationship depicted in the book, making Slim Grisson and Miss Blandish have a hugely melodramatic but consensual romance. Slim, presented as handsome in a melancholic way, owns a flower shop and has been sending Miss Blandish orchids, which she refuses, long before the bungled robbery by Bailey's gang causes her to be kidnapped. Having killed Bailey, in self-defence, Slim offers her freedom but she stays willingly. Living together at the Black Dice club he worries about her effective captivity but she responds: 'This is freedom to what I've ever known. Besides, maybe it's because you're the first *man* I've ever met, I love you.' Their devotion is indicated with numerous passionate clinches. In one scene the couple are presented with a private meal by head waiter Louis (Charles Goldner), who returns to ask after it and then mugs away in the background while the couple continue an extended kiss in the foreground. Their plans to decriminalize their relationship in the eyes of the law are as much Miss Blandish's doing as Slim's and she writes to her father complaining of 'a restricted life she hated' under his roof. She is traumatized rather than jubilant when Fenner (Hugh McDermott) and the police kill Slim and her lover's last words 'Be seeing you, kid' stay with her until she jumps to her death from the hotel they take her to, thus avoiding meeting with her father. Her final shriek stops the jaunty exit of Fenner and Margo (Zoë Gail) as a couple.

Rather than going for the full violence of the police raid in the book the film has cosh-wielding Louis and his staff combat Doc (MacDonald Parke) and Flynn (Danny Green) while Slim kills Eddie (Walter Crisham) with a gun passed to him by Miss Blandish. There is thus less violence in the film than in the book, but much of it is on screen and unusually direct, often with shooter and victim in the same frame. When the victim is not dead, the consequences linger. After Sid James's bartender is smashed over the head with a bottle, he subsequent appears with multiple plasters and a patch indicating he may well lose the sight in that eye.

While the slow reaction of the authorities to the success of Hadley Chase's novels suggests the undergrowth of popular literature was not efficiently policed, reactions to this film adaptation indicate the much higher level of concern about the influence of cinema. The *Monthly Film Bulletin* described *No Orchids* as: 'The most sickening exhibition of brutality, perversion, sex and sadism ever to be shown on the cinema screen' (cited in McFarlane 1999: 38). For C. A. Lejeune 'this repellent piece of work' has 'scraped up all the droppings of the nastier type of Hollywood movie' and the *Manchester Guardian* review described it as 'thoroughly un-British' (both cited in McFarlane 44). Part of this reaction is clearly down to a British film pastiching an American setting. As MacFarlane observes:

> The critical distaste for ersatz American film fodder may again be partially explained on the grounds that, at this time, British cinema was nearer to establishing a reputation as a national cinema than at any time in its history – before or since – and a film like *Miss Blandish* must have appeared to have nothing to do with such an enterprise, to have been irrelevant at best, counter-productive at worst. (44)

Yet there is a sense that the real threat perceived in the film is very different from that of the book; instead of the corrosive selfishness of the criminal, the film presents a class-crossing romance in which the upper-class woman finds the lower-class man irresistible, the same axis of desire that made D. H. Lawrence's *Lady Chatterley's Lover* so controversial (remaining banned for another decade). As Orwell identifies in 'The Lion and the Unicorn': 'the genuinely popular culture of England is something that goes on beneath the surface, unofficially and more or less frowned upon by the authorities' (78). The film version of *No Orchids* taps into this troubling well of unofficial culture. While the British Board of

Film Censors (BBFC), 'a quasi-state apparatus helping ruling interests maintain their hegemony' according to Petley (1986a: 44), approved the film, various local authorities took it upon themselves to ban it.

The outrage around *No Orchids* made it more difficult for later transatlantic collaborations in the crime genre. *Noose* (1948) was based on a successful Richard Llewellyn play, though the idea was initially proposed as a film in the late 1930s (see Murphy 1986b: 300). The film became a truly transatlantic effort importing Carole Landis as a lively American fashion journalist ('two more legs and she'd be running in the Oaks') who gets involved in an investigation of London black marketeer, Sugiani. This villain 'As played by Joseph Calleia, [...] cuts a figure somewhat evocative of the then notorious vice magnate Eugenio Messina, and it is a testament to Calleia's performance that the allusion is only slightly blunted by contemporary censorship's proscription of direct references to prostitution' (Pulleine 29). These American stars each have a British counterpart; her fiancé (Derek Farr) is an ex-commando while Sugiani is organized and restrained by Bar Gorman (Nigel Patrick), a fast-talking spiv rather than an out-and-out gangster. Offering a thwarted detective (Stanley Holloway) champagne he receives a whispered reply and his response is far from the snarl Sugiani would give when he asks, 'What? Bottle an' all?' The film is packed with changes of tone, from comedy to menace and director Edmond T. Greville misses no trick in opening out the play, including expressionistic violence, disorientating audio and visual effects, and even a joke about the Board of Trade heard on the radio. The film ends with Landis and Farr shoeless, picking their way across a street covered in broken glass, an American and Briton whose relationship has survived, but metaphorically walking on eggshells.

The penultimate significant film of this cycle is *The Third Man* (1949) directed by Carol Reed from Graham Greene's screenplay which produced Greene's novella *The Third Man* as part of the process. It is likely to be the best known film discussed in this chapter, and in 1999 it was voted the greatest British film of all time by the BFI. It is, nevertheless, a transatlantic spiv film made partly with American money from David Selznick. The key difference from other films in the cycle is that it was shot on location in Vienna and details that setting remarkably. The narrative follows the investigation of Holly Martins (Joseph Cotten), a hack Western writer, into the death of the friend who had invited him there. He is clearly out of his depth, dwarfed by grandiose Viennese architecture shot at various canted angles to the accompaniment of Anton Karas's distinctive zither score. It is certainly a great British film (made by London Films and distributed by British Lion), but it is carried by American stars, memorably

Orson Welles as Harry Lime but with Joseph Cotten doing much of the heavy lifting with marvellous subtlety, though the contributions of the other top-billed actors, Valli and Trevor Howard, are vitally important, too. Disinclined to rate distinctive directors, British critics of the time are quite grudging in their praise having become disillusioned with Reed making what Jympson Harman called in 1948 'a mere murder story' (Ellis 1996: 72). *The Third Man*'s foreign setting and American villain protected it from the critical ire directed at the rest of the spiv cycle, though that is clearly from where it springs. The setting, a city ruled by four powers, encourages its observations to be understood as internationally applicable. Though Welles's addition to the end of the scene on the Prater wheel about Switzerland, neutrality and cuckoo-clocks is well known, and certainly makes a case for great art coming out of turbulent times, Lime's self-serving cynicism knows no bounds as indicated in his preceding words: 'Nobody thinks in terms of human beings. Governments don't; why should we? They talk about the people and the proletariat. I talk about the suckers and the mugs. It's the same thing. They have their five-year plan and so have I.'

Adaptations of Greene's novels written during the latter half of the 1940s fall beyond the scope of this collection because they were filmed in the 1950s, though it may be noted that *The Heart of the Matter* (1953), starring Trevor Howard, and *The End of the Affair* (1955), with Deborah Kerr and Van Johnson, use the book titles rather than inventing alternatives. This tells its own story about the recognition value the author had earned during the 1940s. Meanwhile Greene would go on to use *The Third Man*'s core idea of the American interloper abroad in his Vietnam-set *The Quiet American* (1955).

The Kersh conclusion

We have encountered Gerald Kersh in the 'Introduction' to this volume. He recurs here because his 1938 novel, *Night and the City*, identified the spiv character as a feature of the London underworld prior to the war, and there is a pleasing symmetry to its 1950 film adaptation being, in the words of Tim Pulleine 'in more ways than one the culmination of the cycle' (33). In the interim Kersh had become a popular writer in a number of genres. His 1940s short stories, collected in *The Horrible Dummy and Other Stories* (1944), *Neither Man nor Dog* (1946) and *Sad Road to the Sea* (1947), range from realistic, plausible crime stories, to army anecdotes, from oblique views of bible stories to speculations on the origins of man and post-apocalyptic science-fiction. Recurrent characters include merciless Siberian peasants, dingy lodgers, loquacious criminals and Kersh himself, if need be, a man interested in stories. All his narratives have a buttonholing quality and their voices – character or narratorial – are engaging: full of great turns of phrase as, for example: 'his resolution expired like a gas-jet at the end of a poor man's last pennyworth, and he felt himself growing limp like a dying tulip' ('Bitter Pink Paper' 1947: 186). Kersh is fascinated by storytelling and credulity, particularly the way people deceive others and deceive themselves.

His first novel, *Jews without Jehovah* (1934), was withdrawn shortly after publication when three uncles and a cousin detected portraits of themselves among the novel's atheist Ratner brothers and threatened to sue. The book's characters are susceptible to cons and get-rich-quick schemes but also support impoverished relatives with artistic aspirations. Kersh's second novel, *Men Are So Ardent* (1935), revisits similar subject matter on a slightly broader canvas, with more emphasis on female characters, one of whom becomes the wife of a fraudulent financier. Kersh's focus is already on crime, but as part of the continuum of society: 'In a nutshell, the apothegm; the entire philosophy in three words – the motto of the swell mobsman, the con-man, the pimp, the racketeer, the gigolo, the prostitute, the share pusher, and the businessman with big ideas – only fools work' (18).

Crooked lowlife rather than active gangsterism is the focus of Kersh's best work of the period, tying him to other British writers of the late 1930s such as Robert Westerby, author of *Wide Boys Never Work* (1937), and James Curtis whose *There Ain't No Justice* (1937) and *They Drive by Night* (1938) were filmed in 1938 and 1939 respectively (see Pulver 78 and Murphy 2013: 87). Their work is set in a defiantly British semi-criminal milieu with an authenticity alien to Hadley Chase's imagined American underworld.

Kersh's 1945 novella, *The Weak and the Strong*, has a disaster movie set-up for the guests at a fancy French Caribbean hotel who visit a cave on a nearby island when they become trapped by a volcanic tremor. The vacationing American gangsters are, however, among the least convincing characters, and there is at least a suspicion it is based on pre-war materials. It is when Kersh thinks about headline crime in Britain and its journalistic treatment that the results are stark and horrifying. The title story of the 1947 collection *Sad Road to the Sea* tells of an impoverished tailor unable to meet his debts who kills the collector with 'a twelve-pound pressing iron' (10) and, thwarted in his desire to swim in the sea at Brighton, is captured and drinks hydrochloric acid. It is a stripped down, lower-class version of Patrick Hamilton's *Hangover Square* (1941). The title story of the 1949 collection of post-war novellas, *Clock without Hands*, is about a witness in a murder trial who, as the actual murderer, becomes frustrated by his lack of recognition and resolves to kill again. It reads like a horrible prediction of the events at 10 Rillington Place (in the sense of a witness being the murderer) that would not fully come to light until 1953. Kersh's British criminals are not ciphers of violence but thoroughly damaged people.

Night and the City dives fully into the underworld from prostitution to blackmail to clip joints to wrestling promotion (as well as the fringes of legitimate business) creating an intense portrait of London's Soho in which Kersh pulls apart his vivid, vital, flawed characters. The central figure, Harry Fabian, is a flash-dressing hustler and pimp who is the very prototype of the wartime spiv. Pursuing a client of his main source of income for blackmail purposes he enters a Turkish bath:

> Fabian was troubled [...] by the fact that his feet were dirty; for in spite of his punctilious shaving, dressing and haircutting, and his almost fanatical aversion to soiled collars, he had not the habit of frequent bathing. As he shed his clothes he felt more and more angry; less and less significant. He pulled the curtains close before taking off his delicate blue silk shorts, and then he felt as feeble and unprotected as an oyster out of its shell. (52–3)

Vividly written throughout, *Night and the City* was a hit but this type of crime fiction (not detective fiction) was too disreputable (and too popular with the wrong people) to bring literary kudos. It was, however, remembered. In 'A Brief Survey of British Feature Films' published in 1947 Julian Maclaren-Ross generously suggests *Night and the City* would make a good screenplay (263), and it was eventually taken up by Twentieth-Century Fox, the rights being bought shortly after its American publication in 1946.

The film version of *Night and the City* that finally emerged postdates the novel on which it is based by more than a decade. The author had revisited the protagonist in the interim in *The Song of the Flea* (1947), and suggested a semi-idyllic later career for him in Monte Carlo, but Kersh was not involved in the various screenplays that were generated and did not like what he saw of them. Hollywood was governed by the morality of the Hays code and, somewhat unjustly (Fabian's main income is as a club tout in the film), he would not be allowed to survive.

Jo Eisinger's adaptation also brought another significant change. In Kersh's novel the protagonist pretends to be American for the associated glamour, though he fools only a small percentage of those he meets. The first chapter emphatically sticks with two of them long enough to hear their opinions of him before rejoining Harry on his travels. There are also several argumentative encounters with a struggling cockney costermonger, Bert, who we eventually learn is Harry's honest brother. In the film, Fabian is played by Richard Widmark and *is* an American post-war hustler. His girlfriend, a singer, is also American, played by Gene Tierney. Googie Withers and Francis L. Sullivan are the British leads and play the dysfunctional couple running the Silver Fox club, adding real emotional heft.

Night and the City was shot in London, directed by Jules Dassin (avoiding the House Un-American Activities Committee (HUAC) hearings in his last film for an American studio). Distinct British and American versions of the film exist, not that unusual in co-productions involving David Selznick. There were British and American versions of *The Third Man*, with the American one having introductory narration by Cotten, the British by Reed (uncredited), but the eleven minutes of cuts for the American market have made the British version the definitive one. The two versions of *Night and the City* have different scores and editing, though in this case the American version is regarded as the definitive one (see Pulver for details).

It is a landmark film noir, overshadowed (not unfairly) by *The Third Man*, but with some suggestive similarities. Like Harry Lime, Harry Fabian is an American abroad, weaving a suspicious path through an old-world underworld he has become accustomed to until he finds himself out of his depth. The upstart American unscrupulously exploits opportunities and overreaches. Lime perishes in the sewers; Fabian is pursued through bomb-damaged streets to be strangled by the river. Crime does not pay, of course, and death cannot be circumvented. But where (as we have seen) the Vienna setting of *The Third Man* absolves Britain, the London of *Night and the City* stands for Britain itself. If thought of as an American film, *Night and the City* accuses HUAC and there is a little of the director, Dassin, in the terrified and doomed attempt of Fabian to escape his fate. But seen as a British film, *Night and the City* conspires to run down the American interloper whose final altruistic act seems futile. Yet underlying this narrative is the source novel in which the crook is only *pretending* to be American, and Harry Fabian might be seen to represent the British film industry's failed attempt to oust American (foreign) dominance from its racket.

The values film critics saw in the cinema of the early and mid-1940s could not be upheld in the economic instability and changed circumstances of the post-war period. John Ellis observes, 'For the critics, it seemed that the good reception given to wartime quality pictures depended on the fact of war rather than the fact of quality' (88). British attitudes could no longer be imposed on the world and American dominance previously seen in the film industry would extend exponentially into other areas. The critics' 'proselytizing humanism' (91) remained influential but, given how much of British popular culture it rejected or ignored, it was never likely to be able to guide the industry into popular success or even to be a reliable guide to what mass audiences would enjoy. Championing an exclusionary focus on British cinema downplayed the British industry's international links and their significant contribution to what Andrew Spicer has called the 'transnational cultural phenomenon' of film noir (2013: 17).

Of the novelists we have focused on in this chapter, Greene's engagement with film built on his work in popular literary genres and ultimately worked for literary critics because he used these forms to critique American attitudes they were hostile to. Other than Orwell, whose novels pointed critiques at the other side in the Cold War, no novelist's reputation was so enlarged by the decade. Meanwhile Hadley Chase would largely confine himself to his imaginary America and under-the-radar genre fiction retaining his sales and the interest of international translators and filmmakers. Finally, Kersh, drawn across the Atlantic by the end of the 1940s but indelibly British, would be left in critical limbo.

Works cited

Barr, Charles. 'Introduction: Amnesia and Schizophrenia'. In Charles Barr (ed.), *All Our Yesterdays: 90 Years of British Cinema*. London: BFI, 1986: 1–29.

Borde, Raymond and Étienne Chaumenton. *Panorama du film noir Américain 1941-53*. Paris: Les Éditions de Minuit, 1955.

Chapman, James. 'Celluloid Shockers'. In Jeffrey Richards (ed.), *The Unknown Thirties: An Alternative History of the British Cinema*. London: I.B. Tauris, 1998: 75–97.

Chapman, James. 'Cinema, Propaganda and National Identity: British Film and the Second World War'. In Justine Ashby and Andrew Higson (eds), *British Cinema: Past and Present*. London: Routledge, 2000: 193–206.

Chase, James Hadley. *No Orchids for Miss Blandish / Twelve Chinamen and a Woman*. Eureka, California: Stark House, 2016 [1939/1941].

Chase, James Hadley. *Miss Callaghan Comes to Grief*. Floyd, Virginia: Black Curtain, 2013 [1942].

Chase, James Hadley. *Make the Corpse Walk*. London: Panther, 1964 [1946].

Chase, James Hadley. *The Flesh of the Orchid*. London: Panther, 1965 [1948].

Crisell, Andrew. *An Introductory History of British Broadcasting*. London: Routledge (2nd Edition), 2002.

Cull, Nicholas John. *Selling War: The British Propaganda Campaign against America 'Neutrality' in World War II*. New York: Oxford University Press, 1995.

Ellis, John. 'Art, Culture and Quality: Terms for a Cinema in the Forties and Seventies'. *Screen* 19 (3), 1978: 9–49.

Ellis, John. 'The Quality Film Adventure: British Critics and the Cinema 1942-1948'. In Andrew Higson (ed.), *Dissolving Views: Key Writings on British Cinema*. London: Bloomsbury 1996: 66–93.

Falk, Quentin. *Travels in Greeneland: A Complete Guide to the Cinema of Graham Greene*. London: Reynolds and Hearn (3rd edition), 2000.

Grant, Ambrose [James Hadley Chase]. *More Deadly than the Male*. London: Eyre and Spottiswoode, 1946.

Harper, Sue. *Picturing the Past: The Rise and Fall of the British Costume Film*. London: BFI, 1994.

Higson, Andrew. '"Britain's Outstanding Contribution to the Film": The Documentary-Realist Tradition'. In Charles Barr (ed.), *All Our Yesterdays: 90 Years of British Cinema*. London: BFI, 1986: 72–97.

Holland, Steve. *The Mushroom Jungle: A History of Postwar Paperback Publishing*. Westbury (Wilts): Zeon, 1993.

Houston, Penelope. *Went the Day Well?* London: BFI Film Classics, 1992.

Kersh, Gerald. *Jews without Jehovah*. London: Wishart, 1934.

Kersh, Gerald. *Men are so Ardent*. London: Wishart, 1935.

Kersh, Gerald. *Night and the City*. London: London Books, 2007 [1938].

Kersh, Gerald. *The Horrible Dummy and Other Stories*. London: Faber Finds, 2013 [1944].

Kersh, Gerald. *The Weak and the Strong*. London: Heinemann, 1945.

Kersh, Gerald. *Neither Man nor Dog*. London: Heinemann, 1946.

Kersh, Gerald. *Sad Road to the Sea*. London: Heinemann, 1947.

Kersh, Gerald. *Clock Without Hands*. Richmond, Virginia: Valancourt, 2015 [1949].

Maclaren-Ross, Julian. 'A Brief Survey of British Feature Films'. In *Bitten by the Tarantula and other writing*. London: Black Spring, 2005: 259–66.

Maltby, Richard. '"D" for Disgusting: American Culture and English Criticism'. In Geoffrey Nowell-Smith and Steven Ricci (eds), *Hollywood and Europe: Economics, Culture, National Identity 1945-95*. London: BFI, 1998: 104–15.

McFarlane, Brian. 'Outrage: *No Orchids for Miss Blandish*'. In Steve Chibnall and Robert Murphy (eds), *British Crime Cinema*. London: Routledge, 1999: 37–50.

Mendel, Ernest. *Delightful Murder: A Social History of the Crime Story*. London: Pluto, 1984.

Murphy, Robert. 'Under the Shadow of Hollywood'. In Charles Barr (ed.), *All Our Yesterdays: 90 Years of British Cinema*, London: BFI, 1986a: 47–71.

Murphy, Robert. 'Riff-Raff: British Cinema and the Underworld'. In Charles Barr (ed.), *All Our Yesterdays: 90 Years of British Cinema*. London: BFI, 1986b: 286–305.

Murphy, Robert. 'British Film Noir'. In Andrew Spicer (ed.), *European Film Noir*. Manchester: MUP, 2013: 84–111.

Orwell, George. 'The Lion and the Unicorn'. In *Collected Essays* vol 2. London: Secker and Warburg, 1968 [1941].

Orwell, George. 'Raffles and Miss Blandish'. The Orwell Foundation. https://www.orwellfoundation.com/?s=raffles+and+miss+blandish [accessed 10 April 2021] [1944].

Orwell, George. 'Decline of British Murder'. The Orwell Foundation. https://www.orwellfoundation.com/?s=decline+of+British+murder [accessed 10 April 2021] [1946].

Petley, Julian. 'Cinema and State'. In Charles Barr (ed.), *All Our Yesterdays: 90 Years of British Cinema*. London: BFI, 1986a: 31–46.

Petley, Julian. 'The Lost Continent'. In Charles Barr (ed.), *All Our Yesterdays: 90 Years of British Cinema*. London: BFI, 1986b: 98–119.

Pulleine, Tim. 'Spin a Dark Web'. In Steve Chibnall and Robert Murphy (eds), *British Crime Cinema*. London: Routledge, 1999: 27–36.

Pulver, Andrew. *Night and the City*. London: BFI Film Classics, 2010.

Richards, Jeffrey. 'Tod Slaughter and the Cinema of Excess'. In Jeffrey Richards (ed.), *The Unknown Thirties: An Alternative History of the British Cinema*. London: I.B. Tauris, 1998: 139–59.

Ryall, Tom. 'England's Dreaming'. *Sight and Sound* 11 (8), August 2001: 30–3.

Spicer, Andrew. *Typical Men: The Representation of Masculinity in Popular British Cinema*. London: I.B. Tauris, 2003.

Spicer, Andrew. 'Introduction'. In Andrew Spicer (ed.), *European Film Noir*. Manchester: MUP, 2013: 1–22.

Street, Sarah. *Transatlantic Crossings: British Feature Films in the USA*. London: Continuum, 2002.

Watson, Colin. *Snobbery with Violence: Crime Stories and Their Audience*. London: Eyre & Spottiswoode, 1971.

Timeline of Works

1939

Eric Ambler, *The Mask of Dimitrios*
Nicholas Blake, *The Smiler with the Knife*
Joyce Cary, *Mister Johnson*
James Hadley Chase, *No Orchids for Miss Blandish*
Agatha Christie, *And Then There Were None*
Graham Greene, *The Confidential Agent*
Geoffrey Household, *Rogue Male*
James Joyce, *Finnegan's Wake*
Robert Neumann, *By the Waters of Babylon*
Anna Reiner, *The Wall*
Mary Renault, *Purposes of Love*
Jean Rhys, *Good Morning Midnight*

1940

Eric Ambler, *Journey into Fear*
Nicholas Blake, *Malice in Wonderland*
Henry Green, *Pack My Bag*
Graham Greene, *The Power and the Glory*
Anna Kavan, *Asylum Piece*
Nancy Mitford, *Pigeon Pie*

1941

Nicholas Blake, *The Case of the Abominable Snowman*
Elizabeth Bowen, *Look at All These Roses*
Ivy Compton-Burnett, *Parents and Children*
James Hadley Chase, *Miss Callaghan Comes to Grief*
Daphne Du Maurier, *Frenchman's Creek*
Patrick Hamilton, *Hangover Square*
James Hanley, *The Ocean*
Gerald Kersh, *They Die With Their Boots Clean*
Helen MacInnes, *Above Suspicion*
Anna Reiner, *Café du Dôme*

1942

Nigel Balchin, *Darkness Falls from the Air*
Monica Dickens, *One Pair of Feet*
Richard Hillary, *The Last Enemy*
Gerald Kersh, *The Nine Lives of Bill Nelson*
Helen MacInnes, *Assignment in Brittany*
Edith Pargeter, *She Goes to War*
Winifred Peck, *House-bound*
Neville Shute, *Pied Piper*
Evelyn Waugh, *Put Out More Flags*

1943

Nigel Balchin, *The Small Back Room*
Daphne Du Maurier, *Hungry Hill*
Stella Gibbons, *Ticky*
Henry Green, *Caught*
Graham Greene, *The Ministry of Fear*
James Hanley, *No Directions*
Gerald Kersh, *The Dead Look On*
Gerald Kersh, *Brain and Ten Fingers*
Nicholas Monsarrat, *HM Corvette*
Nicholas Monsarrat, *East Coast Corvette*
Anthony Thorne, *I'm a Stranger Here Myself*
Denton Welch, *Maiden Voyage*
Hermynia Zur Mühlen, *We Poor Shadows*

1944

Joyce Cary, *The Horse's Mouth*
Ivy Compton-Burnett, *Elders and Betters*
Norah Hoult, *There Were No Windows*
Gerald Kersh, *Faces in a Dusty Picture*
Gerald Kersh, *The Horrible Dummy and Other Stories*
Helen MacInnes, *The Unconquerable*
Julian Maclaren-Ross, *The Stuff to Give the Troops*
J.P.W. Mallalieu, *Very Ordinary Seaman*
Nicholas Monsarrat, *Corvette Command*
Robert Neumann, *The Inquest*
Jocelyn Playfair, *A House in the Country*
Mary Renault, *The Friendly Young Ladies*

1945

Nigel Balchin, *Mine Own Executioner*
Elizabeth Bowen, *The Demon Lover and other stories*
James Hadley Chase, *Eve*
Henry Green, *Loving*
Anna Kavan, *I am Lazarus*
Helen MacInnes, *Horizon*
Betty Miller, *On the Side of the Angels*
Nancy Mitford, *The Pursuit of Love*
George Orwell, *Animal Farm*
Edith Pargeter, *The Eighth Champion of Christendom*
Noel Streatfeild, *Saplings*
Evelyn Waugh, *Brideshead Revisited*
Denton Welch, *In Youth Is Pleasure*

1946

Daphne du Maurier, *The King's General*
Ambrose Grant, *More Deadly Than the Male*
Henry Green, *Back*
Gerald Kersh, *Clean, Bright and Slightly Oiled*
Raymond Marshall, *Make the Corpse Walk*
Robert Neumann, *Children of Vienna*
Edith Pargeter, *Reluctant Odyssey*
Mervyn Peake, *Titus Groan*
Hermynia Zur Mühlen, *Came the Stranger*

1947

Nigel Balchin, *Lord I was Afraid*
Nicholas Blake, *Minute for Murder*
Ivy Compton-Burnett, *Manservant and Maidservant*
Barbara Comyns, *Sisters by a River*
Patrick Hamilton, *The Slaves of Solitude*
Gerald Kersh, *Prelude to Certain Midnight*
Gerald Kersh, *Sad Road to the Sea*
Francis King, *Never Again*
Philip Larkin, *A Girl in Winter*
Helen MacInnes, *Friends and Lovers*
Julian Maclaren-Ross, *Of Love and Hunger*
Naomi Mitchison, *The Bull Calves*

Edith Pargeter, *Warfare Accomplished*
Neville Shute, *The Chequer Board*

1948

Elizabeth Bowen, *The Heat of the Day*
Jocelyn Brooke, *The Scapegoat*
Jocelyn Brooke, *The Military Orchid*
James Hadley Chase, *Flesh of the Orchid*
Graham Greene, *The Heart of the Matter*
Gerald Kersh, *Song of the Flea*
Robin Maugham, *The Servant*
Robert Neumann, *Tibbs*
George Orwell, *Nineteen Eighty-Four*
Evelyn Waugh, *The Loved One*

1949

Nicholas Blake, *Head of a Traveller*
Jocelyn Brooke, *A Mine of Serpents*
Ivy Compton-Burnett, *Two Worlds and Their Ways*
Monica Dickens, *Flowers on the Grass*
Daphne du Maurier, *The Parasites*
Graham Greene, *The Third Man*
Helen MacInnes, *Rest and be Thankful*
Nancy Mitford, *Love in a Cold Climate*
Robert Neumann, *Blind Man's Buff*
Mary Renault, *North Face*
Stevie Smith, *The Holiday*

1950

Jocelyn Brooke, *The Goose Cathedral*
Barbara Comyns, *Our Spoons Came from Woolworths*
William Cooper, *Scenes from Provincial Life*
Elizabeth Jane Howard, *The Beautiful Visit*
Margaret Kennedy, *The Feast*
Doris Lessing, *The Grass Is Singing*
C. S. Lewis, *The Lion, the Witch and the Wardrobe*
Mervyn Peake, *Gormenghast*
Barbara Pym, *Some Tame Gazelle*
Neville Shute, *A Town Like Alice*
Denton Welch, *A Voice Through a Cloud*

Timeline of National Events

1939

1 September	Evacuation of children, expectant and nursing mothers from London and areas vulnerable to air attack
3 September	Britain declares war on Germany after its Nazi government has invaded Poland; first air raid sirens in London (false alarms)

1940

8 January	Food rationing introduced
31 March	33 fascist sympathizers interned, including Oswald Mosley
7 May	Commons debate on recent military failure in Norway
10 May	Chamberlain resigns as Prime Minister; new PM Winston Churchill forms an all-party coalition government
12 May	Internment of all German or Austrian males aged between 16 and 60, starting with those living near south and east coasts
22 May	Emergency Powers (Defence) Act 1940 is passed, granting government authority to control persons and property for the duration of the war
10 June	Italian males aged 17 to 60 arrested and interned after Italy declares war on France and the UK
3 July	First bombing of Cardiff
6 July	Plymouth bombed
9 July	Battle of Britain begins
10 July	Defence Regulation 58AA bans strike action and introduces compulsory arbitration
25 August	First major raid central Birmingham
28 August	First major raid central Liverpool
7 September	First raid sound London; the Blitz begins
18 September	SS *City of Benares* bound for Canada torpedoed and sunk in the Atlantic; 77 evacuee children on board died; overseas evacuation abandoned
31 October	Battle of Britain ends
14 November	Major raid destroys much of central Coventry

1941

10 May	Last major air raid on London
1 June	Civilian clothing rationed

8 December	Britain declares war on Japan
18 December	National Service (No. 2) Act passed; all men 18–60 liable for national service

1942

23 January	US troops start to arrive
23 April	Baedeker Blitz on English provincial towns begins, continuing until 6 June
1 July	Petrol unavailable to public
15 November	Nationwide church bells celebrate victory at the Second Battle of El Alamein
1 December	Sir William Beveridge's Report on *Social Insurance and Allied Services* published

1943

29 July	Women 19–50 liable for compulsory war work
20 December	Devon villages and farms evacuated for training area for D-Day landings

1944

21 January	Operation Steinbock or 'Baby Blitz': Luftwaffe night bombing of southern England; continues until May 1944
10 March	R. A. Butler's Education Act reorganizes secondary schools in a tripartite system (Grammar, Secondary Technical and Secondary Modern)
22–28 April	Exercise Tiger (D-Day training), Slapton Sands, Devon: 746 US servicemen killed in German attacks
12 June	First V-1 flying bomb attack on London
8 September	First V-2 rocket attack on London
17 September	Blackout eased – partial 'dim-out'
3 December	Home Guard stands down

1945

27 March	Last V-2 attack on London
29 March	Last V-1 flying bomb attack on London
2 May	Civil Defence Service stands down
8 May	VE Day
9 May	Liberation of Channel Islands
16 June	Family Allowance Act – payment to mothers
18 June	Demobilization of armed forces begins

5 July	General Election; votes sealed to allow armed forces ballots to be counter overseas
26 July	Landslide Labour victory in General Election; Clement Atlee new PM
15 August	VJ Day
24 October	UK government signs UN charter

1946

1 January	Atomic Energy Research Establishment established, Harwell, near Oxford
10 January	First United Nations General Assembly convenes, Methodist Central Hall Westminster
14 February	Bank of England nationalized
5 March	Winston Churchill's 'Iron Curtain' speech
15 March	Indian independence announced by PM Clement Atlee
27 April	First post-war FA Cup Final at Wembley Stadium: Derby County beat Charlton Athletic 4–1
20 May	*Coal Industry Nationalisation Act 1946* voted for in Commons
31 May	Heathrow Airport opens fully for civilian flights
7 June	TV broadcasts by BBC resume
1 August	*Atomic Energy Act of 1946* established UK-US cooperation
6 August	Family allowance introduced – paid to mothers
9 August	Arts Council established by Royal Charter
31 August	Professional football leagues return
24 September	*Britain Can Make It* design exhibition opens at Victoria & Albert Museum, London, until 31 December
29 September	BBC Third Programme begins broadcasting
7 October	First Woman's Hour transmission on BBC Light Programme

1947

1 January	Coal Industry and Cable & Wireless Ltd nationalized
8 January	High Explosive Research project established to develop independent British atomic bomb
20 January	Earl Mountbatten of Burma appointed last Viceroy of India
1 April	School leaving age set at fifteen
15 June	Wartime restrictions on foreign travel lifted
31 July	National Fire Service established under control of local authorities (from 1948)
24 August	Inaugural Edinburgh Festival of the Arts opens
20 November	Wedding of Princess Elizabeth and Philip Mountbatten, Duke of Edinburgh, televised live to 400,000 viewers
6 December	Women admitted to full membership of the University of Cambridge

1948

1 January	British Railways takes over nationalized system
4 January	London Co-operative Society opens first supermarket, Manor Park, London
1 April	Nationalized electric supply system commences
13 May	National Assistance Act supersedes Poor Law system
13 May	Prof Lillian Penson, first female Vice-Chancellor of UK university
21 June	The Manchester Baby, world's first electronic computer, runs first program
22 June	Arrival of *Empire Windrush* at Tilbury
5 July	National Health Service begins universal free healthcare
29 July	Olympic Games held in London until 14 August
30 July	Gas supply nationalized
6 September	John Derry first British pilot to break sound barrier in de Havilland DH 108 jet
27 October	First post-war Motor Show, Earls Court, London until 6 November; Morris Minor and Land Rover launched
14 November	Princess Elizabeth gives birth to a son, Charles
20 December	Margaret Kidd first female King's Counsel in Britain

1949

1 January	*National Service Act 1947* established eighteen month service in armed forces for men 18–26
25 March	Laurence Olivier's *Hamlet* (1948) first British film to win a 'Best Picture' Oscar
26 April	Première of Ealing comedy, *Passport to Pimlico*
10 May	First self-service launderette opens, Queensway, London
7 June	Dock strike until 25 June; troops deployed to unload cargoes
27 July	Maiden flight of British-built de Havilland Comet, world's first passenger jet, Hatfield, Hertfordshire
30 July	Legal aid system established in England and Wales
2 September	*The Third Man*, with screenplay by Graham Greene, released and wins 1949 Grand Prix at the Cannes Film Festival
19 September	Pound devalued 30 per cent against US dollar
17 December	Sutton Coldfield transmitting station first BBC TV broadcasts outside London area

1950

23 February	Labour wins a second General Election under Clement Attlee with reduced majority

Timeline of International Events

1939

15 March	German troops march into Czechoslovakia
7 April	Conquest of Albania by Italy
23 August	Germany signs non-aggression pact with Soviet Union
1 September	German invasion of Poland
3 September	France declares war on Germany
17 September	Aircraft Carrier *Courageous* torpedoed and sunk in Bristol Channel
29 September	Poland divided by Germany and Soviet Russia
14 October	HMS *Royal Oak* sunk in Scapa Flow
30 November	Russia invades Finland
7 December	German battleship *Graf Spee* scuttled in Montevideo harbour

1940

14 March	End of Russo-Finnish war
9 April	German conquest of Denmark, and entry into Norway
10 May	German invasion of the Netherlands and Belgium
14 May	Germany conquers the Netherlands
28 May	Belgian army capitulates
3 June	End of troop evacuation from Dunkirk
10 June	Italy declares war on Britain and France
14 June	German conquest of Paris
16 June	French leader Marshal Pétain asks Germany for armistice
17 June	*Lancastria* sunk at St. Nazaire while evacuating British troops
22 June	Beginning of Vichy government of remainder of French territory
4 July	British navy sinks French ships at Oran
13 September	Italy invades Egypt
27 September	Tripartite Pact between Germany, Italy and Japan
28 October	Italy invades Greece
5 November	Franklin Delano Roosevelt defeats Wendell Wilkie in US presidential election

1941

7 February	British offensive in North Africa captures 1,30,000 Italian troops
1 March	Germany occupies Bulgaria

11 March	Lend-Lease Act signed by President Roosevelt
24 March	First German offensive in North Africa
28 March	Three Italian cruisers and two destroyers sunk in Mediterranean
5 April	Haile Selassie returned to Addis Ababa in triumph
6 April	Germany invades Yugoslavia and Greece resulting in respective surrenders on 17th and 20th of this month
30 April	Allied troops withdraw from Greece
24 May	HMS *Hood* sunk in North Sea
27 May	*Bismarck* sunk in Atlantic
1 June	German paratroops take Crete
24 June	Germany invades the Soviet Union
13 June	Russia signs treaty with Britain
19 September	Fall of Kiev
18 November	Second British offensive in North Africa
7 December	Japanese attack on Pearl Harbour; USA declares war on Japan
8 December	Germany and Italy declare war on the USA
15 December	German retreat from outside Moscow begins

1942

20 January	Japanese invasion of Burma
15 February	Japanese capture Singapore, capturing 60,000 British troops
8 March	Fall of Rangoon, Burma
28 March	Raid on St Nazaire by British commandos
10 April	US forces on mainland of the Philippines surrender
28 May	Second German offensive in North Africa begins
3-7 June	Battle of Midway
21 June	Fall of Tobruk
3 July	Germans take Sevastopol
27 July	End of month-long First Battle of El Alamein stops German advance into Egypt
9 August	Rioting in India over lack of progress towards independence
19 August	Dieppe raid carried out by mainly Canadian troops
23 October	Second Battle of El Alamein begins, ending in British victory on 11 November
7-8 November	Allies start invade Vichy French territories in North Africa
14 November	French forces in North Africa join allies
27 November	French fleet scuttled at Toulon

1943

14 January	Churchill and Roosevelt meet in Casablanca

23 January	Allies capture Tripoli
7 May	Allies capture Tunis
12 May	German surrender in North Africa
9 July	Allied invasion of Sicily
3 September	Allies invade Italy at Salerno and Italy surrenders
21 November	Allied leaders attend conference at Teheran
26 December	Sinking of *Scharnhorst* off the north coast of Norway

1944

22 January	Allied Landings at Anzio
9 May	Sevastopol liberated by Russian army
4 June	Allied forces liberate Rome
6 June	D-Day Normandy Landings
17 June	Iceland severs union with occupied Denmark
23 August	Liberation of Paris
3 September	Liberation of Brussels
18–26 September	Operation Market Garden in the Netherlands only partially successful
5 October	Allies land in Greece
20 October	Allied liberation of the Philippines begins
7 Nov	Franklin D. Roosevelt defeats Thomas E. Dewey in US presidential election
16 December	German counter-offensive in Ardennes forest

1945

3–10 January	Allied leaders meet at Yalta, Crimea
13 February	Budapest falls to Red Army
24 February	Liberation of Manila
6 March	Cologne taken by Allies
26 March	Battle for Iwo Jima won by Americans
30 March	Russian troops capture Danzig
12 April	US president Franklin D. Roosevelt dies
15 April	Belsen concentration camp liberated by British troops
28 April	Execution of Mussolini by partisans
2 May	Red Army enters Berlin
3 May	Liberation of Rangoon
5 May	Winston Churchill gives 'Iron Curtain' speech in Missouri
8 May	Canadian troops enter Amsterdam
9 May	German surrender completed
11 May	Prague liberated by Russian troops
23 July	Marshal Pétain, head of Vichy government, sentenced to death

17 May	Potsdam conference of allied victors begins
6 August	Atomic bomb dropped on Hiroshima
9 August	Atomic bomb dropped on Nagasaki
15 August	Japanese surrender announced and signed on 2 September

1946

7 January	Austrian territory set at 1937 borders
11 January	People's Republic of Albania declared
31 January	Constitution of Yugoslavia established
1 February	Republic of Hungary established
18 April	League of Nations officially disbands
2 June	Italy becomes a republic
4 July	Independence of the Philippines
2 September	Interim Government of India takes office
8 September	Bulgarian People's Republic established
16 October	Execution of German war criminals convicted at Nuremberg trials

1947

31 January	Communists take over in Poland
21 February	Polaroid camera demonstrated by Edwin Land
22 May	Truman doctrine enacted by US Congress
14–15 August	Partition of India
13 November	Soviet development of AK-47 completed
24 November	Hollywood Ten found in Contempt of Congress and blacklisting begins
29 November	United Nations Partition plan for Palestine

1948

4 January	Independence of Burma
30 January	Assassination of Mahatma Gandhi
4 February	Independence of Ceylon
3 April	US Congress authorizes $5 billion Marshall Plan to aid European reconstruction
28 May	Beginning of Apartheid in South Africa
24 June	Berlin Blockade begins
28 June	Yugoslavia breaks with Russia
26 July	End of racial segregation in US Army
2 November	Harry S. Truman defeats Thomas E. Dewey in US presidential election
10 December	T. S. Eliot wins the Nobel Prize in Literature

1949

1 January	End of Indo-Pakistan war
12 May	End of Berlin Blockade
8 June	Second Hollywood Red scare
1 August	HMS *Amethyst* escapes Yang-tze river blockade
29 August	First Soviet nuclear weapon test
29 August	End of Greek Civil War
7 September	Founding of Federal Republic of Germany
7 October	Founding of German Democratic Republic
10 December	Nobel Prize for Literature awarded to William Faulkner

1950

25 June	Korean War begins
19 October	People's Republic of China enters Korea War
10 December	Nobel Prize for Literature awarded to Bertrand Russell

Biographies of Writers

Elizabeth Bowen (1899–1973) was an Anglo-Irish writer born in Dublin, to parents Florence and Henry Charles Cole Bowen, of Bowen's Court in County Cork. Her early years were spent between Dublin and summers at the 'big house', memorialized in *Seven Winters: Memories of a Dublin Childhood* (1942) and *Bowen's Court* (1942). At seven her father's mental illness led to her departure, with her mother, for England. Her mother died in 1912. Subsequently, Bowen was raised by aunts in Kent. In 1918 she enrolled at London County Council School of Art, but dropped out, though not before finding words could work like painting. She wrote her first stories and, helped by Rose Macauley, her first collection *Encounters* was published in 1923. In 1926 she published *Ann Lee's and Other Stories*, her first novel *The Hotel* in 1927 and in 1929 both *The Last September* and *Joining Charles and Other Stories*. Enjoying both popular and critical success, by the 1930s she was part of London's literary network and intimate with various well-known figures. Indeed, intimacy and its strangeness were major preoccupations in *Friends and Relations* (1931), *To the North* (1932), *The Cat Jumps and Other Stories* (1934), *The House in Paris* (1935), and *The Death of the Heart* (1938). During the war she volunteered as an air-raid warden and reported on Irish neutrality for the Ministry of Information. These experiences informed *Look at All Those Roses* (1941), *The Demon Lover and Other Stories* (1945), and *The Heat of the Day* (1948), a novel set amid the Blitz concerning love, intrigue, sexual blackmail and espionage. She contributed with Graham Greene and V. S. Pritchett to an 'exchange of views' published as *Why Do I Write?* (1948). Post-war Bowen travelled widely and lectured internationally but published just three more novels. Critically neglected until the end of the twentieth century, she is now recognized as a significant mid-century writer.

James Hadley Chase is the best-known pen name of René Raymond (1906–85) who also published as James L. Docherty (1941), Ambrose Grant (1946) and Raymond Marshall (1940–58). During the 1930s he worked in book sales and book distribution and learned what was most successful among the lower middle-class and working-class readers who were members of commercial libraries. His 1939 American-set debut novel *No Orchids for Miss Blandish* was phenomenally successful despite the fact that he had not visited the country. James Hadley Chase and his publishers, Jarrolds of London, were prosecuted for obscenity in 1942, and both were fined £100. A revised edition of *No Orchids* was first published in that year and was adapted for the stage. Its 1948 film adaptation made in the UK was critically reviled. Raymond served in the RAF during the war and contributed to the *RAF Journal*. In 1945 he was obliged to issue an apology in *The Bookseller* to Raymond Chandler for borrowing scenes from his work. Though his collection of short stories *Get a Load of This* (1942) was singularly unsuccessful, there was considerable readership for his output of thrillers, though none equalled the notoriety of *No Orchids*. Married since 1932, Raymond and his wife moved to France in 1956, and to Switzerland in the 1960s. He had written 90 novels by this time and these have been adapted (by others) into upwards of 40 films often in France, but also in Germany, Russia and India. Among the films made from his work the adaptation of *Eve* (1945) as *Eva* (1962) is the most distinguished.

Monica Dickens was born in May 1915, to an upper-middle-class London family, one of three children and the great-granddaughter of Charles Dickens. She was expelled from St Paul's Girls' School after throwing her school uniform into the Thames, but was then sent to finishing school in France in preparation for what she later termed the 'absolute agony' of the debutante round. After being presented at court, she left home determined to enter domestic service, her experiences as a cook-general providing – after a chance meeting with a publisher in 1937 – the material for her best-selling memoir *One Pair of Hands* (1939). Its success, and that of debut novel *Mariana* (1940), led to work as a reviewer for the *Sunday Chronicle* throughout the 1940s. During the war she worked first as a nurse – a period she detailed in *One Pair of Feet* (1942) – and then as a fitter in an aircraft factory, before turning to writing full-time. Her first foray into news journalism at the *Hertfordshire Express* provided both the means and the material for a succession of early novels including the semi-autobiographical *My Turn to Make the Tea* (1951). Soon after its publication, she married United States Naval Commander Roy Stratton – fictionalized in the 1953 novel *No More Meadows* – and moved with him to Washington, before settling in Massachusetts. She was actively involved with the National Society for the Prevention of Cruelty to Children (written about in the 1964 *Kate and Emma*), with the Royal Society for the Prevention of Cruelty to Animals and with the Samaritans writing about the organization in the 1970 novel *The Listeners* and helping to set up the first American branch in 1974. Her autobiography, *An Open Book*, was published in 1978. Despite remaining in America until her husband's death in 1985, she set most of her prodigious output in Britain, including a successful series of equestrian novels for children, the Follyfoot series, which was first televised in 1971, and kept up a weekly column in British magazine *Woman's Own* for twenty years. Dickens continued to write prolifically after her return, her final novel appearing shortly after her death on Christmas Day, 1992.

Daphne du Maurier (1907–89) was the daughter of the actor-manager George du Maurier and the granddaughter of the writer and cartoonist George du Maurier, author of *Trilby* (a background she drew upon for her 1949 novel *The Parasites*). She published her first novel, *The Loving Spirit*, in 1931. Her novels *Jamaica Inn* (1936) and *Rebecca* (1938) were filmed by Alfred Hitchcock, as was 'The Birds', a 1963 short story which draws on her experiences of the bombing raids over Britain in the Blitz. Other films based on Du Maurier's fiction include: *Frenchman's Creek* (1941), *Hungry Hill* (1943), *The Scapegoat* (1957), *My Cousin Rachel* (1951) and *Don't Look Now*, based on a 1971 short story. Du Maurier also wrote two original plays, an adaptation of *Rebecca* for the stage, and nine collections of short stories. She wrote biographies of Branwell Brontë, of her father and other members of her family, two volumes of autobiography and two studies of Cornwall, where much of her fiction is set and where she spent most of her life. Daphne du Maurier married Major (later Lieutenant-General) Frederick 'Boy' Browning in 1932, and they had three children. He was in charge of Operation Market Garden, which was judged a failure; he died in 1965. Du Maurier was an early member of Mebyon Kernow, a Cornish nationalist party. She was awarded the DBE in 1969.

Stella Gibbons (1902–89) went to North London Collegiate School and then trained as a journalist at University College, London, where she began writing poetry. She went on to work for the British United Press news agency while also writing poetry and articles. She worked at the *Evening Standard*, initially as a secretary and was later promoted to feature writer. She continued to write poetry, and in 1928 had a poem published in *The Criterion*, then edited by T. S. Eliot. From 1928 her work was regularly published in *The London Mercury*. Her first published volume of poetry, *The Mountain Beast* (1930), was well reviewed and was followed by another volume in 1934. Gibbons's first novel, *Cold Comfort Farm* (1932), a deft parody of the Hardyesque romances then fashionable, was hailed by Hugh Walpole as 'a minor classic', and, to her resentment, would define her as a writer thereafter. Gibbons saw herself primarily as a poet, publishing another volume of poetry *The Lowland Verses* in 1938. She published three novels over the course of the war, including *Ticky* (1942) which she said was her favourite of her novels. She published her *Collected Poems* in 1950 and became a Fellow of the Royal Society of Literature in the same year. By the time of her death she had written over twenty-five novels, three collections of short stories, four volumes of poetry and a children's book.

Anna Gmeyner (1902–91) was born in Vienna into a middle-class Jewish family. Her initial breakthrough came as a playwright. Having followed her first husband, a biologist, to Scotland, she witnessed a Fifeshire mining community during the General Strike of 1926, and dramatized the events as *Heer ohne Helden*, first performed on 27 October 1929 in Dresden. Gmeyner's involvement in left-wing cultural politics continued after her emigration via France to Britain in 1938. She read from her first exile novel *Manja* (1938) at the launch of the Free German League of Culture in London. *Manja* was first published in German in Amsterdam before being translated as *The Wall* (1939), under the pseudonym of Anna Reiner. The novel was subsequently republished in the UK by Persephone Books in 2003 as *Manja* by Anna Gmeyner. As Reiner, Gmeyner also worked on the screenplay for a Boulting Brothers film, *Pastor Hall* (1940), and published another novel, *Café du Dôme* (1941). This was originally written in German, but only ever published in the English translation by Trevor and Phyllis Blewitt for Hamish Hamilton. After the war, Gmeyner wrote novels in English, such as *A Jar Laden with Water* (1961) and *The Sovereign Adventure* (1970), under her married name Anna Morduch. She remained in Britain until her death aged eighty-eight. Gmeyner's daughter from her first marriage, Eva Ibbotson (1925–2010), also stayed in Britain and became a very successful author of children's fiction.

Henry Green (1905–73), born Henry Vincent Yorke, was an author who produced nine novels between 1926 and 1952. He was raised near Tewkesbury by an educated and wealthy aristocratic family. He attended Eton where he was a friend of Anthony Powell, and later studied at Magdalen College, Oxford, when he knew Evelyn Waugh. Green left without a degree and next worked among the production staff on the factory floor in the family works that produced beer-bottling machines and plumbing supplies. He later became its managing director. During the Second World War Green served in the Auxiliary Fire Service, experiences captured evocatively in his novel *Caught* (1943). He published the autobiographical *Pack My Bag* (1940), and four novels in the 1940s, including *Loving* (1945), *Back* (1946) and *Concluding* (1948). His fiction was admired by many fellow novelists, but a wider readership eluded him. W. H. Auden was quoted as saying that Henry Green was 'the best English novelist alive'. He insisted on anonymity, and for the last twenty years of his life Green was an alcoholic recluse.

Graham Greene (1904–91) was born the fourth of six children to a prominent family in Berkhamsted, Hertfordshire. He attended the boarding school of which his father was headmaster. Following several depressive episodes and attempted suicides, he was sent to live with a London psychoanalyst. Greene later attended Balliol College, Oxford, completing a degree in history. He converted to Catholicism after falling in love with Vivien Dayrell-Browning, a practicing Catholic. He and Vivien married and had two children: Lucy Caroline and Francis. Greene worked as a subeditor at *The Times*, a position he credited with helping him to develop an economy of style. After publishing a book of poetry and a first novel, *The Man Within* (1929), Greene pursued his writing career full time. He and his family often lived apart as Greene travelled widely and carried on long-lasting affairs, most notably with Catherine Walston. During the Second World War, Greene served as an air raid warden during the London Blitz and represented it in *The Ministry of Fear* (1943) and *The End of the Affair* (1951). Later he joined MI6 and was posted to Sierra Leone, the setting of *The Heart of the Matter* (1948). He categorized some of his spy novels and thrillers, from *Stamboul Train* (1932) to *Our Man in Havana* (1958), as 'entertainments.' Ethical dilemmas, Catholic doctrine and global politics feature in most of his twenty-six novels, including *Brighton Rock* (1938), *The Quiet American* (1955) and *The Honorary Consul* (1973). His writing is noted for its cinematic quality, and, with Carol Reed, he wrote the screenplays for *The Fallen Idol* (1948) and *The Third Man* (1949). Critically highly regarded, Greene was shortlisted in 1966 and 1967 for the Nobel Prize for Literature and was awarded the Order of Merit in 1986. He lived for many years in France near his companion, Yvonne Cloetta, and died aged eighty-six in Vevey, Switzerland.

Patrick Hamilton (1904–62) was born in Sussex. He had a disrupted education at several boarding schools until he was fifteen. He was first an actor, then a novelist. His plays *Rope* (1929) and *Gaslight* (1926) were both made into famous films, the former directed by Alfred Hitchcock in 1948, the latter by Thorold Dickinson in 1940. Nine other plays were staged with the last, posthumously, in 1965. He also published thirteen novels between

1925 and 1955. *Hangover Square* (1941), set in seedy late 1930s Earl's Court and Brighton, was filmed in Hollywood in 1945 but transposed to the Edwardian era. *The Slaves of Solitude* (1947) deals directly with the Second World War, set in a seedy boarding house in the suburbs, where various curious individuals avoid the worst of the Blitz. Hamilton's later novels, the Gorse trilogy, focus on a con-man and murderer based on 1940s crimes. On 23 September 1962 he died aged fifty-eight in Sheringham, Norfolk as a result of alcoholism.

James Hanley (1897–1985) was from Liverpool of Irish descent. He joined the merchant navy during the First World War, then joined the Canadian Expeditionary Force and fought in France, but after being gassed, he returned to sea. His first novel was *Drift* (1930), after which twenty-six further novels would be published, including *Boy* (1931) which was successfully prosecuted for obscenity in the UK in 1934. He lived largely in Wales from 1931 until 1963 but was living with his wife in a Chelsea flat from August 1940 to January 1941. His novel *No Directions* (1943) represents the Blitz in London using an avant-garde aesthetic, depicting the bleakness and exhilaration of these events, combining the terror, fear and sexual desire.

Norah Hoult (1898–1984) was born in Dublin. Her Catholic mother had eloped aged twenty-one with her Protestant father. She was nine when they died, and subsequently lived with relatives in England and was educated in boarding school. She became a journalist, and her first book of short stories, *Poor Women!*, appeared in 1928, followed by twenty-seven further books of fiction. She returned to Ireland from 1931 to 1937, moved to New York and returned to Bayswater, London in 1939, where her novel *There Were No Windows* is set. Hoult returned to Ireland in 1957.

Gerald Kersh (1912–68) was born in Teddington-On-Thames into a lower-middle-class London Jewish family and was educated at the Regent Street Polytechnic. In the 1930s Kersh developed an eccentric CV as journalist, cinema manager, wrestler, bouncer and club operator. His first novel *Jews without Jehovah* (1934) was suppressed because members of his family threatened to sue for libel, but he established himself as a novelist with *Night and the City* (1938). During the war he served initially in the Coldstream Guards, but was buried alive by a bomb during the Blitz while on his first leave. After these injuries he was transferred to the War Office, where he ended up writing commentaries for the Army Film Unit, scripts for BBC sketches and accounts of gallantry. He also wrote newspaper columns (initially published under the name Piers England) for *The People* which were read by millions. He published fifteen books of fiction in the 1940s alone, including the bestselling book in the UK during the conflict, *They Die with Their Boots Clean* (1941), drawing on material originally intended for a training manual. After the war he moved to the United States and eventually took up permanent residence in upstate New York. He earned his main income by writing for magazines, and continued to publish collections of short stories but found it difficult to get his novels into print, including *The Implacable Hunter* (1961). In the mid-1960s Kersh suffered from throat cancer and had to have his larynx removed. He was able to complete *The Angel and the Cuckoo* (1967) before cancer returned, but died in debt, largely forgotten in Britain.

Julian Maclaren-Ross (1912–64) was born James McLaren Ross in South Norwood, London, to a middle-class family with links to Cuba and India. Educated in France until the age of nineteen, he rejoined his family now living in Nice until 1933 when he returned to England with the intention of becoming a writer. He married briefly in 1936 but fell on hard times as his family's income dried up in 1938. Having been a vacuum-cleaner salesman on the South Coast (the basis for his 1947 novel *Of Love and Hunger*), he was called up into the army in 1940. His lightly fictionalized accounts of his army experiences found their way into literary magazines and anthologies and were collected as *The Stuff to Give the Troops* in 1944. Maclaren-Ross was, however, physically and mentally unsuited to army life, went absent without leave, experienced military detention and was medically discharged. Thereafter he became a dapper landmark in Soho pubs, living hand to mouth on advances from publishers, journalism, reviewing, literary spoofs, translations from French and script work for film and radio. He married again, and had a son, but it did not last. He is frequently mentioned in memoirs of the period and was fictionalized by both Olivia Manning and Anthony Powell. He died suddenly at the age of fifty-two a third of the way into his *Memoirs of the Forties*.

J.P.W. Mallalieu (1908–80) was born Joseph Percival William Mallalieu (known as William, but always signing his work J.P.W.) into a well-off manufacturing family with political interests. His father was the Liberal MP for Colne Valley between 1916 and 1922, and his brother Lance was a Liberal MP from 1931 to 1933, and from 1948 to 1974. J.P.W was educated at Cheltenham College and at Trinity College, Oxford (where he was elected President of the Union in 1930). Before joining the navy, Mallalieu was a Fleet Street journalist and wrote two books critical of the way in which the British government and big business were conducting the war: *Rats!* (Left Book Club, Gollancz, 1941, five editions) and *'Passed to you, Please': Britain's Red-Tape Machine at War* (Left Book Club, Gollancz, 1942, eight editions). He joined the Navy in 1942 and was commissioned lieutenant in 1943. Mallalieu was elected as Labour MP for Huddersfield in the 1945 elections, while still serving in the Navy (he had been selected as a Labour candidate for the constituency as far back as 1936). He held positions in a number of Labour administrations, including as Navy Minister in Harold Wilson's government (in office 1964 to 1967). He served as an MP until 1979, often speaking to naval issues. The press never forgot his authorship of *Very Ordinary Seaman*, a theme they constantly reworked, sometimes to praise, sometimes to criticize the Labour politician. His autobiography, *On Larkhill* (Allison & Busby, 1983), was published posthumously.

Nancy Mitford (1904–73) was the daughter of the aristocratic family of Lord Redesdale and the eldest of the Mitford sisters. She was largely schooled at home with brief spells at boarding schools; she described herself as 'uneducated', apart from learning to ride and to speak French. Her maternal grandfather was the proprietor and publisher of *Vanity Fair* and *The Lady*. After being presented at court as a debutante she contributed articles to society magazines, a regular column to *The Lady* and compiled two volumes of Victorian letters from members of her family. Encouraged by Evelyn Waugh, Mitford published her first novel in 1931. Alongside her then husband she was a relief worker in the Spanish Civil War in 1939 and during the Second World War volunteered as an army driver and did shifts at a First Aid post. The family's London house was requisitioned for Jewish families bombed out of the East End, and Mitford worked there for much of the war. *The Pursuit of Love* (1945) and its sequel *Love in a Cold Climate* (1949), which drew heavily on her childhood and wartime experiences, established Mitford as a best-selling writer. She had a long affair with a colonel in De Gaulle's Free French Army and moved to Paris in 1946. She lived in France for the rest of her life and wrote a series of biographies of European historical figures: *Madame de Pompadour* (1954), *Voltaire in Love* (1957), *The Sun King* (1966) and *Frederick the Great* (1970). Her final novel *Don't Tell Alfred* (1960) took Fanny, the narrator of *The Pursuit of Love*, to the British Ambassador's residence of Paris.

Nicholas Monsarrat (1910–79) came from a well-off background, and was educated at Winchester and Trinity College, Cambridge. He began work as a trainee solicitor, but soon turned to freelance writing (often writing restaurant reviews) to fund the writing of the four novels he published before the war: *Think of Tomorrow* (Hurst & Blackett, 1934), *At First Sight* (Hurst & Blackett, 1935), *The Whipping Boy* (Jarrold, 1937) and *This Is the Schoolroom* (Cassell, 1939). All four novels had leftist sympathies characteristic of many younger writers of the 1930s (as did his play *The Visitor*, performed as a Sunday evening production at the Aldwych in London in June 1936 and again featuring Greer Garson at Daly's Theatre the following month). None were originally commercial successes, but the latter two novels were reprinted by Pan in the 1960s. He volunteered for the navy in 1940, being directly commissioned as a sub-lieutenant into the Royal Naval Volunteer Reserve (RNVR) on the strength of his peace-time experience of yachting and some consequent navigational certificates. He was quickly promoted lieutenant and by the end of the war was a lieutenant-commander, having served on and been in command of corvettes and frigates. He later said that his service in the navy restored to him a sense of community and tradition which he had lost when he departed from the political beliefs of his upbringing. He left the navy in 1946 and joined the Diplomatic Service. He had some wartime and post-war success as a writer, publishing six books with a naval background during the 1940s, all with Cassell. In 1951, the same publisher brought out his first bestseller, *The Cruel Sea*, which had sold some eleven million copies in eighteen languages by the time of his death. It was also adapted into a popular and acclaimed film by Ealing Studios in 1953, starring Jack Hawkins, Donald Sinden, John Stratton, Denholm Elliot, Stanley Baker and Virginia McKenna. By the end of that decade, with several more books to his name, he left the Diplomatic Service to become a full-time writer. While *The Cruel Sea* was always his best-known book, he had a number of other successes, including *The Kapillan of Malta* in 1973, set during the Second World War. Monsarrat published two volumes of autobiography in 1966 and 1970.

When **Robert Neumann** (1887–1975) left his native Austria for the UK in 1934 he apparently spoke little English, but five of his earlier novels had already been translated from German into English and published by the small British publisher Peter Davies. *Die Macht* (1932) was translated by Dorothy Richardson as *Mammon* (1933). His novel *Struensee* was written in 1934 and published in German by the exile publishing house Querido in Amsterdam in 1935 but reached a wider audience in the English translation by Edwin and Willa Muir as *The Queen's Doctor* (1936). *By the Rivers of Babylon* (1939), which had ten individual stories of Jewish exile at the centre, was written in German, but first published in English. This book finally established Neumann's reputation in Britain: it received praise from H. G. Wells, good reviews in the press, and was the *Evening Standard's* Book of the Month for November 1939. Following internment as an enemy alien, Neumann switched to writing in English and published the novel *Scenes in Passing* (1942). *The Inquest* (1944), in which the main character has to investigate a story of emigration and exile, became his most successful English-language novel. In 1943 he was appointed editor of the Hutchinson International Authors series, which was very successful. Neumann eventually left Britain in 1958 to return to German-speaking regions of Europe, where he was a significant literary critic until his death.

George Orwell was the pen name of Eric Arthur Blair (1903–50). Born in Motihari, India, he grew up in Oxfordshire and studied at Eton before joining the Indian Imperial Police in Burma. In the 1930s, back in Britain, he published five novels, among them his harsh diagnosis of colonial reality, *Burmese Days* (1935), the social satire *Keep the Aspidistra Flying* (1936) and *Coming Up for Air* (1939), a suburban novel that gently puts to rest nostalgic illusions of a pristine, rural England. His 1930s non-fictional output includes *The Road to Wigan Pier* (1937), a key book on class relations in England, and *Homage to Catalonia* (1938), a memoir of his experiences of the Spanish Civil War and of his disillusionment with Soviet communism. During the Second World War, while he worked for the Empire Service of the BBC, he wrote some of his best-known essays, including *The Lion and the Unicorn* (1941), a text that had a crucial influence on twentieth-century revisions of myths of Englishness. His growing international reputation and, by now, unassailable canonical status are based primarily on his two works of fiction written in the 1940s: the satirical allegory *Animal Farm* (1945) and the dystopia *Nineteen Eighty-Four* (1949), a book that has made the adjective "Orwellian" a globally recognizable word.

Winifred Peck (1882–1962) was born in Headington, England; her father was Edmund Arbuthnott Knox, fourth Bishop of Manchester. She attended Wycombe Abbey School, and read Modern History at Lady Margaret Hall, Oxford. In 1911 she married James Peck, a British civil servant, and when he was knighted in 1938, she assumed the title, Lady Peck. In 1918 aged thirty-six she published her first novel, *Twelve Birthdays*, followed by twenty-four more, including *House-bound* (1942).

Jocelyn Playfair (1904–97) was born in Lucknow, British India, daughter of Lieutenant-Colonel Noel Malan. Her mother died when she was nine and she spent two years with a strict evangelical aunt. She married Ian Playfair in 1930, who was in the Royal Engineers and later appointed major-general. After the birth of their two sons, the couple returned to Britain in the late 1930s. She published ten novels, including *A House in the Country* (1944), set at the time of the fall of Tobruk in 1942, and written in 1943 at a low point of the war, when the outcome was still in doubt.

Mary Renault was the pen-name of Eileen Mary Challans, who was born in September 1905 in Forest Gate, London. Evacuated during the Great War only to fall foul of the 1918 flu pandemic shortly after her return, her formal education was somewhat disrupted until she was sent in 1920 to Clifton School for Girls in Bristol. She went on to study English at Oxford, and received a third-class degree from St Hugh's College in 1928, before taking on a series of poorly paid jobs to avoid returning home. In 1933 she began training as a nurse at the Radcliffe Infirmary in Oxford, where she met Julie Mullard, a fellow student-nurse with whom she would forge a lifelong relationship. The relative stability of the profession allowed Renault to combine nursing with writing, and *Purposes of Love* (1939) was just the first of three novels she saw published before the end of the war, despite enrolling in the Emergency Medical Service at its outbreak. She remained a nurse until 1945, treating Dunkirk evacuees in Bristol before returning to the Radcliffe Infirmary to work on its neurosurgery ward, experiences that later inspired *The Charioteer* (1953). When *Return to Night* (1947) won an MGM prize worth £150,000 in 1948, she and Mullard moved to South Africa, where they were able to live together in relative openness. Renault continued to write, but *The Charioteer* would be her last novel to feature a contemporary setting, bestseller *The Last of the Wine* (1956) marking her turn to the historical fiction for which she is now chiefly remembered: it was followed by the Theseus novels (1958–62) and the Alexander the Great trilogy (1969–81). She died in Cape Town in December 1983.

Jean Rhys (1894–1979) was born in the Caribbean island of Dominica and sent to England at the age of sixteen. She briefly attended the Royal Academy of Dramatic Art and had a series of erratic jobs as a model and chorus girl, she then went to Paris in the 1920s. Encouraged by Ford Madox Ford (who would later become her lover) she began writing and he wrote the introduction to her first published writings, a collection of short stories in 1927. Her first novel, *Quartet* (originally titled *Postures*), shaped by her relationship with Madox Ford, was published in 1928, although she had then already begun writing what would be become *Voyage in the Dark*, published in 1934. *Good Morning, Midnight* followed in 1939 but was reviewed as too depressing for the time. This reception led to Rhys withdrawing entirely and her work dropping out of print. She moved to Cornwall, and was rediscovered only when the actor and writer Selma Vaz Dias, in search of the rights to *Good Morning, Midnight*, tracked her down with the help of the writer Francis Wyndham. Rhys credited Vaz Dias with the revival of her writing career. The publication of *Wide Sargasso Sea* in 1966, a reworking of *Jane Eyre* from the point of view of the first Mrs Rochester, led to belated recognition, awards and a reassessment of her work, particularly from feminist and postcolonial critics. Her published work includes five novels and seven collections of short stories. Rhys's *Smile Please: An Unfinished Autobiography* was published posthumously in 1979.

Hilde Spiel (1911–90) was born and grew up in Austria and came from a Jewish background, although her parents had converted to Catholicism. She published one novel, *Kati auf der Brücke* (1933), and completed her doctorate in Vienna before joining her fiancé, the German journalist Peter de Mendessohn, in London in 1936. Until March 1938 she made her living by selling her writing in German to Austrian newspapers and magazines and placing short stories, written in German, then translated by de Mendessohn, in British newspapers. Her first novel published in the UK, *Flute and Drums* (1939), was similarly written in German and translated into English. Shortly thereafter, de Mendessohn and Spiel decided they needed to write directly in English in order to maintain their careers. Both were successful and became accepted within British literary and journalistic circles during the war, including those surrounding the *New Statesman*. However, although Spiel wrote her third novel *The Fruits of Prosperity* in English, it was never published in the UK and only eventually appeared in German as *Die Früchte des Wohlstands* in 1981. Spiel gave birth to a daughter, Christine, in 1939 and a son, Felix, in 1944; and eventually returned to Austria in 1963 and a successful career in journalism and translation.

Noel Streatfeild (1895–1986) was best known for children's fiction, producing twenty-seven novels. Most notable was *Ballet Shoes* (1936) a bestseller, particularly in the United States which by the time of her death had sold almost 10 million copies. She won the third annual Carnegie Medal for *Circus Shoes* (1938), another of the same series. Born in Sussex into a quasi-aristocratic family, her father was later the bishop of Lewes. During the First World War she undertook voluntary kitchen work at a hospital for wounded soldiers, and later as a munitions worker at Woolwich Arsenal. After studying at the Academy of Dramatic Art in 1919, she acted on the professional stage for a decade. Noel drew on these experiences in her work. During the Second World War her flat and most of her possessions were destroyed in a raid on 10 May 1941; she was active in voluntary work as an Air Raid Warden in Mayfair, and in a mobile canteen in Deptford. She produced sixteen novels for adults from 1931 to 1961. One of these, *Saplings* (1945), combines the perspective of various children with a far starker psychological realism, thereby conveying the grim realities of war on the Home Front in the early 1940s. *Ballet Shoes* was made into a six-episode television series by the BBC in 1975, and in 2004, *Saplings* was adapted for a ten-part radio series broadcast on BBC Radio 4.

Jan Struther (1901–53) was the pen name of Joyce Anstruther, a writer and journalist who wrote for *Punch*, *The Spectator* and *New Statesman* magazines. She was invited to write a series of columns for *The Times*, about an 'ordinary' woman's life; married with three children, she created 'Mrs Miniver' in 1937 based on her own experiences, and published a book based on the columns in 1939 which became a bestseller in Britain and America and led to an invitation to lecture in the States. *Mrs Miniver* was filmed by William Wyler in 1942 and won six Oscars, including best film. Although herself an agnostic, Struther contributed hymns to the 1931 edition of *Songs of Praise* and was responsible for the words to 'Lord of All Hopefulness'.

Anthony Thorne (1904–73) was a novelist before the war with two successful novels to his name, both published by Penguin: *Delay in the Sun*, 1935, and *Fruit in Season*, 1938. Both were kept in print by Penguin until the early 1950s. After the war, he published at least seven more novels with Heinemann. These included *So Long at the Fair* (1950), *The Man Who Fought the Monkey* (1951), *Young Man on a Dolphin* (1952) and *The Warm People* (1953). *So Long at the Fair* was made into a film by Sydney Box Productions for Gainsborough Films, directed by Terence Fisher and Anthony Darnborough and starring Jean Simmons and Dirk Bogarde, in 1950. Thorne wrote one further novel about the Royal Navy, also for Heinemann, called *The Baby and the Battleship* (1956). It was a comedy, but was set on the last British battleship, HMS *Vanguard*, which was commissioned in 1946, withdrawn from service in 1955 and scrapped in 1960. The story (as well as eventually reuniting a lost baby accidentally taken aboard the ship with his mother) involves a NATO exercise, the outcome of which suggests that capital ships are still needed in the age of the anti-ship missile. The novel was adapted into a film of the same title by director and producer Jay Lewis also in 1956, with an impressive cast including John Mills, Richard Attenborough and Lisa Gastoni, but *The Times* reviewer was not impressed (anon., 16 July 1956, 5). Thorne seems to have faded from the literary scene during the 1960s, and indeed seems not to have had an obituary in national newspapers.

Evelyn Waugh (1903–66) was born into a literary family: his father Arthur was the managing director of Chapman & Hall and his brother Alec (1898–1981), the author of *The Loom of Youth* (1917), a *succès de scandale* since it featured homosexuality in public schools. Evelyn was educated at Lancing College and Hertford College, Oxford, joining various influential social circles, but left without a degree. Whilst working as schoolmaster he started his first novel, the black comedy *Decline and Fall* (1928). A great success, the money earned allowed him to marry the Hon. Evelyn Gardner, one of the Bright Young Things he would satirize in *Vile Bodies* (1930), which darkens notably as it progresses, being written during the breakdown of his marriage and subsequent divorce. In the Second World War he served in the Royal Marines, in various theatres of operation but with little glory. *Put Out More Flags* (1942) focused on the so-called Phoney War in 1939 and its displacement by the cataclysmic events of 1940. The narrative describes a transition from peacetime boredom and frivolity to the solidarity and serious business of conflict. In 1944 Waugh broke a fibula in parachute training, took unpaid leave in Chagford and completed *Brideshead Revisited: The Sacred & Profane Memories of Captain Charles Ryder* (1945), which was published to great acclaim. His next novel, *The Loved One* (1948), satirizes the British expatriate community in Hollywood and the film industry. It concerns protagonist Dennis Barlow's new job at the Happier Hunting Ground pet cemetery and funeral service but briefly also features reflections on his military service. Waugh later produced a trilogy of novels drawing directly on his experiences of the Second World War: *Men at Arms* (1952), *Officers and Gentlemen* (1955) and *Unconditional Surrender* (1961); all three were revised and published as *The Sword of Honour* trilogy in 1965.

Denton Welch was born Maurice Denton Welch in Shanghai, in March 1915, the youngest of four boys. While he spent portions of his early childhood with his parents in China, in 1926 he was sent as a boarder to preparatory school in Sussex and then on to Repton School in Derbyshire, the death of his mother in Shanghai in 1927 effectively ending family life. After a miserable public-school career cut short when he ran away during his final year, he returned to China to visit his father, a trip that would later inspire his first largely autobiographical novel, *Maiden Voyage* (1943). In 1933 he enrolled at Goldsmiths College in London to study art, with a view to becoming a painter. Only two years into his course, aged just twenty, he was hit by a car while cycling from his digs in Greenwich to an aunt's in Surrey. The accident – later fictionalized in his unfinished novel *A Voice Through a Cloud* (1950) – resulted in temporary paralysis, a fractured spine and damaged kidneys leaving him catheterized, impotent and in near-constant pain for the remainder of his life. Yet it also marked a major turning-point in his artistic development, the process of recovery transforming him into a writer as he sought to rehearse and record the minutiae of his life before the tragedy: *Maiden Voyage* was followed by *In Youth Is Pleasure* (1944) and the short story collection *Brave and Cruel* (1949), which appeared only days after his death, aged thirty-three, from spinal tuberculosis. Indeed, much of Welch's output was posthumous, his partner Eric Oliver working with John Lehmann to publish several volumes including *A Voice Through a Cloud* and a second collection of shorter prose entitled *A Last Sheaf* (1951).

Virginia Woolf (1882–1941) was a well-established novelist with an international reputation at the outbreak of war on 1 September 1939. In May 1935, she had toured Nazi Germany for three days with her Jewish husband, Leonard, and the latter would later identify in *Downhill All the Way* (1967) 'the crude and savage silliness of the country at that time'. Having witnessed the Blitz both in London, where their Bloomsbury home was damaged badly, and near the coast in Rodmell outside Lewes, they retreated to Sussex. There she completed the manuscript of her last (posthumously published) novel, *Between the Acts* (1941), which focuses on a pageant in a small English village, just before the outbreak of the Second World War. Anticipating invasion Woolf drowned herself on 28 March 1941. It appears she feared the couple would be tortured and killed by the invaders, and they had in fact already been listed by the Nazis as undesirables.

Hermynia Zur Mühlen (1883–1951) was born a Countess in the Austrian aristocracy and was married for a short time to Baron Victor von Zur Mühlen. She was a member of the German communist party (KPD) from 1919 onwards, sometimes known as the 'Red Countess', and wrote articles for left-wing and communist newspapers. She wrote the novels *Der Tempel* (1922) and *Licht* (1922) and a collection of novellas entitled *Der Rote Heiland* (1924), as well as detective fiction which she published under the pseudonym

Lawrence H. Desberry. By the time she arrived in London in June 1939 after moving in exile around Europe, Zur Mühlen was not a well woman and had no financial resources. However, she was undoubtedly a well-known writer in the German-speaking world and brought her reputation with her as demonstrated by the fact that the BBC aired a tribute to Zur Mühlen in 1943, on the occasion of her sixtieth birthday. She wrote the historical family saga, *We Poor Shadows* (1943), and its sequel, *Came the Stranger* (1946), in German first before translating the texts, which were published by Frederick Muller in London as by 'Countess' Hermynia Zur Mühlen despite the fact she had long abandoned the title. She lived the remainder of her life in England.

Index

abortion 223, 234, 239
abuse of language 82, 167, 169–70
Achebe, Chinua 198–9
adultery 31, 66, 75, 77, 79, 84 n.13, 245
aerial bombardment *See* air warfare
affect 71, 143, 152, 157–9, 184, 226, 247
Africa 30–1, 191, 192–200, 203, 205–12, 214–18
    Africans 192, 198, 206–7, 209, 211, 212, 214, 218
    North 9, 22
    West 195, 209, 214–15, 218 n.3
Ahmed, Sarah 152, 156
air raids 28, 41, 63–4, 66–7, 73, 75, 79, 97
    after-effects 11, 12, 62, 65, 67, 78
    on Germany 2, 82
air-raid shelters 60, 61, 70
    tube stations used as 2, 65
air warfare 60, 65, 71, 82–3 *See also* Blitz, the
    development of 60, 83 n.1, 83 n.2
    fears of 39, 60, 82
    in Spain 39, 60
Alexander, Jeffrey C. 60, 62
Alexander, A.V., First Lord of the Admiralty 114, 135 n.7
allegory 175, 186 n.12
Allingham, Margery 93
    The Oaken Heart (1941) 60, 83 n.3
altruism 61, 296
AMC (Armed Merchant Cruiser, Royal Navy) 124, 128
America, United States of 8, 18, 26, 50, 61, 83 n.4, 91, 276, 288, 290, 316, 324
    imaginary 281, 283–4, 294
    migration to 27, 47, 218 n.1, 253, 254, 262, 319
American editions 21, 22, 26, 61, 259, 269, 280
    bestselling 277, 324
American entry into the war 48, 82, 310
    British influence on 62, 64, 83 n.4, 109, 156–7, 277
American cinema *See* Hollywood
American characters 50–1, 68–9, 81–2, 283, 292, 293, 296
American Forces Network 275
American Guild for German Cultural Freedom 262, 264
American influence on British culture 197, 275–6, 283–4
American journalists 25, 62, 277
American money 2, 292
American music 275
American print culture 27, 61, 275, 277
American racism 50–1
American reviewers 22, 26
American servicemen 50, 71, 275
American sexual life 227
American underworld 279, 294
Americanization 31, 281, 284, 290
Anand, Mulk Raj 49, 51
Anglo-Irish relations 43, 79, 147, 329
Angry Young Men 101, 166
angst 25, 26 *See also* existential anguish
animals 29–30, 96, 168–74, 183–5, 186 n.11, 187 n.20, 316
    in fables 30
anti-novelistic 30, 175, 177, 180, 181
anti-Semitism
    Austrian 258
    British 251
    German 51, 267
Arendt, Hannah 29, 164, 167
    banality of evil, the 29, 164
    Origins of Totalitarianism (1951) 167
archives 32 n.1, 135 n.5, 142, 156, 160 n.8, 160 n.11, 160 n.14
army 17, 19, 20, 22, 23–5, 63, 94, 121, 131, 139, 197, 293, 320, 321
    captured 2
    discipline 17
    German 285
    hierarchy 113
    Napoleonic 263

Index

Army Bureau of Current Affairs (ABCA) 113, 133
Army Education Corps 113, 135 n.3
Army Film Unit 24, 319
ARP (Air Raid Precautions) warden 71, 78, 81, 146, 195, 315, 318, 324
Arts Council, the 8, 106
Atlantic 51, 114
    U-Boat attacks in 51, 253
Atlee, Clement 126
    Deputy Prime Minister 126
    Prime Minister 307
atomic bomb, the 1, 2, 46-7, 171
Auden, W. H. 8-9, 11, 318
autonomous self / subject, the 175, 182, 186 n.14
Auschwitz 26 See concentration camps
austerity 11, 27, 47, 54 n.2, 100, 107, 203
Austria 31, 146, 249-65, 267, 269, 322, 324, 326
    annexation of/ *Anschluss* (1938) 264
Austro-Hungarian Empire 253, 267
autobiographical fiction 31, 49, 73, 99, 118, 228, 316, 326
autobiography 134, 191, 257, 317, 318, 320, 321, 324
Auxiliary Fire Service (AFS) 76, 318

Battle of Britain, the 42, 60, 107, 280, 305
BBC, the 19, 23, 71, 83, 116, 150-1, 259, 262, 275, 319
    Empire Service 49-50, 51, 322
    European Service 165
    Home Service 145
    Overseas Services for China and the Pacific 145
    remit to inform, educate and entertain 278
    television 324
    Third Programme 145
Beckett, Samuel 5, 52
bedside, hospital 239, 240, 246
Bellanca, Mary Ellen 66-7
Belsen 26, 311 See concentration camps
Benjamin, Walter 180, 186 n. 13
Berlin 40, 193, 268, 312-13
    bombing of 63
Berlin, Isaiah 29, 166-7
Beveridge, William 46, 111, 133
    Beveridge Report (1942) 19, 27, 46, 132

Bevin, Ernest, Minister of Labour 45, 126
Bildungsroman 176, 178
birth *See* childbirth
black Atlantic 49-51
black British 49, 260
blackmail 215, 295, 315
black market 46, 149, 287, 292
blackout, the 8, 50, 71, 72, 80-1
Blitz, the 2, 8, 11, 14, 18, 27, 41-3, 50-1, 53, 54, 59-83, 84, 107, 111, 128, 139, 143, 195, 280, 315, 316. 318, 319, 326
    Baedeker 65
    cultural impact of 43, 60
    mythology of 2, 3, 60-2, 129
    spirit 3, 62
    term 63
Bluemel, Kristin 14-15, 52
boarding house 45, 72, 81, 99, 245-6
boarding-school 229, 316, 320, 326
bodies 30, 228, 230-1, 234, 236
Bohemia (Czech Republic) 262, 265-6
Bohemian upper-class life 28-9, 80, 95-9, 101-3, 105-8
bombing of British cities *See* Blitz
bomb shelters *See* air-raid shelters
Bonaparte, Napoleon 263, 264, 266
Book Production War Economy Agreement 7
Bottome, Phyllis 27
    London Pride (1941) 59, 61
Boulting brothers, filmmakers 31, 269, 288, 317
boundaries 249
    bodily 231-2
    class 265-6
    crossing 95
    dissolved 42
    porous 38
    shifting 47, 51, 74
    transgressed 271
Bowen, Elizabeth 9, 10, 27, 29, 59, 82, 108 n.2, 112, 130, 135 n.6, 139-59, 315
    ARP Warden 78
    Bowen's Court (1942) 145
    'Britain in Autumn' (1940) 155
    'Calico Windows'(1944) 146
    'Careless Talk' (1941) 141, 149
    Collected Impressions (1950) 146
    Collected Stories (1980) 143, 145

critical re-evaluation 142, 143, 145–6
The Demon Lover and Other Stories (1945) 42–3, 143, 149
'The Demon Lover' 143
effect of war on individuals 43–5
'Eire' (1941) 147–8
Elizabeth Bowen Review 143
Elizabeth Bowen Society, 2017 143
English Novelists 145
'The Happy Autumn Fields' 143
The Heat of the Day (1948) 29, 59, 78–9, 144, 146, 149
'I Hear You Say So' (1945) 139–41
intelligence work 142, 146, 147, 151, 159
The Last September draft preface 79
'London, 1940' 146
Look at all those Roses (1941) 144
'Look at all those Roses' 143–4
Ministry of Information 42, 151, 153, 158
'Mysterious Kôr' 143
'Opening of the House' 146
'Panorama of the Novel'
radio work 145
Seven Winters 145
'The Short Story in England' (1945) 43
'Summer Night' 144
'Sunday Afternoon' 43–4
'Unwelcome Idea' (1940) 141, 147, 151
Bradbury, Malcolm 10, 166, 170, 213
Braithwaite, E. R. 48–9
Brazil 252–3
Brighton 22, 24, 294
Brighton Rock
film (1947) 31, 287, 288, 318
novel (1938) (*see* Greene, Graham)
play (1943) 288
British characters in foreign settings 210–11
British cinema 32, 275–9, 284–97
dominated by Hollywood 276
pantheon of wartime films 278
prestige 279, 291
British cities bombed 51
British Commonwealth 48, 219
British costume dramas *See* Gainsborough melodramas
British Council, The 146

British critics 9, 23, 27, 38, 49, 52, 53, 113, 142–6, 195, 223, 228, 260, 323
film 31–2, 277–9, 282, 285, 288, 289, 293, 296–7
British culture 31, 155, 249, 272
British Empire, the 1, 47, 48, 51, 117, 171
dissolution of 1, 51, 171
British Expeditionary Force 2
British film industry *See* British cinema
British Government 2, 82, 147, 196, 251, 277, 320
British history 40, 64
British identity 23, 27, 38, 47, 48, 53, 272
British immigration and refugee policy 251
British Library 7, 252, 164
British nationalism *See* patriotism
Britishness 23, 156
sense of sacrifice 39, 228
stiff-upper-lip / emotional restraint 71, 228
see also Englishness
British newspapers 6, 19, 132, 147, 193, 257, 277, 288, 324
British popular culture 112, 275–6
British propaganda 44, 277 *See also* Ministry of Information
British public 152–3, 155, 247, 253, 258
British publishers *See* publishing industry
British readers 93, 166, 256, 260, 269
British reviewers 23, 129, 131, 145, 297, 321, 322
British Union of Fascists 91
British War Aims 133
British xenophobia 251, 272
broadcasting 49, 83 n.6, 275 *See also* BBC
Brooke, Jocelyn 10, 30
The Military Orchid (1948) 228
A Mine of Serpents (1949) 228
The Scapegoat (1948) 228–31
Burma 9, 310, 312, 322
Burnett, W. R. 279, 286
Little Caesar (1929) 279

Calder, Angus 19, 20, 41, 60, 83 n.2, 83 n.5, 83 n.6, 111,140
The Myth of the Blitz (1991) 60, 62
The People's War: Britain 1939–1945 (1969) 20, 111, 140

care 44, 102–4, 153, 156, 191, 201, 241–3
'careless talk' campaign 29, 149–51, 153–4, 157–9
Carr, Craig L. 181, 186 n.14
Cartesian thought 175, 177
Caserio, Robert L. 44, 46
catastrophe 11, 47, 61, 71, 73, 75, 76
Catholicism 10, 195, 198, 256, 286, 318, 264, 319, 324
   symbolism 215
Cavalcanti, director 285, 288
   They Made me a Fugitive (1947) 288
   Went the Day Well? (1942) 285
Cederwell, William 61–3
censorship 9, 147, 150, 280
   film 279, 292
   postal 151
   self 13, 150
Chamberlain, Neville 1, 17, 21, 305
   Munich trip 1
Chapman, James 278, 282
Chase, James Hadley 31, 275, 279–84, 290, 291, 294, 297, 315
   Figure it out for Yourself (1950) 282
   The Flesh of the Orchid (1948) 283
   horror tropes 282–3
   Lay her Among the Lillies (1950) 283
   Make the Corpse Walk (1946) [as Raymond Marshall] 283
   Miss Callaghan Comes to Grief (1941) 282
   More Deadly than the Male (1946) [as Ambrose Grant] 283
   No Orchids for Miss Blandish (1939) 31, 279–82, 284
      film adaptation (1948) 290–1
   prosecution for obscenity 282
   racism 282
   rape culture 282
Chelsea 71–2
Cherniss, Joshua L. 166–7
childbirth 97, 234, 237, 238
   birth rate, UK 223
China 60, 83 n.1, 145
Christensen, Lis 141, 142
Churchill, Winston 1, 2, 4, 19, 45, 54, 64, 84, 129, 133, 135, 277
   'blood, toil, tears, and sweat' speech 1940, 59

coalition government, 1940, 64, 114, 126, 305
   faith in Empire 48
   Gestapo speech 1945, 46
   'iron curtain' speech 1946, 1, 307
   rhetoric 48, 277
   The Second World War (1948–53) 10
   victory speech 1945, 41
cinema *See* British cinema *and* Hollywood
'citizen sailors' 116, 132
civilian 27, 43, 44, 93, 107, 111, 115, 133, 243, 250
   as combatants 41–2, 65, 84 n.8, 285
   casualties 2, 39, 285
   morale 160 n.13
class 4, 19, 24, 28, 29, 30–1, 41, 44, 51–2, 62, 70, 73, 92, 94–5, 100, 111, 114–21, 123, 130, 133–4, 192, 193, 197, 200–1, 204, 205, 207–8, 210, 219 n.5, 231, 265–6, 270, 278–9, 284
   antagonism 17, 94, 151, 153, 173, 288
   conflict 81, 116, 122, 268
   cooperation 81, 124, 126
   crossing 31, 95, 265, 291
   lower 18, 82, 291, 294
   middle 15, 52, 82, 106, 122, 180, 268, 315, 320, 322
   perspectives 126, 128, 218
   and sex 231, 278–9, 284
   system 69, 81, 118, 123, 193, 279
   underclass 100, 197, 286, 294
   upper 19, 48, 76, 80, 127, 132, 192, 200, 204, 282, 291
   upper-middle 67, 68, 115, 118, 196, 316
   working 18, 20, 24, 25, 42, 52, 70, 82, 122, 124, 125, 128, 183, 194, 195, 197, 218, 231–2, 280, 291, 315
Cleft Chin murder 284, 290
climate of anxiety 39, 147, 151, 167
Clowes, St John Legh, director/ adapter 290
   No Orchids for Miss Blandish (1942) stage play 290
   No Orchids for Miss Blandish (1947) film 290–1
coalition government, wartime 1, 54 n.1, 114, 126, 277
Cold War, the 1, 5, 14, 18, 25, 28, 38, 46–7, 54, 166, 169, 297

colonial 51, 53, 184, 198, 205, 211, 214, 218
  hierarchy 210
  officials 192, 203, 208, 210, 211, 216
  society 212
  troops 2, 208
colonials 22, 48, 201
colonies 15, 30–1, 184, 194, 198, 203, 218
colonized populations 192, 201, 218
common sense, ideology of 108, 122, 130, 134, 167, 175
communism 127–8, 255, 261, 261
communists 21, 97, 126, 255, 270, 312
Communist Party, the 92, 97, 127, 261, 268, 322
  German 261, 268, 326
Commissioned Warrants, CWs 116, 123, 128
Commonwealth 41, 48, 219 n.7
Compton-Burnett, Ivy 10, 30, 193–4
  Manservant and Maidservant (1947) 30, 193–4
Comyns, Barbara 30, 227, 236–8
  Our Spoons Came from Woolworths (1950) 236–8
  Sisters by a River (1947) 237–8
concentration camps 2, 25, 164, 186 n.9, 270
Congress of Vienna (1814–1815) 263, 265, 266
Connor, Steven 174–5
Conrad, Joseph 31, 119, 195, 198–9, 208, 249
  Heart of Darkness (1906) 31, 199, 208–9, 217
  Typhoon (1902) 119
conscription 8, 68
  of colonial troops 208
conservatism 17, 104, 124
corpses 11, 70, 165, 205, 233, 277, 282, 283
cosmopolitan outlook 103, 257
Coventry (bombed) 11, 64, 65, 84 n.8, 277
crime 32, 283, 286, 319
  'does not pay' 282, 296
  fiction 27, 31, 118, 275, 279–84, 288, 294–7
  film 286–93
criminality 100, 284, 287
criminal justice 60, 83 n.3, 294–5

Crisp, Peter 63–65
Cull, Nicholas John 64, 83 n.4, 277
cultural trauma 28, 60–3, 78, 226, 228
Cunningham, Admiral Sir John (C-in-C Mediterranean Fleet) 113, 135 n.4
Curtis, James 294
  There Ain't No Justice (1937) 294
  They Drive by Night (1938) 294
Cvetkovich, Ann 225–7, 228, 231, 234, 237, 247
  'queer trauma' 226–7, 234, 237, 247
Czechoslovakia 21, 146, 262, 267

D-Day *See* Normandy landings
Dachau 270 *See also* concentration camps
Daily Mail 116, 129
Dassin, Jules, director 32, 296
  Night and the City (1950) 32, 295–6
declaration of war on Germany 5, 16, 91
democracy 9, 15, 46, 124, 128, 166–7
democratic 113–15, 122, 126, 127, 131–2, 257, 263, 267
democratization 4, 112, 227
desire 102, 131, 141, 165, 176, 182, 200, 240, 241, 247
  aggression 40
  for anonymity 116
  for comfort 241–2
  critical 143
  to dominate 41
  to laugh 98–9
  oblivion 15
  same-sex 223, 233, 234
  sexual 77, 78, 94, 210, 227, 241, 244, 246, 265, 280, 291, 319
  to travel 197, 199, 202
destruction 11, 60, 70, 73–4, 82, 102, 159 n.3
Dickens, Charles 74
  Dickensian 45, 82
Dickens, Monica 28, 30, 99–101, 107, 227, 239–40, 244, 316
  The Fancy (1943) 99
  Flowers on the Grass (1949) 28, 99–101, 239–40, 242
  One Pair of Hands (1939) 99
  One Pair of Feet (1942) 99
disability 66, 266

disgust 11, 27, 121, 164–5, 201, 210, 227, 229, 232, 238, 247
disorientation 80–1, 231, 286, 292
diversity / diverse voices 20, 50, 51, 53, 121, 130, 260
  sexual 225, 247
documentary
  evidence 247
  films 23, 25, 114
  idea 277
  semi- 133, 278
  wartime wedding with fiction 278
  writing 29, 40, 43–4, 93, 113, 133
  See also Mass Observation
Donnell, Alison 49, 54 n.3
Dove, Richard 251–3, 255–7, 259–61
drugs 218, 281
  cocaine 288
  drug trafficking 287
  reefers 283
Dublin 79, 147–8, 315, 319
du Maurier, Daphne 28, 59, 66–7, 102–4, 107, 108, 316–17
  'The Birds' 59, 66
  Frenchman's Creek (1941) 59, 67
  The Parasites (1949) 28, 102–4
Duncan, Paul xiv, 23, 25
Duncan, Isadora 102–3
Dunkirk 3, 20, 53, 63, 79, 309, 323
Dwan, David 163, 169, 185 n.1, 186 n.8
dystopia 66, 175, 187 n.19, 322

Ealing Studios 131, 284, 321
Easthope, Antony 174–6, 185 n.1, 186 n.15
economic 251, 267, 275–6
  autonomy 92, 107
  balance of trade crisis, 1947 289
  control 4, 42, 122, 264
  instability 1, 2, 5, 16, 296
  privilege 52, 180
Eden, Anthony 123, 126
Edgerton, David 111–12
egalitarianism 69, 130–1, 218
El Alamein 2, 306, 310
Eliot, T. S. 11, 19, 49, 312
  'The Love Song of Alfred Prufrock' 197
  The Waste Land 197
Ellis, John 278, 293, 296
Ellmann, Maud 142, 143
elsewhereness 271–2

Emergency Powers (Defence) Acts 3, 60, 193
emotion 96, 141, 144–5, 165, 185, 232, 237
emotional
  climax 245
  detachment 70, 101, 107, 213
  exposure 238–39
  impact 5, 28, 76, 96–7
  life 227–9, 233, 237, 244, 247
  maturity 246
  melodrama 278, 296
  restraint 71, 151, 154–5, 228–9, 278
Empire Windrush, the 49, 218, 308
English country house, the 16, 67–8, 115
Englishness 14, 29, 175, 228, 322
  post-imperial 15, 47, 166–7
  qualities of 13, 43, 167, 228
English language 82, 170–1, 177, 197, 206, 210, 249, 257–8
  English-speaking world 249, 254, 262
  Standard 121
  translation 252, 256–7, 259, 264, 269
equality 4, 29, 116, 122–3, 129, 169–70, 193–4, 265
espionage 78, 277
Esty, Jed 47–8, 52
euphemism 171, 228
Europe 1, 9, 12, 17, 30, 39, 64, 98, 166, 211, 253, 275
  current relationship with 272
  European views of Africa 199
  pan-European 103, 251, 253
evacuation 8, 17, 67, 70, 148, 305
  of Dunkirk 2–3
Evening Standard, The 259, 290, 317
everyday language 117, 171
everyday life 8, 9, 12, 39, 44, 76, 177–8, 226–8, 230, 239, 246, 247
everyday traumas 234, 236, 282
Exeter 65–6
exile literature 249–50, 260, 262–3, 270–2
existential anguish 26, 69, 149

family 25, 66, 91, 97, 145, 251, 259, 261, 268
  apocalypse 67
  aristocratic 95–7, 318, 324
  Bohemian 102–5
  butler 30, 194, 200
  experience 92, 102, 107
  intersubjectivity 103, 178

money 22, 115
sacrifice 102, 107
saga 262–6
shame 13, 80
survival 100
well-being 125
Faragher, Megan 78–9, 84 n.12
fascism 14, 39, 40–1, 82, 91–2, 129, 166, 169, 251–2, 281
fascist sympathisers 45, 51, 78, 91, 305
fascist tendencies in England 41, 152
Faulkner, William 281, 313
  Sanctuary (1932) 281
FBI, the 280, 282
feeling 3, 10, 29, 32, 42–3, 72–3, 140–59, 165–7, 201, 228–30
  archive of 225, 227, 247
  emotional (*see* emotional)
  of helplessness 65
  of guilt 70, 94, 207, 210
  national (*see* patriotism)
  romantic 100, 119
  of sacrifice 46
  sentimental 96, 128
femininity 94, 99
  conventional 105, 107
  hegemonic 226
  plural 225
  post-war 28, 99, 101, 108
  pre-war 93, 104, 106
Feuchtwanger, Lion 253–5
  Jud Süss (1925) 254
film noir 286–8, 296–7
First World War, the 9, 16, 40, 43, 97, 103, 108, 129, 251, 270, 319, 324
food 122, 153–6, 171, 198
  shortages 63–4, 149
Ford, Ford Madox 84 n.13, 323
Forester, C. S. 115, 130
  The Ship (1943) 115, 130
Forster, E. M. 39, 51, 213
Fowler, Roger 168, 170–1, 173
  '*collective* focalization' 171
  'perversion of language' 168
  'purified language' 170
Fox, Joanna 150–2, 160 n.8, 160 n.9, 160 n.10, 160 n.13
Foyle, Christina 93, 109 n.3, 124
France 22, 64, 218 n.1, 262, 316, 317, 318, 319, 320, 321

freedom 14, 48, 83 n.3, 93, 114, 133, 172, 202, 211, 237, 249, 264, 285, 290
  individual freedom 130, 167, 174–5, 264
  of speech 147
Free French 149, 321
French fleet at Oran 2
French government surrender, 1940 63, 285
French language 23, 121, 206, 255, 261
Freud, Sigmund 72, 75
  Freudian 101

Gainsborough melodramas 278–9, 287, 325
Gandhi, Mahatma 15, 312
gangster films 279, 282, 289–90, 292
gangster novels 31, 279–83
Gardiner, Juliet 60, 63
gender roles
  and class 4, 28, 94, 95, 270
  non-traditional 41, 105, 226, 244, 271
  and sexuality 30, 226, 235
  traditional 4, 226, 234, 250
General Elections UK 19, 126–7, 307, 308
genre 192, 226, 293
  crime (*see* crime fiction)
  film 31, 111, 279, 297
  historical novel 30, 66, 94, 191, 223, 256, 263, 265–7
  literature 27, 31, 52, 93–4, 118–19, 262, 297
  of the novel 175–7, 179–80
  parody 255
  western 101, 292
German characters 13, 17, 82
German collaboration/espionage 74, 193, 285
German language 31, 159, 250, 252–60, 262–4, 269–70, 272 n.1
Germans 16, 17, 67, 164–5, 218 n.1, 253, 267, 285
Germany 1, 14, 29, 63, 66, 146, 164, 241, 249, 261, 262, 264, 270, 316, 326
  bombing of Britain (*see* Blitz, the)
  declaration of war on (*see under* declaration)
  mass bombings, German cities 2
  pre-war 39–40, 316
  refugees from 249–72
  science 83

German and Austrian ex-patriate writers 31, 249–72
Gibbons, Stella 28, 94, 109 n.5, 317
  Cold Comfort Farm (1932) 109 n.5, 317
  Ticky (1943) 28, 94
Gildersleeve, Jessica 79, 143
global powers 47, 166
Gmeyner, Anna (aka Anna Reiner) 31, 250, 261, 268–71
  Automatenbüfett, third play, (1932) 268
  birth and background 268, 317
  Café du Dôme (1941) [as Anna Reiner] 267, 269–71
  in Fifeshire, 1926 268
  and Georg Wilhelm Pabst 268
  Heer ohne Helden, first play (1929) 268
  A Jar Laden With Water (1961) [as Anna Morduch] 269
  in London, 1935 269
  Manja (1938) [as Anna Reiner] 269
  marriage to Jascha Morduch 268–9
  Pastor Hall (1940), film co-writer [as Anna Reiner] 269
  The Sovereign Adventure (1970) [as Anna Morduch] 269
Goldner, Charles 288, 290
Göring, Hermann 63, 84 n.7
Gorra, Michael 75–6
GPO Film Unit 62
Granger, Stewart 278, 287
Great War, the 9, 276 See also First World War
Greene, Graham 10, 27, 30–1, 59, 112, 166, 191–218
  air-raid warden, London blitz 195, 318
  'The Basement Room' (1936) 30, 200–7
  Brighton Rock (1938) 283, 287, 288
  A Burnt-Out Case (1960) 191
  Catholicism 10, 195, 215, 286, 318
  defence of Wodehouse 193
  The End of the Affair (1951) 75–6
  The Fallen Idol (1948) screenplay 30, 193, 200–7
  film adaptations of works by 30, 193, 219 n.7, 284, 286–7, 288
  The Green Cockatoo (1937) screenplay 284
  A Gun for Sale (1936) 282

  The Heart of the Matter (1948) 31, 193, 195, 207–18
    1953 film adaptation 219 n.7
    Orwell review 214
    home bombed 75
    intelligence work MI6 195, 198, 207, 214, 318
  Journey without Maps (1936) 31, 195–5, 196–7, 199, 200, 203
    in Lagos for training 1941 207
  'The Lieutenant Died Last' (1940) 284–5
  The Man Within (1929) 191, 286
  The Ministry of Fear (1943) 59, 73–4
  The Quiet American (1955) 219 n.6
    in Sierra Leone 1941–3 73, 194–5
  Stamboul Train (1931) 284
  The Third Man (1949) 31, 287, 292–3, 296, 308
    novella 292
    screenplay 292
  Twenty-one Days (1937) screenplay 284
  Ways of Escape (1980) 191, 208
Green, Henry 10, 27, 30, 59, 74, 76–7, 112, 226–7, 243–5
  Back (1946) 226, 243–5
  Caught (1943) 59, 62, 74, 76–7
grief 5, 15, 225, 228–30, 233, 241, 244, 247
Gruesser, John Cullen 198, 216

Hallam, Michael Neil 71–3
hallucinatory effects 73, 77
Hamilton, Patrick 27, 45, 59, 294, 318–19
  Hangover Square (1941) 294
  The Slaves of Solitude (1947) 45, 59, 81–2
Hanley, James 27, 59, 71–2, 84 n.14, 319
  No Directions (1943) 71–3
Hartley, Jenny 66, 70, 71
Hartley, L. P. 129–31
Hartnell, William 287, 288
haunted 11–13, 59, 68, 71, 74, 76–7
hauntedness 79
Hayek, Friedrich 30, 167
Hepburn, Allan 139–40, 142, 144–6, 149, 155–7, 159 n.5
heroes 12, 14, 19, 68, 72, 77, 128–9, 178, 281
  anti- 77, 282, 286

heroines 94, 97, 101, 105–8, 224, 228, 234–5, 283
Hewison, Robert 6–8, 19
High-modernist 51–3, 249
Hillary, Richard 9
Hilton, James 276, 277
   Goodbye Mr Chips (1934) 266, 277
   Lost Horizon (193) 277
   Random Harvest (194) 277
Hiroshima 2, 82, 312
His Majesty's Stationary Office (HMSO) 6, 20
historical fiction 30, 66, 94, 191, 223, 256, 263, 265–7
Hitler, Adolf 1, 2, 51, 63, 256, 261, 267
   admirers of 11, 18, 45, 82, 91–2, 97
   'Hitlerism' 41
   'millennial rhetoric' 42
Holland, Steve 7, 279–80, 282
Hollywood 31, 319, 325
   adaptations of British novels 277, 286, 288
   boycott of UK 289
   co-productions 276
   dominance 31–2, 276
   film stars 32, 292–3
   Hays Code/Production Code 290, 295
   hostility to 289–91
   influence 276, 287
   interest in British narratives 276–7
   Ten 286, 312
Holman, Valerie 93, 114
Home Front, the 2, 9, 16, 32 n.1, 41, 42, 46, 59, 63, 65–6, 147, 149, 151–3, 157, 206, 278, 324
Home Guard 59, 285, 306
homosexuality 17, 225, 228, 234, 325
   latent 228
hoogland, renée c. 142–4
Horizon (journal) 8, 22, 23, 63, 185 n.4
hospitals 101, 146, 213, 218 n.1, 223–4, 235–6, 238–40, 242–3, 324
Hoult, Norah 27, 59, 79–81, 319
   There Were No Windows (1944) 59, 79–81
housing crisis 8, 45
House of Commons 48, 83 n.3, 289
House Un-American Activities Committee (HUAC) 32, 296

Howard, Trevor 287, 293
Hungary 146, 262
humanism 166–7, 175, 182, 184, 297

ideology 52, 166, 175, 177, 180, 236, 271
   Nazi 39, 51, 267
illness 99, 230, 237, 242
   and eros 240–4
In Which We Serve (1942) 130, 277, 278
incest 77, 104
India 15, 23, 51, 171, 230, 307, 310, 312, 316, 320, 322
   independence 1947 1, 51, 218
   Partition 15, 312
Imperial Britain 5, 12, 30–1, 47–9, 64, 83 n.4, 322
Ingelbein, Raphaël 11, 13
injury 22, 76, 118, 156, 244
intermodernism 27, 52
   See also Bluemel, Kristin
intimacy 30, 50–1, 117, 178, 223–47, 271, 315
   intimate life 225–7
invasion, threat of 17, 60, 64, 66, 148, 253, 285
Ireland 17, 43, 48, 146–8, 156, 159 n.6, 319
   neutrality 17, 43, 84 n.12, 147, 148
Isherwood, Christopher 8–9, 17, 27, 39–40, 47, 118, 229
   Goodbye to Berlin (1939) 39–40
   Lions and Shadows (1938) 118
   The Memorial (1932) 229
Italy 2, 51, 262, 305, 309–12
   Allied invasion of 2, 311

Jamaica 48–50
Japan 171, 306, 309, 310
Japanese 2, 82, 83 n.1, 286, 310, 312
Jennings, W. Ivor 60, 83 n.3
Joannou, Maroula 40, 42, 234
Johnson, B. S. 70
Jones, Griffith 288, 289
Jordan, Heather Bryant 142, 159 n.4
journalism 19, 29, 62, 146–7, 165, 166, 250, 256–9, 277, 279, 294, 316, 317, 319, 320, 324
Joyce, James 5, 51, 249
   death of 5

Kalliney, Peter 49, 51–2
Kennedy, Alan 174, 186 n.15
Kensington 81, 84 n.13
Kersh, Gerald 19–27, 275, 293–7, 319
  The Angel and the Cuckoo (1966) 27
  Brain and Ten Fingers (1943) 21
  Clean, Bright and Slightly Oiled (1946) 20, 21, 24–5
  'Clock Without Hands' (1949) 294–5
  Coldstream Guards 19, 22, 319
  The Dead Look On (1943) 21
  Faces in a Dusty Picture (1944) 21–2
  Fowlers End (1957) 27
  German Concentration Camps Factual Survey 25
  I Got References (1939) 7
  Jews without Jehovah (1934) 294
  Men are so Ardent (1935) 294
  Night and The City (1938) 26, 293, 295–6
  The Nine Lives of Bill Nelson (1942) 20–1
  Prelude to a Certain Midnight (1947) 25
  Private Life of a Private (1941) 19–20
  reputation 27, 297
  'Sad Road to the Sea' (1947) 294
  Selected Stories (1943) 23
  Song of the Flea (1948) 26
  They Die with Their Boots Clean (1941) 20
  The Thousand Deaths of Mr Small (1951) 26
  The Weak and the Strong (1943) 294
Kindertransport child refugees 251
King, Francis 30, 227–9
  Never Again (1947) 228–9
Kitchen Front Broadcasts, the 153–4, 156, 160 n.8
Klein, Stefan Isidor, Hungarian translator 261–2
Kynaston, David 41, 46, 47, 54
Kyte, Jacqueline 70–1

La Bern, Arthur 288–9
Labica, Thierry 81–2, 84 n.14
Labour government 1, 4, 5, 8, 19, 108, 123, 135
Labour Party
  coalition government roles 126
  electoral defeat 1951 5
  electoral victory 1945 4, 46, 108, 133, 307
Laing, Stuart 93, 108 n.2
Lamming, George 49–50
language 22, 30, 45, 72, 82, 119, 127, 129, 131, 143, 151, 152, 155, 165, 167, 168–73, 175, 181, 183, 186 n.9, 210, 212, 213, 278, 281
Larkin, Philip 11–14
  A Girl in Winter (1947) 11–13
  'New Year Poem' 11
  'On Being Twenty-six' 13
  pro-Nazi father
Lassner, Phyllis 142–4
late Modernism 27, 38, 52–3, 55 n.5
Laughton, Charles 276, 279
Lawrence, D. H. 144, 291
  Lady Chatterley's Lover (1928) 291
Laws, Sophie 235–6
Lea, Daniel 168, 186 n.5
Leavisite literary studies 10, 278
Lehmann, John 49, 326
Lejeune, C. A. 276, 285, 289, 291
Lethbridge, Lucy 68–9
Lewis, Alun 9, 22, 24
Lewis, Wyndham 46
Leys, Ruth 60, 72, 75
liberal humanism 166, 175
Liberal Party 163, 320
Liberia 194, 196, 198–200
Light, Alison 94, 104, 107–8, 124
listening 16, 18, 68, 71, 83 n.3, 123, 129, 139–40, 148, 155, 275
literary magazines 8, 23, 50, 55 n.4, 63, 320
Little Kinsey *See under* Mass Observation
Liverpool 65, 196–7
Lodge, David 82, 200, 218 n.4
lodgers 16, 45, 74, 100, 240–2, 294
London 27, 28, 45, 49, 51, 91, 97, 102, 103, 106, 121, 139, 146, 149, 163, 192, 195, 200, 201, 203–6, 209, 252–3, 257–8, 259, 263, 269, 305–8
  Blitz 7, 14, 50, 60, 62–5, 67, 68, 70–1, 74, 76, 78, 81–2, 83 n.2, 84 n. 9, 149, 195
  born in 22, 316, 319, 320, 323
  capital of free Europe 272
  destination 43–4, 49, 251, 255, 261, 262, 269

medieval churches 179
people of 42, 164, 204
second fire of 61, 83 n.4
seedy underworld 26, 100, 196, 279, 283, 292–6
love 14, 17, 30, 31, 67, 69, 75, 78, 121, 131, 142, 193, 195, 200, 205, 209, 210, 212, 215, 216, 218, 223–7, 229, 235–7, 242–6, 290, 318
lower decks 114, 131
Luftwaffe, the 63, 66, 83–4 n.7, 306

MacKay, Marina 37, 52, 53, 54, 55 n.6, 62, 64
Mackay, Robert 2, 4, 83 n.1
MacInnes, Colin 53–4
　Absolute Beginners (1959) 53–4
MacInnes, Helen 277, 288
　Above Suspicion (1941) 277
　Assignment in Brittany (1942) 277
MacKenzie, S. P. 112–13, 127, 133
McLaine, Ian 112, 135 n.2
McLaren Ross, James *See* Maclaren-Ross, Julian
Maclaren-Ross, Julian 22–6, 278, 281, 295, 320
　Anglo-Indian ancestry 23
　Better Than a Kick in the Pants (1945) 22
　'Bit of a Smash in Madras' 22
　Bitten by the Tarantula (1946) 22
　class boundaries 24
　as critic 278, 281, 295
　financial difficulties 23, 24
　'I Had to Go Sick' 22
　The Nine Men of Soho (1946) 22
　Of Love and Hunger (1947) 22–3
　The Stuff to Give the Troops (1944) 22, 24
　'The Tape' 24
magazines 6, 27, 257, 262, 319, 321, 324
　See also literary magazines
Maidanek 26 *See* concentration camps
Mais, Roger 27, 48–50
　'Blackout' 50
　'Now We Know' 48
Mallalieu, J. P. W. 29, 115–16, 121, 122–3, 128, 131, 133–4, 320
　autobiography *On Larkhill* (1983) 134, 320

Very Ordinary Seaman (1944) 115–16, 121, 122–3, 130
　abridged broadcast on BBC (1944) 116
　postscript to 128–9
Mann, Thomas 180, 251, 253
Mansfield, Katherine 13, 249
Marcus, Jane 259–50, 271
marriage 20, 31, 91–2, 97, 100, 102–3, 106, 206, 207, 213, 214, 223, 236, 237, 241–2, 244–5, 251, 252, 261, 266, 267, 317, 325
Marson, Una 49
　Calling the West Indies 49
　Caribbean Voices, literary programme 49
　first black woman at BBC 49
masculinities 94–5, 225, 226–8, 232–3
Mass-Observation 27, 44–5, 47, 84 n.14, 151
　'an anthropology of ourselves'
　diarists 64, 65
　founding 1937 44
　'Little Kinsey' (1949) 30, 227, 238, 247
master–servant relationship 30, 191–5, 198–9, 201–2, 205, 211–18
Maugham, Robin 30, 194, 218 n.2
　The Servant (1948) 30, 194, 218 n.2
　film adaptation 1963 194, 218 n.2
medical 12, 154, 224, 242, 323
　eros 228, 240, 243, 245
　logos 239, 240, 243
　romance 223, 234–6
Mediterranean 113, 114, 310
memory 12, 18, 41, 72, 77, 80, 106, 170, 178–9, 181, 183, 186 n.16, 187 n.18, 191, 200, 205, 212–13, 233, 286
Mendelssohn, Peter de 256–7, 260, 324
Mengham, Rod 7–9, 60, 73, 76
menstruation 234–5
Merchant Navy 121, 124, 126, 319
Metro-Goldwyn-Mayer (MGM) 276, 323
Michael Joseph, publisher 7, 115
mid-century British fiction 27, 37–8, 44, 47, 49, 52–3, 55 n.5, 144, 227, 228, 315
　imaginary 78
middlebrow 52, 105
migration, 1940s 5, 38, 48, 49, 50, 51, 55 n.4, 250, 251, 252
　emigration 252, 253, 259, 263, 268, 317, 322
migrant workers 192

military
  campaign 2, 82, 224
  service 16, 66, 69, 127, 192, 208, 325
Ministry of Food 154–5
  Food Control Committee 153
  Public Relations 154
  'Kitchen Front' daily broadcasts 153–4, 156
Ministry of Health report 60
Ministry of Home Security 65
Ministry of Information (MoI) 6, 17, 19, 42, 61, 65, 84 n.5, 92, 108, 111, 112, 114, 130, 142, 146–7, 149, 150, 152, 277, 284–5, 315
  archive 29, 156
  Home Intelligence Division 150
  Home Morale Emergency Committee 154
  Policy Committee 151
  Regional Information Officers 150
Ministry of Labour 68
Mise-en-abyme 179–80
Mitford, Deborah 91–2, 107
Mitford, Jessica 91, 97, 107
Mitford, Nancy 10, 28, 30, 95, 102, 107–8, 109 n.6, 226, 236, 320–1
  The Pursuit of Love (1945) 28, 95–7, 107, 226, 236–8
Mitford, Unity 91–2
Modernism 5, 11, 27, 37–8, 52–3, 71, 124
Monsarrat, Nicholas 29, 112, 131–3, 321
  Corvette Command (1944) 115, 132
  The Cruel Sea (1951) 29, 112, 131
  The Cruel Sea (film) (1953) 131
  East Coast Corvette (1943) 115
  H.M. Corvette (1943) 115
  Three Corvettes (1945) 115
  Naval career 321
morale 29, 63, 72, 83 n.2, 111–12, 126, 150–3, 155, 160
morality 163, 170, 176, 199, 279, 287, 295
  ambiguity 39, 95, 282
  black and white 107, 167
  imperative 245
  justice 156
  Kantian 175
  outrage 157
  panic 283
Moretti, Franco 176–7
Morris, David 239–44

Mosley, Oswald 91–2, 305
motherhood 96, 225, 234, 270–1
Muir, Edwin, translator 255–6, 322
Muir, Willa, translator 255–6, 257, 322
Munton, Alan 72–3, 76, 82, 112, 131
Murat, Jean-Christophe 71–2
Murphy, Robert 287, 288, 289, 292, 294
Murrow, Edward R. 62, 83 n.5, 83 n.6
Murrow, Janet 83 n.5
mythology 2, 3, 178, 180, 251, 322
  of the Blitz 2, 3, 27, 60–2, 79
  of Dunkirk 2, 3
  of the People's War 41

Nagasaki 82, 312
narcissism 180–2
National Archives 32 n.1, 160 n.8
National expenditure on books 7, 63
National Government, cross-party 3, 127
National Health Service, the (NHS) 101, 107, 308
National Socialism 249–52, 254, 256–7, 259, 261–3, 267–8
national unity 42, 48, 152, 226, 228
nature 140–1, 172, 174, 183, 225
naval films 114, 130, 133
  novels 29, 111–35
Navy *See* Royal Navy
Nazi bombs 64
  genocide 164
  Germany 262, 305, 326
  ideology 51
  massacre 21
  persecution (*see* National Socialism)
  prisoner 164–5
  sympathizer(s) 11, 17, 82, 91–2
  takeover of Britain 54, 84 n.8
Nazis 15, 39–40, 129
Neumann, Robert 31, 250, 255–60, 262–3, 322
  advised by Zweig 256
  By the Rivers of Babylon (1939) 259
  Children of Vienna (1946) 260
  The Inquest (1944) 259
  interned May 1940 as enemy alien 259
  Die Macht (1932) 255
    Mammon (1933), abridged translation 255
  Scenes in Passing (1942) 259–60
  settled in UK 1934 255

Struensee (1934) 255
The Queen's Doctor (1936), translation 255–6
A Woman Screamed (1938) 259
newspapers 6, 19, 132, 193, 257, 261, 277
New Statesman, The 160 n.7, 258–60, 324
neutrality
  Irish 84 n.12, 147–8, 293, 315
  US 277
1930s 5, 6, 8, 14, 15, 19, 22, 26, 31, 38–40, 52, 60, 97, 108, 132, 141, 166, 192, 194, 214, 223–4, 228, 249, 251–2, 255–6, 263, 267, 272, 276, 282, 284, 292, 294, 315, 319, 321, 322, 323
1920s 97–8, 141, 161, 323
  Roaring Thirties 95
Normandy 9, 25
Normandy landings, the 2, 311
normativity 223, 225, 227, 235, 237, 239, 244, 247
North Africa 9, 22, 309–11
nostalgia 3, 10, 17, 19, 28, 39, 53, 103, 105–6

officer 20, 122, 126, 131–2
  background 115
  billeting 17
  class 24, 27, 119–20, 132
  colonial 211
  commanding 115
  education 113, 133
  information 150
  junior 113, 133
  ranking 24
  senior 113
  SS 164
  training 24, 114, 121, 126, 128
Oliver, Reggie 94–5
omniscient narration 45, 76, 265
orgasm 232, 280
Orwell, George 1, 10, 27, 29–30, 37–8, 46, 49, 163–87, 193, 214, 297, 322
  Animal Farm (1945) 163, 168–74
  Animalism 29, 170
  'As I Please' (1944) 46
  Coming Up for Air (1939) 39
  'Decline of English Murder' 284, 290
  'The English People' (1947) 185 n.3
  Englishness 29, 166–7, 175, 322
  'Four legs good, two legs bad' 30

Homage to Catalonia (1938) 166
'The Lion and the Unicorn' (1941) 291
'Literature and Totalitarianism' 175
meta-novel 175, 181
'Marrakech' 184
Nineteen Eighty-Four (1948) 1, 163, 171, 174–85
obituary 166
personal politics 163
'Politics and the English Language' 167, 170
'Raffles and Miss Blandish' (1944) 31, 280–2, 284
'Revenge Is Sour' 163–5
rise in status 163, 297
'You and the Atom Bomb' 46
Oxford 11–13, 197, 318, 320, 323, 325

Paris 25, 97–8, 199, 237, 253, 261, 268, 323
  Bohemian haunts 98
  cafés 99
  the Dôme 269–70
  liberation of 2, 25
  Peace Conference, 1946 146
Parliament 48, 113
Party politics 3, 124
patriotism 4, 14, 47, 94, 114, 124, 151–2, 156, 289
  false 48
  unpatriotic 192
Pearl Harbour, attack 2, 82, 310
Peck, Winifred 27, 59, 322
  Housebound (1942) 59, 68–9
Penguin New Writing 8, 63, 278
People, The 23, 25
people's war 29, 41–2, 111–12, 114, 121, 124, 129–31, 133–4, 150, 278
periodicals 6, 8, 19, 23
personal and collective 43, 45, 142, 151–2, 177
personal identity 43, 54, 156, 254
Petley, Julian 279, 292
Phillips, Lawrence 75, 79, 179, 185
Phoney War 8, 39, 70, 76, 94, 325
Piette, Adam 11–13, 39, 41, 159 n.4, 226
Plain, Gill 5, 14, 38, 78, 84 n.9, 92, 159 n.4, 228
  Literature of the 1940s (2013) 5, 38, 228

'long' 1940s 5
Women's Fiction of the Second World War (1996) 14, 78
Playfair, Jocelyn 27, 59, 67–8, 322–3
  A House in the Country (1944) 59, 67–8
Poland 23, 218 n.1, 305, 309, 312
  Poles in London 149
political
  activism 271
  analysis 37, 39
  change 32, 52, 114, 252, 265
  context 97, 250
  crisis 92
  critique 15, 142
  discussion 121, 123–6
  guilt 54
  ideals 163, 167
  left 268–70
  rhetoric 168, 170–3
  suppression 28, 197–8
  tensions 91
  utopianism 129
  violence 40
politics 77, 183, 194, 196, 318, 320, 321
  of cold war (*see* Cold War)
  of colonization 214, 219
  of consensus 3
  European 9
  of feeling 96, 140, 142, 145, 155–7, 159
  practices 30
'pongos', Navy slang for soldiers 124–5
popular 3, 4, 27, 132, 163, 215, 254, 315, 321
  culture 276, 297
  fiction 52, 93, 105, 112–16, 133–4, 256, 260–2, 279–80, 282, 291, 293, 295
  success 20
  taste 284
  touch 23
postcolonial 15, 38, 53, 193, 323
postmodernism 5, 53
  post-modernist sensibility 144
post-war 5, 15, 18, 28, 29, 38, 46, 66, 105, 111, 114, 132, 146, 194, 218, 226, 239–40, 245, 251, 267, 269, 272, 287, 296, 315
  angst 25, 27, 47, 125
  aspirations 112, 129, 133
  femininity 94, 101, 108

fiction 49, 55 n.6, 109 n.8, 112, 131, 294, 275
  rationing 287
  reconstruction 31, 38, 97, 105–6, 113, 116, 124, 135 n.3, 267
  state of the nation novel 28, 99
post-war Britain 5, 38, 46, 107, 125, 129, 134
  rationing and austerity 29, 47, 103, 287
Pound, Ezra 5, 51
Powell, Anthony 10, 112, 318, 320
pregnancy 22, 237, 239
  possible 280
pre-war 7, 12, 13, 17, 19, 25–6, 39, 46, 60, 83, 93–5, 97, 100, 101, 105–6, 122, 125, 131, 288, 289, 294
Pritchett, V. S. 166, 315
Priestley, J. B. 3–4
  'Postscript' broadcasts 3–4
Prime Minister 1, 4, 61, 112, 126, 305
prisoners of war (POWs) 240, 243
  POW camps Germany 164–5
private life 39–41, 45, 52, 119, 150
  made public 65, 74, 142, 176–7, 234, 247
Production Code *See under* Hollywood
proletariat 261, 293
propaganda 1, 3, 27, 62, 65, 71, 123–4, 152, 156, 165, 180, 234, 263
  British 44–6, 277
  campaign 3, 149–51
  films 111, 277
psychoanalysis 39, 145, 186 n.15, 236, 318
public libraries 93
publishing industry 6–7, 14, 15, 23, 26, 93, 254, 255, 258, 269, 275, 315, 320, 322
purpose 71, 73, 124, 155, 158
  common 2, 10, 38, 226
  of education 19
  of love 223–7, 239, 241, 246
  lack of 15
  of the war 4, 112, 263

queer adolescence, narratives of 143, 228
  cultures 224, 225, 228, 234, 241
  theory 227
  trauma 226–7, 243, 247
queered 225, 227, 240
Quennell, Peter 116, 129–30
quota system 276, 289
  quota-quickie 276

radio 4, 16, 52, 66, 69, 139–40, 193, 277, 292 *See also* BBC
   news 15, 16–18, 62, 139, 277
   writing for 21, 22, 23, 46, 71, 262, 275–6, 320, 324
RAF (Royal Air Force) 9, 20, 39, 65, 84 n.7, 113, 114, 315
rationing 23, 29, 80, 93, 107, 279, 287
   end of, 1954, 47
   of food 100, 103, 149, 153–4, 305
   of fuel 47
   of paper 6–7, 23, 93, 279
   See also shortages
Rattigan, Neil 111, 134 n.1
Rau, Petra 61
Rawlinson, Mark 9, 20–2, 41–2, 54 n.1
   British Writing of the Second World War (2000) 9, 21
reading boom 7, 23, 63, 93, 280
realism 38, 129
   avant garde 72
   compacted 80
   film 277–8, 285, 289
   pastoral 67, 71
   psychological 142, 324
recuperation 14, 227
Reed, Carol, director 31, 193, 200, 205–6, 287, 292, 293, 296, 319
   The Fallen Idol (1948) 193, 200, 205–7
   The Third Man (1949) 31–2, 287, 292–3, 296
refugee(s) 20, 67, 182
   contribution to British culture 249, 251
   crisis 267
   from National Socialism 249–72
   German-speaking 250
   interned as enemy aliens 259
   Jewish 250–1, 259, 270
   women 250
Regent's Park 146, 157
rehabilitation 223, 225–7, 243, 245–7
Reid, Victor 27, 50
   'Waterfront Bar' 50
Reiner, Anna *See* Gmeyner, Anna
Renault, Mary 28, 30, 94, 101, 223–7, 234–6, 243, 245–6, 323
   The Charioteer (1953) 223
   The Friendly Young Ladies (1944) 28, 94, 101–2, 234–6

   North Face (1949) 243, 245–6
   Purposes of Love (1939) 30, 223–7, 246
repression 30, 228–33, 279
   adolescent 228–33
revenge 29, 163–65, 282, 283
revolution 37, 46, 123, 168, 174, 185 n.12, 225, 261, 267–8, 271
   French 263
   social 4
rhetoric 10, 41, 48, 71, 165, 168, 172, 175, 183
Rhys, Jean 28, 97, 107, 108, 323–4
   After Leaving Mr Mackenzie (1931) 97
   Good Morning Midnight (1939) 28, 97–9
Richardson, Dorothy 144, 255, 322
Right Book Club (RBC) 124, 135 n.9
rocket technology 66, 82–3, 84 n.9, 306
Rodden, John 163, 166, 183, 185 n.1, 185 n.5
romantic 75, 96–7, 100, 104, 141, 183, 196, 236, 240, 262, 266, 271
Rorty, Richard 163, 171, 174
Rose, Sonya O. 41–2, 226
Ross, Alan 10
Royal Navy, the 20, 111–235, 285, 320, 321
   as democratic and meritocratic 29, 115–16, 121–2, 124, 132
   rivalry with RAF 114
   'Senior Service', the 114
Royal Naval Volunteer Reserve, the (R.N.V.R.) 116, 131, 321
Royal Air Force, the *See* RAF
Russia(n) 1, 48, 171
   language 261
   literature 37
   people 45, 269, 270

sadomasochism 231–3, 291
Sage, Lorna 98–9
Said, Edward 198, 203
St John, John 7, 21
St John's Wood 103, 146
St Paul's
   Cathedral 61
   Girls' School 316
Salkey, Andrew 50
   Caribbean Voices presenter 50
   West Indian Stories 50
Santiáñez, Nil 71, 74

Schneider, Karen 41, 159 n.4
Second World War, the 2, 5, 9, 12, 16–17, 38–9, 41, 43, 47, 49, 52–4, 60–1, 92–3, 97, 106, 108, 112, 166, 192, 208, 225, 250, 252–3, 258–9, 272, 280, 318, 319, 321, 322, 324, 325, 326
  and British national identity 53
  poets 9, 23
Seiler, Claire 78–9
sensitive 70, 72, 142, 197, 201, 228
sentimental 20, 61, 96, 117, 120, 128–30, 184
servants 30, 69, 191
  in film 193
  in literature 30, 31, 94, 192–5, 198–219
  shortage of 16, 67, 68, 80
sex 13–14, 30, 41, 72, 77–8, 98, 107, 177, 200, 223–6, 231, 233–4, 239, 241–2, 244–6, 265, 278, 279, 284, 290–1, 315, 319
  behaviour 107, 227, 234, 247, 278–9
  education 236–8
  encounter 72, 98, 233
  experience 200, 231, 239
  and gender 30, 41, 226, 234–5
  homosexual/ity 17, 228, 325 (*see* queer adolescence), (*see* queered)
  incestuous 77
  joyless 98
  Little Kinsey, UK survey 30, 227, 238, 245, 247
  pre-marital 223, 245
  sexism 40, 271, 282
  sexology 145
  urge 243–4, 246
  and violence 280–1, 284
  workers 31, 195, 282
sexism 40, 271, 282
sexual desire *See under* desire
sexuality 17, 30, 41, 101–2, 177, 223, 224–8, 230, 235, 271, 325
Shakespeare(an) 80, 175
Sherry, Norman 195, 207–8
shortages 287
  in Eire 147
  of food 149
  of paper 46
  of reading material 7
short story 8, 22–3, 43, 50, 139, 141, 143–5, 147–53, 200, 284–5, 287, 293–4, 326
Sierra Leone 31, 73, 191, 194–5, 208, 214, 284, 318
Sinclair, Andrew 5, 20
Singapore, surrender of, 1942 2, 310
Smelser, Neil J. 60, 78
Smith, Stevie 14–15
  The Holiday (1949) 15
  Over the Frontier (1938) 14
Smith, Warwick 77–8
snobbery 17, 69, 81–2, 193, 281, 284
socialism 46, 113, 123
  National (*see under* National Socialism)
socialist 24, 113, 135 n.7, 163, 271
Soho 22, 25, 106, 146, 295, 320
soldiers 12, 20, 22, 24–5, 71, 113, 124, 183, 196, 208
somatic experience 227–9, 231
sound 62, 68, 71–2, 140, 169, 279
Soviet Union (USSR) 167, 264, 309–10 *See also* Russia
Spain 60, 91, 124, 166
Spanish Civil War 9, 97, 166, 269–70, 321, 322
  proxy conflict 39
Spark, Muriel 47, 54
  The Girls of Slender Means (1963) 47, 54
Spender, Stephen 37–8, 49
Spicer, Andrew 287, 297
Spiel, Hilde 31, 250, 256–60, 265, 268, 324
  autobiography 1994 257
  Catholic convert parents 256
  children 258
  Flute and Drums (1939) 257–8
  friend of Neumann 256
  The Fruits of Prosperity (1941) 253, 258, 265
    Die Früchte des Wohlstands German publication 1981 258
    Extracts in *Die Zeitung* 1941–46 258
  Kati auf der Brücke (1933) 256
  language switching 258–60
  marriage and move to UK, 1936 257
Spitfire (plane) 9, 83 n.7
spiv 31, 78, 100, 287, 289, 292–3, 295
  black marketeer 31
  film cycle 31–2, 287–93

Stanley, Liz 227, 238, 245, 247
state of the nation 5, 28, 45, 99
Stewart, Anthony 185 n.1, 186 n.10
Stewart, Victoria 67, 74
stoicism 13, 61, 65, 70, 211
Stonebridge, Lyndsey 37, 53, 76–7
Streatfeild, Noel 27, 59, 70–1
   Saplings (1945) 59, 70–1
Struther, Jan 93–4, 107–8, 324–5
   film, *Mrs Miniver* (1942) 94, 107, 109 n.4, 277
   novel, *Mrs Miniver* (1939) 93, 107–8
Sturgeon, Sinéad 140–1
Stürzer, Anne 268–70
subjectivity 141, 144–5, 153, 167, 175, 177–8, 179, 185
Sunday Pictorial 30, 227, 247
surreal 14, 71, 74
Sussex 64, 78, 318, 324, 326
Switzerland 91, 254, 261, 262, 293, 316, 318

Tatler, The 13, 135 n.6
technology 77, 141, 159
Teeling, William 124, 135 n.9
terror 13, 28, 60, 66, 72, 80, 129, 200, 319
Thames 65, 81, 199, 316, 319
The Man Within
   film (1947) aka *The Smugglers* 286–7
   novel (1929) (*see* Greene, Graham)
'their finest hour' 41, 47, 54, 60
This Gun for Hire, film (1942) 286
   adaptation of *A Gun for Sale* (1936) (*see* Greene, Graham)
   influence on film noir 286
Thorne, Anthony 29, 115–26, 128–9, 131, 325
   I'm a Stranger Here Myself (1943) 115–28, 131
   postscript 128
thriller, the 73, 119, 262, 282, 316, 318
Times, The 94, 151, 197, 318, 324, 325
TLS (*Times Literary Supplement*) 26, 259, 263, 281
Tobruk, fall of, 1942 2, 67, 310, 323
total war 3, 107–8
totalitarianism 45, 166–7, 171, 175, 180, 186 n.9, 186 n.14, 272, 281
Townsend Warner, Sylvia 41–2
traditional class and gender roles 4, 100, 109 n.7, 192, 240

transnational 50, 297
transport 18, 92–93
trauma 13, 28, 30, 60, 67, 74, 78, 95, 98, 144, 225–8, 234, 240–2, 247, 280
   collective 61–2, 224–7, 246
   'incubation' or latency period 75
   novel 59, 67
   physical 237, 244
   queer (*see under* queer trauma)
   rehabilitation 223, 225, 227
   theory 59–60
traumatic 12, 15, 22, 61, 72, 73, 76, 79, 231
   childbirth 238
   memory 72, 77
traumatized 1, 6, 26–7, 71, 155, 226, 239, 259, 280, 290
travel writing, late 1930s 31, 39, 192, 194–7, 199–200, 203
Tredell, Nicolas 73–4
Tribune 42, 163, 284
tube stations 2, 65
Twentieth-Century Fox 284, 295

uncanny, the 74, 182
understatement 228, 278
United States of America *See* America, United States of
utility 223–5
utopia 74, 175
   utopian spirit 17, 46, 129

Vichy government 285, 309, 310, 311
Victor Gollancz, publisher 116, 134, 255–6, 320
Victorian 28, 68, 69, 94, 321
Vienna 251, 255, 256, 261, 262, 267, 268, 317, 324
   Congress of 1814–15 262, 265–6
   filmed in 292, 296
'Vengeance weapons' (*Vergeltungswaffen*) 66, 84 n.9
   V1 attacks 65, 75–6, 79, 82, 306
   V2 attacks 65, 82, 306

Walker, Ronald G. 75–6
Wallace-Johnson, I. T. A. 214–15
   African Standard 214
   arrested 1939 under Emergency Act 214

founder West African Youth League (WAYL) 214
Negro Worker 214
War Cabinet 37, 64, 126
warfare state 106, 111, 116
wartime solidarity 3, 44, 45, 54, 61, 117–20, 131, 325
Weeks, Jeffrey 223, 225, 227
Welch, Denton 10, 30, 227, 228–32, 326
  In Youth is Pleasure (1944) 228–32
Welfare State, the 5, 26, 52, 54, 105–8, 116
  plans for 46
  See Beveridge Report
Wells, H. G. 84 n.13, 144–5, 183, 251, 259, 322
Went the Day Well? 285
  book about film (1992) 285
  film (1942) 285
West Indian authors 49–51
West Indian literature 51, 55 n.4
West Indians 48–50, 209
Waugh, Evelyn 10, 15–19, 46, 54, 67, 95, 109 n.6, 112, 318, 321, 325
  Brideshead Revisited (1945) 17–19, 67
  and Catholicism 10
  The Loved One (1948) 18
  Put Out More Flags (1942) 15–17, 95
Whittington, Ian 3–4
widower 28, 240
widow 67, 78, 100, 107, 139, 213, 242, 244
William Heinemann, publisher 7, 20, 23, 117, 325
Wilson, Elizabeth 105–7
Wilson, Harold 289, 320
Wilson, Angus 43, 54
  The Old Men at the Zoo (1961) 54
Windrush generation 49, 218, 308
Wodehouse, P. G. 30, 193, 218 n.1
  1940s novels 218 n.1
  arrested by French police, 1944 218 n.1
  German collaboration, accused of post-war 193
  interned by Germans 218 n.1
  wartime radio broadcasts, Berlin 193
women workers in
  agriculture and horticulture 92
  aircraft industry 16, 92, 99
  auxiliary services 92
  chemical and explosives industry 92
  civil defence 92
  librarians 12
  munitions 92
  nursing 101
  secretarial 261
  shipbuilding and heavy engineering 92
  welfare 97
Women's Liberation Movement 102
Women's pride in work 28, 93, 99
women's writing 28, 92, 94, 102
  cheerful register 107
  fatalistic 108
  refusal of seriousness 108
Woolf, Leonard 326
Woolf, Virginia 5, 11, 27, 40–1, 51–2, 59, 64, 84 n.8, 144, 145, 250, 326
  Between the Acts (1941) 40, 59, 64
  death of 5, 51, 326
  Jacob's Room (1922) 40
  speech, Workers' Educational Association 1940 51–2
  'Thoughts on Peace in an Air Raid' (1940) 40–1
  Three Guineas (1938) 40
Woolton, Frederick James Marquis, 1st Earl of 45
working-class *See* class
W.V.S. canteen 70

Yorke, Henry *See* Green, Henry
young women 12, 28, 44, 94–5, 98, 99, 100. 101–2, 105–6, 107, 194, 200, 202, 209– 10, 234–7
Yugoslavia 21, 262, 310, 312
  Relief Society 145

Zaharoff, Sir Basil 255
Zeitgeist viii, 12, 250, 272
Žindžiuvienė, Ingrida 59, 67
Zur Mühlen, Hermynia 31, 250, 253, 261–7, 268, 271–2, 302, 303, 326–7
  birth 261
  BBC birthday tribute (1943) 262
  Came the Stranger (1946) 263, 264, 267–8, 303, 327
  escape to London 262
  marriage and divorce 261
  member German communist party (KPD) 261

partner 261
work in popular genres in 1920s
  262
We Poor Shadows (1943) 253, 263,
  264–7, 302, 327
Zweig, Stefan 31, 250, 251–4, 255, 256,
  262–3, 266
  applied for British citizenship 252
  arrives London 1933 251
  Balzac manuscript (2000) 253
  Beware of Pity (1939) 252
  English translation entitled *The Queen
    of Scots* 252
  first marriage 251
  Magellan (1938) 252
  Marie Antoinette (1932) 252, 256
  Maria Stuart (1935) 252
  on National Socialist prohibited texts
    list 251
  The Right to Heresy (1936) 252
  sails to New York and South America
    253
  suicide of Zweig and second wife, 1942
    254
  The World of Yesterday, memoir (1943)
    253

This index was compiled by the volume editors in September and October 2021.

www.ingramcontent.com/pod-product-compliance
Lightning Source LLC
Chambersburg PA
CBHW052142300426
44115CB00011B/1479